Introduction to Christianity

FOURTH EDITION

Mary Jo Weaver
David Brakke
Indiana University

WADSWORTH
CENGAGE Learning™

Australia • Brazil • Japan • Korea • Mexico • Singapore • Spain • United Kingdom • United States

WADSWORTH
CENGAGE Learning™

Introduction to Christianity, Fourth Edition
Mary Jo Weaver and David Brakke

Religion Editor: Worth Hawes

Assistant Editor: Patrick Stockstill

Editorial Assistant: Kamilah Lee

Marketing Manager: Christina Shea

Marketing Assistant: Mary Ann Payumo

Marketing Communications Manager: Darlene Amidon-Brent

Project Manager, Editorial Production: Hal Humphrey

Art Director: Maria Epes

Print Buyer: Linda Hsu

Permissions Editor: Timothy Sisler

Production Service: Matrix Productions Inc.

Copy Editor: Frank Hubert

Cover Designer: Yvo Riezebos Design

Cover Image: Jeffrey Becom/ Lonely Planet Images/Getty Images, Inc.

Compositor: International Typesetting and Composition

Library of Congress Control Number: 2007935512

ISBN-13: 978-0-495-09726-6

ISBN-10: 0-495-09726-8

Wadsworth
10 Davis Drive
Belmont, CA 94002-3098
USA

Cengage Learning is a leading provider of customized learning solutions with office locations around the globe, including Singapore, the United Kingdom, Australia, Mexico, Brazil, and Japan. Locate your local office at **international.cengage.com/region.**

Cengage Learning products are represented in Canada by Nelson Education, Ltd.

For your course and learning solutions, visit **academic.cengage.com.**

Purchase any of our products at your local college store or at our preferred online store **www.ichapters.com.**

Printed in the United States of America
1 2 3 4 5 6 7 12 11 10 09 08

Dedicated to our students
in the Religious Studies Department
Indiana University

Contents

Introduction for the Teacher

This revised fourth edition of what has become a popular textbook has the same goal as its predecessors: to provide a general introduction to Christianity that relieves the teacher's frustration at having to lay a substantial foundation and then having little time to build on it. Our experience with students suggests that many of them come to a religious studies class knowing very little about religion. We cannot assume much prior knowledge and so must begin with basic information. Students who enroll in a Christianity class because they believe they already know what Christianity is often need to have their horizons expanded, and those who enroll because they know nothing need to begin simply.

The strength of this book has been its usefulness and flexibility; it is also written for students and is quite readable. We have tried to set forth the historical development of the Christian tradition in lucid prose that presents a clear narrative without oversimplification. At the same time, we have tried to pose correctly the major issues within contemporary Christianity, the ones that engage the interest of today's students, though without attempting to solve them. Issues are not boxed and tied neatly with a ribbon; rather, they are presented from a number of different standpoints so that students and teachers can follow their own interests in and out of the classroom.

This new edition of *Introduction to Christianity* builds on these strengths. This revision is a collaborative effort of Mary Jo Weaver, the original author, and David Brakke, who specializes in early Christianity. Users of the book have appreciated its readability, and we have maintained it as we revised chapters clarifying difficult ideas, updating material, and introducing new topics (like globalization) where needed. In the third edition, we added a new feature: sidebars in each chapter featured an important person, concept, and controversy. In this new edition, we have added a fourth sidebar called "Spirituality" that explores a significant experience of the divine from ancient times to the present. At a time when many students claim to be "spiritual but not religious," we thought it a good idea to explore what being spiritual meant to people in the past. All the sidebars illustrate themes in the main text, and we hope that they entice students into additional areas of Christian studies and provide material for class discussions or lectures. Sidebars are challenging to write because we have to explain someone as complicated as, say, Thomas Aquinas or Darwin in about four hundred words. As such, we have to be selective and a little provocative, hoping that teachers and students will turn to the Web or other sources to begin to fill in the gaps, to get a more nuanced understanding, or to identify ideas and persons that we have only been able to mention. At the end of each chapter are focus questions, some of them new to this edition, to help students not only review the covered material but also think critically about it; the questions are deliberately challenging. We have removed the footnotes and suggestions for further reading from this edition because we know that most people turn to computer-generated sources of information and we see how quickly books are eclipsed by newer ones. We have put material from the notes into the text when appropriate. Finally, although learning dates and events is never fun, we have tried to make it less intimidating by streamlining the time line and placing it within the book's front and back covers for easy access.

This book continues to be historical but not exclusively so. In fact, the book divides neatly into two parts: a mostly historical section (Parts I and II) and an increasingly political section (Parts III and IV). We think this aspect of the book is well suited for today's students. On the one hand, they need the history because they usually do not know it and because it explains the origins of denominational differences among Christians. Although twenty-first-century students might want to know why there are Roman Catholics, Methodists, and Eastern Orthodox Christians, they might also find it hard to understand what all the fuss was about over justification or credal formulations. Our historical discussions try not only to explain these theological issues clearly but also to show why they have engaged the hearts and minds of Christians. On the other hand, students today often understand Christianity through the various controversies over social and economic issues, such as abortion, gender and sexuality questions, school prayer, and other matters that dominate some political debates and are presented regularly on television and in the newspapers. These controversies divide contemporary Christians along lines that are perhaps more political and cultural than they are denominational. The more political sections of this text try to clarify why conservative Roman Catholics may have more in common with evangelical Protestants than with liberal Catholics on these high-profile issues. These divisions dominate the Christian story as it enters its third millennium. So this book's seemingly "split personality" matches well the moment in Christian history in which our students, especially U.S. students, find themselves.

This edition, then, has the needs of the modern classroom in view. It provides a clear, readable introduction to the varieties of Christianity while its sidebars invite teachers and students to adapt it to their own interests.

Organization and Content

The book is divided into four parts: two tell the story of Christianity up to the modern period, and two contain material designed to help students understand modernity and contemporary issues.

Part I focuses on the Bible, the religious experience of the ancient Jews, the place of Jesus within that Jewish context, and the emergence of the Christian community. Modern Christian students need to be reminded that Christianity began as a Jewish sect in a Greco-Roman world. Chapter 1, although not meant to be a complete introduction to the Old Testament or Israelite history, does introduce concepts crucial for understanding the Jewish and Christian traditions: revelation and the Bible, the complex character of God, and the theological interpretation of history. Chapter 2 tells the story of Jesus as it fits in the diverse Judaism of his day, highlights the origin of Christianity in Jewish apocalypticism, and explains the creation of the New Testament. Chapter 3 studies the emergence of Christianity as a new religion that had to settle internal matters of structure and leadership and had to meet external challenges from rival philosophies and religions. We stress diversity in Christian origins by featuring sidebars on Gnosticism, women in the early church, the experience of the Holy Spirit, and the divinity of Jesus. We also examine the nature of God in Part I, from the tension between immanence and transcendence in God's character to the ways the divine was experienced from Moses to Philo.

Part II gives a wide-ranging and relatively brief historical overview of Christianity up to the eighteenth century, focusing on core moments and issues. Chapter 4 explains the differences between Eastern Orthodox and Roman Catholic Christianity and then explores the key features of medieval Catholicism. The concept of "new Rome" has proved to be a successful way to understand this period as a time when Christians, east and west, tried to create Christian cultures with unified theologies and politics. Chapter 5 surveys the Reformation and thus introduces students to the major Protestant denominations. Chapter 6 continues this story of diversification in early modern Europe and shows how it carried over to early America. In contrast to its predecessors, this edition does a better job of conveying the spiritual experience of historical Christians (such as mysticism and the Great Awakening) and of highlighting how Christian groups and issues that may be familiar to students (monks, Jesuits, science versus religion) have their roots in the past.

Part III marks an important transition: it brings the historical survey to a close and presents modernity in its many aspects, the challenges of which Christianity is still facing. Chapter 7 introduces students to a modern world in which the separation of church and state means that churches must now compete with one another for members and loyalty and in which the critical inquiry of the Enlightenment has brought new challenges to Christian doctrine. Chapter 8 unfolds the complex religious diversity of America: it presents a lot of information in a compact space, which can be tough for students exhausted from midterms, but some relief is provided by the new material on figures like Aimee Semple McPherson and the popular understandings of Jesus as friend and businessman. Chapter 9 focuses on two central aspects of modern Christianity, missions and globalization, showing how they have engendered fresh movements such as liberation theology, and new challenges as Christianity in the Two-Thirds World becomes a dominant force in global Christianity. In this edition, the complexity of this big picture is rendered more manageable by the sidebars, which provide focused examples of such broad themes as mission in reverse, divine healing, and Our Lady of Guadalupe.

In Part IV, on contemporary issues, the political focus of the book comes to the fore. We again organized this part through the church/world diagram, which may be imperfect but does help students understand in religious terms the political divisions among American Christians. Each chapter uses the axes of this diagram to clarify contemporary diversity. In Chapter 10, the distinction between withdrawal and domination ties together the different ways that Christians have responded to U.S. political, economic, and cultural life. Chapter 11 places such vexing modern problems as racism and war into the context of adaptation and nonconformity within American Christianity. Chapter 12 turns to the division that may be most familiar to today's students—that between liberal and conservative Christians—and explores how this division plays out in areas like women's ordination, sexuality, and televangelism. Although students have always found these chapters "relevant" to their own time, we have tried in this revision to make them even more so with separate profiles of people and movements, like Martin Luther King and the Amish school shooting, that are prominent in the media.

Mary Jo Weaver
David Brakke

A Note from the Authors

The very last discussion question, at the end of Chapter 12, reminds students that this book divides Christianity into its historical and political aspects and asks them whether it is possible to tell the story of Christianity without both of them. Through years of teaching and writing, we are convinced that it is not. If you are using this book because you agree with us, we are encouraged, but if you are using this book as a foil to show students how wrong we are, that's fine, too. This book is now nearly 25 years old as it ventures into the world as a fourth edition. Mary Jo Weaver retired last year and will likely not be working on subsequent editions, but trust her friend and colleague David Brakke to continue to make improvements and to find ways to speak realistically about Christianity in all its messy and amazing glory.

ACKNOWLEDGMENTS

In his classic text *American Renaissance*, E. O. Mathiessen said this:

> During the course of this long volume I have undoubtedly plagiarized from many sources—to use the ugly term that did not bother Shakespeare's age. I doubt whether any criticism or cultural history has ever been written without such plagiary, which inevitably results from assimilating the contributions of your countless fellow-workers, past and present. The true function of scholarship as of society is not to stake out claims on which others must not trespass, but to provide a community of knowledge in which others may share.[1]

Without elevating ourselves to the stature of Mathiessen, we must acknowledge that we share his general feeling. This book was produced from research and teaching experience, anecdotes told to us individually by friends, and informative arguments from colleagues. Many of those who have used other editions have written over the

---

[1](Oxford: Oxford University Press, 1968), pbk. p. xv.

years to suggest better ways of explaining things or to save us from ignorant conclusions. We are grateful to them and realize that many of the improvements in this edition are due to their kindness. We thank the following reviewers of this edition: Liyakat Takim of the University of Denver, Betsy Perabo of Western Illinois University, Julia Lambert Fogg of California Lutheran University, and Ronald H. Miller of Lake Forest College.

In the first edition, Weaver mentioned debts to Gershom Scholem[2] and William E. Hordern,[3] and she renews her thanks to them in this edition. Some of the material originally appeared in an Indiana University Independent Study Division text, and we thank the trustees of the university for allowing us to use it again here. Many of the refinements, however, have been suggested by colleagues and students over the years. We are grateful for their intelligence and generosity, and are indebted to their support and good grace as we attempted to make generalizations in areas they believed needed much more sophistication than we could bring to the task. In particular, we appreciate the careful reading of sidebars by Candy Gunther Brown and Kathryn Lofton and the substantive suggestions given to us by our partner on the third edition, Jason Bivins, now at North Carolina State. Barbara Nelson Gingerich of Associated Mennonite Biblical Seminaries was a huge help to Mary Jo Weaver on the very first edition of this book and helped us a great deal on this edition as well.

Weaver asked many friends to read the first edition so that she could profit from a wide variety of viewpoints. We have not burdened them with subsequent editions but are still in their debt and acknowledge new sources of inspiration and information, especially from the graduate students who have assisted us in the course over the last few years, particularly Holly Folk, Doug Winiarski, and Stephen Taysom. Weaver's life support system, her friends, have been steady through this process: Jean Alice McGoff, Therese Gullickson, Gena DiLabio, Julie Bloom, and Susan Gubar. Thanks also to Donald Gray, who made cogent suggestions. Brakke thanks Bert Harrill for his love and support. The staff at Wadsworth was wonderful during the production of all editions, including this one. We are indebted to the good spirits and competence of Patrick Stockstill, assistant editor; Hal Humphrey, production manager; Worth Hawes, editor; and Kamilah Lee, editorial assistant. Thanks also to Aaron Downey at Matrix Productions and our copyeditor, Frank Hubert. This book and its earlier versions would not have been possible outside the atmosphere of Indiana University. Colleagues in the Department of Religious Studies deserve our thanks. To our students over the years, we can only make a small gesture of gratitude by dedicating this book to them.

[2]"Revelation and Tradition as Religious Categories in Judaism" in *The Messianic Idea in Judaism and Other Essays on Jewish Spirituality* (New York: Schocken Books, 1971), pp. 282–303.

[3]*A Layman's Guide to Protestant Theology* (New York: Macmillan, 1968).

Note to Students

All religions can be looked at from either the inside or the outside. When Christianity is viewed from the inside, one gets a believer's perspective and sees Christianity as *the* religion, the only possible truth. If Christianity is viewed from the outside, one gets a nonbeliever's perspective and sees Christianity as *a* religion, one perception of the truth among many. A clear and determined choice between these two approaches leads to considerable distortion from the very outset. To avoid this distortion, this book attempts to incorporate both perspectives, though within limits. This book takes an outsider's perspective insofar as it does not attempt to proclaim Christianity or prove it to be true. At the same time, it is faithful to an insider's viewpoint as it tries to read and understand the doctrines and practices of Christians as they are understood within the believing community.

Christianity has a doctrine about God that includes a belief in the life, death, and resurrection of Jesus, and it offers a method for getting in touch with God that involves a relationship with Jesus. Christians agree that it is important to know, to believe in, or to experience Jesus, but they disagree about how that is done. There are, accordingly, many varieties of Christian belief and practice, most of which reflect differences in biblical interpretation, historical experience, and Christian self-understanding.

An introduction to Christianity can do many things, some of them more ambitious than others. This book is modest in intention and general in scope: it intends to *introduce* Christianity from a number of perspectives so that students can have some appreciation of its richness and diversity without being overwhelmed by its differences of opinion and practice. Christians are extraordinarily diverse in their beliefs and behavior, but they also share common understandings. This book delineates the historical differences and commonalities to introduce the dynamism and diversity of one of the world's largest religions.

A book like this is bound to be controversial however hard the authors try to be fair-minded and judicious in choosing material, examples, and topics. We can only hope that those who see significant gaps in interpretation and historical awareness will fill those gaps with supplementary reading. We wrote this book with a definite audience in mind—the college freshman who has little knowledge about Christianity and perhaps a minimal understanding of religion—and have kept the needs of the student uppermost in mind while writing.

Accordingly, though we usually allude to the fact that most issues are more complex than they may appear to be in this general introduction, we do not raise difficult questions of scriptural exegesis (critical explanation) or sophisticated historical argumentation in the body of the text itself. We realize that most students use the Web as an information source and expect them to consult sources there to deepen their understanding of issues and of gaps necessarily left in sidebars. The appendices at the back of the book give more nuances and further explain certain aspects of historical Christianity. Our approach to the Bible is informed by historical and critical scholarship and grounded in a deep appreciation of the ways Scripture is used by believing communities of Christians. Different groups of Christians read certain texts differently, and we have tried to recognize that fact without attempting to solve the issues. We have tried to raise some questions about scriptural interpretation without urging one interpretation over another. We have not taken time to explain some historical material or to identify certain personalities, but we have added a glossary of terms and names to elaborate on areas not covered in depth in the text. Use the glossary like a dictionary: when you find a word or the name of a person in the text that you want to know more about, turn to the glossary for a further explanation.

Finally, we have accepted the statements from each religious group about itself and have made no speculations about the possible truth or falsehood of certain claims. Our intention is to give each group an impartial reading and to present its history and its positions straightforwardly. We have been more interested in practical issues than in theological ones and more interested in presenting an explanation for Christian diversity and unity than we have been in writing a comprehensive history of Christianity. Our hope is that you will find the text clear, accurate, and challenging.

Biblical and Historical Background for Christianity

PART I

The first part of this book introduces the background against which the varieties of Christianity have emerged. Christianity is a revealed religion: Christians believe that God has communicated with them and has been manifested in words and in a history of saving actions. For Christians, the most important self-communication of God is Jesus Christ, whose life, death, and resurrection form the foundation of the Christian religion.

The first three chapters focus on the work of God, the life of Jesus, and the presence of the Holy Spirit in the church. Most Christians believe that God is the creator and savior of people, that Jesus Christ is God's most important self-disclosure, and that the Holy Spirit is God's power at work in the Christian community. Christians trace their roots through Judaism back to the Creation. So we will begin with some general perceptions about God as creator, as providentially interested in the world and in the history of the Jews. The second chapter situates Jesus within his historical context: the apocalyptic mood and messianic hopes of the Jews provided Christians with a way to understand Jesus and to interpret his mission. The third chapter outlines the emergence of the Christian church and the importance of the Holy Spirit within the church.

Christianity did not develop easily or smoothly. There were serious arguments among Christians and between Christians and Jews about the person and mission of Jesus. Christianity is a complex religion that has been growing and changing from its beginning. The first part of this book explains the basis of the dynamic growth within Christianity and introduces the foundations of the Christian experience.

God as Revealed in the Bible

CHAPTER **I**

Western religions aim to help believers follow the will of God. And how do believers know the will of God? If you ask that question of followers in any revealed religion (Judaism, Christianity, Islam), they will tell you that God has spoken, has been made manifest, has communicated with people. That is the claim of *revelation,* a word that comes from the Latin *revelare,* which means to unveil or to disclose. When people criticize a bathing suit for being too *revealing,* they mean it unveils or uncovers too much. When the word is applied to God, it means that God unveils—not by disrobing but by disclosing the divine will and personality through words and actions. Believers, therefore, know the will of God because it has been revealed to them.

REVELATION AND RELIGIOUS EXPERIENCE

Revelation is an article of faith for believers and a complex problem for theologians. Since there is no single way to explain it, students have a variety of ways to understand it. Furthermore, because revelation is linked to complicated and sometimes emotional issues like inspiration, a person's religious background often suggests that one particular interpretation is better or more adequate than another. In terms of a person's private beliefs, that observation is quite true: some explanations *are* more satisfying than others. For our purposes here, however, we have to see whether we can put aside personal preferences and try to understand revelation in very general terms. What do people mean when they say that they have had a direct communication from God? What do they mean when they say that their lives and beliefs are based on God's will for them?

Because we are considering the very beginnings of Christianity, and because Christianity traces its understanding of itself back through Judaism to the beginning of time, we have to start by trying to understand Judaism as a revealed religion. Judaism began in a conviction that God had actually appeared in some fashion or done something—that a vision of God had been seen or that God's voice had been heard.

The first clue to understanding revelation, therefore, is *experience*. Theories of revelation tell us that an experience of God is often awe-ful and demanding: one feels bound to respond to the event and to keep it alive for oneself and one's community.

Those whose stories form the basis of Judaism and Christianity usually believe that their experience has helped them understand the will of a *personal* God. The stories of Abraham, Moses, Jesus, and Paul do not lead to the conclusion that they had some vague encounter with "something out there." Rather, they all believed that God spoke to them directly and demanded some action on their part. They experienced God as a person who initiated a relationship with them. According to these great religious figures and others, God revealed a desire for partnership and demanded a response.

Skeptics, of course, would dismiss such religious experiences as madness or illusion, but those whose stories we find in the Bible were *believers,* though perhaps not always immediately and not without a struggle on their part. Revelation is not a one-way street but the beginning of a partnership. God reveals, but people must choose whether to live in accordance with that revelation, a choice that often involves whether to believe that a revelation has occurred.

If people choose to accept the revelation, they usually reflect on it, remember it ritually with feasts or celebrations, tell it as a story to later generations, write it down, refine it, edit it, and apply it to new situations. They may even receive new revelations and come to deeper understandings of God over a long period of time. In Judaism and Christianity both, there is a sense of ongoing revelation: God continues to disclose Godself and to call believers into deeper levels of understanding and partnership.

Revelation is God's self-communication and can apparently occur in a number of ways. Each time, however, the pattern recurs: direct communication from God on the one hand and the response of people on the other. Revelation, insofar as we understand it in Judaism and Christianity, is a direct communication of God *intended for a group of people.* It may have originally been experienced by a single individual, but the content applies to a whole people and invites response and belief from that entire group.

Once it is accepted by a group, revelation is interpreted. An incident of God's action may be interpreted differently by groups of believers. For example, Jews, Christians, and Muslims all agree that Abraham is extraordinarily important as an early partner of God's self-communication, but they interpret Abraham's life and history differently. Muslims trace their connections with Abraham through Ishmael (see Gen. 16, 17, and 21), whereas Jews trace their lineage to Abraham through Isaac (Gen. 17–22). Jews have interpreted the story of the sacrifice of Isaac (Gen. 22) as a test of Abraham's obedience and a strengthening of the covenant, whereas Christians have tended to see the same story as a typology for the sacrifice of Jesus on the cross.

Whatever particular interpretations have shaped Judaism, Christianity, and Islam, however, each religion bases itself on revelation: in each religion, one can find stories of God speaking to a group through the experience of special people; what God has said and what God has done are foundational for each group. Jews, Christians, and Muslims all believe that they have discerned God's intentions for their lives because of the ways God has spoken and acted in history. Finally, each of these groups has preserved its understanding of God in ritual celebration, and each has produced a sacred text that, it claims, contains "the word of God." Because Christianity grew out of Judaism and the Israelite experience of revelation, Christians reverence the Hebrew Bible, albeit in different form. Our understanding of Christianity must begin, therefore, with an examination of the Bible as the primary account of God's revelation.

THE BIBLE

Tanakh is the Jewish Bible, consisting of the Torah, Nevi'im (prophets), and Ketuvim (writings); therefore, the Bible is divided into three parts: the Torah, the Prophets, and the Writings. Christians rearranged the Jewish Bible and renamed it the Old Testament. For Christians, the Bible is made up of two parts: the Old Testament and the New Testament. Because they use different versions of the Hebrew Bible, Catholics and Protestants disagree about how many books should be in the Old Testament (see Appendix 1). The New Revised Standard Version, the most reliable scholarly edition of the Bible, has different editions for different faiths. (See Appendix 2 for a list of books.)

The word *Bible* means "book." To Jews and Christians, it is a holy book, set apart from others because of its sacred content and origin. The Bible has a central place in Jewish and Christian worship all over the world. Worshipers believe that the use of biblical texts in liturgy puts them in touch with God's actions in history. Since those actions are regarded as saving ones, liturgical use of Scripture enables believers to be touched by God's saving acts. The Bible has been translated into more languages than any other book; it exists in a variety of versions and is constantly studied, read, quoted from, and treasured. For all that, however, it is rare to find many people who can understand the whole book, especially the Old Testament. Parts of it seem obscure or peculiar, some of it is hard to read, and some of it (for example, lists of ancient genealogies) appears irrelevant to life in the present.

Jews and Christians agree that the Old Testament is inspired, though they disagree about which parts are and which are not. Whether there is inspiration and how it occurred or functions are matters of theological dispute. Some believers are content with the idea that God dictated every word of the Bible to chosen authors; others prefer to understand inspiration as a more subtle psychological process. For the most part, however, all these people believe that somehow, through an infusion of divine breath or spirit, God directed the writing of the book; that is what inspiration means. We need not belabor the way inspiration is explained by various religious groups and theologians. A broad, working definition might see inspiration as God acting and revealing through a particular community. Within that community, authors reflect on their collective experience, treasure it, and write it down. What the author writes and the way it is written are inspired, have divine influence behind it. The issue is not simple; the debate about it and refinement of its definition continue.

Even though Jews and Christians agree that the Old Testament is inspired, that God is revealed in it, this does not mean biblical content and meaning will be immediately evident to the reader. Any reader of the Bible needs to understand the enormous range of history and literature it contains. One help in understanding a particular book or passage is discovering the author's intention. Not all books were written to respond to the same circumstances. They may all deal with God's relationship with people, but they have been written in a number of different styles and in different contexts, with probable differences of purpose.

There is considerable disagreement among Christians about how to read the Bible. Some believe that the Bible, as God's word, need only be read and understood simply and literally—that every word and explanation is absolutely true. Others believe the Bible was written for and by a particular people and that one needs to understand this historical context before the real message can be understood. Still others approach the Bible with tools of scholarship—ancient languages, archaeology, history—to understand different strands of the stories and the levels of intention behind those stories.

For example, the first book, Genesis, begins by telling the story of the creation of the world and the "fall" of humankind. The biblical author wanted to explain the wonders of the universe as the actions of a powerful, generous God—in other words, to show the essential goodness of creation. At the same time, that author needed to explain the sense of frustration and alienation people sometimes suffer—in other words, to show that the bad things that happen in this world are not God's fault but are the result of human error or sin. Whether the author meant to describe actual events in historical and scientific terms is a matter of dispute among Christians, but Christians do not dispute the power and beauty of the creation account and the profound way the story of Eden explains the presence of evil in the world.

When one turns to the Bible, therefore, one finds a great variety of literature. The Bible contains straightforward historical information as well as poetry and prose. Law and lore are included along with prophetic and devotional books; there are books that deal with serious human problems (like suffering) and books that describe ancient battles and dynasties. But for all the differences of style and literary types, one finds some central themes. Throughout the Bible, God is revealed in history as generous, eager to save people from bondage and to draw them into a relationship. God is also demanding and mysterious, capable of anger and frustration. One general theme in the Bible is covenant: God makes agreements with human beings that promise divine protection in return for trust and obedience. Belonging to God's people, therefore, requires fidelity to the terms of the covenant.

The great variety of literature in the Bible tells us something about the many ways in which God was experienced by biblical people and understood by biblical authors. Scholars may spend their entire lives trying to fathom one particular type of biblical literature—poetry, for example, or ancient history—and still not have a full understanding of the text. As we look at two major aspects of divine purpose as revealed in the Bible, therefore, let us realize that we are dealing in very general terms.

This introductory sketch of God's personality and purpose is meant, in the long run, to stir your interest and encourage further study; for the present, we need only form an elementary understanding of God's personality as it emerged in the life of the people of Israel. The two aspects of the divine personality that are particularly helpful are creation and providence. On the one hand, God is the powerful, transcendent creator of the world who stands, as it were, above and outside human existence. On the other hand, God is interested in history and is apparently willing to enter into its unfolding in partnership with people. These two aspects of the divine personality—remote yet intimately involved—are known in theological language as *transcendence* and *immanence*. We need not get distracted by a technical discussion of terms here: suffice it to say that God's personality has been, from the beginning, disclosed in both ways. Jews and Christians need not feel forced to choose between an awesome, powerful being and an intimate partner since God's personality encompasses both possibilities.

As we look at the creative and provident aspects of God's self-disclosure, a word about the chronology of events is in order. The Bible begins with a story about the

SPIRITUALITY

Immanence and Transcendence: The Paradox of God

Belief in God is as old as humanity, and understandings about God have changed over time, as we will discover. God's personality, as it unfolds in the Bible, has two aspects that Christians have sometimes seen as contradictory. On the one hand, God is *transcendent:* a supreme and powerful being who exists apart from this world and removed from human experience. On the other hand, God is *immanent:* a personal being who enters into the world and shares a mysterious kinship with humanity. These two aspects of God appear throughout the Old Testament. The immanent God bargains with Abraham (Gen. 18:16–33) and is felt to be so close that the psalmist longs to see his face (27:8). The transcendent God upbraids Job for questioning the divine majesty and tells Moses, "No one may see me and live" (Exod. 33:20).

These two aspects of God appear in the very first chapters of the Bible, in the creation stories. In the first chapter of Genesis, a majestic, transcendent God creates merely by speaking and then pronouncing the created order good. In the second and third chapters, an immanent and more personal God forms a man from mud and breathes life into him, walks in the garden, and needs to ask Adam and Eve where they are hiding. Biblical scholars believe that two originally separate stories of creation have been combined to create this one complex and rich picture of God the creator.

Imagining God as transcendent prevents God from being identified too closely with any one particular group of people or their point of view: God is above all human assertions and cannot be confined by definitions. At the same time, too much stress on transcendence tends to separate God completely from the created world so that God appears untouched by its events. Believers can usually relate more easily to an immanent God who understands their problems like a caring parent. But thinking about God in personal terms can lead to other difficulties, such as thinking God is really just like us only bigger or imagining that "God the Father" is really male and that men are more like God than women. Perhaps you can think to other benefits and drawbacks of each aspect of God.

The paradox of God understood both as transcendent and immanent reflects the endless fascination people have with a God who is beyond anything they can imagine yet is intimately concerned for their welfare.

creation of the world that makes sense chronologically—all good stories begin "once upon a time"—but probably does not reflect the religious reality of the situation. Remember what we said about revelation being rooted in experience. The people whose stories fill the Bible first of all had an *experience* of God as one who yearns for a relationship (the story of Abraham) or as one who hears the cries of the oppressed and acts to liberate a captive people (the story of Moses). That experience was kept alive in ritual celebration and in the constant retelling of events. In fact, the story was circulated in a variety of forms or editions for hundreds of years before it was written down, edited, and spliced together to form what we know today as the Tanakh.

As the stories of the original religious experiences were told and retold, nuances were added, new incidents were woven into the fabric of the narrative, and the life of the community became part of the unfolding story of God's revelation. As later generations speculated about God's presence in the world, they brought their experience to that speculation. When they had questions they could not answer from historical documents—the details of the creation of the world, for example—they invented a story based on their experience of God as powerful, sustaining, nurturing, involved, and available. The order of events as found in the Bible, therefore, beginning with creation, is probably *not* accurate. The way the story unfolds in the Bible, however, does have a clear historical flow, and we will follow the biblical chronology because of that feature. The only other thing to keep in mind is this: our purpose here is to get a general understanding of God, not to have a full-scale recital of the history of biblical peoples.

GOD AS CREATOR

The first three chapters of Genesis give us a complex picture of God as creator. We notice that

1. *God masters chaos or creates out of nothing.* Scholars read the creation account in two ways, depending on how they translate Genesis 1:1. In one, God masters primal chaos; in the other, God creates out of nothing. God is the one who can assert creative mastery over the universe.
2. *God creates in both word and deed.* In the first chapter of Genesis, God does not conjure up a spell but simply says the word, and what is spoken happens; in the second chapter of Genesis, God fashions a man from the earth—makes a person from already-existing material.
3. *God says that creation is good.* The world is not an evil place, and the material universe is not to be disparaged. One need not have a dreary attitude toward the world or think of it as a prison; it is seen by God as a good place.
4. *Man and woman are created in God's own image.* People have been made as the crowning glory of God's creative activity, to act as God's representatives in this world.

All these aspects testify to the power and goodness of God. They also connect creation with the power of God's word, a rich biblical concept. "By the word of the Lord the heavens were made," says the psalmist (Ps. 33:6). God's word is connected with revelation and with the law: Psalm 119 is a long meditation on the law, replete with references to God's word. Psalm 19 compares the brightness of the sun to the enlightenment brought by God's word in the Torah. God's word is also bound up with prophecy: all the prophets speak God's word and are prophets precisely because "the word of the Lord" came to them and empowered them. In the New Testament, Jesus is described as the preexistent "word of God" and is said to be "the word made flesh." Christians believe that Jesus is the Son of God, that he incarnates the creative power of God's word.

The biblical authors tell us about God's goodness, power, and generosity, but in attempting to explain the human condition, they also explain that the creative act of God was disrupted. The Christian term usually used to describe this disruption is *the Fall,* a falling away from the original intention of creation. If the world began as a good thing but is not as good as it once was, then something must have happened to account for the fact that God created a paradise, yet people live in a world of pain and suffering. The biblical authors knew from their own experience that something happened because they did not live in a paradise. They knew that life is hard work; that people can be wicked, aggressive, and selfish; and that no matter how much people have, they want more. Biblical writers were able to incorporate these human experiences into their descriptions of the dim beginnings of world history The experience of the community and their understanding of God shaped the way they explained the beginnings of the world. The story of creation and the Fall belongs to a period usually designated as prehistory, the time for which we have no written records. All ancient peoples had some explanation for the creation of the world and the status of people within that world. When the story of creation was finally written down by the biblical authors, it reflected the experience and beliefs of their own community.

Let's look at some of the ways the Israelites might have explained creation and the presence of evil in the world. Like other peoples of the ancient Near East, they could have reasoned that the gods are like people, both good and bad, which accounts for evil in the world. They could have said, "Life is hard and people are wicked, and that must be God's fault." Both of these explanations appear in ancient literature written around the same time as the biblical story of creation. Since Israel knew from its experience as a community and from God's self-communication that God was good and that the created order was good, the Israelites could not blame God for the mess of the world. They knew just as well from experience that the world was a mess. How could it be explained so that God's goodness was not put in doubt? The creation story in Genesis accounts for both kinds of experience. In that story, God remains good and powerful and creates people as an act of generosity. Evil gets into the world but not through God's fault. The story tells us three things:

1. People were made in the image of God (they are wonderful, like God in some way, and God longs for a relationship with them).
2. People freely, as an act of curiosity and willfulness, chose their own will over God's will and disrupted creation.
3. God promised to restore good relations among them.

To retell the story briefly: God created a man and a woman, gave them everything they could possibly want in terms of comfort and power, and added one more gift, freedom. God wanted them to respond freely, not by force. Now, the biblical authors tell us, this gift of freedom was put to a test in a very direct way. God told them they could eat the fruit of every tree in the garden except one. It is the doctrine of conditional joy, rather like a fairy tale: "You can have the beautiful princess if you bring her a magic radish," or "You can have three wishes if you bring me the little blue light." According to the Bible, the people failed the test, and in failing it, they acted as we all act. We all know what it is to have someone say, "You can do anything but . . ." In *The Magician's Nephew*, by C. S. Lewis, two children are exploring an underground world where everyone is asleep and the whole atmosphere is mysterious. In the middle of a courtyard, they find a little silver bell and a hammer and an inscription that reads:

> Make your choice, adventurous Stranger;
> Strike the bell and bide the danger,
> Or wonder, till it drives you mad,
> What would have followed if you had. (chapter 4)

Lewis's ditty clarifies the dilemma the biblical author was trying to convey, exquisitely evoking the first problem of human freedom. In religious language, we say that the first man and woman were tempted, egged on to do something they were not supposed to do. In the biblical story, the man and woman weakened and gave in, and the biblical author says it was because they were tempted by a clever serpent. How can we interpret this story, then? Were the man and woman outsmarted? Were they just weak and curious? Did they sin? Some believers interpret the action of the first man and woman as one of pride and self-deception, others as an expression of the desire of people to set their own limits, be their own God. Whatever the interpretation, their action changed things—life was no longer lived in a beautiful garden. Painful realities entered into human life: work now included frustration and might be fruitless as well as difficult, birth occurred within a context of pain, and sickness and death became part of human existence. In Christian religious language, this moment of separation and alienation is called Original Sin; it is the religious explanation for the facts of life as the biblical authors and the community experienced them.

The story tells us about God and humanity. God the Creator is powerful and good and wants people to have good relationships with each other and with the deity. We know that human beings are created in the image of God and that they are free to reject God and go their own ways. We also learn about the reality of sin: people are capable of it through weakness and willfulness, and it does damage by pulling people in a direction away from God.

Many times in the Bible, sin is explained in terms of direction: people turn away from God, go astray, follow the wrong leaders, or worship false gods. To return to God's good graces requires repentance and conversion, literally a change of direction, a move back toward God. Repentance is an important concept throughout the Old Testament. The prophets especially, speaking to those who have turned away from God, call upon people to remember the covenant and turn back to God. In the New Testament, Jesus calls people to repentance and conversion, which is precisely a change of direction and a turning away from sin to embrace God's word.

GOD AS PROVIDENT

In the creation account, we learned that things began well, but because of sin, people found themselves in a muddle. God's response to this situation discloses another divine attribute. When people ruined a good situation, God (as all powerful) could have let them die and then could have started over or could have left them to their own devices. Some explanations about God's relationship with the world argue that God created the world and then left it to itself; some explanations of human life rely on concepts of fate or determinism. The biblical account, however, says something different and extraordinary: God is willing to enter into the muddle and bring the divine creative energy to bear on it without interfering with human freedom. God re-created their good options; when people moved away from God, God was willing to help them find the road back. God moved into the history of these people. God created a world, watched people make a mess of it, and then entered into that mess creatively, fashioning out of it a people, a law, and a way. Christians call God's involvement in the world *providence,* the divine provision for humanity.

Some people have wondered how an all-powerful God relates to people without violating their freedom. God's actions in history come as calls, not demands. The Bible does not usually picture God as manipulative or overbearing but as interested and compassionate. People are invited to be in partnership with God. The pattern of

Controversy

Creating the Creator: Inspiration at Work

Bible stories reflect the religious experience of the ancient Israelites as they interacted with other cultures and interpreted their own history. Celebration of and reflection on these experiences led to new insights and eventually to the Bible we have today. The attributes of God affirmed in the creation stories are a good example of inspired writing. The ancient writers knew about gods and creation stories in other cultures, but they were also quite sure that their God was different. Here's how it worked.

The Babylonians were ancient neighbors of the Israelites whose creation myth is found in a book called the *Enuma Elish*. Their story involves many gods, a council of divinities presided over by Marduk (the storm god) and Tiamat (the sea goddess). When these two engaged in a furious battle, Marduk won and formed the created world from Tiamat's corpse. He filled her belly with wind and "opened her like a clam" so that the front of her body became the sky (with waters above it) and the back of her body became the earth (with waters beneath it). Marduk then took mud and Tiamat's blood to create human beings, created to be slaves to the gods. The striking features of this story are that there were multiple gods, that creation resulted from a struggle between order (Marduk) and chaos (Tiamat), and that humans were created from mud and blood so that they could serve the gods forever.

The biblical authors knew this story, but they also had a much different experience of God. Their God had rescued them from slavery in Egypt, brought them into freedom, and called them into a special relationship. When they wrote their own story of creation, they revised the Babylonian myth in light of their own experience. Inspiration led them not to make up a whole new story but to infuse an old story with very different features.

The creation story in the Bible has only one supreme God who needs only to speak in order to create. Human beings are created in the divine image, from mud and divine breath. Furthermore, they are beings whose freedom allows them to serve God or not, as they choose. We can find echoes of the Babylonian story in the Hebrew Bible (God speaking in plural terms, for example, saying, "Let us create humankind"), and there are obvious wordplays (God's spirit hovers over a "deep," which is *tehom* in Hebrew, a word that comes from Tiamat). What makes the story inspired is the way it reflects Israel's unique religious experience.

providence and continuing revelation in the Bible, therefore, can be interpreted as a pattern of call and response. God still initiates the conversation and relationship, but human freedom is intact because people may choose to reject the invitation or to accept it.

The fifth book of the Old Testament, Deuteronomy, contains a summary statement about what God has done for a particular people (26:5–10). It begins by saying, "A wandering Aramean was my father" and goes on to explain what happened to him. He became the father of a great nation. That nation or people was in the course of time welcomed into the land of Egypt but later made slaves. The passage goes on to say, "And the Egyptians treated us harshly, and afflicted us, and laid upon us hard bondage. . . . Then we cried to the Lord the God of our ancestors, and the Lord heard our voice, saw our affliction, our toil and our oppression and the Lord brought us out of Egypt with a mighty hand and an outstretched arm, with great terror, with signs and wonders . . . and he brought us into this place and gave us this land, a land flowing with milk and honey." Something has happened in the lives of this particular people that reveals how God's providence works. The creation story was about all people, the first people of the human race; it offered an explanation for universal destiny. The summary of God's works in Deuteronomy is about a specific people, a people called by God to be special and to be the bearers of God's self-communication, to begin the work of restoring what was lost in the Fall.

The Story of Abraham

In Genesis 9, we see that God promised to do something about the havoc people brought upon themselves through disobedience. What God would do is not clear, but there are grounds for anticipation of some action in the future. The first specific idea we get about the divine plan occurs in Genesis 12, when God called Abraham.

The Abraham story has five important elements. First, God's intervention into Abraham's life came with no explanation; it was pure gift—gratuitous. Second, Abraham was an old man with an old, childless wife when God told him that he would be the father of a great nation. The story tells us that Abraham found God's promise confusing, funny, and awesome, but that in spite of misgivings, he responded. In religious terms, we can say that he responded in *trust*. We might note here that many biblical heroes initially had doubts but finally trusted that God would be with them and help them fulfill their call. Third, Abraham did have a son (two of them, in fact, though the first, Ishmael, drops out of this story) and named him Isaac. This child was born when Abraham's wife, Sarah, was old and barren, so a *miraculous element* was involved: God acts with power and demonstrates divine lordship. Fourth, God made a pact with Abraham, a *covenant*. Finally, God *tested* Abraham's faith and obedience by asking him to sacrifice Isaac. Faith and trust in God are not a one-time event but part of an ongoing relationship that requires heroic obedience.

The word *covenant* occurs repeatedly in the Bible. Covenants spell out the terms of God's relationship with people; they are partnership agreements, contracts. In the modern world, contracts are written down with the terms specified and penalties explained for breaking the agreement. In the ancient world, there *were* written contracts, but there were also spoken agreements, which were solemn and sacred. In contracts and covenants, there are witnesses to the signing and to the terms. Often, covenants were enacted before the gods (who acted as witnesses); all parties bound themselves rigorously to the terms. A covenant, therefore, is a solemn form of the spoken word, a binding and sacred agreement.

The terms of God's covenant with Abraham were clear: God would see that Abraham was the father of a great nation, which God would then bless and protect. Abraham in turn was to honor God and see that every male member of his family was circumcised as a sign that he belonged to God. A further divine promise was that through Abraham and his descendants, the nations of the world would be blessed; the promise was universal as well as particular.

When Abraham agreed to the terms, responded to God's specific step toward partnership with a people, he made it possible for God to do something about the muddle. You can read the rest of the story in Genesis, which tells how this chosen people were eventually enslaved in Egypt.

The Story of Moses

The Moses story (Exodus) has some parallels to the Abraham story and clear links with it. Abraham was the father of Isaac and the grandfather of Jacob. The biblical tradition maintains that Jacob had twelve sons, who were the fathers of the twelve tribes of Israel (God changed Jacob's name to Israel). They continued to honor God and to follow the terms of the covenant, and so, through them, the covenant between God and Abraham passed down through history and the God of the Hebrews came to be known as the God of Abraham, Isaac, and Jacob. One of Jacob's sons, Joseph (see Gen. 37–50), is the main character in the story of the Hebrews in Egypt, which is where we must go for the Moses story.

The covenant with Abraham occurred some time between 1850 and 1600 B.C.E. (before the common era), and the flight from Egypt under the direction of Moses probably took place between 1250 and 1200 B.C.E. The Hebrews had lived in Egypt for many generations, first as welcome guests and finally as slaves. Moses enters the story as God's chosen liberator, sent to free the Hebrews and bring them to a new land and a new covenant. We can find some of the same elements in the Moses story that we found in the Abraham story. First, according to the biblical authors, God's intervention into Moses' life is gratuitous. His birth was no different from any other Hebrew boy's, and nothing explains why a hidden providence protected him and eventually selected him as the mediator for the covenant. Second, when Moses first heard God's voice (Exod. 3), he was awestruck and impressed but also confused and afraid. His decision to return to Egypt to lead people out was a trusting response made in spite of his hesitation about what God wanted him to do. Third, the great events in Egypt—the plagues, the Passover, the Red Sea event (see Exod. 7–15)—were miraculous. God acted with power, and the Hebrews and Egyptians saw God's power in those events. Fourth, God made a *covenant* with the whole people at Mount Sinai. Finally, these people were *tested* in the wilderness. Almost immediately after accepting the covenant, the people who agreed to keep it broke it. Furthermore (as reported in stories in Num.), their lack of faith finally resulted in their not being permitted to enter the promised land; instead, they were forced to wander in the desert for 40 years.

Besides these parallels with the Abraham story, other features of the Moses story stand out. The Hebrew people in bondage in Egypt "cried out," and God "heard them" and determined to help them. Because of the covenant with Abraham, because God promised to protect this people, they had a claim on God and could cry out with reminders of the divine obligation to them. When God responded to the people and sent Moses to liberate them, God said, "I am the God of Abraham, Isaac, and Jacob," thereby showing a continuity between the Mosaic and the Abrahamic covenants.

Three months after the people left Egypt, God brought them to the wilderness at Sinai, and the high point of the Moses story is the covenant made at Sinai. God not only delivered the Israelites but called them into a partnership agreement. At Sinai, through the giving of covenant law (including the Ten Commandments), the relationship between God and Israel took on a new dimension of particularity. While the people camped below, Moses went up the mountain, "up to God." There God told Moses to say this to the Hebrews: "You have seen what I did to the Egyptians and how I bore you on eagles' wings and brought you to myself. Now therefore, if you will obey my voice and keep my covenant you shall be my own possession among all peoples; for all the earth is mine, and you shall be to me a kingdom of priests and a holy nation" (Exod. 19:4–5). Moses went down the mountain and gave that message to the people, and they responded, "All that the Lord has spoken, we will do" (see Exod. 19 and 24:3). It is clear that the people responded on the basis of their experience of God's liberation. They heard thunder and understood it as the divine voice; they demanded a mediator to interpret God's words for them, and Moses brought them the terms of the contract; they agreed to the terms of the covenant and willingly bound themselves in a relationship with God that required them to keep the commandments.

The People of the Covenant

God entered into history to make these former slaves into a special people and did so through the covenant. Biblical tradition sees the Law as an act of divine providence enabling Israel to maintain the covenant relationship with God. The people had been set free in Egypt by an act of divine justice; the Law was given to help them maintain that freedom and justice within their new society.

The history of Israel from the covenant at Sinai onward is one of keeping and violating the covenant and of God's continued intervention to restore a proper relationship. People read the Bible for many reasons, one of which is that it discloses parts of the divine personality; the Bible also shows a deep understanding of human nature and conveys the two-steps-forward-one-step-backward kind of progress most people experience in life. Even with God as their protector and guide, the people of Israel continually went astray. Why? The story in Genesis about the first man and woman helps explain the tension people find themselves in: people are attracted to good (because they were made in the image of God, who is good) and to evil (because of their sinfulness). Israel's experience demonstrates that those attractions can be equally strong, that human beings are easily confused. Is good more attractive than wickedness? The Bible is not clear on this question, and the history of Israel bears out the ambivalence. Israel's history is not unique. All human history reveals similar patterns of fidelity and betrayal.

The rest of the history of Israel builds on the same themes. During the first two centuries in the promised land, the people of Israel led a varied existence, both politically and religiously. When they were in trouble and cried out, the Lord sent help by way of heroes and heroines (see Judges). As the small band of nomadic slaves brought out of Egypt grew into a larger people and settled into the land, they were torn between wanting to maintain their uniqueness (as God's people) and their desire to be like their neighbors. The story of Israel's move toward kingship is ambivalent. For a number of reasons, and with mixed results, Israel solidified into a kingdom that reached its zenith of organization and power under David and Solomon around the year 1000 B.C.E. David's son Solomon was the last king to rule over a united Israel. For political reasons (that had theological significance for Israel), the twelve tribes split into two separate kingdoms: ten tribes in the north (called Israel) and two in the south (called Judah). Although early Israel felt deep ambivalence about the kingship of David (as a dethroning of the divine king), the later biblical tradition generally sees it as an important part of God's plan.

The two kingdoms did not last because they were conquered by foreign powers. The northern kingdom fell to the Assyrians, and the southern kingdom was conquered

Concept

Contracts with God: Covenant Theology

Although the books of the Bible differ in audience and intention, a primary theme in the Bible is God's covenant with Israel. A covenant is a contract that binds both parties to certain terms. In general, the people of Israel agreed to bind themselves to only one God, the Lord: they shall "have no other gods before" the Lord (Exod. 20:3). Note that the Bible assumes the existence of other gods: the people must choose to follow the Lord alone (Josh. 24:15). In return, God promised to protect Israel in return for their fidelity to God and the Law.

When we read the history of Israel, however, we see that they were not always under divine protection. How can this be explained? As the biblical authors saw it, the ups and downs of their history were a result of Israel's wavering fidelity to their promises. That is why we find different covenants in the Bible: they provide theological explanations for the social and political history of Israel. Notice the differences in how God sets the terms.

Genesis 9:1–9. After the flood, God made a promise to Noah that included all humanity, indeed, all sentient life. The world would never again be destroyed by flood, and the rainbow was God's sign of this promise. Humanity was now to be fruitful and multiply. This covenant was made unconditionally; it would always be true.

Genesis 17. God promised Abraham that he would be the father of many nations and that he would be given a promised land. The sign of this covenant was circumcision, a bodily ritual that makes a male a descendant of Abraham and thus an heir to the promises of God. This covenant was made unconditionally; God would keep the promise no matter what Abraham and his descendants did.

Exodus 10–20. Through Moses, God promised the Israelites that they would be God's treasured possession out of all the peoples on the earth. This group that God brought out of slavery in Egypt was destined to become "a holy nation." Unlike the previous covenants, this promise was made conditionally; to gain the benefits promised by God, Israel had to obey the covenant laws that were given to Moses and summarized in the Ten Commandments.

2 Samuel 7. The covenant with David, like those with Noah and Abraham, was made unconditionally. God promised David that his dynasty would last forever: the kings of Israel—descendants of David—would be like sons to God. They could be punished for their sins (as David was), but God would always love them.

During the Exile, these covenants seem to be over. The Jews lived under the domination of foreign powers, they did not control the land promised to Abraham, and no descendant of David ruled as king. In this situation, groups of Jews began to reinterpret the covenants in terms of apocalyptic eschatology. In other words, they began to think not so much about what God had done for them in the past but about what God would do for them in the future. In that time, they believed, God would restore all these promises through a Messiah. Christians, in their desire to explain Jesus in light of Jewish expectations, also reinterpreted the covenants. According to them, the covenants with Abraham and David refer to Jesus (see Matt. 1:1; Rom. 1:3; Gal. 3:16).

by the Babylonians. Why did God let this happen to this chosen people? Here we must turn to the prophets and enter a new phase of Israelite history. The word *prophet* comes from the Hebrew word *nabi*, which perhaps means "called by God" and usually implies someone who is called to speak God's word to those who seem to have forgotten it.

People

King David

Important biblical figures are remembered for their parts in God's actions for Israel. David is the classic king, whose tumultuous career and wavering fidelity to God made him a symbol for the nation as a whole. His narrative occupies a large part of the Hebrew Bible from 1 Samuel 16 through 1 Kings 2 and portions of 1 Chronicles. David's story, like that of many biblical characters, is a mosaic of historical material, folklore, and legend. According to the Bible, David was a poet who wrote the Psalms and a courageous young man who slew the giant Goliath with a slingshot.

God chose David when he was a boy tending his father's sheep. He was anointed by Samuel, became a rival to Saul, and eventually succeeded him as king. Confident that God was on his side, David expanded the kingdom of Israel and unified it around a new city, Jerusalem, the "city of David," to which he brought the Ark of the Covenant. David made his own covenant with God, who promised that his dynasty would be eternal. He thus became a symbol of the Jewish kingdom and the focus of later hopes for a Messiah, a "son of David" who would reestablish God's kingdom.

Yet, wary of the close connection between him and the idea of a divinely favored kingdom, the Bible raises questions about David. For example, God made David king, yet is not God the true and only King of Israel? Are David's violent efforts to establish his rule admirable? David is morally upbraided by the prophet Nathan for his affair with Bathsheba. His troubles with his son Absalom make him a tragic figure as well as a hero.

The complexity of David's life and character is reflected in the book of Psalms, of which he is traditionally (if incorrectly) seen as author. Some convey trust and love between God and his "son"; others attack and wish harm against enemies; and still others cry out to God in anguish. As psalmist, David has given words to generations of Jews and Christians seeking to express to God the full range of their feelings.

Prophets were thus sent on missions by God to recall people to the covenant. Part of their message was the dire warning that unfaithfulness to the covenant would lead to destruction. As God's people neglected the covenant and ignored God, the prophets tried, often poetically and with a sense of desperate urgency, to get people to remember their relationship with God.

The northern kingdom (Israel), which lasted from about 922 to 721 B.C.E., was successful in economic and military terms but was unfaithful to the covenant. Two important prophets were sent by God to recall Israel to the covenant. Amos, a shepherd from Judah, preached there in the 750s and warned Israel of its impending doom. He was a poor man preaching to rich people, and his message was angry and harsh. Hosea, a native of Israel, preached a message of divine compassion 20 years later, when his people were in the midst of war with Assyria. His life dramatized his message: he married a prostitute who was totally unfaithful to him, yet he brought her back to his house, loved her, and would not let her go. You can already see in these two prophets the outlines of what will become a later interpretation of the covenant. On the one hand, God warns an unfaithful people and allows them to be conquered, but on the other hand, God continues to love them and longs to take them back.

The southern kingdom (Judah) lasted from 922 to 587 B.C.E., when it was destroyed by the Babylonians and its people carried off into Exile. Again, God called prophets to warn and comfort people. Two of the most famous prophets exercised their ministry in this context. Jeremiah, whose preaching began c. 627 B.C.E., is famous for his oracles and lamentations in which he sees the coming destruction but also imagines that eventually there would be a new and deeper relationship with God. The book of Isaiah reflects the ministry of at least two different prophets in two different time frames. First Isaiah (chapters 1–39) entreats Judah to return to the covenant and warns them against social injustice. The kingdom of Judah was destroyed by the Babylonians and its people carried off into exile because God's people failed to heed the warnings of the prophets, failed to return to their covenant obligations. Did the Exile mark the end of the covenant?

The People in Exile

What is the relationship between God and an exiled people? Is it possible to continue to believe in the covenant after being nearly destroyed and removed from the promised land? During and after the Exile, many Jews looking at the grim events of history tended to see their hardships as punishment for their sins. Paradoxically, for them, the Exile was not a sign that God had forgotten the covenant but a sign of God's abiding care. The Exile was a punishment for disobedience, a purification. God's word—spoken by the prophets, before, during, and after the Exile—helped the Jews understand their painful and confusing experience. We can see clearly here the interrelationship between historical experience and ways a group understood God's role in their lives. In all of Israel's history and in the Bible, there is a connection between the Jews' historical experience, their self-understanding, and their perceptions about God. Even when things were at their worst—when the people were in exile in Babylon being taunted by their captors—God continued to send prophets to keep God's word alive. When the people wondered what would happen to them after the Exile, prophets like Ezekiel had visions of a renewed Israel where the original purposes of the Abrahamic covenant would be fulfilled and where Israel would become a universal blessing to all nations. Ezekiel's famous vision of the "valley of the dry bones," who "hear the Word of the Lord" and are restored by God's breath (Ezek. 37:1–14) is a dramatic account of what a faithful people can expect from God. Thus, around 537 B.C.E., when a small group was returned to Palestine, many Jews felt they were being brought back and given another chance, a fresh start. They would never again have a kingdom or much political power, but they were still God's people, and they still had the covenant.

Their history from their return onward is one of domination by foreign powers—Persians, Greeks, and Romans. During one brief period (143–63 B.C.E.; see Chapter 2), the Jews were in control of their political lives, but in 63 B.C.E., Pompey, a Roman general, captured Jerusalem, and the Romans were in control of the country when Jesus was born.

When we look at the Hebrew Bible, we can find books that tell these stories in much more elaborate detail (see Appendix 2). The books of the Torah and the Prophets tell us about Israel's history and prophetic experience. The Writings fill in another dimension of Israel's experience of God. The Psalms, a magnificent, poetic prayerbook containing hymns for almost every occasion and feeling; the so-called Wisdom literature with its philosophical reflections (for example, Job); moral maxims (for example, Proverbs); the erotic poetry of the Song of Songs (or Song of Solomon); the apocalyptic visions of Daniel—all indicate an extraordinarily rich experience of God's action and presence in their lives. All of these books and most of this experience were used later by Christians to explain Jesus. For the time being, however, it is enough to know the main outline of the story, to realize that it is inexhaustibly rich and amenable to a wide variety of interpretations, and to remember that, according to the Bible, God did not abandon the Jewish people.

CONCLUSION

This chapter has set forth the ancient context and foundation of Christianity, along with some basic concepts. We have seen what revelation means and noted that the Bible is a record of God's revelation. Since both Christians and Jews look to the Bible as the record of God's revelation, we looked there to find out some of its basic perceptions of God. We found that the God of Jews and Christians is the powerful, transcendent creator of the world. More important, however, we found that God did not leave people to their own devices but remained interested in them even when they made a mess of God's good creative work. We have focused on the Abraham and Moses stories in the history of Israel as demonstrations of divine providence: the initial promise, the covenant with Abraham, the rescue of Abraham's descendants, and the covenant at Sinai all disclose God's personality. We have seen that being in a covenant relationship with God did not mean that all went smoothly or that people were never tempted to do anything wrong. On the contrary, people, even though they were in a relationship with God, continued to go astray and to follow the wrong paths. An important insight from the Bible is that God continues to be interested in a people even when they fail to keep the covenant. God judges them and redeems them; God's self-communication is revealed in an ongoing history of invitation and response.

Focal Points for Discussion

1. Consider the examples of transcendence and immanence in this chapter and on page 7. Is it possible to conceptualize God using only one of these categories?
2. The Israelites had a tumultuous history and yet believed that God was always present among them. How did their notion of God or covenant change in different historical circumstances?
3. Religion is first grounded in experience, then celebrated in ritual, and then elaborated in a text. How does this formula work to explain the development of the Hebrew Bible?

The Context for and Life of Jesus

CHAPTER 2

Jesus was born into a volatile political situation and a complex religious milieu. The Jews had been exiled to Babylon in 587 B.C.E. after the Babylonians destroyed the southern kingdom (Judah); they remained in exile until 537 B.C.E. When the Jews returned from Babylon to Palestine, they were faced with problems of survival and of interpreting the meaning of the Exile. Their attempts to resolve those problems had a bearing on how they perceived Jesus' life and teaching. Since their interpretations of the Exile and their reactions to their new historical circumstances were bound up with renewed seriousness about the Law, Jesus' relationship to the Law was also very important to them. Jewish ideas about the kingdom of God along with the divided political situation within Judaism itself made gaining acceptance difficult for any powerful preacher: no matter what the preacher said, there was always a different but equally valid interpretation. Jesus' life and teaching, therefore, must be understood against this complicated background. Similarly, writings about Jesus (and early Christians) have to be read in light of the religious and political situation of the times. One of the important questions for early Christian interpreters was where Jesus fit with regard to Jewish expectations. In this chapter, we will see what those expectations were, where they came from, and how they were reinterpreted by early Christian writers to fit the life and message of Jesus.

JEWISH INTERPRETATION OF THE EXILE

The covenant at Sinai was the major event that shaped the lives and understanding of the Jewish people. It not only provided them with their specific identity as God's people but also gave them a perspective from which to interpret their history. Whatever happened to them, they could look back to the covenant, to the basis of their relationship with God, and find a way to explain it. What did the Jews think about the Exile? And what do you think their captors thought of the Jews and their religion?

How do you think the belief that they worshiped the one true God and were God's people looked in light of their defeat and exile? It is not hard to imagine that many people wondered just what had happened: Had God deserted them? Was God no longer interested in the Jews? Psalm 137 tells us how the Jews themselves felt: "By the waters of Babylon, there we sat down and wept when we remembered Zion" (137:1).

It must have been tempting, even for the Jews, to think that God had lost interest in them. Because of the covenant, however, and because of their long experience of God's faithfulness and mercy, the Jews did not interpret the Exile as a sign of divine abandonment. In fact, they interpreted it in just the opposite way. When they reflected on their dislocation and their return to Palestine, they saw a sign of God's continuing interest in the covenant relationship. God was, indeed, bound up with them, repeatedly warning them and reminding them of the terms of the covenant. God continually sent messengers, the prophets, to call the people back to observance of the Law and to a better relationship. Only because they would not listen and because there was no other way, God was constrained to punish them, to uproot and replant them. Their sinfulness, their "going astray," meant that they had to be redirected. The Exile was seen as the means God used to cleanse the people, forcing them to develop a clearer vision of the relationship between God and Israel. When they were brought back from Babylon (in 537 B.C.E.), it was with a renewed sense of obligation to be loyal and obedient to the commandments.

How did they intend to be God's faithful people in the future? How would they be true to the one God in their belief, worship, and everyday life? The answer—present in the terms of the covenant—lay in keeping the Law. Since they were no longer one people in one land with one ruler, the Law provided internal coherence for them. They had learned that keeping the Law was sometimes difficult when they were surrounded and tempted by a foreign culture. Their renewed efforts to keep the Law, therefore, were coupled with an intense effort to keep themselves apart from influences that might seduce them or force them away from the Law. This meant, in effect, that the Jews had a strong interest in keeping themselves separate from other people. They might be forced to live under foreign political domination, but they could resist any attempts at religious domination; by obedience to the Law, they could refuse to intermarry and become part of another culture.

When the Jews were restored to Palestine in 537 B.C.E., they were subject to a number of different foreign powers. The most serious threat to their resolution to remain faithful observers of the Law, however, occurred during the Hellenistic period, which began with the death of Alexander the Great (323 B.C.E.) and is usually thought to have ended politically with the conquest of Alexandria by the Romans in the first century B.C.E.

HELLENIZATION AND THE JEWS

The conquests of Alexander the Great spread Greek ideas, culture, philosophy, manners, language, and art to the Near East and well into Asia. The Jews were touched by Hellenistic civilization as evidenced in the Bible by the so-called Wisdom literature (Proverbs and Ecclesiastes, for example). During the Hellenistic era, the descendants of Alexander's generals hoped to consolidate their empire, unifying it in language, customs, law, and philosophy. They hoped to do this by insinuating their culture and practices into the lands they conquered and by pursuing a policy of intermarriage with the peoples they ruled. Their policies were thus in direct conflict with the Jewish resolve to keep themselves separate.

One can imagine that some of the Greek ideas and philosophy must have seemed appealing to some of the Jews. The impulse of Hellenism, along with the power and beauty of Greek culture, was felt in Israel as everywhere else. The Jews continued to keep themselves apart from some of its demands, but at the same time, they began to disagree about how far they *could* go in accommodating themselves to this new cultural influence. Could a Jew be true to the Law and study Greek philosophy? Could a young Jewish boy participate in the athletic games at the local Greek-styled gymnasium? Could Jews allow *some* statues of Greek gods in their towns? Issues like these divided the Jews not only in theory but in practice. Some Jews felt that they could enter into the spirit of the Greek culture and maintain their Jewish identity; others believed that any participation in Hellenistic civilization violated the covenant and displeased God. A strong opposition party, the predecessors of the Pharisees, arose against Hellenization and those Jews who favored it. They argued that Greek customs were foreign and idolatrous and that no Jew could legitimately participate in them.

Once aversion to Hellenization took the form of a political party, the arguments against Greek ways had a more political character. The opposition to Hellenization grew stronger and more vocal; in the minds of Greek officials, at least, it began to appear that things could not be resolved without a showdown, or test of power. In 168 B.C.E., therefore, Antiochus IV—whose rule extended over Jerusalem, from Palestine to Syria and eastward to the Euphrates, and who had already offended the Jews by selling the office of high priest (in direct violation of Jewish practice and law)—began a campaign to destroy the religion of the Jews. He issued an edict that forbade Jews to practice circumcision, to celebrate any festivals, or to keep the Sabbath. All copies of the Torah were to be destroyed and the Jewish temple turned into a Greek temple. A statue of the Greek god Zeus was put up in the Jerusalem temple, and Jews were forced to worship the pagan gods.

In this appalling turn of events, even the Jews who had favored Hellenization found the policies of Antiochus IV abominable. Opposition to Antiochus solidified behind the leadership of Judas Maccabaeus and his four brothers, who revolted against foreign domination. The revolt and their victory, which are recorded in the first book of Maccabees, are celebrated each year in the Jewish feast of Hanukkah. The struggle for religious freedom turned into a battle for political freedom. From 143 to 63 B.C.E., the Jews retained political control of Israel. The Jewish defeat of the Greeks led to 80 years of political freedom, but it did not end foreign domination. In 63 B.C.E., the Roman general Pompey captured Jerusalem and began Roman domination of the Jews.

At the time of Jesus, Herod the Great, whose father had gained political power as an ally of Julius Caesar, was the ruler of all Palestine. Although he was the ruler of the Jews, he was despised by them. Furthermore, the Romans, who had always allowed the Jews to practice their religion in relative freedom, were beginning to find the Jews a political nuisance. It was possible, the Romans thought, that the Jews might be secret political allies of the Syrians—an alliance that would constitute a serious threat to the Romans that either the Syrians or the Jews alone would not. Remember that the Jews had a stake in maintaining their own identity, in refusing to intermarry and to take on customs of the conquering power. Since they had maintained their own identity, they had not been absorbed into the empire. Such political autonomy, therefore, made them appear dangerous to the Romans. It was into this Jewish world, politically unstable and ruled by Romans, that Jesus was born.

JEWISH HOPES FOR A KINGDOM OF GOD

To understand fully the religious context into which Jesus was born, you must understand that faithfulness to the Law was bound up with the popular Jewish expectation that God would somehow and at some time act decisively in their behalf through an agent chosen by God. God had rescued them from the land of Egypt and had restored them to Israel after the Exile. Thus, they had reason to expect that God would continue to act for them. Whereas most Jews searched the Law for guidance about everyday behavior, some searched other parts of Scripture for what God might do in the future. A strong vocal minority centered their hopes on the concept of a *kingdom of God,* perhaps because it recaptured the old ideal of a chosen people in a promised land under a divinely sanctioned king. However it was understood, the kingdom of God became a slogan for what would happen in a new age. The coming of the kingdom would mark the establishment of God's rule forever, everywhere. Some groups of Jews did not believe this because it was not written in the Torah itself, and it is not altogether clear just how many Jews *did* believe that God would act in this way.

Within this general understanding of divine victory, however, there were differences of opinion. Some Jews believed that the Messiah would be a wise and ideal king who would establish justice all over the world. Some thought a Messiah-king would surely be of the Davidic line, since David had been the greatest of the ancient kings. Some believed that the establishment of the kingdom of God would mean Jewish political prestige throughout the world: Israel would be the most powerful nation on earth, ruling over everyone.

As the Jews became more threatened by political events, especially in the second and first centuries before the common era, popular beliefs about the kingdom of God began to take on more militant aspects. Since Jews were involved in crucial political and military struggles, their ideas about the Messiah and the kingdom of God increasingly incorporated political and military expectations. Some people began to see the kingdom of God not so much as an ideal kingdom of righteousness but as some kind of powerful event. The kingdom of God began to be tied up with the expectation that God would perform some great act. Since the world was in such a mess, God would have to bring about a complete transformation of people and of the world.

During this time, a literature and outlook called *apocalyptic* began to flourish. The second and first centuries before the common era were times in which the influence of religious dualism began to be felt and an apocalyptic tone heard: people began to look at the world as a place under the influence of evil powers that could not be defeated by human powers alone. To defeat these evil powers, God would have to intervene and conquer them with divine power. People saw the world as a battleground between the forces of good and evil; they believed the universe was divided between the kingdom of God (whom they hoped was coming to the rescue) and the kingdom of Satan (whom

CONCEPT

Living on the Edge of Time: Apocalypticism

Happy people do not write apocalypses. Apocalyptic groups are oppressed by governmental authorities and usually by others in their society as well. They explain their sufferings as part of the necessary turmoil that will precede the end of the world, and they tell their readers that God will eventually intervene on the side of the elect. Although outsiders cannot understand the bizarre symbolism of apocalyptic visions, the elect can read the secret plan of God. When outsiders react negatively to apocalyptic writing, the elect see this as additional confirmation of their beliefs; as the righteous ones, they must suffer at the hands of outsiders, but God will punish their oppressors when the kingdom comes.

Jewish and Christian apocalyptic writings, composed between 200 B.C.E. and 150 C.E., treat the world as a battleground between the forces of good and evil. The authors write about horrendous suffering and injustice and long for a divine intervention to usher in a new age—usually called the kingdom of God—where good people would flourish and the wicked would suffer terrible torments. Jesus preached that the kingdom of God was at hand, and when he appeared to his disciples after his death, the first Christians believed that Jesus had risen from the dead and would soon return as the "Messiah" to usher in a new kingdom. Thus, apocalypticism has been called "the mother of Christian theology."

The letters of Paul are filled with apocalypticism. When his followers in Thessalonica felt rejected by the people around them, Paul told them that their afflictions constituted "evidence of the righteous judgment of God." Christians, he said, were the elect, and God would repay their tormentors with "eternal destruction" (2 Thess. 1:4–10). Paul's purpose was to comfort and to offer hope to a small group of Christians in a hostile world. He offers words of comfort and says that outsiders are condemned to destruction. Apocalyptic literature has that double theme of comfort for the saints and punishment for the wicked.

The best-known apocalyptic writing in the Old Testament is the book of Daniel, and the apocalyptic text of the New Testament is the book of Revelation (sometimes called the Apocalypse), with its omens about the end of the world. But apocalypticism did not come to an end in the early church and has appeared numerous times as a recurrent feature of Christianity. Christians have claimed to receive new revelations about the end times, often in the form of new understandings of the visions in Daniel or Revelation. For example, in twelfth-century Italy, the monk Joachim of Fiore (1135–1202) applied the symbolism of Revelation to his own day and predicted a new age would come in 1260. In 1995, television evangelist Pat Robertson published a novel called, *The End of the Age,* which interpreted Revelation as referring to events that would unfold in the United States in 2007.

they believed was now in power). The day was surely coming, they thought, when God would destroy the power of Satan and master the evil that abounded.

During the two centuries before the birth of Jesus, an enormous body of literature developed about the coming of the kingdom and the overthrow of the demonic powers. There was a popular concept of what would happen. The world, dominated by evil powers, would be a place of great suffering and hardship until God rose up and overthrew the kingdom of Satan. In this mood, many ideas about the Messiah focused on military conquest. The Messiah might be wise, but most of all he would be a powerful warrior-king who could conquer evil and begin the age of bliss.

THE JEWS DIVIDED

Judaism at the time of Jesus' birth was not monolithic but varied, especially in attitudes toward Roman domination and in expectations about the Messiah. There were probably about five hundred thousand Jews in Palestine at the time of Jesus, divided into many different groups. Descriptions of four of them will give you some idea of the situation and help you to appreciate the position of ordinary Jews.

The Sadducees

The Sadducees were the small aristocratic ruling class. In modern terms, they might be called the Establishment. They were wealthy conservatives who kept the Torah strictly, allowed no doctrinal innovations, and were strongly associated with the temple. They controlled the office of high priest and held a dominant position in the Jewish governing body, the Sanhedrin. Because of their political power over the Jewish community, they were the Jews the Roman politicians dealt with. Because the Sadducees were wealthy and established, they tended to deal with the Romans in a polite way. They were political collaborationists who were willing to adapt to Roman rule because the status quo worked in their favor. In terms of their religious beliefs, the Sadducees thought the Torah (the Law, the first five books of the Bible) was the single most important religious text and were not, therefore, interested in apocalyptic literature or Jewish tradition. It is not altogether clear what they expected in a Messiah, but it is safe to assume that they did *not* expect a Palestinian peasant from Nazareth.

The Pharisees

The Pharisees (approximately six thousand) were made up of artisans and merchants, descended from the party that opposed Greek ideas at the time of Antiochus. To keep the Jews faithful to the Law and away from any foreign influence, they were inclined to extend the Law to every phase of life, and they insisted on perfect observance. They were liberal in that they constantly applied the Torah to new situations and built up a whole new tradition of interpretation. The Pharisees associated not so much with priests but with laypeople, with scholars and teachers. They believed that every decision in life could be governed by the Torah, and they developed a system of elaborate interpretation (which later became the Mishnah and Talmud). They did not approve of political collaboration with the Romans and desired separatism. They accepted as authoritative the prophetic and other writings of the Bible, which the Sadducees did not accept, and incorporated some of the apocalyptic notions of the time into their religious understanding. Since they were not as interested in political matters and were not established economically as the Sadducees were, they had different expectations of a Messiah. The Pharisees were more religious than political, and their opinion of the future of Israel was a religious one. The Messiah, for them, would probably be a religious leader and teacher who perfectly observed the Law and who could lead people to repentance and the power of the Torah.

People

The Prophets and Messiahs of the First Century

Jesus proclaimed the kingdom of God and is reported to have performed miracles to back up his message. Whether or not Jesus called himself the Messiah, some Jews thought he was the agent of God they were waiting for. Roman authorities saw Jesus as enough of a threat to have him executed; in this respect, Jesus' career was similar to that of his teacher, John the Baptist, who was beheaded by Herod.

Jesus and John were not the only Jews of the first century who proclaimed the kingdom of God and provoked the wrath of the Roman government. Ten years or so after the death of Jesus, a prophet named Theudas led a nonviolent movement that looked for God's deliverance of Israel. He told his disciples to follow him to the Jordan River, which he promised to part. This miracle would indicate that Theudas was a new Moses leading a second exodus, this time away from Roman rule. The Roman governor sent some soldiers to the Jordan, who killed several people and cut off Theudas's head. Some time later, another Jew, known only as "the Egyptian," called on his listeners to march around the walls of Jerusalem, promising them that the walls would fall down. He saw himself as a new Joshua once again conquering the land for Israel. Although the Roman army killed many of the marchers, the Egyptian escaped. The careers of Jesus and John follow this pattern: they gathered a group of disciples, promised imminent deliverance of Israel from God, and were killed by Roman authorities.

Somewhat later, in 131–132 C.E., a man named Simon bar Kochba led a revolt of Jews against Roman rule in Palestine. Simon waged guerrilla warfare against the Roman armies by hiding out in caves and avoiding any direct, full-scale battles with the Romans. According to Jewish tradition, the esteemed Rabbi Akiva called Simon the Messiah and identified him as the "star" (*kochba*) that had been promised in the Torah as a deliverance for Israel (Num. 24:17–18). The Romans subdued Simon's revolt by 135 C.E., destroyed Jewish Jerusalem, and built a new city (Aelia Capitolina) in its place.

Jesus, therefore, was not unique. He was one of several prophets, or "messiah" figures, who raised Jewish hopes for liberation from Roman rule. Unlike the movements led by John the Baptist, Theudas, or Simon bar Kochba, however, the movement led by Jesus did not end with his death. Instead, Jesus became a figure worshiped after his death by a religious movement made up mostly of Gentiles.

The Essenes

The Essenes (approximately four thousand) were disenchanted ascetics and apocalyptic visionaries who withdrew from general society to form communes in the desert, where they waited for the Messiah and the destruction of the Romans. We know something about this group because of the discovery of the Dead Sea Scrolls, documents of the ancient Essene desert community of Qumran. Like the Pharisees, the Essenes had been part of the revolt against Greek customs, and their protest finally took the form of complete withdrawal from society.

They lived by themselves in the wilderness, preparing for the coming of the kingdom of God. Their expectation was apocalyptic, believing that the end of the world was near and that their lives should be lived in perfect obedience to God in the short time remaining. They believed that God was about to begin the messianic kingdom on earth and would form a new covenant with them. The new covenant and the Messiah would be bound up with the defeat of the Romans and with the promise of eternal life. They believed they had been called by God into the desert to be recipients of the new covenant. Thus, they called themselves the community of the new covenant and thought they were the true Israel.

The Zealots

The Zealots were a small band of underground activists whose roots can be traced back to the Maccabean revolts in the second century B.C.E. They were strict followers of the Torah who hated heathens and who had organized themselves into a political party to resist idolatrous practices. They expected to lead an armed uprising against the Romans in Israel. In modern terms, they were potential guerrilla warriors, collecting arms and soldiers for an impending struggle. They looked on the Romans as enemies to be overthrown, and they expected the Messiah to be a warrior-king who would lead them into battle against the Romans. They were annihilated in the Jewish wars of 70 C.E.

Ordinary Jews

The common people, who were the bulk of the Jewish population, were variously influenced by these and other groups and by apocalyptic literature. These people probably had a number of different ideas of what a Messiah should be, and biblical authors had drawn *some* ordinary people into messianic expectation in a special way by emphasizing God's concern for the *anawim,* the lowly and downtrodden people to whom the Messiah would eventually appear (Amos 2:7; Isa. 61:1). Most Jews in Palestine at the time of Jesus were not associated with any particular group. Most Jews were peasants who were not heavily invested in religion.

SUMMARY OF THE CONTEXT

The Jews saw the covenant as the central event of their lives; it provided the central motif for their interpretation of history. The most important part of the covenant was the keeping of the commandments. To avoid foreign corruption of their practices and beliefs, the Jews held themselves apart and maintained religious and ethnic purity. The Jews were looking for God to enter into history in a radical and transforming way, for a Messiah who would defeat the powers of evil, and for the establishment of a new kingdom. Finally, the Jews had differing expectations about the Messiah. Some thought he should be a warrior-king, others expected a strict observer of the Torah, others thought he should be a man of the temple, and still others expected a revolutionary or the one who would usher in the end of the age. When Jesus came, those who believed in him, who became Christians, perceived that he was none of these—that he did not at all fit into the expectations of the time—but they claimed that he was the Messiah nevertheless.

THE LIFE OF JESUS

Jesus was born into the situation described above. Although scholars generally agree that he was born in 4 B.C.E., they disagree about the date of his death; some say he died in 30 C.E., and others in 33 C.E. He is not mentioned in non-Christian literature until the end of the first century C.E., and when he is mentioned, references to him are vague. Most of what we know about Jesus was written down by Christians, and most of the New Testament material was not written until at least 35 years after his death. The earliest Gospel, Mark, was probably not written until about 70 C.E.; Matthew and Luke were both composed about 85 C.E.; and John was probably not written until sometime between 80 and 100 C.E.

There is no one story of Jesus; each of the Gospels has a different idea about him. We could, however, piece together a story based on reading all four Gospels. Jesus was born in Bethlehem during the reign of Herod the Great. He was born into obscurity, and some traditions assert that he was conceived through the Holy Spirit (that his mother's pregnancy was a direct act of God and a miracle) and that he was born of a virgin named Mary (who had not had intercourse with her husband, Joseph, before her pregnancy).

Jesus grew up in a small town, Nazareth, where he was the son of a carpenter. Whether or not he had any education or was ever part of a particular religious group within Judaism, we do not know. A few years before his death, perhaps somewhere between 27 and 29 C.E., Jesus was drawn to the preaching of John the Baptist, a Jewish preacher calling people to repent and believe that the kingdom of God was at hand. John the Baptist embodied some of the apocalyptic and messianic hopes of the time and was, according to Luke, a cousin of Jesus. The writers of the Gospels understood John as one sent to prepare the way for Jesus, to attract those with messianic hopes and then point them to Jesus.

John baptized Jesus in the Jordan River, an event of great significance for the Gospel writers. They interpreted Jesus' baptism as the time when Jesus was anointed as Messiah: according to them, the heavens opened, the Holy Spirit descended on Jesus, and God said, "This is my beloved Son." In the Old Testament, the Spirit's presence indicated a special calling or mission. It is clear from the Gospels that Jesus spent some time in a special ministry around Galilee and northern Palestine, where he was renowned for his teaching and powers of healing. Pharisees and Sadducees sought him out to ask questions and were astonished at the depth of his answers. He was, apparently, a threat to both groups and a disappointment to the Zealots. We know nothing about his relationship to the Essenes. Like John, he preached the coming of the kingdom of God and called people to repent. The significance of his words and actions was not always clear. Even his close friends and disciples did not always understand his mission. Still, he attracted crowds and had many followers.

For reasons clear only to himself, he was determined to go up to Jerusalem and preach there. His friends warned him against this because he was not in favor with the authorities there, but he believed that his mission called him to Jerusalem. We might note the similarity between Jesus, Abraham, and Moses: all had intense religious experiences and felt called by God to radical action. The people of Jerusalem welcomed him, and some of them may even have been drawn to him as the Messiah; but within a week, he was arrested, accused of blasphemy and sedition, tried, and executed. He celebrated the Passover with his disciples one night and the next day was flogged, mocked, and sent back and forth between Pontius Pilate and Herod as a strange and interesting prisoner. He was then crucified by the Roman officers stationed in Jerusalem.

After he died, his body was sealed in a tomb with a great stone in front of it. His followers were stunned and afraid. The Gospels affirm that three days after his death, however, the tomb was empty. Some people said that his disciples stole the body and were going to claim that Jesus had risen from the dead. His followers, however, said that they did not steal the body but that Jesus in fact had risen from the dead and appeared to some of them. The resurrection of Jesus was the sign to his followers that he was the chosen one of God, the Messiah. The early preaching about Jesus was simple: Jesus, who was crucified, has been raised from the dead; repent and believe that he is Lord and Messiah.

THE ACCOUNT OF JESUS IN THE NEW TESTAMENT

The New Testament is the Christian holy book. It contains twenty-seven books, some about the life of Jesus, others about practical problems within the young Christian community; it ends with an apocalyptic vision, a Christian version of the end of the world. Taken together, these books are the canonical literature of Christianity and are considered to be inspired by God. Most of what we know about Jesus comes to us from the Gospels; much of what we know about the early Christians comes to us from the Epistles. The book of Revelation is in a class by itself; it is representative of an apocalyptic consciousness and was probably written during a severe persecution of the Christian churches.

The Gospels

The Gospels (the first four books of the New Testament) are not biographical materials in any sense of the word. They are, rather, specific reflections on the life, death, and resurrection of Jesus written by people who were mainly interested in the last few years (or even months) of his life. They all reflect the perspective of faith: the Gospel writers believed that Jesus was the Messiah and that he had been crucified in Jerusalem and had risen from the dead. They based their perspective of Jesus on their belief in his resurrection, and they shaped the material available to them about his life according to that belief and to the needs of their audience.

No one Gospel contains a complete, objective account of the life, death, and resurrection of Jesus. Each Gospel was written from a specific perspective and used the material about Jesus to emphasize particular things about him. The first three Gospels—Mark, Matthew, and Luke—are similar in content and tell many of the same stories about Jesus. If you put these Gospels in parallel columns, you can see how similar they are. Because they can be seen together, they are called *synoptic* (from the Greek for "seeing together"). The style and content of the synoptic Gospels are different from that of the fourth Gospel, John.

The Gospel of Mark is the shortest and probably the earliest Gospel. It presents Jesus as the Son of God tragically misunderstood by his followers, and its picture of Jesus has an apocalyptic edge: he expects the end of the age to come soon. In the Gospel

CONTROVERSY

What Books Are Authentic? The Formation of the New Testament

The twenty-seven books that now compose the New Testament were not the only books written about the life and work of Jesus or the young Christian community. The earliest piece of Christian literature that survives today is Paul's first letter to the Thessalonians, written in 51 C.E., nearly 20 years after the death of Jesus. Scholars disagree about which New Testament book is the latest, but a good candidate is 2 Peter, probably written around 125 C.E. In the 75 years between these two texts, Christians produced all sorts of literature: they wrote letters, gospels, sermons, church handbooks, a church history (Acts), and some mystical revelations. They wrote about their own lives in the community, collected sayings of Jesus, and wrote what they had heard about him. Some authors wrote books about Jesus or his mother, Mary, as children. The *Infancy Gospel of Thomas,* for example, grapples with the problem of what it would have meant for God to become a little boy.

The process of selecting some of these books and discarding others was a long one because many of the books written at this time were good candidates for a book of Christian scriptures. By around the year 200, most Christian churches had at least an informal New Testament (usually including the four Gospels and Paul's letters). At the same time, many of these churches also used other books as if they were Scripture, and there was no way to enforce a definitive list because no one was in charge of the universal church at this time.

That situation changed in the early fourth century, when Constantine, the first Christian emperor, worked to form a single, worldwide church. Since he believed that a universal institution should have an agreed-upon set of sacred texts, he ordered Bishop Eusebius of Caesarea to produce an official list, and he hired copyists and artisans to produce several ornate Bibles.

The bishop, however, had trouble producing a clear list. He realized that several books—2 and 3 John, for example, or 2 Peter—were "disputed," accepted by some Christians but not by others. It was not until 367 that Bishop Athanasius of Alexandria listed precisely the twenty-seven books that make up the present New Testament. Although having a definite list was probably good for Christian organization, it was not a good way to preserve early Christian culture. Once Athanasius's list was accepted, many of the "other" books disappeared. They were destroyed or scribes stopped copying them. The occasional rediscovery of a lost text, like the *Gospel of Judas* in 2006, only reminds us of the probably hundreds of books from earliest Christianity that we no longer have.

of Mark, Jesus is pictured as *a Messiah who must suffer.* Jesus is clearly the Messiah, but he does not conform to any of the expectations of some groups; he is not a warrior-king or a revolutionary but a man with power to work miracles, the Son of God, who must suffer and die. The resurrection is a sign of his power over death. In Mark, the powers of evil (demons being exorcised) recognize Jesus before people do. People expected God to establish his kingdom by overthrowing the powers of evil. Jesus, in Mark, has the power to do that, and the demons see that their reign is about to end.

The Gospel of Matthew sees Jesus as *the new Moses,* the giver of the new law. For Matthew, Jesus is the fulfillment of the biblical prophecies; for many of Jesus' sayings and actions, Matthew finds a parallel in the Jewish Scriptures. All the expectations about where the Messiah would be born, how he would enter Jerusalem, and what he would do are used by Matthew to explain Jesus. The parallels between Jesus and Moses are strong in this Gospel: Moses gave the people the old law from Mount Sinai, and Jesus delivers the new law in the Sermon on the Mount. The main emphasis in Matthew is on God's generosity to people manifested in Jesus and the kingdom. Human beings are to respond to that generosity by loving one another joyfully.

The Gospel of Luke and the book of Acts should be read together as the first conscious history of the Christian movement. Scholars agree that the same author wrote both books. Jesus, for Luke, is a merciful savior who grants forgiveness to those who repent. There is a special focus on Jesus' compassion and tenderness. Luke emphasizes universality—Jesus came for everyone, not just for the Jews—in his account of Jesus' work and message; Luke traces the genealogy of Jesus back to Adam (the father of the human race), rather than back to Abraham (the father of the Jewish people) as Matthew does. Luke has many stories about the poor and downcast; in his view, Jesus relates positively to the Samaritans (a despised people) and gives women a place of importance. The great parable of forgiveness, the parable of the prodigal son, is found only in Luke. In the resurrection, God reveals Jesus as the one who brings mercy for all. The message of Jesus is to be taken to the ends of the earth. The book of Acts takes up the theme of the universal mission of the Christians (it will be discussed in the next chapter).

The Gospel of John differs from the synoptics in organization, style, and content. John presents the *mystery* of Jesus, who is like other people but above them in some way. John focuses on the eternal origin and divine nature of Jesus. The Gospel begins with Jesus as the preexistent word of God—an important concept when you remember that the world was created through God's *word.* John says the word through whom the world was made had now been made flesh. Jesus was more powerful than death even before his resurrection: the story about Jesus raising Lazarus from the dead is found only in John. Remember that many Jews believed that to establish the kingdom, God would have to enter the world in some radical, transforming way. The Gospel of John says Jesus is God become a man—God entering the world in a radical, transforming way. John also structures his Gospel differently. Some interpreters say the Gospel of John contains two books, a book of signs (John 1–12; see, for example, the miracle at Cana, 2:1–12) and a book of glory (John 12–21; see, for example, the farewell discourse, 17:1–26).

The Epistles

The other literature found in the New Testament is in the form of a series of letters. There are twenty-one letters in the New Testament; at least nine of the major ones were written by the apostle Paul. The Epistles are not about the life of Jesus as the Gospels are. They reflect the life, questions, and conflicts of the early community, and they show a developing theology or reflection about Jesus and his mission. The resurrection is central to them as it is to the Christian message as a whole, as a sign of God's action and a vindication of Jesus' life and work. It was the resurrection that enabled Jesus' followers to understand him as the Messiah and Lord, and the resurrection provided the key to his authority—his teachings and his miracles all pointed to his power over death and his divinity. Death and the resurrection make Jesus the Savior. His power to forgive sins and to restore the created order is tied up with his victory over death.

And the resurrection shows people that God does not mean for death to be the end of things but indicates that God calls people to fellowship even beyond death. Paul said that nothing can separate the believer from the love of God, not even death.

The Book of Revelation

Revelation, the last book of the New Testament, pictures the end of the world and is written in highly symbolic language. Its author had visions of God's merciful government of all creation and wrote this book to sustain Christian hope during severe persecution. It has functioned to sustain Christian hope ever since. It is not an easy book to read because it is full of symbols, numerical calculations, strange beasts, and other apocalyptic figures. Many contemporary Christians use it to predict the end of the world, to speculate about what Jesus will do when he comes back to judge people, though its probable purpose, like the rest of the New Testament, is to reveal the Gospel and to inspire Christians to check their lives and see whether they are living according to the Gospel.

JESUS AND JEWISH EXPECTATION

Some Christians think that Jesus was so clearly the Messiah that no one could fail to recognize him as such. People who believe this often see Jews as stubborn, blind, or deprived of their chance for salvation. This hostile interpretation of Judaism, which has been present in Christianity from the beginning, has led to a long and painful history of atrocities against the Jewish people. Since the time of Jesus, Christian history has been marred by serious crimes against the Jews, often perpetrated in the name of religion. A necessary step in the understanding of Christianity is a better appreciation of Judaism.

Christians who see Jews as a "problem" might be surprised to learn that Jesus has been a continual puzzle for Jews. Medieval Jews tended to picture Jesus as an apostate Jew, a man who had lost his faith; nineteenth-century Jewish scholars had an image of Jesus as a great ethical teacher. They could not agree whether he claimed to be the Messiah or not, though modern scholars agree that Jesus did *not* make that claim for himself. Today, some Jewish scholars study the Gospels as sources for studying Jewish life in the first century and find parallels between the life and work of Jesus and that of other charismatic Jewish leaders at the time. The issue of whether or not Jesus was the Messiah, therefore, is not the only point of discussion between Jews and Christians, though it is still an important one.

When Jesus lived and died, some people were expecting a Messiah. Christians believed that Jesus had been raised from the dead and was the promised Messiah. Belief in the resurrection was not a matter of evidence; it was a matter of faith: if one did not first accept the resurrection, the messianic claims made no sense. Jews who did not accept Jesus as the Messiah had good reasons for not doing so. Not everyone, after all, was expecting a Messiah. Jesus' life and teaching, therefore, were of no interest to some and were unconvincing to others. Insofar as Jewish history was full of God's action on their behalf and also full of hope for a *decisive act of God,* there were, in some quarters, hopes for a Messiah. Whether Jesus lived up to those hopes is precisely the dividing issue. The earliest Christians were also rooted in Jewish history. Jesus was a Jew. His apostles were Jewish—they knew the biblical stories about Abraham, Isaac, and Jacob; they understood deeply the meaning of the covenant and the experience of the Exile. Their belief in the resurrection of Jesus enabled them to believe that he was the Messiah and to interpret their Scriptures accordingly. When they preached about Jesus, they said that with Jesus a *new* history—built upon the old but also different from it—began.

It is important to see what this means. The Jews believe that history has a purpose, that God has acted and will continue to act in it. Christians claim that history has a purpose, that God has acted in it so decisively in Jesus that a new history has begun. Jews are still waiting for the messianic age to begin because they do not accept the Christian claim that Jesus was the promised one of God. For Jews, many of the messianic promises were *not* fulfilled in Jesus: in Isaiah (11: 6–7), for example, it says that people will live together in peace when the Messiah comes, that the lion will lie down with the lamb; those events did not happen with Jesus. In that way, Jesus was a *scandal* to messianic expectations. After his death, nothing changed: the Jews were *not* restored to political power; Jesus did *not* meet the personal qualifications of messianic hope because he was not righteous (according to the Pharisees); and Jesus' death on a cross made him unacceptable to Jews because the Torah says that a man hanged upon a tree is cursed by God (Deut. 21:23).

Christians and Jews interpret the Bible differently. For Christians, Jesus shakes up the old order of things and makes it possible to see everything that went before him as pointing essentially toward him. For Jews, the events of the Bible do not point toward Jesus at all but beyond him, to a future Messiah. The differences in interpretation are profound: for the Jews, the Hebrew Bible points toward something still to come; but for Christians, it sets the stage and provides an explanation for someone who has already arrived.

Look, for example, at Jeremiah 31:31–33: " 'Behold the days are coming,' says the Lord, 'when I will make a new covenant with Israel . . . not like the covenant which I made with their ancestors when I took them by the hand to bring them out of the land of Egypt . . . but I will put my law within them, and I will write it upon their hearts; and I will be their God, and they shall be my people.' " For Jews, this new covenant is yet to come, but Christians have, from earliest times, applied these words to Jesus. The early eucharistic formulas (in 1 Corinthians, for example) relate that Jesus, on the night before he died, blessed the cup and said, "This cup is the new covenant in my blood" (11:25). Later, in Hebrews (8:8–12), the author quotes from Jeremiah explicitly to draw theological conclusions from it: if there is a new covenant found in the New Testament, it is based on an experience of Jesus and is not understandable apart from that experience. One cannot expect non-Christians, therefore, to read those texts in the same way.

Early Christian authors used the Hebrew Bible as a typological gold mine: events in Israelite history were interpreted as "types" or symbols for what would happen to Jesus. The Hebrews passed through the Red Sea during the Exodus. This event was taken as a symbol that Jesus would pass through death. Similarly, the sacrifice of Isaac might symbolize the Crucifixion. Again, these events become types only in a specifically Christian interpretation.

The new perspective of the Christians is most evident in what they did to the Hebrew Bible (see Appendix 1). They adopted it as their own book but renamed it the

SPIRITUALITY

Experiencing God: From Moses to Philo

The Bible has a rich legacy of images and metaphors by which people might understand their relationship to the divine. Hebrew slaves fleeing from Egypt experienced God in terrifying terms (lightning, thunder, trumpet blasts) before Moses was summoned to meet God and receive the Ten Commandments (Exod. 19). At Sinai, God was an utterly powerful, protective figure who could not be seen but who demanded fidelity and obedience. As the Hebrews took possession of the land of Canaan, they imagined God as a warrior who led them into battle against their enemies. In Deuteronomy and Leviticus, God speaks as a lawgiver, demanding that the people participate in the divine holiness.

Changing times disclosed more personal images of God. Elijah, for example, did not find God in wind and fire but in a "still, small voice" (1 Kings 19:12). In the kingdoms of Israel and Judah, prophets such as Amos, Hosea, Isaiah, and Jeremiah had direct experiences of a God who called them to preach justice and compassion. Jews began to understand God as deeply personal and merciful, more interested in justice for the oppressed than in prayers and sacrifices (1sa. 1:15–17). After the conquests of Israel and Judah, exiled Jews found connection to God through suffering. Although the Song of Songs, a very late book, was written as a celebration of love between a man and a woman, later Jews and Christians saw in it a metaphor for the intimacy between God and the human soul.

At the time of Jesus, some Jews were looking for ways to combine the remote, powerful God of Sinai and the intimate, personal God of the prophets. Philo of Alexandria (d. 45 C.E.) was a Jewish theologian and contemporary of Jesus and Paul (although he did not know them). He believed that although God's nature is beyond human comprehension, God chooses to relate to people through divine "powers" or activities. These powers draw one to want to know God, but when people try to do so, they always fall short. The seeker, however, finds fulfillment in the never-ending desire and search for a God who cannot be known and yet reaches out to humankind.

Old Testament (old covenant), a name that implies the existence of a new one. And they changed the order of the books. The Jewish Bible ends with the Exile, with the expectation that God will act in the future. The Christian Old Testament ends with the books of the so-called minor prophets (those whose books are shorter compared to those of the "major" prophets), which are full of references Christians apply to Jesus. Micah, for example, says, "But you, O Bethlehem . . . who are little . . . from you shall come forth for me one who is to be ruler in Israel" (5:2). Where does the New Testament say Jesus was born? In Bethlehem. The book of Habakkuk is about the sovereignty of God and contains the phrase that appears later in the Epistle to the Romans: "The righteous shall live by faith" (Hab. 2:4; Rom. 1:17). The book of Haggai records God's promise, "I am about to shake the heavens and the earth" (2:21), interpreted in Hebrews (12:26) as accomplished in Jesus.

All these books have an edge of expectation. The book of Zechariah pictures the Messiah as prince of peace and a good shepherd and contains the quotation "Lo, your king comes to you, triumphant and victorious is he, humble and riding on an ass, on a colt the foal of an ass" (9:9). The New Testament authors used that quotation to describe Jesus' entry into Jerusalem. The book of Malachi is about the impending coming of the Lord and about a forerunner. All these books were written in the sixth or fifth centuries B.C.E. and were therefore full of meaning for the Jews quite apart from any link with messianic hopes, but Christians saw them as an immediate foreshadowing of the coming of Jesus. It is a big step from the end of the Jewish Bible to the New Testament, from the Exile to Jesus; but when a Christian reads the Old Testament minor prophets, he or she expects something to happen. To Christians, Jesus appears as the proper and natural end of these prophecies. That was the Christian intention in reordering the books. But one can see how both the Jewish and the Christian interpretation of the life of Jesus could have grown out of the same Scripture.

CONCLUSION

The Jewish context of the life of Jesus was, of course, a great deal more complex than we have indicated here: Judaism at the time of Jesus was enormously varied, politically, religiously, and sociologically. The groups described here, for example, were composed of relatively few Jews, and the purpose in presenting them was to give you some indication of the variety within Judaism at the time. It is tempting to think that there was a normative Judaism, very neat and tidy, and that Jesus offered a clear alternative to it. Such thinking indulges in fantasy, though. There was no single Judaism at the time of Jesus; people were incredibly divided on all sorts of issues; and whatever alternative Jesus offered, it was probably no clearer than anything else at the time.

In major matters, Jewish opinion was divided. Most Jews were moved by Israel's institutions and were loyal to the temple, the Law, feasts, Jerusalem itself, and the idea of a holy land but differed over theological concepts and methods of interpretation. It is not clear, for example, how many Jews were waiting for a Messiah. Christian interpretation is most congenial to a view that many were, but it is likely that very many Jews scarcely gave it a thought. You might compare it to a contemporary Christian interest in the end of the world. Do most Christians think often about the end of the world? Would you say that most of them are eagerly or even consciously waiting for it? Some are, of course, but are most of them? Probably not, even though, as a concept, it is part of their tradition. The same thing was probably true of the Jews and messianic expectations. At the same time, since the goal of this chapter was to situate Jesus in a clear and relatively simple context, messianic expectations were emphasized here.

There were certainly major differences of opinion within Judaism about the appropriateness of an apocalyptic edge in scriptural interpretation, just as there are major differences within Christianity on the same issue. The apocalyptic vision was the focus here because the intertestamental period (100 years before Jesus to 100 years after) *was* a time when hundreds of apocalyptic books were written and when it did seem to be "in the air."

Finally, a word about the Torah. The Torah as such—the first five books of the Bible—was being edited, refined, and written down about the same time the Jews were returning to Palestine from the Exile. When we talk about their hope to be more faithful to the Torah, therefore, we are speaking in a general way about fidelity to the covenant and the commandments. Even on this crucial issue of the Law, Jews were of different minds—Sadducees (conservatives) kept to the letter of the Torah as *it was written* and did not allow for refinements or interpretations or extensions, whereas Pharisees (liberals) extended applications of the Torah to every phase of life and generated a body of interpretation that, in time, became as binding as the Torah itself.

We have simplified the life of Jesus to present a fairly coherent view of him and his work. On the level of pure story, this is quite possible: We have woven strands together to come up with a composite picture that is, itself, an interpretation. We think it is appropriate at this level to look at the life of Jesus in this way, but one should also do so with certain cautions. Scholars argue about almost everything—which Gospel was earliest, where the Gospel writers got their material, how accurate they were, who their audiences were—and we have tried to spare you those arguments here. At the same time, we have to say that it is very hard to reconstruct the life of Jesus. The Gospels are not biographies; they are theological interpretations that tell us more about what Jesus meant than what he actually did. How many of the words attributed to Jesus are actually his is disputed not only by scholars but by Christians in general. Even the *geographical* details cannot be taken without further investigation: for example, did Jesus have a mission in Galilee and then "go up to Jerusalem"? Most scholars are not quite sure about this. Luke's journey motif is brilliant and rich, but that does not make it historically precise.

This chapter, therefore, has given you a simplified version of the context for and life of Jesus—what we hope is a good beginning for your understanding. As you read more widely, you will discover some of the nuances we have tried to allude to here.

Focal Points for Discussion

1. As Christianity developed, it grew further away from and increasingly hostile toward Judaism. How might a better understanding of Christianity's Jewish origins affect contemporary Jewish-Christian relations?
2. Imagine that you are a Sadducee, Pharisee, Zealot, or Essene. Write a want ad for a Messiah that reflects the values and needs of your group. On the basis of that description, would you hire Jesus?
3. Why does the Christian community need all four Gospels to describe Jesus adequately? Which aspects would you lose if you omitted Matthew, Mark, Luke, or John?

CHAPTER 3

The Emergence of the Christian Church

Christians interpreted the Bible as they did because they believed that Jesus was the Messiah, a belief supported by their experience of Jesus as risen from the dead. Christians today sometimes think the apostles saw the risen Jesus, obtained a blueprint from him, and proceeded in happy agreement to construct the Christian church. The truth is that members of the early Christian community disagreed with and misunderstood each other. They were no more compatible than any other group, no less immune to argument, and no more peaceful.

The early Christian community began with the energizing belief that God's spirit had been sent to them in Jesus, and the first believers were enthusiastic, eager to share their good news. Although they were unified in their belief in Jesus, they were divided over other issues. This chapter discusses some of those issues and also introduces some of the complex questions Christians had to face as they encountered other religions, incredulous reactions, and persecution.

THE EXPERIENCE OF THE APOSTLES

According to the Acts of the Apostles, Jesus, after he was raised from the dead, stayed on earth for 40 days and then ascended into the heavens (1:1–12). We can speculate that the apostles were overjoyed about the resurrection but, at the same time, were mystified about what it really meant. They were convinced that Jesus had risen from the dead—they had heard about it, seen him, eaten with him, touched him—but they were not sure what the implications of that experience were. What did the resurrection mean, for example, for their behavior? What were they now to *do?* Relate this for a minute to some biblical stories. Abraham believed that God had spoken to him, but he wasn't initially sure what that meant; God led him to understand it step by step. Moses believed that he had had an encounter with the "God of Abraham, Isaac, and Jacob" but was appalled to find out that God wanted him to go back to Egypt and confront the powerful pharaoh there. The prophets, too, were sure about their encounters with God but were mystified or reluctant about what those meant for their mission. So it was with the experience of the risen Lord. The apostles believed it, experienced it as a miracle of prodigious proportions, but were also stunned by it. Even after the resurrection, there was not such clarity that there were no questions and not such charity that there were no arguments.

The experience of the resurrection empowered human beings with God's spirit (life) so that their lives were changed. Not all New Testament writings agree on exactly what that meant. The Acts of the Apostles talks about the role of the Holy Spirit a great deal by means of a narrative recounting of the church's beginnings. It is clear that things are idealized considerably. We suspect, for example, that the first believers were not so completely united as Luke suggests (see Acts 5:1–5). But the story does help us see how the history of the Christian movement was perceived as a continuation of the story of Israel, precisely because the same Holy Spirit was at work in both.

The Old Testament tells us that the Spirit was sent to people who had a special mission (prophets and judges, for example), but it was to be shared with all people in the final age. The prophet Joel states an especially clear prophecy about the Spirit: "And it shall come to pass, afterward, that I will pour out my spirit on all flesh; your sons and your daughters shall prophesy, your old men shall dream dreams, and your young men shall see visions" (Joel 2:28). The coming of the Spirit to the apostles, therefore, is set within the context of God's promises about the last days. Throughout Acts, one can see how the power of the Spirit is interpreted. The Spirit is the driving force behind the proclamation of the Gospel, the agent who brings about conversion and faith in Jesus as the Christ; the Spirit strengthens people and helps them endure persecution, guides the early missionary efforts—especially those of Paul—and inspires the Gentile mission. Through the Spirit's work, the unorganized group of early believers begins to form the Christian church.

The story of the coming of the Spirit to the apostles is found in Acts 2. Just looking at the story, we are struck by certain things. Notice that the Spirit came to the apostles on the Jewish festival of Weeks, Shevu'ot, also known as *Pentecost.* This feast commemorates and celebrates the giving of the Law at Sinai. The New Testament account is written to stress this parallel. It conveys the sense of something new happening, something that can replace or go beyond the old way (the old covenant).

The outline of the story is this: The apostles were gathered together in one place and were confused and frightened. All of a sudden, they heard a sound like a mighty wind (the Hebrew word *ru'ah* and the Greek word *pneuma* mean both spirit and wind) that filled the house, and tongues of fire hovered over the head of each of them. God's appearances in the Bible are often accompanied by wind and fire; the New Testament account, therefore, is surely meant to convey that the apostles experienced the presence of God in wind and fire. The apostles were filled with the Holy Spirit and began to speak, not according to their own designs but as the Spirit directed them. They spoke in languages they did not know, and visitors to Jerusalem from all over the Middle East heard them speaking about the mighty works of God.

After they received the Spirit, the apostles spoke to the crowd. The most famous speech was delivered by Peter, who quoted Joel's words about the pouring out of the Spirit and ended by saying, "And it shall be that whoever calls on the name of the Lord shall be saved" (Acts 2:21). Notice the word *whoever:* not just Jews but all who call upon the name of the Lord will be saved. This is a radically new idea and one, the author suggests, that the Spirit gave to Peter. The apostles are supposed to go beyond the terms of the covenant at Sinai and extend the saving message of Jesus to everyone. The Acts of the Apostles is a partisan record of this extension.

After that startling statement, Peter told his audience the story of Jesus, especially how he was crucified but had been raised up from the dead. Imagine the impact of a statement like this! Some listeners thought the apostles were drunk or crazy; others were moved and asked what they should do. Peter told them to repent (to change their direction, to turn toward God by following Jesus) and to be baptized. According to the Pentecost story in Acts, three thousand people were baptized that day.

Acts 2 summarizes the enthusiasm characteristic of the early Christian community, but it also gives the impression that it was united in mind and heart from the beginning. The account in Acts implies that the coming of the Holy Spirit clarified the meaning of Jesus' words and life. It is historically naive to think this was the case. The New Testament says the apostles were enlightened, had an experience of the risen Lord, received the Holy Spirit, and were filled with a desire to carry the saving message of Jesus to others. Acts presents Pentecost as the inauguration of a truly universal preaching about Jesus that ultimately transcended all boundaries of nationality, speech, and religion. That universalist understanding about Jesus, however, was not something clearly evident at the outset. The argument about who should hear the Gospel was the most serious controversy in the young community.

INTERNAL CONFLICTS IN THE EARLY CHURCH

A popular picture of earliest Christianity is that it began in perfect uniformity and split into groups. A better picture is that it began with *variety* and only in the course of generations came to an explicit sense of unity. Some deep issues caused conflict among the first believers, and only time and the accidents of history brought them to a shared view.

Three general questions arose within the early community:

1. Who can hear the Gospel? (universality)
2. Who is in charge? (authority and doctrine)
3. What does it mean to be free? (law and freedom)

Because these questions caused conflicts, a principle emerged that came to be used as a norm against which to measure everything. That principle was *apostolicity:* when people wanted to know whether a writing was reliable, whether the right person was in authority, and so on, they asked whether it was apostolic, clearly connected with the work and intentions of the apostles. Understanding the conflicts is essential to understanding the principle, which developed along with the community.

Universality of the Gospel

For whom was the Gospel intended? Did Jesus offer his message for everyone or just for Jews? There is no single answer to this question in the Gospels themselves because the Gospels reflect, in part, the life of the early community, which was divided on this question. So in some parts of the Gospels, it seems as if Jesus has come only to preach to the Jews (Matt. 10:5–7), and in others, his words seem intended for all who believe (Matt. 28:19). Jesus, remember, was Jewish and so were his apostles; his life and mission were interpreted in the light of Jewish prophecies and expectations. It was logical to assume—as some did—that the message of Jesus was intended only for the Jews. Yet the account of Pentecost in Acts includes "all who call upon the name of the Lord." That statement represents a position adopted by the early community only after a severe struggle.

A particularly vivid account of this argument is found in the Epistle to the Galatians (chapters 1 and 2), where Paul recounts his own growth in understanding. He began, he tells his readers, hating Christians and persecuting them precisely because he was "so extremely zealous for the traditions of my fathers" (1:14). God called him, converted him, and made it clear that he was to "preach among the Gentiles" (1:16). He was asked by God to do an extremely difficult task—namely, to abandon his background, training, and beliefs to set out on a daring new path. He did not do so without approval from the rest of the community, and Galatians tells the story of his approval by the Jerusalem community, especially by Peter (who was preaching to the Jews). Peter himself, however, was not free from ambivalent feelings on this issue. He welcomed Paul's approach in Jerusalem, but on a visit to Antioch, he reverted to an anti-Gentile position (Gal. 2:11–17) and was confronted by Paul. The early community made no attempt to hide the fact that they argued over this issue, and we should remember the arguments as we read those stories that make the concept of a universal mission seem much smoother.

In Acts, for example, one finds the story of Philip going to Samaria and bringing about a remarkable conversion there (chapter 6). Most Jews regarded the Samaritans as heretics and enemies, yet according to the story, the Samaritans received the word of the Lord eagerly and were converted. The author's point is that the power of God's word and the Spirit are not put off by religiously imposed boundaries: this Spirit can work in any situation. Later in Acts, there is an even more dramatic story. Peter was preaching—for the most part, to Jews—but one day received a message from a Roman soldier, Cornelius, inviting him to dinner. It is hard for us, perhaps, to grasp the impact of the invitation. Jewish dietary regulations were considered part of God's will. The terms of the covenant forbade Jews to eat certain foods and to eat with non-Jews. A Jew could not eat dinner in a Roman house, therefore, without being in serious violation of divine law. What was Peter to do? In Acts (chapter 10), the author takes the question out of Peter's hands and says that the Spirit instructed Peter to go, that he did go, ate, preached to Cornelius, and saw that "God shows no partiality . . . the Spirit has been poured out even on the Gentiles" (10:34 and 10:44).

The stories in Acts make the decision to pursue a universal mission look much easier than it was because Acts was written after the fact and from a perspective that favored universality. The climax to this question occurs in Acts 15, when some members of the Jerusalem community said, "Unless you are circumcised according to Moses, you cannot be saved" (15:1). In other words, the message of Jesus could be extended but only through Judaism. To be a Christian, one had first to be Jewish, to be circumcised, and to follow the Law of Moses. This position of the so-called Judaizers precipitated a clash, and an important meeting was held in Jerusalem to resolve the issue. When all sides had been heard, they deliberated and decided that the Gospel was to be extended freely to all and that one did not have to become Jewish to become a

Christian. In the letter written to different Christian communities about this meeting, the leaders assembled in Jerusalem used a very telling phrase. Describing the process of decision making, they said, "It seemed good to the Holy Spirit and to us...." The implications of that statement are large: the young community considered itself in *partnership* with the Spirit. They decided this important matter together and would decide future matters together.

This assertion about the presence and guidance of the Holy Spirit is a fundamental principle within Christianity. God is continually present to Christians by way of the Holy Spirit, who resides in the church. The continual presence of the Spirit keeps the church alive and faithful to God's commands and leads it to deeper understandings. Christians agree about the importance of the Spirit in the church, but as we shall see, they disagree intensely about where the Spirit resides, how it is experienced, and what its powers are. For now, it is enough to see that the early church resolved the issue of a universal mission and, in the process, established the principle of the abiding and guiding presence of the Spirit in the church.

Authority and Doctrine

The Christian church, as you can imagine, grew increasingly complex as it grew in numbers and extended itself to a wide range of cultures and peoples. All religions are, to some extent, shaped by the cultural milieu in which they thrive; Christianity in Syria was different from Christianity in Rome and from Christianity in Egypt or Palestine. Questions arose about behavior and practice. How should the Lord's Supper be observed? Who may participate? Must one practice perpetual virginity after baptism? How is the forgiveness of sins to be enacted? How is discipline to be maintained? What prayer forms are appropriate? Which stories about Jesus are trustworthy? To complicate the situation, Christianity arose at a time when many different religions were practiced and in an environment where interchange and cross-fertilization were inevitable.

Should the Christian community be seen as an organization needing officers or as a community of believers trusting the guidance of the Spirit and willing to attempt consensual decision making? Both views were present in the early church and continue to be present in the modern Christian church. Some think Christians should form themselves into small, manageable groups of believers who are "of one heart and soul" (Acts 4:32). Others believe that the church needs an organizational model with certain people in charge and streamlined, hierarchical methods of decision making.

Structures of authority grew along with the church: they were not there from the beginning, nor was it immediately clear that such structures were needed. Paul's first letter to the Thessalonians makes no mention of church leaders. Yet in the Acts of the Apostles, we find not only leaders but several kinds with different functions—elders and deacons, for example. Paul's farewell address to the elders at Ephesus (as reported in Acts) is a handing on of his authority, and it pictures Paul as an authority figure. By the time the pastoral Epistles were written (two letters to Timothy and one to Titus), we find a strong, directive interest in church administration. These letters were not written by Paul—scholars are nearly unanimous in their agreement about this point—and so do not show a development in Paul himself, but they do show a development within the early community. The first letter to Timothy not only mentions bishops but

People

Women in the Early Church

In his letter to the Galatians, Paul quoted from the early Christian ritual of baptism: "There is no longer male and female, for all of you are one in Christ Jesus" (3:29). It looks, therefore, as if men and women shared a fundamental equality in the new religion centered on Jesus.

Did the reality in early Christian communities match this declaration? The evidence is ambiguous even within Paul's letters. On the one hand, Paul insisted that women may pray and prophesy in church meetings but must wear traditional head coverings (signs of subordination) when they do so (1 Cor. 11: 7). Elsewhere, he says that "women should be silent in the churches" (1 Cor. 14:3–4), a command that may not have been written by Paul himself but was added later by more conservative Christians.

On the other hand, Paul knew and approved of several women who held prominent positions in his churches. Phoebe carried the now-famous letter from Paul to the Christians in Rome. Paul calls Phoebe a "deacon of the church" and notes her financial support of himself and other Christians (Rom. 16:1–2). He also praises the husband-and-wife missionary team of Priscilla and Aquila, who hosted a church in their house in Rome (Rom. 16:3–5). Most dramatically, Paul refers to Andronicus (a man) and Junia (a woman) as "prominent among the apostles" (Rom. 16:6).

When a later Christian wrote the first letter to Timothy in Paul's name, he resolved the ambiguity about the role of women in a clearly misogynist direction. He says that men should pray and that women "are to learn in silence and full submission" (1 Tim. 2:8–11).

In later centuries, as the church developed the offices of bishop and priest, it officially excluded women from them. But this did not mean that there were no longer women leaders in the church. Thanks to their wealth, learning, and virtue, several women gained authority in the early centuries. For example, Macrina the Younger (d. 379/380) helped her mother turn their large estate in Asia Minor into an important monastery. Her famous brothers, Basil of Caesarea and Gregory of Nyssa, acknowledged her theological learning and influence on them. Melania the Elder (d. c. 410), a wealthy Roman matron, established a monastery on the Mount of Olives in Jerusalem and played a major role in the theological controversies of her day. In Constantinople, the deaconess Olympias (d. c. 410) spent her great wealth on charity and religious causes and so acquired great influence in church affairs; in the process, she made enemies who arranged to get her exiled. These women may not have been ordained clergy, but their power and authority sometimes exceeded that of bishops and priests.

also lays down qualifications for them (3:1–7) and suggests some regulations for worship (2:1–15); the letter to Titus also specifies qualifications for bishops and elders. Christian literature not included in the New Testament—the *Didache,* for example, or the *Apostolic Constitutions*—is primarily devoted to administrative matters and questions of true teaching and practice.

As the church developed, a certain organizational model eventually emerged as the dominant one. Officers (bishops) were elected by congregations to teach and to supervise. You can imagine that as long as a particular community remained fairly homogeneous, few problems arose. Once the Christian church began to attract large numbers of new members from all classes and occupations, however, controversies and questions arose on every conceivable issue. We can see already in Paul's letter to the Corinthians that Christians had to *learn* how to celebrate the Lord's Supper properly (chapter 11), and that is an early letter. Imagine the complex problems that would arise in a church that had communities throughout the ancient world and members who were from all social and economic classes, with different educational and religious backgrounds.

Questions arose at all levels. Within the structure of the church, there were questions of discipline (what to do if someone violated a commandment), of jurisdiction (whether priests from one place could work in another without the permission of the local bishop), membership (whether a soldier could be a Christian without resigning from the army), and doctrine (whether Jesus was truly the Son of God), to name a few. Sometimes, questions were handled locally within the church or within the district, but as time went on and as questions grew more complex, church leaders from a large region met to discuss them. In later centuries (beginning in 325 C.E. at Nicaea), worldwide meetings (or councils) were held to decide important matters of doctrine and practice (see Appendix 4).

Little by little, the ancient equivalent of a corporate flowchart emerged within the Christian church. In terms of regional organization, the church owed some debts to Roman imperial structures, which, after all, had enhanced the smooth administration of a massive empire. In terms of teaching and moral authority, the bishops, individually or collectively, came to decide things. In matters that involved the entire Christian world—especially matters of doctrine—all the bishops of the world gathered to debate, reflect, and decide. In their decision-making process, they were conscious of the partnership they had with the Spirit, so their decisions were considered extensions and refinements of divine will.

Law and Freedom in the Spirit

The apostle Paul preached a Gospel of freedom and believed that God had given him the authority to do so. "It is no longer I who live," he said, "but Christ who lives in me" (Gal. 2:20). As a serious young Jew, Paul knew the Law and upheld it; as a Christian, converted by God to preach to the Gentiles (Acts 9), he was constrained to explain, from many different perspectives, the relation between the Law and the Gospel. One gets some sense of the brilliance with which he held these two concepts together in his Epistle to the Romans: in chapter 7, he discusses the Law and its place in Christian life, and in chapter 8, he discusses life in the Spirit.

Paul's claim that his authority was God-given rested on two things: his vision of the risen Christ and his style of servant leadership (following Jesus' model). On his missionary journeys, he founded churches and he thought of himself as a nurturing parent (1 Thess. 2:7, "like a nurse"; 2:11, "like a father") to those congregations. He was loath to build a superstructure of rules or legal authority but not at all afraid to give his opinions about specific questions. Some groups in Christian history point to their reading of the early Pauline model precisely to argue for Christian freedom. Some Christians see Pauline congregations as congregations in which the chief presiding officer was Christ and his Spirit, not priests or bishops or even Paul. He told communities they were called to freedom (Gal. 5:13), but a freedom that did not lie in doing whatever one pleases. The freedom of the Gospel is the freedom to love one another, to be servants, to be solicitous for each other's needs. Care for one another does not mean slavery; rather, people are called to "freedom in the Spirit," freedom from the old law, freedom from attempts to domineer over other people's faith, freedom to support one another.

Paul did not create a new norm but saw Christ as a new standard. He exhorted people to live in communities of freedom and to be faithful, to "be imitators of me as I am of Christ" (1 Cor. 11:1). The ancient moral commandments are not up for discussion—they hold; yet in Romans 10:4, he says that Christ is the end of the Law. The new law of Christ is Paul's Gospel of freedom.

EXTERNAL CONFLICTS OF THE EARLY COMMUNITY

The church in its first three centuries, from New Testament times to the reign of the first Christian emperor, Constantine (d. 337), grew from a small group of dedicated believers with no uniform structure to a worldwide movement with organized hierarchies of management and established norms of behavior. As we have seen, early believers differed, sometimes radically, about practice and doctrine, and one can understand their differences from two perspectives: from looking at some of the early conflicts (as we have just done) or from looking at the context in which these and other conflicts were worked out.

The world of early Christianity was geographically large, religiously diverse, and culturally heterogeneous. In a variety of ways, Christians had to learn to answer for themselves. How were they different from Jews? What did Christianity have in common with Judaism? How could their beliefs be reconciled with Hellenistic philosophy: how could they explain Jesus to someone who read and loved Plato? How were they going to define their beliefs? And what relationship was there between doctrinal and practical matters: what kind of structure or teaching authority would work best? Why were Christians rigidly monotheistic? Why did they refuse to worship any other gods? How would they adapt to the rich and enticing variety of Roman religions?

No matter what cultural context they found themselves in, they had to address these and other questions. This section will discuss three different cultural contexts and three specific facets of Christian identity. Like all simplifying generalizations, this one is imperfect because much more was going on in each of these contexts than we can discuss here. But it is also useful to give a general sense of developing Christian identity. Christians developed their religious, philosophical, and political identity as they grew and interacted in the complex ancient world. Let us focus on their *religious* identity within the Jewish context, their *philosophical* identity within the Greek context, and their *political* identity within the Roman context.

The Jewish Context and Religious Identity

Christianity was born into a Jewish context and eventually established a separate religious identity. Early Christians thought of themselves not as separable from Judaism but as a Jewish sect distinguished by their belief that Jesus was the Messiah. Their worship was modeled on Jewish services, and their understanding of the mission of Jesus was derived from the Hebrew Bible. Although Christians believed Jesus had come to gather the Jews together in preparation for the final days, they voted to extend his saving act beyond the Jewish community.

What do you think a universalist position meant to Jewish Christians? Their position was determined to some extent by the political and religious situation, especially growing Roman antipathy and their own apocalyptic expectations. Because of political and religious tensions, Christianity's relationship to Judaism was precarious from the outset. The early Christian community in Jerusalem perceived itself as a temporary community living in the interim between the coming of the Messiah and the final coming of the kingdom of God, the end of the age. It is not clear that Jewish Christians welcomed the mission to the Gentiles or saw much reason to set up enduring structures or policies.

The Jews were in a volatile political situation punctuated by periodic outbreaks of insurrection. Any rebellion could give the Romans the excuse they wanted for crushing the Jews, and from 66 to 70 C.E., an unprecedented revolt of the Jews against the Romans took place. It was one of the most savage wars in history: massive numbers of Jews were killed or sold into slavery. Since a large part of the early Christian community was Jewish, this war of national liberation presented a serious problem to the early church. Jewish Christians were caught between the demands of national identity and the words of the Gospel. Full of apocalyptic expectation and reminded of the words of Jesus about the last days (Matt. 24:15–21), Jewish Christians felt obliged to flee the city, an action that made them traitors in the eyes of the Jews.

The fall of Jerusalem in 70 C.E. marked the end of any Jewish Christian hope to convert the Jews. In the minds of Gentile Christians, it vindicated the decision for universality. Gentile Christians pointed to the fall of Jerusalem to argue that Jewish Christian apocalyptic hopes were false; later, they claimed that the Jewish aspects of Christianity were unnecessary. Jewish Christians were homeless: they were not welcome in Judaism and not comfortable with a universalist Christianity. Accordingly, the Jewish Christian discussion of early Christianity diminished, and the way was paved for a separate Christian church.

When the Sanhedrin was restored in Jerusalem (90 C.E.), many Jews wanted to condemn any Jew who had accepted Jesus and to rid Judaism of any trace of Christianity. Liturgical practices that had been in any way contaminated by Christian usage were changed; a formal curse against Christians was added to Jewish morning prayer. Christians were no longer able to associate with Jews.

The de facto and de jure segregation of the Jews from Christians gave the Christians a profound cultural shock. Christians regarded their faith as the extension of the covenant between God and Abraham; they believed they were part of the Jewish heritage even if they did not agree with Jewish cultural exclusivity. When the Jews severed connection with *them,* Christians were forced to rethink their position.

Christians made a variety of responses to their dilemma, as reflected in early Christian writings (see Appendix 3). In the heat of the controversy, some writers disparaged Judaism, arguing that it was worthless and unnecessary to Christianity. Christians made changes in the practical order to complete the severance: they celebrated the Lord's Day (the Sabbath) on Sunday instead of Saturday and celebrated their main ritual meal, the Lord's Supper (Eucharist), every week instead of once a year (at Passover).

Christianity, therefore, developed an identity separate from Judaism, but it could never leave Judaism totally behind. Christians were indebted to Jews for liturgical consciousness and forms of worship, for a sense of roots, and for the Bible. Like Jews, Christians believe in one God, the Creator and Judge of the universe; like Jews,

Controversy

Salvation Through Knowledge: Gnosticism

Early Christian theologians, in an effort to make their beliefs understandable to different cultures, worked to relate Christian doctrines to the Jewish tradition, to Hellenistic culture, or to the Roman world. Justin Martyr's *Dialogue with Trypho* is an example of a Christian apologist appealing to Jewish sensibilities, as Origen's philosophical writing is an example of a Christian thinker working in the Greek intellectual tradition. By far the most radical theologians in this regard were the Gnostics, a Christian sect that originated in the second century. Gnostics (from the Greek *gnosis,* meaning "to know") preached a salvation through knowledge; to get to heaven, one had to learn a secret wisdom. Their teachings were so unusual and esoteric that the Gnostics were later outlawed and condemned as heretics.

The Gnostics were Platonists who believed that reality was spiritual and that the physical universe—including the human body—was a dreadful mistake. In their view, the "god" of Israel who created the universe was not the ultimate God but a lesser supernatural being named Ialdabaoth, who was demonic, vain, and foolish enough to believe that he was God. When Ialdabaoth and his angels created Adam and Eve, they unwittingly placed a stolen share of divine spiritual power in human beings. Sparks of this divine power, they believed, survived through human history in the descendants of Adam and Eve's third son, Seth. Thus, Gnostics called themselves the "children of Seth." They would be saved when an emissary from the divine realm came to call them home. For them, Jesus was that person—God incarnate who summoned the Gnostics to "wake up" to their true nature as divine beings trapped in a material world.

To those whose existence was miserable, Gnostics offered the hope that this world was not their true home. Indeed, they were destined for reunion with a perfect spiritual universe where the life of the body (and all its ills) would be left behind forever. Those who did not accept this message were called "children of Cain," human beings with no hope of salvation. Although Gnostic schools appealed to intellectual Christians who sought a deeper, more philosophical version of their faith, their hostility toward the God of Israel and their tendency to restrict salvation to members of their own group were distinctly at odds with mainline Christian teaching. Furthermore, it was important for the early Christian community to see itself linked to the creation of the world and to God's providential plan for humanity; they believed in the goodness of creation and believed that Jesus identified the God of Israel as his father. Finally, the apostolic preaching invited people to salvation through faith, not through esoteric knowledge.

Thus, even when a revised version of Gnosticism was taught by the brilliant teacher Valentinus (c. 100–175), who invited Christians to experience mystical union with God the Father, mainline Christian churches rejected it.

Christians accept providence, free will, and a history of salvation. Without the Hebrew Bible, Christians would have been unable to make sense of the life, death, and resurrection of Jesus.

The Greek Context and Philosophical Identity

Christianity matured in a Hellenistic world of pagan philosophy and ideas. Since the Greeks respected philosophical sophistication, members of the early Christian community began to adapt themselves to the task of making Christian faith philosophically

Concept

The Divinity of Jesus

When the early Christians said that the crucified Jesus of Nazareth was the promised Messiah, the "anointed one" who would bring God's kingdom, most Jews did not believe such a bold claim. But the Christians did not stop there: they proclaimed that Jesus was divine and should be worshiped as God.

Christians came to believe in Jesus' divinity as they read the Jewish Scriptures in light of their experience. For example, they believed that God had raised Jesus from the dead and taken him up to heaven and that this event fulfilled Psalm 110:1: "The Lord says to my lord, 'Sit at my right hand until I make your enemies your footstool.'" Christians argued that this verse shows God ("the Lord") speaking to Jesus ("my lord") at the resurrection. Because God calls Jesus "lord," which is also how the Bible refers to God, Jesus must also have the name of God and be divine. The New Testament quotes Psalm 110:1 more than any other verse from the Old Testament.

As Christians began to express their faith in philosophical terms, they developed sophisticated ways of explaining the divinity of Christ. For example, Platonist philosophers said that God was too remote and spiritual to be involved with this material world, and thus, God interacts with the world through a divine emanation called God's *Logos,* meaning "word" or "reason." It is the *Logos,* they said, who actually created the world, and human beings can know the highest God only through the *Logos.* Ancient Jews thought of God's Wisdom in a similar way: Wisdom helped God to create the world, and people learn the ways of God through Wisdom (Prov. 8). The Gospel of John identifies Jesus as God's *Logos,* through whom God created the world (1:1–4), and Paul calls Jesus God's Wisdom (1 Cor. 1:24).

Justin Martyr (d. 165) developed a "Logos theology" that explained Jesus as a "second God." God the Creator cannot appear on earth, so the Word of God appeared to Moses in the burning bush. The Word of God (God's son) became human in Jesus. For Justin, Jesus the Word is clearly divine and to be worshiped as God but is less divine than the ultimate God. This way of thinking and the questions it raised would become a major source of controversy in the fourth-century Arian crisis.

respectable. We can see some attempts at this kind of adaptation already in the Acts of the Apostlels, in Paul's speech to the Athenians (17:16–34). In their encounters with Greek philosophy, early Christian writers and scholars laid the philosophical foundations for what would later become an elaborate Christian theology.

The task was a difficult one because of internal and external opposition. Externally, Christian philosophers had to learn to talk to people who had just freed their understanding of the divine from a mythological tradition: when Christians arrived on the scene talking about the Son of God, Greek philosophers thought they were dealing with a backward people. Internally, there were problems of definition and interpretation: what did it mean to be free from the Law or to be free in the Lord? Some people thought they were bound by no laws and could, in effect, be a law unto themselves; others felt free to pick and choose parts of the Bible or parts of Jesus' teaching to suit their own particular philosophical interpretation. Some people thought they were saved by faith; Gnostics thought they were saved by knowledge (from the Greek *gnosis)* and developed elaborate systems of secret knowledge, passwords, and esoteric doctrine.

In an effort to define orthodox Christian views *and* to make their beliefs understandable to a philosophically sophisticated audience, early Christian writers borrowed some of the philosophical ideas of the time and attempted to present a systematic Christianity. Justin Martyr (100–165 C.E.) arranged the sayings of the Gospel under the headings of "self-control," "universal love," and "being blameless." Theophilus of Antioch (late second century) did much the same thing, adding insights from the Ten Commandments. Once they had a set of Christian maxims, writers could combine them with Greek philosophical ideas about spiritual perfection through the cultivation of the soul. Clement of Alexandria (d. 215 C.E.) and Origen (185–254 C.E.) interpreted the Christian life as one beginning in faith and ending with a real likeness to God; many tried to synthesize Christianity and philosophy.

Christian philosophers were relating to the outside world effectively, but there were other pressing matters; internal problems plagued the Christian church. Early Christian writers wrote philosophical works; they also wrote treatises on behavior, decorum, and Christian practice. Originally, members of a local church handled problems of belief and discipline in that congregation. In the second and third centuries, however, bishops began to exercise their power and authority more strongly. The Christian church became larger and more complex; the bishops believed that the church needed centralized authority, which rested in the office and administrative power of the bishop. With authority to judge doctrinal matters, bishops believed they could protect people from dangerous doctrines and practices. Accordingly, the early church moved slowly but surely toward a monarchical episcopacy: the bishop was like a king, a man with high authority who could decide (by himself or in consultation with other bishops) whether a certain position was right or wrong.

In the context of the Hellenistic world, then, Christianity developed a structure for handling problems. The office of the bishop and the authority of the bishops culminated in a series of meetings called councils (see Appendix 4), where Christian doctrine was defined and Christian practice regulated. Philosophically, the church adopted new vocabulary and ideas. Christian philosophy and apologetics (explaining Christianity to a potentially hostile audience) were the work of theologians and were central to the church's development in both East and West.

The Roman Context and Political Identity

Christianity was born into a Jewish religious context and learned how to negotiate in a Hellenistic philosophical environment, but the real rulers of the world into which Christianity emerged were the Romans. At the beginning of the second century, the Roman Empire stretched from Mesopotamia to Scotland, from the Danube to the Sahara Desert. Within this area lived many peoples with different cultures and worldviews. The Roman Empire was one of the most highly organized, well-ruled, sophisticated civilizations the world has ever seen. Two languages dominated: Latin in the West and Greek in the East. The emperor, an absolute ruler with pretensions to divinity, stood at the top of this large edifice.

The ideals of human decency (called *philanthropeia* in Greek, *humanitas* in Latin) and universal brotherhood were supported by the power and uniformity of Roman law. The empire was not without problems: huge slave populations, horrible slums, and terrible poverty existed side by side with Roman elegance. In addition to social ills, there were serious political problems. Lack of a peaceful way to choose a successor to the emperor caused periodic anarchy and instability; a nonindustrial base caused a gold drainage and severe inflation; a farm crisis and decimating plagues undermined the empire; and the army was mercenary rather than composed of Roman citizens. The political reforms of Diocletian in the third century helped to ease some of these situations, but the real reform came in the fourth century with Emperor Constantine, who chose to favor Christianity over all the other religions in the empire.

Roman religion, an amalgam of various cults throughout the empire, was often more concerned with form and rite than with spiritual teaching; in some ways, it focused more on devotional practices than on inner experience. As the empire expanded, the mystery religions of the Mediterranean peoples gained influence precisely because they emphasized internal aspects of religion: a savior God, mysterious rites (sacraments—*sacramentum* is the Latin translation of the Greek word *mysterion*), intimacy, and emotional response. The spiritual side of Roman religion was shaped by outside influences, by the beliefs and practices of conquered peoples. The most important outside influences were Stoicism, Epicureanism, Mithraism, the mystery religions, and Christianity.

Stoicism and Epicureanism, philosophical systems developed in the Greek world, both rested on a theory of human perfectibility. Epicureans thought that everything hung on *fate,* and since there was no given order in the universe, they advocated the freedom to pick and choose the very best things in life. Stoics, on the other hand, believed in an ordered universe, a cosmic intelligence or world soul that permeated the universe and made it possible for people to attain perfect freedom by living in total harmony with reason. Stoics are sometimes pictured in our minds as withstanding pain and refusing to admit their feelings or fears. They *did* attempt to control their passions by living fully in accord with reason, but a more accurate picture would show them trying to get in touch with the universe, feel its vibrations, and resonate with its harmonies. Both these attitudes continue to appeal to people today (though not, perhaps, in their pure philosophical form), and you can imagine that they appealed to the Romans as well.

The mystery cults were an entirely different matter and appealed on a more experiential level. Through their mysterious rites, they not only offered a way to an emotional religious experience but also immortality: if one believed in the savior-God and followed the mysteries, one could live forever. The fertility cult of Cybele celebrated its feasts orgiastically; the Egyptian cult of Isis had magical initial rites including a ceremony of death and rebirth. The most important mystery religion for the Romans was probably Mithraism, a dualistic system that may have developed in Persia. Dualism divides the world into two parts, good and evil, and the followers of Mithraism believed that there were powers of light and powers of darkness at work in the universe. What one hoped to do, through religious rites, was to get in touch with the powers of light and withstand the powers of darkness.

Christianity developed in the Roman Empire on the heels of these other religions and philosophical systems and learned to adapt some of the best parts of them to its own belief system. In some ways of looking at it, Christianity did not have to prepare its own ground but was able to grow in the soil prepared by others. Hellenized Judaism in Alexandria brought a consciousness of monotheism to the empire and provided it with a Greek translation of the Bible. Stoicism, with its concept of universal

SPIRITUALITY

Experience of the Holy Spirit: Inspiration and Renewal

The New Testament is filled with extraordinary experiences that early Christians attributed to the Spirit of God. In the Old Testament, God's Spirit is a wind or breath that can create things (Gen. 1:2) and inspire people to lead (Judges 3:10). As the disciples of Jesus gathered to celebrate the Jewish festival of Pentecost after the resurrection, their meeting place was filled with a rush of wind, tongues of fire appeared among them, and they began to speak in foreign languages (Acts 2:1–4). Paul became an apostle of Jesus after a revelation of God (Gal. 1:15–16), and he continued to experience visions, including one of "the third heaven," where Paradise is located (2 Cor. 12:1–4). Peter became convinced that even Gentiles could receive the Spirit when he heard new Gentile converts speaking in tongues without even being baptized (Acts 10:44–48).

Speaking in tongues, that is, speaking a divine language that cannot be understood without inspired interpretation, was a regular feature of meetings in Paul's churches. Paul considered it a gift of the Spirit (in Greek, *charisma*), although he considered it of lower value than other spiritual gifts such as prophecy, healing, and even "forms of assistance" (1 Cor. 12:27–31). In Paul's view, God's Spirit was active in all baptized Christians, causing them to cry out in joy, "Abba! Father!" (Rom. 8:15–16). It bestowed a variety of gifts on different people, and so Paul's communities were loosely organized: people took on tasks as the Spirit inspired them.

As the church grew more formal and structured, such experiences of the Spirit became less frequent but did not disappear. For example, in the 170s, three Christian prophets in Asia Minor—Priscilla, Maximilla, and Montanus—began to speak for God by the Holy Spirit. For example, Maximilla said, "Hear not me; rather hear Christ [through me]." The prophets told Christians to prepare for the return of Christ and that the New Jerusalem would descend on the village of Pepuza. Although Christ did not return as predicted, the movement that the prophets began, called New Prophecy, spread throughout the Mediterranean world, inspiring men and women to renew their commitment to Christianity. Many clergy, however, distrusted the unpredictable and uncontrollable manifestations of the Spirit and could not accept women in leadership positions. When some bishops later labeled New Prophecy a heresy, its followers formed their own churches.

Manifestations of gifts from the Spirit have sparked movements from the ancient world into modern times. Spirit renewal can be found in Christian churches in Africa and Latin America today, and in some mainline denominations as well, sometimes provoking opposition from official leaders.

brotherhood, prepared the Romans for a universalism unknown in other religious circles. Neoplatonism, with its quest for ultimate perfection and mystical awareness of the divine, introduced an aspect of spiritual exaltation. The mystery religions were especially important: they had emotional appeal, a concept that everyone could be saved, a savior-God who died and was reborn, and a sacramental rite that brought believers immortality by association with the sufferings and eventual triumph of God.

Christianity knew how to adapt itself, where to borrow, and how to shape its message into the atmosphere of the times. It was universalist and aimed (in some quarters) at ultimate perfection through mystical union. Baptism and the Lord's Supper developed into sacramental rites, with ceremony and emotional appeal. Christianity was ancient because it was rooted in the Hebrew Bible: it could trace itself back to the creation of the world and the first inklings of a divine-human partnership. Most of all, however, Christians offered a savior-God who was historically concrete. According to Christians, Jesus was not a mythical savior but a real person, a man who had lived and died on earth and in history (*not* "once upon a time"), one who talked and suffered in the sight of others, who died publicly and rose again where people could see and touch him. Christianity endured longer than these other religions and was eventually declared the official religion of the empire. In the second and third centuries, few people could have predicted the *survival* of the Christian religion, let alone its rise to a position of favoritism. To understand how phenomenal the rise of Christianity was, we must look back at the first 300 years of its life when the Christian church was persecuted.

The Romans were essentially tolerant of different religions, yet their policy toward Christians in various parts of the empire was one of periodic but severe persecution. Christians were strict monotheists who refused to recognize the Roman gods; in times when *everyone* in the empire was supposed to make some sacrifice to the gods—to ensure victory or forestall harm—Christians refused to offer sacrifice. Christians also refused to worship the emperor. Instead, they held their own unauthorized gatherings on the Lord's Day and were regarded with suspicion by both the Roman populace and the authorities. Christians were sometimes killed or tortured by officers of the state. Why? Some Romans believed that Christians subverted good order and that the Romans should attempt to eliminate Christianity by killing its bishops and burning its books.

Christians responded in different ways to persecution. Some witnessed to the truth of their beliefs by suffering and dying and are remembered as martyrs (the Greek word *martus* means witness); others endured torture and were honored as confessors (they confessed their Christian faith and were tortured but not killed for doing so). Another group escaped persecution either by denying their beliefs or by finding some loophole in the law that allowed them to avoid a confrontation. When these people are remembered at all—many people believe the persecutions produced only heroes—they are recalled as the *lapsi,* people who lapsed from their religion. Because of the martyrs, the Christian church developed a cult and theology of martyrdom: their deaths were interpreted as heroic imitations of the passion and death of Jesus; the martyr was the true disciple who followed Jesus even into death at the hands of the state. Because of the *lapsi,* the Christian church was challenged to a more systematic administration of the sacrament of reconciliation, or penance.

In the Roman context, therefore, Christians had sufficient freedom to adapt a variety of religious ideas and practices to their own beliefs, but they also suffered persecution because their religious stance put them at odds with the empire. Their survival convinced them even more of their special mission to the world.

CONCLUSION

The early Christian community was small, adapted to new situations, was courageous in the face of death, and was agile in adopting new solutions to problems. Despite differences, a catholic consensus about doctrine and discipline was growing. Ancient ecclesiastical functions and early models of church structure—a bishop, a board of elders, and a college of deacons—eventually gave way to a monarchical episcopacy. By the beginning of the fourth century, the small group of believers had become a large body with members in all parts of the Roman Empire and beyond its bounds; it was universal in outlook, well organized, and theologically complex. Christians developed methods of discipline, a growing philosophical literature, and political autonomy. Early in the fourth century, Christians were probably less than 10 percent of the Latin-speaking population of the West and not more than 35 percent of the Greek-speaking East. But with the support of the state, Christianity's ascendancy as the dominant religion of the Roman Empire was assured, and Christianity became the universal religion of the Mediterranean.

As Christianity moved into a more complex world and spread, the challenges and problems presented to it by new cultures and religions increased. Christians in New Testament times thought the world would end soon; after that, many had a negative view of the world, regarding it as presenting a strong temptation to sin. By the end of the third century, Christians had a more positive response to the world; they had learned to live with it, to adapt to it, and to a great extent, were ready to conquer it.

Focal Points for Discussion

1. The original apostles believed in Jesus because they had an experience of him as the risen Lord. How does the Christian community enable new believers to have contact with that experience?
2. Early Christianity was not a fully unified group. The community argued over very important issues, like whether to admit pagan Gentiles. What kinds of inclusion/exclusion questions do Christians face today in their churches?
3. The Greek, Roman, and Jewish idioms are all different ways of explaining human life. How did early Christianity make itself understandable within each of these cultural contexts?

Historical Roots of Christian Diversity: From Constantine to Modern Times

PART II

The second part of this book introduces the variety of Christian belief and expression by focusing on the roots of Christian diversity. It is not meant to be a comprehensive history of Christianity but a general explanation for the major divisions among the various expressions of Christian belief that have grown up since the fourth century. Christians differ substantially in doctrine, practice, and ecclesiastical structures, and those differences all arose within specific historical contexts. The more serious arguments among Christians led to major divisions within Christianity itself and to the formation of separate churches and denominations. These chapters explain those differences.

The first major rift in Christianity occurred between what are now called the Roman Catholic church and the Eastern Orthodox church. These groups grew up in different parts of the vast Roman Empire and, from the early fourth century especially, confronted radically different problems: Western Christians battled to survive, while Eastern Christianity, protected by the state, hammered out the foundations for Christian doctrine (see Appendix 4). They developed different liturgical practices and patterns of ecclesiastical authority and eventually separated into two distinct forms of Christianity.

The second major division occurred in the West during the Reformation. Reform attempts within and outside the church led to the development of several new forms of Christianity distinguishable from one another in governance, belief, and practice. We will follow the Reformation itself and then watch the reforming spirit of the sixteenth century move dynamically through the seventeenth and eighteenth centuries. By the beginning of the nineteenth century, there were many new varieties of Christianity.

These chapters cover an enormous range of history and development and were written specifically to explain how and why there are so many different kinds of Christianity. Part II should therefore be read not as a history of Christianity but as an attempt to look historically at Christian controversy over fifteen centuries and to explain how some of those controversies led to the formation of separate denominations.

One important principle to keep in mind is that conflict and controversy characterize any living religion. We have already seen that the young Christian community was shaped by many different questions and defined itself in various contexts. The fact that the early Christians had to figure things out rather than follow some predisposed plan of action is not a negative judgment but is a testament to the complicated realities of community life. As we will see in this part of the book, conflict and controversy sometimes became so acute that breaks occurred and new denominations were formed. Some people see this proliferation of denominations as tragic, as a betrayal of the essential unity of Christianity. One can wonder, however, whether there ever was the kind of unity that some people project into the distant past. Christians have always argued heatedly over important issues and have often treated one another with hostility, suspicion, and anger. The point of this part of the book is to explain how and why there came to be so many different kinds of Christianity, to present each new group sympathetically, and to identify its special understanding of the Christian life.

CHAPTER 4

ORTHODOX CHRISTIANITY AND ROMAN CATHOLICISM: FROM THE FOURTH TO THE FOURTEENTH CENTURIES

Two distinct forms of Christianity grew up in the eastern and western parts of the Roman Empire: Orthodox Christians in the East and Roman Catholics in the West are the largest and most ancient forms of Christianity. They share central assumptions, but because they developed in radically different religious and political climates, they also have significant differences and represent conflicting orientations. Roman Catholic Christianity tends to be more legalistic in the structures of church life and in its approach to the sacraments; Orthodox Christianity is more mystical in its liturgical preoccupations and more concerned with inner spiritual content. Differences in perspective have shaped the way each group articulates doctrine and celebrates liturgy. One general example may make this difference clearer. Western Christianity explains that the word of God became flesh to save people from their sins; thus, Western Christians stress salvation. Eastern Christianity explains that the word of God became flesh so that people could become like God; thus, Eastern Orthodox Christians stress deification.

Our approach to the material in this chapter is somewhat different from our approach in later chapters and perhaps deserves some word of explanation. Because we will not *specifically* follow later developments in Orthodox Christianity—especially in relation to Roman Catholicism—and because Roman Catholicism and Orthodoxy (in contrast to Protestantism) put a premium on the development and canonization of tradition and on the model of sanctity represented by the monastic tradition, our discussion of these two groups is meant to give you some idea of the deep unity of ancient Christianity. At the same time, because these two groups developed in very different geographical and political situations, they became, for all their shared heritage, two quite distinct expressions of Christianity. Those differences are most evident in their styles of authority and worship. This chapter, therefore, does not simply describe a profound historical breach; it attempts to show some of the consequences of that break in terms of different structural and liturgical expressions.

POINTS OF CORRESPONDENCE

Belief in the authority of tradition distinguishes Roman Catholics and Orthodox Christians from most other Christian groups. Both Roman Catholics and Orthodox Christians posit the need for a religious authority alongside the Bible based on postbiblical experience and practice. They share an ancient doctrinal system and have liturgical preoccupations that are accepted only in part (if at all) by other Christian denominations. Both also place a high value on monasticism and avowed religious life, institutions that have not been important in other Christian groups. We explore these points of similarity between the two churches first.

Tradition as a Religious Authority

The Bible is the most important source of religious authority for Christians but not the only one. In these ancient churches, a parallel stream of religious authority was generated by Christians applying the Bible to new situations. The religious authority produced in this way is called tradition. Put another way, since biblical stories and teachings were written to respond to the spiritual and practical needs of the people to whom they were addressed, those words must be continually studied and applied to new situations, a process that creates some new applications and guidelines.

The Bible and tradition are not opposed to one another. Indeed, tradition is the way the Bible is interpreted and applied to questions of belief and practice. You might say that tradition is the Bible lived out in a community, and most Christians see the need for it. The debate arises, however, over how much authority to invest in tradition. For example, are the decrees of ecumenical councils (see Appendix 4) a binding part of sacred tradition? Orthodox and Roman Catholic Christians accept the teachings of the first seven councils as authentic interpretations of the Gospel, but only Roman Catholics accept conciliar decrees formulated after the ninth century. As we shall see, Protestant reformers were especially critical of the Roman Catholic acceptance of traditions (like the claims of the papacy or the existence of purgatory), which (as they perceived it) had no roots in the New Testament.

Tradition is a specific interpretation of Scripture as elaborated within the Christian community and affirmed by the church. Since tradition originally allowed for new interpretations to meet questions not specifically addressed in Scripture, tradition was meant to be fluid rather than fixed. Tension can result when a group shows a tendency to absolutize or canonize tradition, to make it appear unbending. The development of tradition was not meant to lead to ecclesiastical rigidity but instead developed precisely to recognize the dynamic interplay between the concrete, fixed authority of Scripture and the fluid, developing authority of daily practice.

Because it is dynamic, tradition adds something new to Christianity: it enlarges upon Scripture. Human ingenuity is a factor in the development of tradition as well: people often expand a concrete communication beyond its original scope.

You should remember that tradition builds up slowly, almost imperceptibly, until it becomes authoritative and, in the minds of some Christians, a source of religious authority equal to Scripture. The postbiblical collection of opinions, practices, and dogmatic definitions that we find in the early ecumenical councils and the writings of the church Fathers (see Appendix 3) took hundreds of years to develop into a tried and tested body of revered Christian teaching.

Orthodox and Roman Catholic Christians disagree about some parts of tradition—especially about the authority of the pope—but they agree on the principle of tradition. Both see a need for an extrabiblical religious authority. For them, Scripture without tradition lacks vitality, tradition without Scripture lacks foundation, and either of them without observance and practice lacks credibility.

Models of Sanctity

One model of the Christian life portrayed in the New Testament is life in common: people shared work, prayer, and food, lived simply, and grew in fellowship. Another New Testament concept is the life of perfection. Jesus once said, "You, therefore, must be perfect, as your heavenly Father is perfect" (Matt. 5:48). Christian monasticism derives from these two concepts as they developed in a world where an ascetic ideal already existed. Greek philosophers used the word *asceticism* to describe a system of discipline intended to combat vice and enhance virtue. The word comes from the Greek word for training or exercise; ascetics are people who train themselves for virtue. In Christianity, the words of Jesus about denying oneself, taking up one's cross, and following him (Mark 8:34) provide inspiration for Christian ascetic life: negative self-denial on the one hand and positive following of Jesus on the other. But what does it mean to deny self and follow Jesus? For some early Christians, it meant living in anticipation of martyrdom; for others, it meant living an ascetic life: being alert and watchful, praying and fasting, giving up earthly possessions, and turning away from pleasures of the flesh (food, drink, and sex). Those who chose asceticism were monks.

Monks sought a life of perfection in faraway places removed from the cares and stresses of worldly life. Although the first people to withdraw from the world were hermits, living alone in caves in remote areas of Syria and Egypt, monasticism soon became defined by small communities of men and women sharing a common rule. The first monastic communities formed when groups of hermits came together for safety or fellowship and then built a wall around their hermitages. Eventually, these communities lived in monasteries where monks slept, ate, and prayed under the same roof. Monastic life was open to both men (monks) and women (nuns) who spent their days in prayer and work and who took solemn vows of *poverty* (without private possessions or money), *chastity* (no sex), and *obedience* (to the will of the local superior). These vows are sometimes called the counsels of perfection, a phrase that indicates that those who follow them desire to follow the command of Jesus to "be perfect" (Matt. 5:48).

As the ascetic life flourished, some of the early Christian writers undergirded it with theoretical and theological support. In the third century, Clement of Alexandria and Origen both extolled asceticism and encouraged Christians to live pure and perfect lives. Because Clement and Origen lived and wrote in a Neoplatonic environment, they

Concept

Monasticism and the Resistance to Culture

Just as Christianity emerged as the dominant religion in the Roman Empire, tens of thousands of men and women abandoned ordinary life to live as monks, many in the harsh deserts of Egypt and Syria. The word *monk* comes from the Greek *monachos,* meaning "solitary one." Monks seek a life apart from society to focus on their relationship with God.

From its beginnings, Christianity rejected elements of the culture that surrounded it. Jesus devalued family ties, praised celibacy, and recommended the proper way to fast (Matt. 6:16–18; 19:12; Luke 14:26). Paul urged his followers who were not married to remain so, calling the celibate life a "gift" and claiming that marriage divides the believer's loyalty between God and spouse (1 Cor. 7). Such ascetic practices as celibacy and fasting trained the soul in virtue and rejected the values of this world.

It is no surprise, then, that when the church became more of a dominant and bureaucratic institution, some Christians sought a lifestyle that embraced simplicity and the freedom to seek God. Monastic life appealed especially to idealistic, spiritual young people like Augustine of Hippo (354–430) who turned away from worldly rewards of wealth and status to pursue lives of prayer and fellowship with other monks.

From antiquity to today, men and women attracted to monastic life have lived in a variety of ways. They have been hermits in deserts, caves, and enclosed chambers; some have chosen to live as groups in small houses or large monasteries. Whatever the setting, monks follow a daily discipline, sometimes written in a "rule," that includes frequent prayer, regular work, and simple meals. Some monks and nuns also observe extended periods of silence. Although monastic discipline may appear regimented, monks experience its regularity and predictability as freeing: they learn to quiet their own desires and to concentrate on God and other people.

Monks may reject many of the values of the wider culture, but most do not flee from society. Instead, monasteries have often served others as hospitals and places of refuge, and during the Middle Ages, monks preserved ancient culture by copying the manuscripts of classical texts. All members of monastic communities pray in behalf of the wider world.

The appeal of monasticism continues into the modern period as people are drawn to spiritual disciplines like meditation, lives of simplicity, and periodic retreats from ordinary life. Christians have experimented with a variety of ways of being "alone" with God in the midst of a changing world.

combined their interest in asceticism with the Neoplatonic concept of contemplation. For them, monasticism combined a desire for perfection (the ascetic life) with mystical ascent (the contemplative life). In the Eastern church, contemplation and mysticism were always the central preoccupations of monastic life, and Eastern monasticism has remained contemplative. Monastic life in the West was similar but also developed a more active concept of religious community life: Western Christianity supported religious congregations and orders of friars and canons who lived under a semimonastic rule (life in common and specific vows) but followed specific active vocations in the church, like preaching or teaching.

Monastic life in both East and West contained some extremists. Some extravagant ascetics in the East spent years atop high pillars in one position to discipline their flesh and draw closer to God in attitudes of eternal prayer. Irish monks in the West who rowed out into the open sea and scuttled their oars to see "where God would send them" embodied the idea of an individual pilgrimage to God found in a life of wandering. In both East and West, we can find monks and nuns who thought the ascetic life required extreme penances: long fasts, the wearing of spiked chains next to the skin, and so on. For the most part, however, monasticism was simple community life under a sensible rule. Furthermore, however much Eastern and Western monks stressed avoidance of worldly temptations, each also stressed hospitality: all monks and nuns, whether living alone or in community, were to be ready to share their material and spiritual goods with those in need of them. If monks and nuns found the demands of hospitality distracting, they could only move to a more remote area and limit accessibility to themselves. Refusing hospitality to those in need was never an option in monastic life.

Monasticism in Orthodox Christianity has been based, essentially, on the writings of Basil the Great (330–379 C.E.). Some people refer to the "Rule" of St. Basil, but his writings really constitute letters of spiritual advice to those trying to find a deeper union with God through prayer and ascetic practices. Although there have always been—and still are—hermits in the Orthodox tradition, Basil stressed communal life and encouraged monks to practice manual labor and obedience, prayer, and work. Since Orthodox monasteries were protected and often financed by the government, and since Orthodox Christianity grew in a relatively peaceful environment, Orthodox monks have been free to pursue the mystical life to the exclusion of other concerns. Orthodox monasteries are usually not great centers of learning or scholarship; they are places where people can dedicate themselves totally to prayer and contemplation. Eastern monasticism is much the same today as in its origins: monks still follow the wisdom of St. Basil, wear the same clothing, and live simply. Their lives combine asceticism, mysticism, and discipline in search of a direct experience of God. The chief mystical experience is the vision of divine light, and the main preoccupation of the monk is the desire for union with God.

In contrast to Orthodox monasticism, Western monasticism is based on a clear rule devised by Benedict of Nursia (480–550 C.E.). Benedict stressed work and prayer, and monks were required to bind themselves to a single monastery for life. According to the Benedictine Rule, the first piece of Western monastic legislation developed for monks living in politically unstable Europe, monks were supposed to lead a traditional monastic life. In fact, however, monks in the West often lived unconventional monastic lives because their situation demanded it. Western monks, however much they may have wanted to devote their entire lives to union with God, often were called upon to act as teachers, political advisers, and missionaries. Monks were the great librarians of the West, primarily responsible for the preservation of learning during the Dark Ages and entrusted with copying and preserving ancient manuscripts.

Furthermore, since the politically unstable situation of the Western church created an environment for change and creative adaptation, monasticism in the West inspired a variety of experiments in religious life. Some of these new groups devoted most of their energy to teaching or begging, to crusading or spiritual knighthood, to religious or political reform. It is hard to imagine Western civilization without monks: they were teachers, administrators, reformers, inventors, and religious leaders.

THE POWER OF ROME AS AN IDEA: TWO CHRISTIAN MODELS

Jesus was born into a Mediterranean world ruled by Rome at a time when the Roman mystique was at its apex. The world had never experienced an empire so vast or so efficient, and when people thought of "Rome," they envisioned a set of associated ideas. Rome was vast, peaceful, beautifully organized, and ruled by a great legal system; it was religiously complex, with impressive shrines and monuments celebrating its own glory and providing inspirational spaces for its people; it was distinguished by a highly developed intellectual and cultural life where playwrights, poets, and philosophers spoke classical Latin and wrote essays and histories that were so good we still read them today. Rome was presided over by Caesar, a central ruling authority who stood close to divinity and who symbolized in his person the glory of Rome. As that glory dimmed—Marcus Aurelius, the "last good emperor," died in 180 and so began a period of decline and political anarchy—and then appeared to be restored to some degree by Constantine, it was natural to wonder whether the old Rome might, indeed, reclaim the attention of the world.

If we can see Rome more as an idea than as a place, perhaps we can understand why it was very powerful and attractive. Rome was a goal, an ideal to shape policy. It is not surprising that it attracted Constantine, and it probably should not be disconcerting that it attracted Christians in general. As we begin to look at political arrangements, East and West, it might help to keep the "idea of Rome" in the back of our minds as a kind of explanation for events. If we ask who could have revived Roman dreams or restored Roman glory in the context of the fourth century, we will find several answers. As the Roman emperor, Constantine clearly had the best claim on the project, but when he moved his capital from the city of Rome to a new site in the Eastern part of the Roman Empire, he left a political vacuum in the West and invited rival claimants. In the West, several groups were inspired to restore Roman glory: old senatorial families, new barbarian families, and most of all, the bishops of Rome, later known as popes.

For all their shared heritage in tradition and monasticism, therefore, the two ancient forms of Christianity grew into distinct churches mostly because of widely differing political experiences. The Orthodox church organized itself in two ways: at the local level, ecclesiastical organization was based on the local community with the bishop as its head. In an ideal form, local churches are united by a community of love rather than by an institutional bond. At the same time, the broader version of the Orthodox church organized itself along the administrative lines of the Roman Empire, wherein the chief administrative officer was the emperor, thought to be God's agent on earth. The patriarch of Constantinople, the highest-ranking church official in the Eastern church, understood that his standing was tied to the emperor, who could approve patriarchal elections, call councils, and pass ecclesiastical laws. In matters of faith, however, Christ was understood to be the head of the church, and Christ's will for the church was stated and defended by the patriarchs.

The Roman church organized itself according to the claims of apostolicity, especially the claims that Peter was *the* most important apostle and that his territory (Rome) was *the* seat of religious authority. The patriarch of Rome, the highest-ranking church official in the Western church, understood that his standing was greater than the emperor's and that he (the bishop of Rome, later called the pope) was the head of the church. Both pope and patriarch thought of themselves as Roman and as heirs of the greatest political empire in the history of the world. We look next in greater detail at each of the two systems of church-state relations as they developed in their historical contexts. We can see how this led to a great schism between the two churches that has endured until the present day.

Constantinople as the New Rome: The Greek Orthodox System

When Constantine reunited the fragments of the Roman Empire in the early part of the fourth century, he did so under the sign of the cross. The claim made by Constantine's biographer, Eusebius, was that Constantine—like Paul in the New Testament—was called directly by God to embrace Christianity. The political results of this claim were momentous for the church: it meant that Constantine ruled by divine right, that he considered himself appointed by God, and that his government was a theocracy (that is, the people believed that God, through a mediator, the emperor, ruled Byzantium). Neither Constantine nor the emperors after him ever claimed to be divine, but they did see themselves as God's representatives on earth, ranking just below Christ in the administration of earthly justice. The office of the emperor was, in a sense, the visible manifestation of God on earth. The emperor was like God because God's business was to bring the heavens into a peaceful unity and harmony, and the emperor's business was to create a state in which all people coexisted in unity and harmony. God ruled the cosmos and the emperor ruled the earth.

Through a series of victories and treaties, Constantine, who worshiped the sun god, became the sole master of the western half of the empire by 313 C.E. and master of the entire Roman Empire—East and West—by 324. The decisive battle in which Constantine won control of the West was the Battle of the Milvian Bridge (outside Rome). Before this battle, Constantine had a dream or vision, which he later understood as a revelation: he saw a cross superimposed on the sun and heard the words "In this sign conquer." Constantine took control of the West under the Christian sign of the cross, and from that time, he was more sympathetic to Christianity than to any other religion. It was Constantine who passed the Edict of Milan, which granted religious freedom to all and ended the persecution of Christians; it was Constantine who began the process of making the empire Christian. He began gradually to transfer all the religious revenues of the ancient world to the Christian church and by 324 began a massive church-building program so the most impressive buildings in the empire were Christian places of worship.

Constantine called the first ecumenical council at Nicaea in 325 (see Appendix 4). Politically astute, he saw that the Roman Empire needed a unifying ideology, that a geographically massive empire with a variety of philosophical schools and cultures needed some common belief to bind people together. Constantine saw Christianity as the perfect unifying force. Universal in scope, it was beginning to take hold of people's religious imaginations. It combined some rituals and beliefs of the mystery religions with belief in a historically concrete savior-God, and it had developed a sophisticated philosophical and political framework that enabled discussion of issues and evaluation of positions. And it was *organized*. Besides, Constantine believed he had been called by God, blessed with a revelation experience, and appointed to build a Christian empire.

The religious symbols associated with the Christian empire solidified his claims. Constantine's mother, Helena, made a pilgrimage to Jerusalem and found there some of the implements of Jesus' death—the cross, the nails, and the sign of the cross that identified Jesus as king of the Jews—which became the great religious talismans of the empire and tokens of divine favor. The people of Byzantium, renamed Constantinople when Constantine moved the capital of the empire there in 333, considered themselves both Romans and the chosen people of God. Coins were stamped with pictures of Jesus and the motto Jesus Christ, King of Rulers. The actions of the emperor took on a sacred and symbolic character; military expeditions were sacred and the ceremonies of war were holy. People believed the real ruler of the empire was Christ: the cross was carried into battle as a standard and laws were passed in the name of the Lord Jesus Christ, Our Master.

Constantinople, the capital of the eastern part of the Roman Empire, was called the new Rome. All the weight and civilizing importance of Roman history was adopted by Byzantium. The new Rome differed from the old in that the new one was Christian; the task was no longer just to civilize but to bring all people to salvation in Christ. Constantine perceived himself as an apostle sent by Christ to bring the Gospel to the world; one of his titles, carved on his tomb when he died, was "Equal of the Apostles." When Constantinople fell to the Turks in 1453, the title and the claims to be the new Rome—the third Rome—fell to Moscow and the Russian Orthodox church. In the fifteenth century, Russia was the only politically independent power remaining in the Orthodox world. The czar called himself "Beloved of Christ," as the emperor of Constantinople had done. The claims and tasks of the Orthodox system fell to the czar and the Russian Orthodox church, and in Russia, religious and political destinies were intertwined as in old Byzantium. The idea of an Orthodox Christian state lasted until July 16, 1918, when the last Russian czar, Nicholas II, was executed.

Where was the church in this theocratic system? It was bound up with the state, supporting and reinforcing the state's power. The head of the church, the patriarch of Constantinople, seldom had occasion to exercise direct *political* power because the East always had a strong emperor. When Constantine moved the capital to the East, a political vacuum was created in the West. Rome and the West lacked a strong political system, and the result was political chaos. The head of the church in the West, the bishop of Rome, finally managed to rise to power, to make order of the political disorder. The patriarch of Constantinople seldom had that opportunity; as head of the church, he had full spiritual power, but what political influence he had, he exercised in support of the emperor in the East. No independent religious authority in conflict with the emperor's political authority emerged in the East.

In the Eastern system, the church was protected and established by the state: it was supported by state-collected taxes, met with no persecutions, and feared no attack from outside. But sometimes, the state became overprotective, and the church had to deal with emperors who wanted to take on spiritual functions and make spiritual decisions. It was not the patriarch of Constantinople or the bishop of Rome who called the first ecumenical council; it was the emperor. When Constantine entered the hall where the bishops were meeting in Nicaea to open the council, Eusebius described him as "an angel of God descended from heaven, radiant in the fiery glow of the purple and adorned with gold and precious gems—such was his outward appearance. But his soul was visibly ornamented with the fear and adoration of God." This description is both political and spiritual, and it emphasizes the enormous power of the emperor in both political and spiritual realms.

The patriarch of Constantinople was the chief celebrant of the sacraments and the one who presided over the synod of bishops; he was the leader of the church, but it was the emperor who bore the title Vicar of God on Earth. The power of the patriarch of Constantinople was to be exercised in the spiritual realm; he was not to interfere with political decisions. Even his spiritual functions were to be exercised in cooperation with the emperor, who was—by virtue of his titles and power—permitted to operate within the spiritual realm. At its best, the cooperation between patriarch and emperor on the spiritual front was what the Greeks called a *symphonia,* a harmony of spirits.

Things were not always at their best, however, and the patriarch often had to struggle against the emperor and to safeguard the spiritual freedom of the church. By definition, the patriarch was to be spiritually free, but sometimes, that freedom was encroached upon by the powers of the state. When the Orthodox system moved to Russia in the fifteenth century, the harmony between patriarch and emperor (czar) was destroyed; the czars took full control of the church. In the eighteenth century, Czar Peter the Great abolished the patriarchate and established the internal life of the church along lines he thought were better suited to it and to an enlightened view of church structure.

In summary, then, the Orthodox system conformed to the model of the Roman Empire; Constantinople was the new Rome, and Constantine was appointed by and beloved of God. The old Roman emperors sometimes proclaimed themselves gods; Constantine and his successors did not need to make such a claim because, even without it, they held an enormous amount of power and prestige in an essentially theocratic state. As the Vicar of God on Earth, the emperor also held a central position in the church. He protected and subsidized the church, called and presided over the ecumenical councils, and promulgated all the conciliar dogmas. In this situation, the church could not compete for political power and sometimes had to fight even to maintain its own spiritual power, defending matters of doctrine from imperial interference. A much different situation obtained in the West.

The West as Roman Catholic: The Rise of the Papacy

Constantine sought to establish a new Rome in Constantinople and to be the earthly ruler of a theocratic state. He wanted to replace the old (pagan) Roman Empire with a new (Christian) one, and he succeeded in the eastern half of the empire. The situation in the West, however, did not support the same kind of result. When Constantine moved the capital of the empire to Byzantium, he abandoned the old center of imperial power. In the resulting chaotic situation, the bishop of Rome tried desperately to bring various barbarian chieftains and their peoples into the Christian communion so that religious and political unity would again flourish in the West as they were then doing in the East. To establish his claim to moral authority in the Western world, the bishop of Rome began to interpret Jesus' words in Matthew 16—"You are Peter, and on this rock I will build my church"—to justify his attempt to control and supervise the Latin church and the peoples in the western part of the empire. Constantine claimed to rule by divine appointment, citing his revelation experience before the Battle of the Milvian Bridge; the bishops of Rome also claimed to rule by divine appointment, citing the words of Jesus about Peter. The popes interpreted Matthew 16:19 to mean that they had the "power of the keys." Peter, and by extension, his successors, the popes, were meant to have supreme authority over the whole church since Jesus gave Peter the power to rule as well as to forgive sins.

In the East, the emperor's political power was so strong that it sometimes spilled over into the spiritual realm; in the West, the bishop of Rome's power inevitably embraced the political realm. In both parts of the empire, spiritual and political power overlapped; at best, there was a harmonious cooperation of interests, but at worst—in the chaotic Dark Ages—confusion and a battle for power resulted. The political situation in the West was precarious; the collapse of the Roman Empire, the devastating effect of the barbarian invasions, an unstable economy, and other serious problems created a need for a strong leader located in the West. The leader who emerged was the bishop of Rome, a spiritual leader who found it necessary to become politically powerful as well. The first task in the West was not unity (as in the East) but survival; beyond that, the church in the West set itself the task of making the Gospel known to tribes of unsophisticated peoples. The bishop of Rome began to insinuate himself into the political vacuum and to suggest that the most natural place to look for moral leadership was to the old capital of the empire, Rome. By the fourth century, the bishop of Rome began to call himself the pope, the president of the whole Western Christian church.

The hierarchical system of governance that developed in the early Christian church and was legislated at the council of Chalcedon (451 C.E.) rested on the authority of five supreme patriarchs. The leaders of the church in Rome, Constantinople, Alexandria, Antioch, and Jerusalem together shared authority over the entire Christian church. An earlier council (Nicaea, 325 C.E.) taught that the patriarch (or bishop) of Rome had a *primacy of honor*, a special reverence because the Roman church had been founded by Peter and Paul. Since their bones were buried there, Rome was a popular place of pilgrimage for Christians, and it is not surprising that the bishop of Rome was called "first among equals" and held an honored place among the patriarchs. Eventually, however, the bishops of Rome began to claim that, as successors of Peter (leader of and chief among the apostles), they should be leader and chief among the patriarchs. The bishop of Rome did not want to be first among equals; he wanted to be above all others in honor and authority.

The other four patriarchs recognized the bishop of Rome as the undisputed leader of the Western church but did not acknowledge jurisdiction in their territories. The *patriarchal* claim is the assertion that the bishop of Rome is the head of the Western church, something accepted by Orthodox Christians and later rejected by Protestants. The *papal* claim is the assertion by the bishop of Rome of his authority over the entire universal church, a claim rejected by Orthodox Christians and Protestants. Friction between East and West, even today, usually involves the papal claim.

The history of the papacy is the story of attempts on the part of the bishops of Rome to exercise authority over the western part of the empire, to claim jurisdiction over all bishops, monastic houses, and Christians there. In establishing this authority, however, they began to press their claims over the entire Christian church. By the end of the sixth century, they had worked out theological claims for this authority based on texts from the Gospel of Matthew, claims supported by their increasing religious and political dominance and their reforming and evangelistic initiatives.

Although the popes had great spiritual power, they struggled to assert their political authority. The strongest assertion of political power did not come until the year 800, when the pope made an alliance with a Frankish tribe and sealed it by elevating their king, Charlemagne, to the rank of emperor. By crowning Charlemagne as "Holy Roman Emperor," the pope claimed the power to confer the imperial title upon whomever he wished. This daring moved proved disastrous for the papacy for a number of reasons. First, it created a genuine political rival in his own backyard: whereas the pope formerly argued with an emperor thousands of miles away, Charlemagne was close at hand. Second, rather like the emperors in the East who protected and subsidized the church, Charlemagne and his successors adopted some of the titles and functions of the emperor in the East, including a tendency to interfere in internal church matters. Finally, once the pope claimed he could name the emperor, the office of the papacy took on enormous political importance. When Charlemagne's empire collapsed, the papacy became a pawn in a ruthless political struggle that lasted throughout the so-called Dark Ages. Some of the worst stories of papal corruption come from the ninth and tenth centuries.

The first reform attempts were made by Otto the Great, a tenth-century Holy Roman emperor who saw the value of a reformed papacy. The strongest of the reforming popes was Gregory VII (1073–1085), whose energies devoted to reforming the church eventually spilled over into a desire to reform the state as well. That desire led to a myriad of church-state controversies that characterized the Christian church in the West up to and beyond the reformations of the sixteenth century. During the hundreds of years of church-state conflict, the popes were sometimes strong enough to control the secular ruler and sometimes were controlled by the secular power.

The ever-present danger in the Eastern Orthodox system was that the emperor would use his power to interfere in spiritual matters; in the West, the danger was both that the pope would use his spiritual power to interfere unduly in politics *and* that the emperor (or king) would use political power to interfere with the life of the church. Neither the popes nor the kings would relinquish their powers in the name of peace for roughly the same reasons that the leaders of the modern world insist they cannot disarm unilaterally. In the West, neither pope nor king ever had a total victory, just as in the East the patriarch never had an opportunity to develop political independence. Whether the popes should have been involved in the political order to the extent that they were is a matter of dispute among Christians. Some argue that the church had no business wielding political power, and some argue that without papal involvement the state would have controlled the church in the West as it had in the East. Whatever the merits of each side of the argument, the history of the papacy is an integral part of Western political *and* spiritual history.

The East-West Schism and Contemporary Relations

To review the preceding two sections, the types of church government in Eastern and Western Christianity were remarkably similar but were distinguished from one another by their relationship to the emperor. In the East, the emperor often acted as if he were the head of the church and as if the patriarchs were no more than liturgical leaders; in the West, the pope was clearly the head of the church, though he sometimes had to defend himself from imperial interference. Both churches tended to think of themselves as the kingdom of God on earth.

Given the role of the pope in the West and the claims he made for jurisdiction over the universal church, it is not surprising that a schism arose between East and West. Orthodox Christians never acknowledged the theological claims of the papacy, yet the church in the West grew up assuming those claims were true. The Roman Catholic and Eastern Orthodox churches thus became increasingly unrecognizable to one another. They were separated by growing cultural and linguistic differences so that when they did meet, they could not understand each other's language, nor could they recognize each other's system of church authority. Since their liturgies developed very differently as well, they were not able to pray together with any ease. They tended to argue heatedly about peripheral matters—whether priests should have beards—and about substantive disciplinary issues like clerical celibacy.

Historical events were interpreted by each group as divine vindications. For example, when the old Roman Empire collapsed at the end of the fifth century, Christians in Constantinople (the "new Rome") saw it as God's vengeance upon the West and a sign that the Orthodox church was called to carry forth God's plan in the world. When the popes managed to emerge from the ruins of that old empire as leaders in the West, Roman Catholics saw God's favor upon *them*. As they interpreted it, God clearly intended the power of Peter to be passed down through the line of bishops in Rome. Each church developed claims and counterclaims and was at pains to deny the positions of the other.

There were jurisdictional disputes between East and West about new Christian territories, especially Bulgaria, Moravia, and Byzantine provinces in southern Italy; some old ethnic rivalries—between Serbians and Croatians, for example—date back to religious arguments. The frequent clashes between East and West over religious matters led to a formal schism between Rome and Constantinople in 1054.

The great rift between Orthodox Christianity and Roman Catholicism occurred during the Crusades. In 1204, Constantinople was captured by crusaders from the West; monasteries, churches, palaces, and libraries were robbed, and fire destroyed many of the Byzantine art treasures. The crushing blow was the establishment of a Latin patriarch and emperor in the city. When the Turks threatened to capture Constantinople in the early part of the fifteenth century, an attempt was made to reunite the two churches, but it did not last. The rift between them was too old and too deep. The Turks captured Constantinople in 1453. Thus ended the Byzantine Empire, but the "third Rome," Moscow, took over the Byzantine tradition and the principles of the Orthodox church and gave them soil in which to survive and flourish.

Besides some real theological and liturgical differences, the main stumbling block between Roman Catholic and Orthodox reunion today is church authority. The Orthodox churches cannot accept the office and universal authority of the pope, and although there has been more dialogue between these two ancient churches since the Second Vatican Council (1962–1965), a major sticking point continues to be the status of the pope. The eighth meeting of a joint theological commission for dialogue between the two churches (July 2000) did not publish an expected declaration on progress but rather seemed to indicate that dialogue had come to a standstill. There are some Orthodox churches that accept the authority of the pope (see Uniate churches in

Controversy

How Can Christ Be Both Divine and Human?

By the third century, Christians had come to believe that Christ was the divine Son of God but wondered how he related to God the Father. And if divine, then how could Christ also be human? How would the divinity of Christ affect the oneness of God? How could the humanity of Christ explain redemption?

These questions and others like them led to intense debates not only among church leaders but among ordinary people. The person and nature of Jesus were as engaging to ancient Christians as politics or sports are to some people today. For more than 200 years, Christians tried to settle these arguments, but divisions about them continue today.

The *divinity* of Christ was a problem for Arius (d. 336). Since there is only one God, he argued, the Son cannot be the same as God the Father. God must have created the Son as a creature so unique that he can be called divine and worshiped as God. Justin Martyr and other early theologians held similar opinions. Athanasius (d. 373) opposed this idea and condemned Arius as a heretic. The Son was *not made* by God, nor is he a creature like us. Indeed, God begets him as a father begets a son, which means that the Son is as divine as God the Father. Furthermore, since God cannot be divided, the Father and the Son are one God.

When the argument between Arius and Athanasius became an international crisis, Constantine, whose imperial plans did not welcome a divided church, called the Council of Nicaea (325) to settle the dispute. The bishops agreed with Athanasius, condemned Arius, and taught that the Son is "begotten, not made" and "of one substance" with the Father. Jesus was fully divine.

The *humanity* of Christ was a problem for Apollinaris (d. 392). If the Son of God is fully divine, he asked, then how could he also be fully human? He concluded that Jesus had a human body and soul, but his mind was replaced by the word of God. Bishops at the Council of Constantinople (381) denied this idea and taught that Jesus had a human mind that united with the Word. Jesus was fully human.

Conciliar decisions settled disputes but did not quell questions. If Christ is both human and divine, then can one say that God was born in Bethlehem and that a human being had raised Lazarus from the dead? Was Mary the "mother of God" or just the mother of Jesus? It took another century and more church councils to sort out these problems. Finally, Chalcedon (451) affirmed that Christ is one person "in two natures," human and divine. The Coptic Orthodox church, however, rejected Chalcedon and remains separate from the Roman Catholic and Greek Orthodox churches.

glossary), but they constitute a minority. A variety of Orthodox churches exist in the United States today: Russian, Greek, Romanian, and so forth. Although these groups share a rich liturgical heritage, they have been unable to achieve any structural unity: attempts to form an American Orthodox church have failed.

LITURGY AND DOCTRINE IN THE TWO CHURCHES

Roman Catholicism and the Orthodox church each have distinctive patterns of worship and ancient systems of doctrine. They display some crucial differences in liturgical art and practice, as well as in doctrinal issues. Some of these differences are culturally explainable, but many derive from orientations established in the early Christian church. We look at these differences next.

Icons and Divinization: The Orthodox Perspective

One of the most beautiful manifestations of Orthodox piety is the icon. The artistic style and place of icons in Orthodox life and worship grew out of the mosaic tradition of early Byzantine art. Used to decorate Orthodox churches, they are images of Christ, the Virgin Mary, and the saints painted in a highly stylized way. Christianity, growing as it did from Judaism, was very much against the veneration of pictures of holy persons. Indeed, the Iconoclast controversy of the eighth and ninth centuries (see glossary) illustrates the close ties between religion and politics as they arose around these images. The fight between Christians who loved and venerated icons and those who feared that such devotion violated the commandment against "graven images" erupted at a time when Muslim invasions had considerably diminished the territory of the Byzantine state. Could the veneration of icons be blamed for political defeats? Were icons forbidden? Or were icons crucial to instruct and assist believers? John of Damascus, a monk theologian living in Muslim-controlled Palestine, supported icons on the basis of the Incarnation. Because Jesus, the Son of God, had taken human form, he said, those who deny the power of the icons deny the Incarnation itself. The ecumenical council Nicaea II (see Appendix 4) permitted the veneration of images and secured the place of icons in Orthodox Christianity.

According to pious Orthodox belief, icons are not made by human hands. Theologically, icons are an expression of a central Christian belief, the union of the divine and human natures in Christ. As it says in the Gospel of John, "The Word became flesh" (1:14); God became visible in Christ. Icons, therefore, are thought to be manifestations of heavenly archetypes. They are always painted on a gold background (to represent a heavenly atmosphere), and they are recopied as they are, not embellished or made subject to new artistic styles. They are consecrated sacred images, not art objects. In Orthodox belief, heaven comes down to earth, especially in the celebration of the Eucharist, where the earthly congregation meets and eats with the heavenly congregation. The icons represent this coming to earth of God and the angels and saints.

Orthodox believers venerate icons (bowing in front of them, kissing them, lighting candles before them) both at home and in church. In an Orthodox home, the eastern corner of the living room and/or bedroom is the so-called beautiful corner, with a series of icons and candles, often decorated with flowers. An Orthodox church has an *iconostasis,* originally a low barrier but currently a high wall completely separating the sanctuary from the rest of the church. Icons are arranged on the iconostasis in a fixed order. On the center door of the iconostasis are icons of the angels Michael and Gabriel, to the right of the door is an icon of Christ, and to the right of that is an icon of John the Baptist. On the left side of the door is an icon of the Mother of God, and to the left of that is an icon of the saint to whom the church is dedicated. Above these major icons are rows of smaller icons representing the story of redemption and presenting a visible image of eucharistic piety and belief.

Icons are an integral part of Orthodox dogma and a focal point for prayer. Remember that Orthodox piety is rooted in contemplation and directed toward divinization. Icons provided Orthodox Christians with a glimpse into the divine world and deepened their appreciation of the mysterious and beautiful nature of God. The book of Genesis says that humanity was made in the image of God, and the

Orthodox interpretation of this text was that human beings carried an icon of God within themselves. This idea explains sin as a distortion of the image of God within oneself.

Though for political reasons Constantinople was considered the new Rome, for liturgical reasons it was more of a new Jerusalem, a holy city. There were many different churches, all of which were filled with tangible reminders of the saints (relics) and decorated with icons. Religion was a way of life for people: religious controversies were not so much abstract arguments as they were matters of great popular interest. The notion that the divine energy was present in everything fostered a piety that tended to revere the whole created order. The bond between the resurrection and the sacred meal celebrated in the Eucharist made the liturgy essentially a joyful event. The endless reenactment of the Christian mysteries in the liturgy was the way the corporate life of the people found its religious expression.

Orthodox liturgy is elaborate, rich in gestures, vestments, and hymns. Many forms developed in the context of certain historical preferences and prohibitions. A ban on instrumental music in Orthodox churches led to a highly developed tradition of choral singing and chanting that uses the human voice as an instrument of praise; a preference for certain types of art led to an elaborate range of art in murals, mosaics, and icons. A ban against the theater and drama encouraged people to use their dramatic energies and talents in the celebration of the liturgy. In both East and West came rich, dramatic developments of liturgical prayer and style and a proliferation of different liturgies. In both cases, the liturgy was finally standardized and celebrated in the same way everywhere. Both Orthodox and Roman Catholic liturgies are substantially different from most Protestant worship.

The doctrinal complexion of the Orthodox church is mystical: the great dogmatic preoccupations are deification, sanctification, rebirth, resurrection, and transfiguration. The emphasis is not so much on truth and justice as on beauty and love. The Orthodox believer's aim is to become a new creation, to be transfigured by grace. God did not become human to satisfy divine justice but to enable people to become like God. Sin is not so much a violation of a law as a diminishment of the original image of God in a person; redemption is, therefore, bound up with renewal and transfiguration. Orthodox Christians lack a concept of predestination and do not emphasize eternal punishment of sinners. They expect the final judgment to be a time of grace and love more than separation and judgment. This doctrinal view is very much at odds with that of Roman Catholicism.

Survival and Salvation: The Roman Perspective

Recall that the circumstances in which Roman Catholic Christianity developed differed greatly from those of Orthodox Christianity. Where Orthodox Christianity interacted with Hellenistic philosophy and mystery religions, the Roman church faced barbarian tribes. Where Orthodox Christianity developed within a stable government system, the Roman church built upon the old Roman legal system to prevent the total collapse of civilization in the West. Where religious life in the East was confined to monasticism, it developed into monasticism plus a variety of functional religious orders in the West. The liturgical preoccupations of Orthodox Christianity were

Spirituality

Contemplating the Hidden God

At the heart of spiritual longing, a transcendent yet immanent God puzzles and attracts those who long for a relationship that feels important and yet impossible. Pseudo-Dionysius, the anonymous fifth-century Greek monk who virtually invented mystical theology, understood the paradoxical nature of spiritual desire. He began his most famous treatise with a plea to be led "into the brilliant darkness of a hidden silence" (*The Mystical Theology*, chapter 1). Because humanity can know nothing about a being so vast and mysterious as God, because the divine nature is beyond all words, then anything one can say about God must be immediately denied and then denied again. For example, the statement "God is light" must be denied by saying "God is darkness." Then one must deny the denial to get "God is a blinding ray of darkness." The result honors the distance between divine and human nature and draws the seeker toward the deep silence of mystery.

Like Gregory of Nyssa (c. 335–394) before him, Dionysius understood Moses as a man who sought God by going alone into the mysterious darkness. He did not try to see or to know God with his mind but rather allowed himself to be enveloped by God's presence. Furthermore, the encounter Moses desired would not have been possible without God's initiative. This sense that a connection with God can be felt, that the deeper meanings of one's faith can best be apprehended by way of religious experience, is the basis for mystical longing and reflects the paradoxical God of the Bible. God as transcendent demands a relinquishing of the desire to figure things out; God as immanent turns toward humanity and draws humankind toward ecstasy.

Dionysius had a profound influence on several Western mystical writers, including the anonymous fourteenth-century English author of *The Cloud of Unknowing* and the German Dominican priest and master of paradox, Meister Eckhart (c. 1260–1327). A contemporary practice called "Centering Prayer" is designed to help people find a receptive space like that described by the *Cloud* author. As such, it prepares modern seekers to be silent to receive the hidden God.

essentially mystical; the church in the West developed a fascination with practical understandings of doctrine and worship.

One can find both mystical and practical aspects in the New Testament; Roman Catholicism was more moved by definitions and ordinary Christian life, though it was not without a mystical tradition. Roman pagan religion had been legalistic: the priest knew the correct forms of prayers and sacrifice, how to please the gods. Pagan piety was concerned not with dogma and ethics but with proper cultic acts scrupulously performed, with precise rules and rigorous exactitude in religion. Influenced somewhat by old Roman religious concerns, Western Catholicism was preoccupied with sin and justification. In Orthodox Christianity, the church is the place where one can become transfigured by meeting with the heavenly community. In Roman Catholicism, the church is a place of justice; God has laws, people break them, and justice demands that people make reparation. The church is the place where reparation is made possible: the bishop—or his agent, the priest—determines the degree of sin and the kind of reparation necessary. Penance (which in Orthodox Christianity is more pedagogical than punitive) developed into a system very much like jurisprudence: sins, like crimes, were weighed, and punishments (penances) determined for them. The priest was the legitimate agent of divine law.

Western Christianity also rallied its resources to define doctrines as precisely as possible. In the Orthodox tradition after the great councils, the elements of the Nicene Creed (see Appendix 5) have never been rigorously rationalized and defined; in Roman Catholicism, the need to explain doctrines to new and primitive peoples and the fascination with logic and Scholasticism tended to foster doctrinal definitions and systems of theology. Doctrines of sin, grace, eschatology, and predestination, as well as explanations of sacramental power and papal primacy, were all based to some extent on a legal interpretation of the relationship between God and people. Anselm of Canterbury (1033–1109) made the legal understanding of this relationship the key to his theological explanation of the Incarnation. For Anselm, the word of God became flesh to satisfy the demands of divine justice: when people sinned and upset God's original plan (the Original Sin story in Genesis), they so offended divine justice that only a perfect sacrifice could satisfy its demands. Christ, therefore, is the perfect victim, the one who died to satisfy divine justice and save people from their sins.

The practical perspective is evident in Roman liturgy and in the more general life of the church. Whereas the observance of the Eucharist in the Orthodox church was a joyous celebration of Christ's presence and the resurrection, in the Roman church it emphasized the sacrifice of Christ on the cross. Both the Orthodox and Roman churches hold that the bread and wine are transformed into the body and blood of Christ, but only the Roman church developed a precise theory of how and when this transformation occurs, the doctrine of transubstantiation.

The doctrinal complexion of the Catholic church was shaped by the practical realities of survival. Whereas Orthodox Christians tended to emphasize the divinity of Christ and to imagine Christianity as a means of divinization, Roman Catholics tended to focus on the humanity of Jesus and to experience Christianity as a comfort in a life of sorrow. Western Christians found consolation in the fact that Jesus was like them in some ways, a human being who suffered and died but who triumphed over death and was even now waiting to reward their patience. Sin was a transgression against the laws of God that, at the very least, could diminish one's chances for an afterlife in heaven and, at the worst, might lead straight to the eternal punishment of hell. Catholics learned to obey the laws of God and the laws of the church to avoid damnation.

MEDIEVAL CHRISTIANITY IN THE WEST

For practical reasons, we now leave the world of Orthodox Christianity to concentrate on Roman Catholicism in the centuries preceding the Reformation. The differences between these two ancient forms of Christianity are fascinating ones. The perception of deification as opposed to salvation and the Orthodox tendency to value knowledge gained through prayer and fasting as opposed to the Catholic preference for rational reflection or ecclesiastical pronouncement are only two examples of the many ways that Orthodoxy and Catholicism represent two conflicting orientations that would probably find reunion very difficult. At this point, however, we need not speculate about the future but should turn our attention to the dim past of medieval Christianity.

We have seen how Constantine attempted to rebuild Rome in his new city of Constantinople. How did the bishops of Rome attempt to restore Roman glory in the West? They had a much harder problem for several reasons: they were not primarily political leaders and so had no armies and no clear mandate; they lived in a situation that was politically unstable (remember that the Roman Empire in the West fell in 476 after nearly 300 years of turmoil and chaos) and dangerous; they were besieged by barbarian tribes looking for new land and for a share of old Roman glory; and they were faced with a massive missionary problem in their hope to convert the West to Christianity.

At the same time, the religious leaders of the West, the bishops in general and the pope in particular, had some strong support: they presided over a church that was, on the whole, well organized, philosophically sophisticated, and liturgically attractive; Christians had a history of survival and expansion, and they had the support of the emperor, wherever he was located. In addition, Catholicism, through its monastic system, had a large, relatively well-educated group of functionaries to help with the expansion of the Christian mission. Finally, the popes and bishops were often men with political savvy and high reputation: they were able to press their claims for Rome as the holiest city in Christendom (after Jerusalem) and strengthen their position as the supreme leaders of all Christians based on Jesus' words to Peter in Matthew 16.

Up to the Reformation, the Roman Catholic church was involved first in survival and then in consolidating church authority. Since no comprehensive vision of church history can be given in a limited space, we need to focus on an idea that can help organize our understanding. Recall the aspects associated with the idea of Rome: vastness, peace, organization, jurisprudence, religious sensibility, glory, beauty, intellectual life, a common language, and Caesar. At some level, this set of characteristics is what the popes attempted to achieve for the Roman Catholic church. We will deal with them individually to say something about the various ways different parts of the church cooperated in the great adventure of the Middle Ages.

The Catholic church was *vast*. We have seen how Christianity spread and adapted itself to a variety of different cultural situations. The missionary impulse was part of Christianity from the beginning: Constantine supported missionaries throughout the eastern part of the empire, and the popes and bishops sent their ablest priests to the remote regions of the West. You may have heard about St. Patrick (d. 461) converting the Irish to Christianity, but perhaps you do not know about other early missionaries. For example, St. Boniface (d. 755), a Saxon monk, was sent to convert German tribes, and St. Augustine of Canterbury (d. 605) was sent to England. In each of these places, influential, powerful women acting as abbesses in innovative monasteries were crucial to the success of the mission: St. Brigid of Kildare in Ireland; Leoba, St. Boniface's cousin, at Bischofsheim in Germany; and Hilda of Whidby in England. Because of the work of missionary men and women, thousands of people became Christians and whole countries were eventually "won" for Christianity. By the time of the Reformation, the entire Western world, as it was then known, along with great stretches of the "New World" discovered at the end of the fifteenth century, belonged to the Catholic church.

Catholicism was, in theory at least, *peaceful*. The impressive strength of the Roman military made the old Roman Empire so relatively free from war that the term *Pax Romana*, meaning "the Roman peace," was part of the description of the empire. *Pax vobiscum*, meaning "peace be with you," was a phrase in the Catholic liturgy. All those in monasteries and convents were forbidden to engage in warfare and were

People

Thomas Aquinas

Thomas Aquinas (1225–1274) lived and wrote during a particularly creative century of Christian history: works of Aristotle translated into Latin were challenging traditional ways of understanding religious faith; universities were replacing monasteries and cathedral schools as centers of Christian learning; and new forms of vowed religious life were attracting bright young men to lives of poverty and service. Aquinas was the foremost interpreter of Aristotle, a brilliant teacher at the University of Paris, and a member of the new Dominican order (founded c. 1215).

An oversimplified version of the question that occupied Christian thinkers throughout the centuries has to do with how one knows God. Does a believer best approach the divine through silent contemplation, or can one understand God through reason and ordinary experience? More than a century before the birth of Aquinas, Anselm (1033–1109), a philosopher and church leader, prayed to understand what he already believed. His phrase "faith seeking understanding" was at the heart of the scientific study of God (theology). Recall that in monastic and mystical locations, God was essentially an object of contemplation. In the university environment, however, God was primarily an object of thought.

Aquinas was a genius who saw that traditional education and methods could not handle the issues raised by Aristotle's logic, ethics, and metaphysics (translated into Latin for the first time in the twelfth and thirteenth centuries). He also understood that failure to link the God of the philosophers to the God of the Bible would put religious faith in an isolated and defensive position. Faith, he argued, is grounded in and moving toward God and is therefore supernatural, but it is also intellectual. One can contemplate the mystery of God and still create rational arguments for God's existence. In other words, it is possible to combine faith and reason.

Thomas wrote many works but is best known for his *Summa Theologica,* a comprehensive synthesis of biblical, patristic, and medieval understandings of Christianity. His teaching, though predominantly philosophical and theological, embraces worship, morals, preaching, and spiritual practice. After a lifetime of brilliant teaching and writing, Aquinas abruptly stopped working on the *Summa* before it was finished. He could not go on, he said, because while celebrating Mass in early December 1273, he had a religious experience wherein his own work seemed "like so much straw" compared to what was revealed to him in that moment.

---

encouraged to avoid even the feelings of hostility. Those who were dedicated to fighting were urged to engage in "holy wars" or crusades, which were fought far away from European soil. The church itself, through a series of pronouncements, forbade any fighting during Lent (6 weeks in the spring), during Advent (4 weeks before Christmas), on all Sundays and Fridays, and on other notable feast days.

This system of peacekeeping worked remarkably well for a long time, partly because the church had a weapon of its own: excommunication. Those who disobeyed the laws of the church could be expelled from the communion of the church. Anyone who died in a state of excommunication, so it was believed, went to hell forever. Besides the threat of excommunication, the church had the power of its popes, who had learned over the years to become skilled negotiators and shrewd political operators. After some early setbacks—the compromise with Charlemagne and the ensuing horror of the Dark Ages—popes emerged in the eleventh century as strong men able to keep the peace in the West precisely because they refused to be dominated by secular rulers.

The Catholic church was splendidly *organized* along old Roman imperial lines. The local churches in the vast territory of Christendom were organized into dioceses presided over by bishops. The bishops themselves were organized into districts or along national lines and reported directly to the pope, the chief bishop and supreme ruler of Christendom. As you can imagine, the church as an institution needed bureaucrats: little by little, an organized body of men dedicated to running the internal affairs of the church developed into the Curia, a complex entity with a variety of offices, concerns, procedures, and personnel intent on keeping the machinery of ecclesiastical life running smoothly. Some critics find the very idea of church bureaucracies scandalous, as if a religious institution has no need of such offices, but it is safe to say that every church organization, even at the local level, has some kind of governing body. Furthermore, from the eleventh century onward, the Catholic church developed a system to ensure the peaceful election of popes: the College of Cardinals (established by Nicholas II in 1059) was not always perfect, but it did function often in an orderly way to ensure peaceful succession of papal authority.

Christianity in the West administered its own *legal system,* eventually known as Canon Law. The development of legal structures in the West was long and arduous. The church, as it converted and interacted with various new peoples, adopted some of their legal procedures and also inserted some of its own into new law codes as they developed. The theoretical principle for church-state interaction was the one attributed to Jesus in Matthew 22:21: "Render to Caesar the things that are Caesar's, and to God the things that are God's."

The problem, of course, lay in the application of the principle. Were the laws governing marriage civil or religious ones? What part of the taxes collected by a secular ruler had to be turned over to the church? If the church in a particular place needed the protection of the local baron, and if he had to raise an army for that protection, who paid for the army? If the archbishop of Milan was also, by historical precedent, the chancellor of the empire, to whom did his loyalty belong in case of conflict? Was it appropriate for the pope to collect taxes from the churches in France? If so, was it also appropriate for the pope to lend that money to the king of England so that he could wage war against France? A list of such questions could fill volumes. Eventually, the church in the West worked out a system of ecclesiastical law that was meant to make justice available to everyone. Peasants who were treated badly or paid so poorly that they nearly starved could bring suit against wealthy landowners in ecclesiastical courts. Needless to say, questions about divorce, the legitimacy of children—often important in matters of imperial succession—and other matters of religious interest were a major concern of this legal system. Ameliorations of social life—laws about the ways landowners had to treat serfs or the ways husbands were to treat their wives—were also concerns of ecclesiastical law.

The Catholic church was characterized by great *religious sensibility* and creativity. In the early years, it had been difficult to make the liturgy and the sacraments available to all Christians in the West. Furthermore, the years of the barbarian invasions and the Dark Ages tended to destabilize religious life along with political life. By the tenth century, at the end of the Dark Ages, monastic life was often lived in unconventional if not clearly corrupt terms: the rules of chastity, poverty, and obedience were not fully practiced.

Liturgy and prayer life for ordinary people were in a poor state: priests were few; many were ill prepared and so did not preach effectively or celebrate the sacraments properly. Convents and monasteries were no longer centers of learning and piety. In the tenth and eleventh centuries, however, a great surge of religious reform began when a small band of French Benedictine monks founded the monastery of Cluny. Monastic life and practice were reinvigorated throughout Europe because of Cluny. In addition, various commercial centers began to plan for and build impressive cathedrals, and a new group of reforming popes—Leo IX, Nicholas II, and Gregory VII—encouraged the growth of the reforming spirit throughout Europe. With monastic reform, new churches, and the support of the popes, religion in the West flourished.

Men and women were drawn to new religious orders to devote their lives to God and to work on some vexing problems in the world. Francis and Clare, two idealistic young people in Assisi, founded groups devoted to prayer and simplicity. Franciscan friars and Poor Clare nuns were devoted to helping the poor as well. Dominican friars were devoted to preaching and teaching. In addition, new forms of prayer and devotional life attracted Western Christians: some went on pilgrimages to the shrines of powerful saints or to Jerusalem to walk on the ground that Jesus had walked during his lifetime. Churches were decorated with paintings and statues depicting events in the life of Jesus and making popular saints "visible" and available for prayer or petition.

At a different level of sensibility, many churches collected and housed *relics* of sanctity, pieces of clothing or hair or bones associated with some holy person and sometimes reputed to have almost magical powers. It is easy to laugh at the medieval devotion to relics and to use stories of extreme credulity to dismiss this particular kind of piety. At the same time, if you know someone who has tried to get close enough to touch a rock star, perhaps you understand a little bit of what people felt in the thirteenth century when someone told them that the local church had a relic of the very cross on which Jesus was crucified.

Catholicism was full of *glory* and *beauty*. The pomp and ceremony increasingly associated with the papacy and with the various church functions testified to lavish wealth. Did the church go too far in promoting splendor in itself? Who paid for all the glory? Were church taxes too high? One medieval king is reported to have written to the pope and said, "You are supposed to feed the sheep, not fleece them." At the same time, the buildings in Rome—especially St. Peter's, the Vatican museum, and the cathedrals—are monuments to an era in which religion was thought to be the most important activity on earth. Kings and queens endowed churches specifically so that they would be richly adorned and thus would glorify God. Because of royal money and the tithes of the people, the liturgy was impressive: The cups and plates used for communion were made of pure gold, and the vestments of the priest were fashioned from rare silk and embroidered with pearls and golden threads. Music was written especially for church services and sung by highly trained choirs. Hildegard of Bingen (d. 1179), a visionary and a powerful German abbess, was a genius who was revered for her writings and especially for her music (one of the largest repertoires among medieval composers). The overall effect of these displays of visual and aural beauty was splendid, precisely the mood church leaders wanted to convey.

Catholicism had a rich *intellectual life* from the earliest days of the church Fathers (see Appendix 3) through the founding of the great European university system. The official language of the church was Latin—as it was in the Roman Empire—and the scholarly language of the university was Latin. Charlemagne had been a great patron of education. He invited a famous monk and scholar, Alcuin of York (d. 804), to his court in Aachen. Alcuin set up a new form of elementary education and a plan of higher education based on the study of the seven liberal arts. His system, which was divided into two parts, the *trivium* and *quadrivium,* became the basis of medieval intellectual life. The first part of the curriculum gave a student certain tools—language, logic, disputation, and clarity of expression—and the second required mastery of certain subjects, usually practical ones like arithmetic and geometry.

Little by little, Alcuin's system was applied to religious and philosophical questions, and a new way of doing theology was born. Whereas mystics attempted to understand God through direct experience and monks spent their lives in dedicated work and prayerful reflection on the Bible to achieve union with God, university life produced something new: theologians engaged in rational argument about God's personality and about the ways the divine design offered certain opportunities to the human race.

Scholasticism was the *method* medieval scholars used to arrive at logical conclusions about the deepest mysteries of Christian faith. The great universities of Europe were devoted to the study of many subjects, but the most respected was theology. The greatest theologians were those who were able to combine the tools of logic and disputation—aided from the twelfth century onward by the use of the philosophical works of Aristotle and Plato—with their insights about God as revealed in the Bible and in the classical writings of the church Fathers. Peter Abelard (d. 1142) was one pioneer of scholastic philosophy whose contributions have been overshadowed by the account of his tragic affair with his gifted student, Heloise. As such, he is more famous as a romantic figure than as a theologian, but his early work was instrumental in the development of Scholasticism. Thomas Aquinas (d. 1274) was the most prominent of all medieval theologians, so influential and brilliant that in the nineteenth century, when the Roman Catholic church was looking for a way to answer the modern critics of religion, Leo XIII (d. 1904) called for a revival of the study of Thomas Aquinas as the best and most effective way Catholic theology might cope with the modern world.

The influence of the church on intellectual life and vice versa is one of the great stories of the medieval period. Here, as in other quarters of the Western world, differing opinions sometimes led to conflict and condemnation. New theories were subject to ecclesiastical approval—strange as that may seem to us today—and those who attempted to apply their new understandings without the permission of the church were sometimes condemned to death. Medieval intellectual life, therefore, should not be confused with the modern concept of intellectual freedom. At the same time, the idea behind the church's involvement—that the church, guided by the Holy Spirit, was a divinely guaranteed teaching authority that could guard against mistakes in any quarter—made perfect sense at the time and was supposed to lead to an atmosphere of intellectual play and discovery.

For many years, this concept of university life worked very well: scholars were able to debate one another with zest and to submit the most important of life's questions—God's purpose, human nature, the meaning of love and will—to rational scrutiny and public argument. As we will see in the next chapter, scholars began to ask serious questions not only about intellectual matters—nature and grace, for example—but also about practical issues like ecclesiastical authority and the papacy. The university system, therefore, however much it may have upheld "the church's truth" in some ways, also carried within it the potential to disrupt that status quo in times that seemed to cry for reform.

Finally, the Catholic church had its Caesar in the person of the pope. From the early writings of Pope Leo I (d. 461), who laid the theoretical foundations for the medieval papacy; through the work of Pope Gregory I (d. 604), who strengthened the secular or temporal power of the papacy; to Gregory VII (d. 1085), who asserted his authority by excommunicating the Holy Roman Emperor, Henry IV, and forcing Henry to stand barefoot in the snow begging papal forgiveness, the power of the papacy had been strong. In these early years, however, the popes had no major political rivals, and their moral authority in the West was enough to ensure their political success. Pope Urban II (d. 1099) called the first Crusade, which was an enormous event. By urging princes and soldiers from all over Europe to liberate Jerusalem from the Turks, he basically proclaimed himself the personal leader of Christendom.

Secular rulers sometimes fought with the popes, and it was clear that the church could be attacked and resisted, but it could not be ignored as a political power. Pope Innocent III (d. 1216), perhaps the most powerful of the medieval popes, was constantly involved in important political questions and presided over a church that was at its religious and theological apex. After Innocent III, papal power held its own for a while, but from the thirteenth century on, strong national rulers were increasingly in a position to challenge papal authority in political matters. As we shall see in the next chapter, religious reformers from the fourteenth to the sixteenth century were also increasingly in the position to challenge the pope's spiritual authority.

CONCLUSION

The break between the Greek Orthodox church and the Roman Catholic church in 1054 was the first major split in the Christian church. It continues to the present day. The church in the East developed under the protection of the emperor and had no chance to assert its independence from the empire; the church in the West was able to become more politically independent. In the course of its history, the Roman church asserted the primacy of the pope as the supreme leader of the entire Christian church, a claim that Orthodox Christians could not—and still cannot—accept. In addition to the issue of church authority, concepts and traditions crucial to both churches developed differently in East and West: monasticism and liturgy are ancient and central in both churches, but they have become quite different in ethos and practice.

The difference in general perspective between East and West reflects the history and early environment of each church. The tasks of the Christian church were different for both groups, and they developed different outlooks. At the same time, however, they are remarkably similar: both are committed to certain doctrinal positions, though they have different emphases; both observe an ancient, fixed liturgy;

both recognize the importance of tradition; and both believe the church includes the communion of saints (dead and alive). The Christian groups that emerged from the Reformation disagreed with the Roman church on nearly all of these issues. It is important, therefore, to see the points of correspondence between the Orthodox and the Roman Catholic churches as well as to know where their differences lie.

Medieval Catholic Christianity, as it has been sketched here in brief form, was an elaborate system that involved everyone in a cosmic scheme of salvation. The church encompassed life in every quarter and was involved in intellectual development, political action, religious practice, and cultural expression. As the foundation and patron of all aspects of life, the Catholic church exercised enormous influence and wielded great power. As we shall see in the next chapter, great power led to great corruption and eventual reform. It is important to remember, however, that at its best, medieval Catholicism encouraged most of the activities and qualities associated with Western civilization.

Focal Points for Discussion

1. Constantine ceased the persecutions and brought the church and the empire together to act toward a common goal. Who gained the most from this alliance: the church or the empire?
2. Monasticism was a protest movement and a yearning for a purer form of the Christian life that ultimately created two classes of Christians: perfect monks and less than perfect ordinary folk. Is this development inconsistent with what you know of earliest Christianity?
3. Theologians in the East and in the West explained the mission of Jesus in quite different terms. For Orthodox Christians, Jesus offers the opportunity to become more like God, whereas for Western Christians, Jesus died to satisfy the demands of God's justice. How do the different forms of worship and artistic expression in East and West reflect these different understandings?

Aspects of the Reformation

CHAPTER 5

The Reformation was not so much an isolated incident of protest as a series of reform attempts and movements between the fourteenth and seventeenth centuries. During that time, the political and cultural climate changed substantially; old connections between church and state broke down in the face of emerging nationalism, and the issue of religious authority finally divided Christianity into a variety of factions that persist to this day.

We have chosen to highlight only a few of the factors that made these times so intensely creative and chaotic. We left the medieval world with an impression of stability but with a few hints that maybe everything was not as settled as it looked. As we enter the fourteenth century, we find a much more volatile situation. The rise of strong national rulers led to a variety of political problems between nations and within the church. New sources of money and employment gave people more mobility, and the invention of printing contributed to a higher rate of literacy: people were more inclined to ask questions and to demand answers. Intellectual life was vibrant as scholars began to challenge old methods like Scholasticism and to encourage new reliance on biblical scholarship. Finally, preachers and religious figures added new dimensions to their understanding of spirituality and so fed an increasing interest in the means of salvation. All of these changes, and others, led to two centuries of religious reformation.

This chapter focuses on the historical context for these great reform movements and on aspects of each of the reform movements themselves. The protests of Wycliffe and Hus, the reforming efforts of the conciliar movement, and the atmosphere of humanism and the Renaissance all provided support for some creative reforms within Christianity. Those reforms also led to a severe break within Christendom, and from the sixteenth century on, there would no longer be just two branches of Christianity (Roman Catholic and Eastern Orthodox) divided geographically; the Protestant Reformation resulted in new churches and distinct denominations. We will look briefly here at the four major strands of the Protestant Reformation and at the reformation of the Catholic church from within.

THE HISTORICAL SITUATION

From the fourth to eleventh centuries, the church in the West had been challenged to survive, to withstand political pressure from outside, and to convert barbarian tribes to Christianity. To some ways of thinking, the church had been a remarkable success: most Europeans were Christians, a system of international church law tried to ensure justice and fairness, liturgical life and ecclesiastical discipline were being made uniform, religious life flourished in a variety of forms, and the church had managed to secure autonomy by becoming a powerful political entity as well as the highest spiritual authority in the West. To other ways of thinking, the church had assumed too much power, meddled in the wrong issues, and devoted insufficient attention to spiritual matters. This perception, prominent from the late eleventh century on, increased markedly throughout the Reformation.

From the eleventh to fourteenth centuries, the Western Catholic church was in a process of consolidating its power. Because the political world was changing so dramatically, the church found itself involved in intense political struggles. The image of an international church presided over by a wise pope was being challenged by the emergence of a new kind of *national* ruler. Kings, in England and France particularly, resented what they considered papal intrusion in their own political affairs. There was no longer a political vacuum in the West for the pope to fill, as had been the case earlier, and there was no longer a predictable political struggle between the *one* secular ruler (the Holy Roman Emperor) and the pope, as had been initiated with the crowning of Charlemagne. Some people, especially scholars in universities, believed that the pope ought to give up all political power, leave politics to kings, and become a strictly spiritual ruler. They argued this position on both political and religious grounds. The response on the part of the official church was to exaggerate the papal claims: popes declared they had power over the entire world (as vicars of Christ) or that they could step into any situation in which sin had been committed—in other words, anywhere, anytime.

At the beginning of the fourteenth century, a startling response to papal claims was made by Philip IV, king of France. Pope Boniface VIII and the king had been involved in a series of moves and countermoves against each other for some time, and animosity was growing on both sides. The conflict was over power and money and had long since passed the point where polite conversation or arbitration could resolve it. The pope, counting on power that had worked in centuries past (power he no longer had), threatened to depose the king. In 1302, the pope issued a document, *Unam Sanctam,* which ended thus: "We therefore declare, say and affirm that submission on the part of every human creature to the bishop of Rome is altogether necessary for his salvation." In earlier times, the king might have capitulated; this time, the king began a plan to depose the pope. Boniface VIII was arrested and died on his way to Paris to stand trial. The new pope was not Italian but French, and the papacy moved from Rome to Avignon, a small town in France. The papacy was now under the control of the French monarchy; the popes in effect became agents of the king.

King Philip's defiance of the papacy was the dramatic end to the powers of the medieval popes. If you will remember that Pope Gregory VII forced the Holy Roman

Emperor to stand barefoot in the snow begging papal forgiveness (1077), you can appreciate the power that popes were able to exercise over secular rulers. Now, imagine Boniface VIII being forcibly taken to Paris to stand trial for his crimes (1302), and you can see how much things had changed in 200 years.

The Avignon papacy is remembered as one of the great scandals of Christendom. It lasted from 1304 to 1377, when Catherine of Siena, among others, persuaded the pope to return to Rome and restore some sort of normalcy to a church that was increasingly divided. Within 14 months, the pope died in Rome and a new election was called: the College of Cardinals, under some pressure from the Romans, elected an Italian, Urban VI. For a number of reasons—Urban's plans for reform, his general lack of tact, rivalries between Italian and French cardinals—this same College of Cardinals returned to Avignon and elected a second pope, Clement VII. From 1378 until 1415, the Roman Catholic church was divided between two men, one in Rome and one in France, both claiming to be the true pope.

This further scandal, known as the Great Western Schism, tended to divide Europe along religious and political lines: England, the traditional enemy of France, backed the Roman pope, for example, while Scotland, the traditional enemy of England, backed the French pope. Unless you have read widely in the history of the period, you cannot begin to imagine the turmoil. Suffice it to say that the church was clearly in need of *institutional* reform.

The situation in the fourteenth century was unusual, to say the least. In addition to political and institutional turmoil, Europe was just recovering from an outbreak of bubonic plague that had struck in the 1340s. The Black Death, as it was called, was quick and fatal: it killed nearly one-half of the European population in a short time. Not surprisingly, this period was characterized by great religious anxiety: many people believed that the plague had been a divine punishment and so were terrified about their own survival and chances for salvation. Others called for massive repentance and joined movements of extremists who went from town to town whipping themselves (literally) into a frenzy and frightening people with visions of the end of the world.

There was an explosion of mystical experience and writing at this time, especially in England (Julian of Norwich, Richard Rolle, Walter Hilton, and the author of *The Cloud of Unknowing*) and in Germany (Henry Suso, Gertrude the Great, John Tauler, Marguerite Porete, and Meister Eckhart). In other parts of Europe, new forms of religious life emerged that encouraged profound consciousness of a deep personal relationship with God. Some of those who were influenced by popular religious movements became anti-institutional and so were condemned as heretics. Many of those following the new devotionalism, however, were simply looking for a different kind of piety, one with an inward dimension that could not be shaken by external institutional abuses. The book that best exemplifies the kind of religious life many people were yearning for is *The Imitation of Christ,* by Thomas à Kempis (d. 1471).

Finally, the fourteenth century was characterized by deep social unrest and intellectual upheaval. During this time, a series of peasant revolts and uprisings took place as people attempted to gain more power or protection in a changing political situation. Intellectually, the fourteenth century was a time of birth: some focus on the rebirth (renaissance) of classical learning, and others on the new birth of biblical scholarship. The invention of the printing press, the availability of books, and the

SPIRITUALITY

Imitation of Christ

In the first thousand years or so, Christ was generally pictured as a distant and frightening champion who had conquered death and was poised to return at the end of the world to judge the living and the dead. That image has persisted, but from the twelfth century onward, Christians increasingly thought of Christ as a suffering man who needs compassion or as a loving Lord who understands human pain. Holiness was imagined as an imitation of Christ, and desire for a loving relationship with him became an important part of Christian spirituality.

Then as now, some Christians asked themselves what Jesus would do in a particular situation and then did it. Monasteries and convents had always based their imitation of Christ on vows of poverty, chastity, and obedience and had tested themselves in virtues of love and humility, but new ways of being religious were now being formed to follow Jesus in new ways. For example, Francis of Assisi (d. 1226) saw Jesus as a poor man who asked his followers to preach the Gospel without worrying about money, food, or shelter. His followers (Franciscans) were dedicated to poverty and simplicity. An experimental community of women (Beguines) in the thirteenth and fourteenth centuries lived outside convents and took no vows but ministered to the poor and the sick and led prayerful lives. Menno Simons (d. 1561) and his followers (Mennonites) obeyed the ethics of Jesus literally through pacifism and sharing all they had with anyone in need. *The Imitation of Christ,* by Thomas à Kempis (d. 1471), was written to encourage Christians to renounce worldly values for heavenly truths. That book, second only to the Bible as a source of Christian life, said that imitating Christ means leaving oneself behind, being more interested in practicing virtues than in defining them.

A fascination with the life of Jesus drew many Christians into his final days by way of devotional practices like the Stations of the Cross, meditations on events surrounding his suffering and death. The vulnerable humanity of Christ could be found in graphic descriptions of divine suffering in the writings of women mystics like Bridget of Sweden and Julian of Norwich. A tormented yet patient Jesus, found in pious practices or in works of art, became a model for faithful Christian life.

tremendous influx of Greek manuscripts after the fall of Constantinople (1453) all gave scholars new things to discuss and new ways to discuss them. It is within this general context that we must understand a series of religious reform movements that began in the fourteenth century. These were not the *only* such movements, but they are perhaps most characteristic.

RELIGIOUS REFORM BEFORE LUTHER

The two most important reform movements that began in the fourteenth and extended into the fifteenth century were those of John Wycliffe and John Hus, on the one hand, and the conciliarist movement, on the other. Wycliffe and Hus wished to free the church from control of the ecclesiastical officials, from specified forms of liturgy, and from complex creeds and dogmatic tests. The conciliarist movement aimed to reform the institutional church and to restructure it. One of the central questions concerned religious authority: Where did one turn for the truth? Some of the answers to that question included the pope, ecumenical councils, the Bible, classical antiquity, tradition, mystical experience, and one's own conscience. These answers are not unlike the options available in the modern Christian church, nor are they peculiar to the fourteenth century; some of them had been present within Christianity from the beginning. In the climate of the Reformation years, however, the variety of answers divided Christians from one another and split apart what had once been a united Christendom.

Reforms of Wycliffe and Hus

One of the most significant protest movements before Luther was that associated with two university professors, John Wycliffe (c. 1330–1384) in England and John Hus (c. 1372–1415) in Bohemia (present-day Czech Republic). Wycliffe was a philosopher at Oxford who gained support and fame by arguing that religious authority ought to be reserved for the righteous and that unworthy, immoral people (like the Avignon pope and wayward priests) had no legitimate right to exercise religious authority over people. Since he believed that religion had become too much a matter of clerical authority and esoteric doctrines, he attacked the authority of the pope and extolled the authority of the Bible. He argued that the office and claims of the pope had no support from Scripture and that the only way one could judge holiness was by whether or not one's behavior accorded with the Gospel, not by whether one possessed a certain ecclesiastical title.

One of the most daring reforms associated with Wycliffe was a translation of the Bible into the language of the people (in this case, English). For centuries, the Catholic church had used the Latin translation of the Bible known as the Vulgate and discouraged translations into vernacular languages. Since most people could not read Latin, however, they were unable to read the Bible for themselves. Instead, they had to depend on church authorities to read and interpret texts for them. Wycliffe thought all Christians should be free to read the Bible for themselves and that to do so they needed to read it in their own languages. In arguing that Scripture is the highest authority for every Christian, Wycliffe was not anticipating Luther's appeal to *sola Scriptura* (Scripture alone). Wycliffe accepted the interpretive authority of the church Fathers (see Appendix 3), and he respected many of the church's theologians. His criticism was directed against those parts of the church that were, in his view, *unscriptural*. The papacy was not to be found in Scripture, and the greed and corruption of the papacy in Wycliffe's day convinced him that a pope who grasps for power and wealth is an anti-Christ.

Wycliffe's followers were called Lollards (mumblers, a word of derision with a Dutch origin). The Lollard movement is remembered as one of ecclesiastical reform. Their chief authority in religious matters was the Bible as they read and interpreted it. On the basis of their reading of the Bible, they attacked unscriptural *doctrines* (like transubstantiation and clerical celibacy) and unscriptural *practices* (like indulgences and pilgrimages). They extolled evangelical poverty and contrasted the poverty of early Christians (and many contemporary Christians) with the wealth of church officials. The Lollard movement was at first one of academic criticism (which was denounced by the church and persecuted) and later a more popular religious reform movement. People from the poorer classes were drawn to it, and for a while, it looked as if it might lead to an active revolt against the institutional church. By the middle of the fifteenth century, however, the movement had dwindled and effectively ended. But not before it had influenced John Hus.

Hus was a reforming priest in Bohemia who had been deeply moved by the teachings of Wycliffe. His life coincided with the Great Western Schism and the political divisions caused by that schism, so his reform attempts were, to some extent, linked with political issues. He denounced the hierarchical organization of the church and preached against an immoral clergy. In the middle of a stormy religious controversy, he was invited to the Council of Constance (see Appendix 4), where his safety was guaranteed by the emperor and betrayed by churchmen. Constance was a dangerous place for reformers and reforming ideas like those of Hus. The council condemned Wycliffe posthumously and demanded that his remains be dug up, burned, and thrown into a river. Hus was brought to trial for heresy but refused to recant unless the council fathers could prove to him, from Scripture, that he was wrong. He was burned at the stake in 1415.

While Hus was in prison, his followers in Prague took the daring step of administering the cup of wine to the laity during Communion services. For hundreds of years, laypeople in the Catholic church received only the eucharistic bread. Hus and his followers found this practice unscriptural and so returned to receiving Communion in both forms. The council forbade laypeople to receive the cup, a move that only fueled the fires of rebellion. What followed were a series of Hussite wars in which the Communion cup (or chalice) became an emblem of resistance. The Hussite wars lasted throughout the Reformation period and were the first consistent armed attack on feudal politics and the Roman Catholic church. People claimed the right to make religious decisions for themselves rather than accept the practices decreed to them by a hierarchical church. As such, the Hussite movement helped pave the way for the Protestant Reformation.

Conciliarism

Conciliarism was the most notable internal reform movement to arise out of the chaotic situation of the Great Western Schism. Wycliffe and Hus were not so much interested in reforming the existing church as in denouncing it as unreformable: their message, in general, encouraged people to leave the corrupt church, read the Scriptures, and live a decent Christian life. The conciliarist movement, on the other hand, believed that the institutional church was necessary but that it needed a basic constitutional reform, one that would limit papal power and restore a more ancient—collegial—type of church government.

Gregory VII (pope from 1073 to 1085) had set the tone of the medieval papacy by arguing that the pope was the supreme authority within the church. He decreed that no council could be called without papal permission, that papal decrees could be annulled by no one, and that the pope could be judged by no one. The conciliarists opposed this position. Armed with a growing body of reform literature and opinion, they set out to argue that an ecumenical council is superior to the pope as a religious authority.

The first council called to heal the schism and restore the church under the leadership of one pope was the Council of Pisa (1409). People loyal to both popes came to Pisa, deposed both popes, and elected a new one, who, unfortunately, died within months. Most people attending the council had already gone home, and those who were left at Pisa elected another man, a powerful leader who, they thought, could heal the schism by force if not by persuasion. He took the name John XXIII. His election and the Council of Pisa did not heal the schism but made it worse; after Pisa, *three* men claimed to be the pope—John XXIII, the French pope, and the Roman pope. At the urging of the emperor, Sigismund, John XXIII called the Council of Constance in 1414, which deposed all three popes and elected a new one, Martin V. The new pope pronounced Constance a valid ecumenical council, thereby approving its aims and decrees.

Constance affirmed the authority of ecumenical councils by passing two important conciliar documents. The first, *Haec Sancta* (1415), asserted the supremacy of the council over the pope as a religious authority; the second, *Frequens* (1416), declared that ecumenical councils should be held at least every 10 years. Finally, the council drew up a list of abuses and called for significant reform in the church. It looked, for a while, as if the Council of Constance would lead to a major reformation in church structure and policy. As it turned out, however, the council did *not* reform the church. Indeed, in 1516, Pope Leo X (who would later condemn Martin Luther) issued a decree that condemned conciliarism *(Pastor Aeternus)*. According to some interpreters, the failure to enact the reform agenda of the Council of Constance led directly to the Protestant Reformation.

HUMANISM AND THE RENAISSANCE

Lord Acton, a famous nineteenth-century historian, said, "Power tends to corrupt and absolute power corrupts absolutely." Perhaps that explains why popes did not reform the church along lines that limited their power. It may also explain why national leaders developed into national despots when they assumed broad political power. Whatever the reasons, the battles between church and state in the fifteenth and sixteenth centuries were mostly fought over political power. The old prerogatives from the medieval papacy were at odds with the spiritual and intellectual uneasiness of an awakening world. The agent of that awakening was a loosely defined movement known as humanism and, later, as the Renaissance. Humanists responded to the religious and political chaos around them by remembering ancient conceptions of humanity, culture, ideals, and destiny. Their goal was to rediscover the sources of and to delight in the type of life portrayed in classical Greek and Roman documents. Their efforts led to a rebirth of classical learning, the Renaissance.

We can simplify the Renaissance by looking at two different geographical settings with two different agendas: the southern or Italian Renaissance was primarily devoted to literature and texts, whereas the Renaissance in Germany and England was religious in scope. The excitement about the recovery of classical literature first blossomed in Italy, typified by the work of two poets and a priest. Francesco Petrarch (1304–1374) was a genius whose love of Latin antiquity led to a scorn for medieval methods and attitudes. His friend, Giovanni Boccaccio (1313–1375), brought the same enthusiasm to Greek classics. Both of them were decidedly more interested in the mystery of humanity than in the study of divinity, intent more on the ways human beings adapted to life on earth than on the ways they worried about heaven and hell. Lorenzo Valla (1407–1457), a priest drawn to the Christian literature of Greece, shows us how research into ancient texts can be alarming to religious authorities. As an avid reader of the Fathers (see Appendix 3) and one of the first to study different versions of the Greek New Testament, Valla shocked church leaders in three areas: he questioned tradition by showing that the Apostles' Creed was not actually written by the apostles; he questioned the authority of Scripture by noticing that there were major differences in ancient New Testament manuscripts; and he undermined the authority of the papacy by exposing the "Donation of Constantine" as a forgery.

The northern Renaissance was nourished in the great universities of Germany and England and centered primarily on religious topics. German Renaissance scholars, interested in theological issues, were drawn by classical antiquity to study the Bible. Their combining of theological interest with human scholarship also led to a passion for reform: German scholars were especially interested in a reform of church and society. The breadth of the northern Renaissance can be seen in the work of a German Old Testament scholar, a Dutch humanist, and an English lawyer, Johannes Reuchlin (1455–1522), one of the first Christian scholars to study Hebrew to understand the Old Testament. His Hebrew grammar and dictionary opened up a whole new vista of historical and critical work in biblical studies. Desiderius Erasmus (c. 1466–1536), born in Rotterdam, the greatest of the northern humanists, was an avid student of Greek who eventually published a Greek edition of the New Testament. More important for us, he was a reformer at heart who longed for a church that was not riddled with superstition, corruption, and error. Thomas More (1478–1535), English statesman and author, wrote *Utopia* (about an imaginary island where inhabitants share their goods and practice religious toleration) but is most famous as the chancellor of England under Henry VIII. When More refused to recognize Henry's claim to be head of the church in England, he was beheaded for treason.

Neither the southern nor the northern humanists sought to overthrow the Catholic church. They believed that ancient texts could strengthen Christian beliefs and that new scholarship would make the church stronger, less vulnerable to charges of corruption, and better able to acquit itself in intellectual discussions. Although they tended to reject medieval methods (like Scholasticism), they did not reject basic Christian doctrines.

How did Catholics react to the Renaissance? Many scholars were enthusiastic about it. Ordinary people, so far as we can tell, were drawn to new currents of popular piety grounded, to some extent, on a return to earlier embodiments of Christianity. Because of the printing press, many more people were aware of these new currents than ever before. Scholastic theologians, we can suppose, might have been threatened by them. The Renaissance popes reacted to the Renaissance in an unusual way. Popes began to believe that they need no longer confine themselves to religion and politics. The Renaissance gave them a new job description, an opportunity to become great patrons of the arts.

Remember the "idea of Rome" as we discussed it in Chapter 4? Rome was the great ideal of ancient civilization, and the medieval church was fashioned to be its religious successor. During the Renaissance, the popes believed that Rome should be the spiritual and cultural capital of the universe. They set out to rebuild the city, endow museums, build magnificent buildings, and patronize artists.

To accomplish this goal, popes believed they had to oppose two major threats to their power: rising nationalism (an external threat) and growing conciliarism (an internal threat). Accordingly, the popes created a competitive national power of their

PEOPLE

Erasmus: Faithful Humanist

Not all Christians who saw corruption and abuses in the church chose to challenge it as directly as Luther and Calvin. Catholic humanists like the Dutch scholar Desiderius Erasmus (1466–1536) remained faithful to the church even as they criticized it through their scholarship.

Although he was an ordained priest and took monastic vows, Erasmus lived and worked as an independent scholar. Educated in Paris, he taught at Cambridge for a time and then traveled and worked throughout Europe. He studied classical literature and the early church Fathers, and he wrote in graceful Latin. Like the Protestant reformers, he wanted the church to return to the teachings of the early Christians, but he remained committed to changing the church from within.

For example, Erasmus encouraged Christians to study the New Testament in the original Greek. He examined the manuscripts that he could find in Europe and produced the first critical edition of the Greek New Testament with his own Latin translation. Erasmus dedicated his work to Pope Leo X, but it was Martin Luther who used Erasmus's edition to translate the New Testament into German.

Erasmus frankly condemned practices and beliefs that he considered corrupt or superstitious in such works as the satire *In Praise of Folly.* Pilgrimage to shrines of saints was a very popular act of religious devotion, celebrated in Chaucer's *Canterbury Tales.* In *Pilgrimage for Religion's Sake,* Erasmus criticized abuses of this practice, especially fraudulent shrines that took money from pilgrims. Christians would serve God better, Erasmus suggested, by attending to their jobs and families, not making pilgrimages.

When Luther began to criticize the church, Erasmus was sympathetic to many of his points, but when Luther pressed him to join the Protestants, Erasmus would not. Instead, he and Luther engaged in a fierce debate over the issue of free will and salvation, and Erasmus affirmed his belief in the traditional view of the presence of Christ in the Eucharist.

Erasmus hoped that study of the great tradition of Western Christianity, including the Greek and Latin classics, would lead the church to reform itself. He exemplifies the ideals of the humanist movement.

---

own in Italy. They refused to implement the decrees of the Council of Constance and set themselves the task of becoming Renaissance princes. They engaged in battles, maintained an army, and pursued political power. Many of them used their financial success to enrich their own families: Renaissance popes have not gone down in history as great spiritual leaders. In a world of emerging power claims, they believed that they were protecting the church by developing a strong, independent papacy free from secular control.

Recall that the Catholic church understood itself to be ruled by men who were direct successors to St. Peter. According to the popes, Jesus had given a mandate to Peter to build and protect the church, a mandate that needed to be carried out if the church was to remain free and able to pursue its spiritual journey. Could it still be so? Reformers thought not and argued that the medieval conception of the papacy had simply outlived its usefulness; others believed it needed simply to be refortified. That disagreement, in some ways, was at the heart of the Protestant Reformation. And the humanist/Renaissance movement supported that reformation by providing an alternate reading of the sources of papal power. Martin Luther's position was not fundamentally new—Wycliffe and Hus had said many of the same things before—but he backed up his protest with the fruit of humanist/Renaissance labor. He was able to supply some of the critical scholarship from which real reform and (to some ways of thinking) revolution would come.

THE PROTESTANT REFORMATION

The reform movements before Luther did not lead to separate and distinct groups within Christianity; Luther himself did not intend to found a different church but hoped to reform the existing one. Because the reform movements of the sixteenth century led to a major break in Western Christianity, because they were protests with more severe consequences than earlier movements, we mark them with a distinctive title and call those who departed from prevailing Christian beliefs Protestants.

The Protestant Reformation drew the arguments in the church back to *religious* issues, always with an impact on political arrangements. There were four main channels of the Reformation: Lutheran, Reformed (associated with Zwingli and then Calvin), Tudor (or Anglican), and Radical (or Anabaptist). All of these movements were interested in the same basic issues, but their approaches differed. They were united in their opposition to traditional Roman Catholic notions of the nature of salvation, the church, and religious authority. We look at each of these four movements in greater detail next.

The Lutheran Reformation

As we have seen, humanist scholars rediscovered the Greek New Testament and began to see what it means to understand a text in its historical setting. Furthermore, beginning in the middle of the fifteenth century, there was more general interest in the Bible: many more copies than ever before were available, and the Bible was circulated both in its Latin version (the Vulgate) and in vernacular translations. Scholars began to wonder what it might mean to the church if doctrinal teachings were based on the Greek original rather than on a Latin translation. Increasingly, young reformist scholars began to use the Bible to question the church's teaching authority, to wonder whether the church's teaching tradition was consistent with the Scriptures.

Martin Luther (1483–1546), a young German monk and professor of Scripture at the University of Wittenberg, was one of those scholars influenced by German humanists. His Scripture studies and the humanist atmosphere of the German universities helped him articulate a strong new position, *sola scriptura*. Earlier humanist scholars like Erasmus deplored abuses, studied the Greek New Testament, and argued that some of the conclusions of scholastic theologians were false, but they did not deny the authority of church tradition. Luther, however, went further: he concluded that the entire teaching tradition of the church might be wrong, that judged against the teaching authority of Scripture alone, tradition was often erroneous.

Luther did not arrive at his position all at once or alone. By the time he was ready to engage in debate about a specific issue, he was nearly thirty four and his university was clearly supportive of his conclusions and goals. The first target of Luther's public protest was not an esoteric point of scriptural interpretation but an abuse of an old system related to salvation and popular piety. Luther's immediate protest was raised against Johann Tetzel (1470–1519), a Dominican monk and a high-powered ecclesiastical peddler of *indulgences* in a town near Wittenberg.

Over a long period of time and for a variety of philosophical and historical reasons, the Roman Catholic church had developed the doctrine of purgatory, a place where the punishment due for sins could be worked off after death. The reasoning was that God's *justice* demands that sinners pay a penalty (in this life or the next) for sins, while God's *mercy* will not allow a repentant (but not fully paid-up) sinner to spend eternity in hell. Therefore, it was speculated, there must be a state en route to heaven where sinners can stop for a while and pay their penalties in full. This speculation seemed logical at a time when the task of theology was rational inquiry about God and the divine relationship to humanity and when scholars worked to formulate systematic, all-encompassing explanations. The idea of purgatory was one such logical speculation. When it was combined with ideas about the church's power, the rationale for indulgences was developed.

The church believed that the obedient sacrificial death of Jesus and the good works of Mary and the saints had built up a treasury of merit, like a bank account that the church could draw on to pay the debts of sinners. Indulgences were a withdrawal from the account. Sinners could earn indulgences by doing what the church suggested: good works, prayers, and devotions. People who went on pilgrimages received indulgences, as did those who did good works, bore their sufferings patiently, or said certain prayers. During the Avignon papacy, the popes, in need of money for a variety of projects, began to *sell* indulgences; one wit noted that the popes had discovered the fiscal possibilities of purgatory. The practice of selling indulgences went from bad to worse and was in a scandalous state when Luther began his public protest against the church's corruption in 1517.

Luther's protest against indulgences was inspired partly by his disgust with a greedy practice but also by his new understanding about the Christian life. The sixteenth century was a time of deep and paradoxical religious energy: many people were attracted to a new devotional life that stressed a personal relationship to God and a kind of inner fervor, yet they experienced great anxiety about their own salvation. The Catholic church taught that one was saved through a faith that activated itself in good works. Christians did not save themselves by doing good works, but their pious deeds, their prayers, and their devotions all were indications that their faith was genuine. One can see how many people were confused about the relationship between faith and works in an atmosphere full of the paraphernalia of religious practice—relics, indulgences, pilgrimages. Anxious people could ask themselves whether they had "done enough" to merit heaven. Indulgence peddlers like Tetzel gave Christians the impression that they could bargain with God about their salvation, somehow appease divine anger with certificates. Indulgences made it look as if one could buy peace of mind, and Luther's experience contradicted that implication radically.

Luther originally intended to be a lawyer, but in a profound spiritual crisis, he gave up the study of law and entered a monastery (in 1505) and was ordained a priest (1507). Anxious about his own salvation, Luther thought that monastic life was the best way to overcome doubts about his relationship with God. He was an exemplary young monk, scrupulous about his devotions and duties, obedient, and thoughtful.

Yet he did not gain any confidence about his relationship with God and was often in a mood of despair and pessimism about his own salvation. In this melancholy context, he finished his doctorate in theology and began to teach Scripture at Wittenberg.

Slowly, as he worked as an exegete and teacher, he had a breakthrough experience. Scholars differ about what actually happened to him, when it happened, and how it can be explained in terms of scriptural exegesis. Classically stated, Luther came to see that one is saved by faith alone. Good works—including the whole theological foundation for the theory of indulgences—were, as he saw it, absolutely useless for one's salvation. Indulgences harm Christian belief in two ways: they give Christians a false sense about their salvation, and they pervert a right understanding of God.

If medieval Catholics sometimes saw God as an avenging judge who needed to be appeased, Luther finally experienced God as a loving father who forgives freely. Luther understood salvation as a relationship in which the individual sinners have "faith" (trusting absolutely in God's mercy) and God "justifies" them (forgives them even though they do not cease to be sinners). The scriptural passage often cited as Luther's key to this understanding is Romans 1:17: "For in [the Gospel] the righteousness of God is revealed through faith for faith; as it is written, 'He who through faith is righteous shall live.' " Faith is not a "work," not something that one can "do," but is, rather, a gift from God that one accepts in surrendered trust.

The freedom and sense of release Luther felt in the wake of his insight were phenomenal. His experience obviously touched a chord in the hearts of many Christians at the time, since it was a message of religious consolation. Add to the sense of relief a zeal for reforming some of the abuses in the church, and you have an idea of why Luther's protest generated a new and compelling movement within Christianity.

Luther believed that Roman Catholic doctrine and practice put up walls around religion, that the church operated as a power structure that so controlled the means of religious experience that it was virtually impossible for people to have an assurance of God's love and their own salvation. The church, as he perceived it, controlled *Scripture* by insisting that it be read only in Latin and not translated into the vernacular, and the church was the sole authorized interpreter; it controlled *doctrine* by means of theological complexity and clerical formulations; and it controlled *grace* by binding grace to reception of the sacraments and the practice of acts that would secure merit. All of this control was tied up with the power of the priesthood, a power that extended up and down a hierarchical ladder from pope to bishops and from bishops to priests.

Luther set out to free the Gospel from the control exercised over it by the Roman church; he wanted to extend the freedom and assurance of faith-alone salvation to others. He translated the Bible into German and made it available to the people. For Luther, hearing Scripture was a kind of sacrament; he believed that if people could just hear the word of God in Scripture, in language they understood, it would have a powerful effect on them. Scripture, he argued, creates its own unity; people do not need to be confined to the official interpretations of the church, nor do they need to have their own interpretations of the Gospel regulated in some way. He shared his own insights and told people what the best interpretations were; those interpretations, he believed, could be discovered and bear fruit in a more scriptural model of the church. He insisted that the church was not a hierarchy but a "priesthood of all believers" and a fellowship. Finally, he insisted that salvation was granted to believers on the basis of faith alone. People did not need to rely on complex doctrines or on a system of sacraments and indulgences dispensed by priests; they had only to trust that God would regard them as righteous.

Luther did not intend to form a new church but to reform the existing one. By 1519, however, it was clear that his positions were radically at odds with Roman Catholic doctrines, and a break from Rome seemed inevitable. In 1520, he wrote three famous treatises—*Address to the Christian Nobility of the German Nation, The Babylonian Captivity of the Church,* and *The Freedom of a Christian Man*—which spelled out his political and religious positions. Luther argued for German *(not* Roman) control of the German churches; he denied the power of the pope as the final interpreter of Scripture; he denied the power of priests to mediate between the believer and God; and he rejected all sacraments except baptism and the Eucharist. He was excommunicated from the Roman church in 1521.

Luther spent most of the rest of his life alternately supporting and curbing his reform movement, translating the Scriptures into German, and writing catechisms and hymns. His reading of Scripture and his experiences led him to support certain theological conclusions and fortified his conviction of the uselessness of human effort and reason in matters of salvation. His religious experience convinced him that God is gracious and looks upon people as if they were righteous, if only they have faith and confidence in God's goodness and Christ's atonement. Righteousness was granted to people freely through the grace of Christ. Luther drew religion away from its political entanglements in the Roman church and insisted that it was based on Scripture and faith alone; religion, therefore, was a personal matter between God and the individual believer. At the same time, however, he did not free it from political involvement: he allowed the church to be subordinate to the political power of the state and appealed to the political power of the German princes to suppress quasi-religious uprisings like the Peasants' Revolt (1524).

Luther's reform movement led to the formation of a separate church and inspired similar revolutions by other reformers. Lutheranism was systematically defined in various Lutheran creeds (see Appendix 5), all of which were combined in the Book of Concord (1580). Justification by faith alone and the primacy of Scripture as a religious authority are major tenets of Lutheranism. Luther was essentially conservative within his own movement; he did not support those who argued for extreme spiritualization. He was also cautious in relation to other reform movements; he did not support what he considered the extreme reforms of Zwingli, our next topic.

The Reformed Tradition

The man who initiated the movement that later became associated with the Reformed church was a contemporary of Luther's, Ulrich Zwingli (1484–1531), a Swiss reformer. Zwingli had been influenced by the humanists, especially by Erasmus, and was drawn to the reform movement through his studies of Scripture. On the basis of these studies, he argued against clerical celibacy, monasticism, and indulgences. In 1519, he gave a series of lectures on Scripture using Erasmus's edition of the Greek New Testament. Zwingli's position was simple: the word alone is enough, and one does not need the accumulated interpretations of the church and the commentaries of scholars. Zwingli, like Luther, argued that churches should be freed from Roman control. In 1523, the city council of Zurich approved Zwingli's positions about restoring the practice of the primitive church and ordered all priests to comply with them: organs were destroyed and images and statues removed from churches, priests were encouraged to marry, the liturgy was simplified, and monasticism abolished.

Whereas Luther's protest was inspired by his own questions of personal salvation, Zwingli's desire for reform was motivated by his conviction that Christians could be bound only by what they found in the Bible. Accordingly, their views about the Christian life differed: Luther emphasized reconciliation and freedom, while Zwingli put more stress on the obligation of the Christian to conform to God's will as found in the Bible. Even though they agreed about many things—the need for reform, the scandal of indulgences, the centrality of the Bible—they disagreed profoundly about others, and their theological arguments led to the first rift within Protestantism, the break between the Lutheran and the Reformed traditions.

A central point of disagreement between Luther and Zwingli was the presence of Christ in the Eucharist. Roman Catholics believed the actual body and blood of Christ were present in the bread and wine consecrated in the Divine Liturgy. Catholics even had a philosophical explanation for *how* that happened. Luther rejected the metaphysical explanation but not the belief: for him, the body and blood of Christ were really present in the bread and wine and received by the faithful. Zwingli located the presence of Christ in the hearts of the believers rather than in the elements of bread and wine. For him, the Eucharist was a *memorial* meal that unites the faithful by means of a common bond with the Lord.

These different interpretations led to a severe break between Luther and Zwingli: as Luther perceived it, Zwingli had simply gone too far. Those who would later be called Anabaptists believed that Zwingli had not gone far enough, and they, too, broke away from his movement to form a fellowship of their own. When Zwingli was killed in a religious war in 1531, the Swiss wing of the Reformation—Zwingli's ideas and points of emphasis—was adopted, modified, and developed by a second-generation reformer, John Calvin.

Calvin (1509–1564) was a French Protestant theologian and the person most closely associated with the Reformed tradition. He originally intended to be a Roman Catholic priest but apparently had some doubts about his vocation and about the Roman Catholic church. He studied to be a lawyer, even though he was more attracted to Hebrew and classical studies; as a student, he was influenced by the humanists. His active role in the Reformation was precipitated by a religious experience in 1533, in which he felt himself called to join the movement to restore the Christian church to its original purity. When he turned his energies to the Reformation, he used them to systematize Protestant theology—his *Institutes of the Christian Religion,* 1536–1559, were revised several times during his lifetime—and to develop his doctrinal system in the context of a theocratic state, the Geneva experiment, 1541–1564.

Calvin continued the disagreement with Luther about the Eucharist. That argument led to the separation of the Protestant church in Germany into the Lutheran church on the one hand and the Reformed church (Calvinist) on the other. A more serious disagreement between Luther and Calvin, however, involved politics and the relation of the state to the church. Calvin restored the political power of the church and organized a church-dominated society. For Calvin, it was not enough to define

Concept

Making Saints Out of Sinners: Justification

Protestant reformers and their Roman Catholic opponents differed on many issues, such as the authority of Scripture and the organization of the church. But at the center of the conflict was a debate over how God justifies ("makes right") sinful human beings. Although Roman Catholics taught that justification was *intrinsic,* an internal change of the person, Protestants said that justification was *extrinsic,* an external change in how God sees the person.

The key question is whether or not something really happens to human nature through grace. Let's start with the premise that human nature is sinful to begin with (a dungheap): extrinsic justification says that if you have faith, then even though you remain a dungheap, you smell like a bed of roses to God; nothing really changes you, but by virtue of the grace of Christ, God treats you as a garden. As Luther saw it, the baptized Christian is covered with Christ's righteousness so that God sees the sinful person as righteous even though the person is still a sinner. Luther could say that a Christian was *simul justus et peccator* ("at the same time a righteous person and a sinner"): in your nature, you are still completely sinful, but from God's perspective, you are completely righteous.

Intrinsic justification starts with human nature as equally sinful, a dungheap, but it says that the sacraments of the church give you grace so that you will be changed into a rose garden. Something really happens to you, or to put it in the religious language of the times, "grace transforms nature." Christians are being healed of sin, changed from sinners into saints. This is not what Luther believed.

You can see how this fundamental difference could lead to many other conflicts. For example, Luther's view limits the role of the church: basically, God looks at each individual sinner and pronounces the Christian not guilty (even though he or she really is guilty). The Roman Catholic view makes the church essential to salvation: the grace that transforms sinful human nature is available only in the sacraments of the church.

the church as a "priesthood of all believers"; the church, he believed, needed power as well as fellowship.

Calvin was invited to Geneva, Switzerland, to create a refuge for French Protestants (who were being persecuted by the Catholic government of France) and to design a city government based on early Christian polity. An initial attempt (1536–1538) failed, but from 1541 until his death, Calvin governed Geneva and was able to develop a theocratic government there: God was the supreme authority, and God's laws were clear; Calvin interpreted them and utilized the secular powers to enforce them. He organized a constitutional government based on New Testament offices and hoped that the state would be subordinated to the church. Calvin had far-reaching powers not only in religious matters but over the private lives of all the citizens of Geneva. He established disciplines for everything, religious and secular; his laws were based on the Bible and enforced by civil magistrates. Any deviation from the law was punished, and opposition was punished severely. Geneva was a haven for religious refugees, a place for a new beginning. In a chaotic time full of injustice, persecution, and religious confusion, it promised a visible and godly order and a chance for a well-regulated Christian life under the providence and sovereignty of God.

In Calvin's theology, God's providence governs everything, and the fate of everything and everyone in the world is in God's hands; the believer should strive to have his or her own will taken up into the sovereign will of God. But how does one know God's will? Calvin proceeded from the premise that the Bible contained God's will and divine laws for every facet of human life: everything necessary for salvation has been revealed in Scripture in a clear and certain way. The Bible is read and understood in the church, which is a community under the sovereignty and grace of God. The church, therefore, is essential for salvation: it is the locus of God's covenant of grace because it is supported by the person and work of Christ. People are freed from anxiety about their salvation because it lies in God's hands.

To people who look at it from the outside, one of the striking features of Calvin's theology—a logical extension of his beliefs about the absolute sovereignty of God—is the theory of divine election and predestination. Since God knows everything and is absolutely powerful, it follows that God knows who will be saved and who will be damned. In fact, Calvin argued, God elected those to be saved and predestined those to be damned, and then God saw to it that those on the road to damnation were sinners and those on the road to salvation were saints. God's people—the elect—have been put on earth to work out the divine plan; election, therefore, is a calling and the Christian life a serious vocation.

Both Luther and Calvin had a gloomy view of human nature: both believed that people were sinful by nature and unable to do any good of their own accord; both perceived the Roman Catholic doctrine of intrinsic justification as unbiblical and hopelessly wrong. According to Luther, salvation was accomplished by Christ and was granted freely to people on the basis of faith. Calvin agreed but emphasized that faith and salvation depended on election. The teaching about predestination has borne most of the anti-Calvinist criticism, but it should not be taken out of context or given disproportionate attention: it was meant to release people from anxiety about their salvation, to give them a sense of sinfulness and a profound sense of God's forgiveness, an experience that resulted in feelings of thankfulness and joy. The doctrine was also meant to divert their attention from worries about personal worthiness and to focus it on Christian life as a calling and on God's sovereign role in the salvation of a person.

One of the followers of Calvin, Jacob Arminius (1560–1609), changed his mind about the doctrine of predestination even while he was trying to defend it. He and his followers in the Dutch Reformed church argued for conditional predestination and a more liberal theology. Arminianism is usually associated with honoring the role of free will (as opposed to Calvinistic determinism) and the concept of unlimited atonement. Arminius's followers were condemned at the Synod of Dort (1618–1619) in Holland.

From this Reformed synod, one can find a clear expression, in brief form, of Calvinist doctrine. There are five major points, which can be remembered with the acronym TULIP:

1. *Total depravity of humankind:* Since the Fall, people can only sin; they are incapable of sinless acts.
2. *Unconditional election:* Once a person is saved (by faith), that person is always saved.
3. *Limited atonement:* Christ died to save the elect, not to save everyone.
4. *Irresistible grace:* There is no freedom to resist God's grace.

5. *Perseverance of the saints*: The elect must lead saintly lives and persevere to the end; they cannot assume they are saved, nor can they rest in an assurance of salvation.

Once one accepts the sovereignty of God and the certainty that Scripture is the supreme rule of faith, one is to accept the world as created by God and is challenged to maintain its order. If the Bible is normative for every facet of human life, following the Bible allows one to uphold and glory in God's sovereignty and world order. The Calvinist system blended well with the demands of emerging capitalism: Calvin extolled thrift, hard work, sobriety, responsibility, and self-reliance, the very virtues that were crucial for those who wished to make substantial progress in modern mercantile society.

Calvin wrote a systematic theology of major Reformation positions and laid the groundwork for a theocratic society. Calvinism has been defined in various creeds (see Appendix 5), the most famous of which is probably the Westminster Confession. The form of church government Calvin proposed—Presbyterianism—and his religious ideas had a major impact on the religious future of English Protestants in the sixteenth and seventeenth centuries. The principles of the Synod of Dort and some of the ideas associated with the Geneva experiment—new beginnings, a refuge from religious persecution, and a visible, godly society under divine sovereignty—were the predominant influence in the minds and intentions of the Puritan founders of the American colonies.

The Tudor Reformation

The reformations of Luther and Calvin were doctrinal, liturgical, and disciplinary as well as structural, and they were pursued for predominantly religious reasons. Both Luther and Calvin set out to change the situation in the church. Luther hoped to reform the Catholic church by calling it back to its religious roles and informing it with more scriptural understanding; Calvin set out to purify Christianity and to organize Protestant Christianity into a theocratic system. The Tudor (Anglican) Reformation was not like either of its European cousins. It took place in England, and when it was over, much of what was Roman remained in liturgy, doctrine, and practice, despite its break with the papacy. Like Catholics, Anglicans continued to accept the episcopal structure of the church whereby authority moved from the top down; the liturgy was not substantially altered and there were, at first, no great doctrinal changes as in Lutheranism and the Reformed tradition.

The Roman Catholic church in England had been a rich and powerful institution dating back to the sixth century. One of the first missions of Pope Gregory I had been to organize the English church on the model of papal primacy. At the same time, England was the first country to have a strong monarchy (able to oppose the pope on some issues) and a strong parliamentary government (able to oppose the monarch on some issues). England was a religiously vibrant country: the first significant reform movements occurred there (with Wycliffe and the Lollards), and an impressive array of mystics flourished in fourteenth-century England (Julian of Norwich, Richard Rolle, Walter Hilton, and the author of *The Cloud of Unknowing*).

The precipitating cause of the Tudor Reformation was a conflict between King Henry VIII (1491–1547) and the pope about divorce. Henry wanted to divorce his wife, Catherine of Aragon, to marry Anne Boleyn. The breakdown in negotiations between the king and the pope led to an administrative and judicial change in the structure of church government in England. Henry asserted the royal primacy over the church, declaring that the king (or queen), *not* the pope, was to be head of the church in England. Theologically, Anglicans attempted to find a middle way between Roman Catholicism and continental Protestantism. Accordingly, they kept much of the Roman Catholic doctrine and liturgical celebration, adopted a significant structural change, and allowed changes in some disciplinary matters like clerical celibacy.

When Henry VIII died, his son Edward VI (age ten) was king, and England was ruled by regents. The regents were substantially more sympathetic to European Protestants—especially to the Reformed tradition—than Henry VIII had been. At this time, some changes were introduced into the Anglican Book of Common Prayer, and it looked as if the Anglican church might become more thoroughly reformed. Edward VI died in 1553 and Mary Tudor, Henry's oldest daughter, granddaughter of the king of Catholic Spain, and a strong Roman Catholic supporter, became queen. With her ascension to the throne, the stage was set for a confrontation between Anglicans (who had accepted the Reformation and the changes in the Church of England) and Roman Catholics (who had not accepted Henry's changes but had remained loyal to Rome). Mary at first simply forbade the practice of the Protestant religion, but within a year, she established ecclesiastical courts to find and sentence heretics. She is remembered as Bloody Mary because of the severe persecutions during her reign. John Foxe's *Book of Martyrs* (1563) was written to chronicle the stories of many Protestants who were cruelly tortured and executed for their religious beliefs.

Mary was succeeded by her half-sister Elizabeth I, daughter of Anne Boleyn. Elizabeth (queen from 1558 to 1603) was suspicious both of Catholics (who judged that she was not the legitimate monarch) and of Protestants (who would have destroyed some of the protection offered to her by the episcopal polity of the Anglican church). As she tried to negotiate a course between various religious factions in England, Pope Pius V issued a formal condemnation and excommunication of Elizabeth in 1570. In this decree, *Regnans in Excelsio*, the pope released all English people from allegiance to her. Catholics were forced to choose between their citizenship (loyalty to the queen) and their religion (loyalty to the pope), and Queen Elizabeth had no choice but to see Roman Catholics as traitors. Up to this time, English Protestantism and Roman Catholicism existed side by side; after the condemnation, Roman liturgy (the Mass) was forbidden and Catholics met increased persecution. By the end of Elizabeth's reign, England was the foremost Protestant country in Europe.

The Radical Reformation

The word *radical* comes from a Latin word meaning "root." Radical reformers separated from other reform movements because they did not believe those reform movements really returned to the root of primitive Christian faith. Some radical reformers were called Anabaptists, a derogatory name from a Greek word meaning "to *re*baptize." Anabaptists did not believe that it was scriptural to baptize babies and so rebaptized one another and from then on baptized only adults. They wanted more than a structural and doctrinal reform: they wanted to restore apostolic Christianity, to live in conformity with Scripture and the faith of the first Christians. To do this, they saw the New Testament as the sole norm for Christian life and understood their relationship to Jesus as one of discipleship. For the Anabaptists, the life, death, and resurrection of Jesus were important not merely as elements in a doctrine of justification but as norms for Christian behavior: the Christian was one who lived as Jesus had lived.

Several disparate groups of Anabaptists formed in the early part of the sixteenth century, some of which were not typical of later Anabaptist practice. The Zwickau Prophets, for example, joined the Peasants' Revolt, and a group of Münster Anabaptists under the leadership of John Leyden established a theocracy and practiced polygamy. Two important early groups were the Mennonites and the Hutterites. Mennonites were named for Menno Simons (c. 1496–1561), a Dutch reformer. Their views were similar to those of the Swiss Brethren, a group that split from the state church in Zurich (Zwingli's church) because the Reformation there hadn't been radical enough and because they regarded the whole notion of having church affairs subordinate to state control as unscriptural. The Hutterites took their name from Jacob Hutter (d. 1536) and were distinguished from other Anabaptist groups by their adoption of common ownership of property.

Anabaptists differed radically from other reform groups in practice and behavior. Their reading of the New Testament and their determination to follow the ethics of Jesus literally led them to some positions that were at odds with the practices of both Catholics and Protestants. Anabaptists were persecuted by both Protestants and Catholics who found their teachings and vision uncompromising and politically destabilizing. Five Anabaptist beliefs were particularly threatening:

1. *Separation from the world:* The world was perceived as a place controlled by evil, and Anabaptists believed they should separate themselves from it—that is, be disinterested in politics or the affairs of the state.
2. *Refusal to swear oaths:* Taking Jesus' words "Do not swear at all. . . . Let what you say be simply 'Yes' or 'No'" (Matt. 5:34, 37) literally, they refused to swear oaths; since the oath was the basis of the juridical feudal system, it looked as if they stood against the basic organization of society.
3. *Nonresistance:* Doing as Jesus did and refusing to fight evil with evil, they refused to do anything violent; that is, they refused to fight in wars for any reason.
4. *Adult baptism:* They regarded baptism and responsible faith as matters of adult conviction, not the province of children, who were regarded as innocent until they reached an age of accountability.
5. *Community of goods:* They believed in sharing one's goods with everyone, friend and foe alike; in its extreme form, everything was owned in common, as with the Hutterites.

Anabaptists were a small but important strand of the Reformation. Their beliefs and their radical discipleship distinguished them from other groups and had the effect of keeping their numbers small. As we shall see in later chapters, Mennonites and Amish (a later Anabaptist group) continue the traditions of the Radical Reformation not only in terms of belief and religious practice but sometimes in the very old-fashioned way they live in the contemporary world.

These four major strands of the Protestant Reformation all grew into separate denominations, which, as we shall see, inspired the growth of other churches. The creative protests of Wycliffe and Hus, the reforming decisions of the conciliar movement, and the supportive atmosphere of the Renaissance all worked together to energize the reforming impulses of Christianity. The Protestant Reformation was the beginning of a rich period of religious growth that, for Protestant denominations, was especially vibrant in nineteenth-century America. Catholicism was also urged to reform during this time, and it is to that group that we now turn.

THE CATHOLIC REFORMATION

The Catholic Reformation is sometimes called the Counter-Reformation, a term that implies little more than a reaction to Protestant reform movements. It would be more accurate to say that reform movements had been going on within and outside Catholicism for some time and that some of the early Protestant reform movements were originally attempts to reform the Catholic church. Still, there *was* a significant Roman Catholic response to the Protestant Reformation.

The charter of the Roman response was contained in the decrees of the Council of Trent (1545–1563), a reforming council that met on and off for nearly 20 years. Although the council began with realistic hopes for constructive conversation, positions quickly hardened and made mutual understanding impossible. Roman Catholics refused to meet Protestant reformers halfway on any issue and used Trent instead to reassert church authority, to clarify traditional doctrine, and to establish a solid basis for the renewal of discipline and spiritual life within Catholicism. After Trent, the Roman Catholic church emerged with a clear system of doctrine and discipline and some significant moral and administrative reforms. Among the doctrines and practices affirmed by the Council of Trent were the following (notice that they respond to Protestant questions or positions by denying them):

1. A creed is important, and the official creed is the Nicene Creed.
2. Scripture is *not* the only source of divine revelation; *tradition* is on an equal footing with Scripture as a source of religious authority.
3. Individuals may *not* interpret the Bible for themselves: the church is the sole interpreter of the Bible, and the official Bible is the Vulgate.
4. The Protestant doctrine of sin and justification is false; people have free will, and justification is intrinsic and related to grace.
5. There are *seven* sacraments instituted by Jesus Christ, and sacraments are necessary for salvation.
6. The doctrine of transubstantiation is the official explanation for the real presence of Christ in the Eucharist.
7. The eucharistic doctrines of Luther, Calvin, and Zwingli were condemned.
8. The chalice (wine) was denied to the laity.
9. The value and importance of the liturgy (the Mass) were reaffirmed.
10. Reforming moves aimed at bishops, seminaries, and diocesan synods were established.
11. The doctrines that supported purgatory and the use of relics and indulgences, all of which were severely criticized by Protestant reformers, were upheld.

Controversy

Soldiers of the Catholic Reformation: The Jesuits

Although Protestants criticized the monastic institutions of the Roman Catholic church, the Catholic Reformation gave birth to several new religious orders. The most famous of these is the Society of Jesus, whose members are known as Jesuits.

The Jesuits were founded by Ignatius of Loyola (1491–1556), a soldier who decided to devote his life to Christ through poverty, celibacy, obedience, and service. The new order was organized as an army, led by a "general" who was elected for life. Ignatius did not require any special clothing or devotional program, but he did stress obedience to the pope and rigorous training of recruits based on a program of meditations found in Ignatius's book *Spiritual Exercises*. The order grew rapidly: by Ignatius's death in 1556, there were more than 1,000 Jesuits; by 1626, there were more than 15,000; and membership reached a peak of more than 36,000 in the 1960s.

The society became known for three major activities: anti-Protestant work, missions, and education. Ignatius did not found the society to fight Protestants, but the Jesuits soon took a leading role in this area. Several Jesuits represented the pope in negotiations with countries, like Ireland, that the pope wished to tie more closely to the Vatican. Jesuit theologians such as Peter Canisius and Robert Bellarmine wrote catechisms and anti-Protestant theological treatises. Bellarmine also gained fame in the trial of the scientist Galileo (see Chapter 6). Perhaps unfairly, the Jesuits have been called "the storm troopers" of the Catholic Reformation.

Missionary work was the major focus of the Jesuits throughout the nineteenth century. The society pioneered missionary methods that adapted Christian doctrine and practice to local cultures. Francis Xavier (1506–1552) was a courageous man who preached the Gospel in India, Indonesia, and Japan. Matteo Ricci (1552–1610) led the mission to China (see Chapter 9). The Jesuits also led the conversion of Brazil and Paraguay to Christianity. All this work was dangerous: more than 1,000 Jesuits are listed as martyrs, mostly in mission areas.

Contemporary Americans are most familiar with the Jesuits' role in education. By 1626, the Jesuits ran four hundred colleges, and their schools today (including high schools, colleges, and seminaries) number in the thousands worldwide. The Jesuits advocated high-quality education that combined the best of Renaissance humanism with Catholic moral and religious values. There can be no doubt that numerous educated people have found it possible to embrace Roman Catholicism thanks to their Jesuit education. According to one Jesuit saying, "Give me a child until he is seven, and he will remain a Catholic the rest of his life."

To ensure the success of the Catholic Reformation, two offices were established (or reestablished under different rules): the Inquisition (a final court of appeals for heresy cases, not to be confused with the Spanish Inquisition, which was instituted in the late fifteenth century by the Spanish crown as a means of using state power against Muslims and Jews) and the Index (an official list of books that members of the Roman church were forbidden to read).

Protestant reformers had protested that religious orders and monastic institutions in Catholicism were corrupt. In the sixteenth century, a number of new reformed religious orders were established; a particular one, the Jesuits, was established for the energetic support of the church. In all of these religious groups, members had a reputation for piety and austerity as well as great preaching and teaching ability. On a popular level, as a tangible example of reform in the church, they were effective.

The Catholic church made no significant overtures to Protestants or to members of the Orthodox church until the Second Vatican Council (1962–1965). At that council, efforts were made to talk with and understand Protestants, and much of what has been characterized as the "siege mentality" of Trent began to disappear. The primary importance of Scripture was affirmed, the importance and role of laypeople in the church was stated, Protestants were recognized as true Christians, it was declared permissible to celebrate the liturgy in the vernacular, more congregational participation in worship was encouraged, and the Index was abolished. The changes of the Second Vatican Council were sweeping, and the effects of those changes as well as the development of some of them into significantly different practices and attitudes continue to be felt.

CONCLUSION

Throughout his public life, Jesus was often asked, "By whose *authority* do you do these things?" Questions of religious authority have marked the Christian church from the beginning and have contributed to the variety in its life. During the Reformation, questions of religious authority were bound up with questions of doctrine and practice and led to a full-scale division of the Christian church into Protestant and Catholic in the West. Orthodox Christians were interested in the reformers' protests against papal power but not much inspired to make doctrinal and liturgical changes; the Reformation, therefore, did not significantly influence them.

By the middle of the sixteenth century, Protestants and Catholics had begun wars against one another; each group understood itself as the instrument of God's will and wrath, commissioned to bring the other group to its knees. Both Catholics and Protestants persecuted Anabaptists whenever they could and otherwise killed and tortured each other in the name of religion. The wars of religion (involved with political issues as well) formally ended with the Peace of Westphalia in 1648. The wars ended but not the controversy and not the proliferation of Christian churches.

Focal Points for Discussion

1. Catholic and Protestant reformers believed that they were continuing or returning to the original beliefs and practices of the earliest Christians. What could each group point to in defense of its position?
2. To protect the church and ensure the spread of the Gospel, the medieval papacy tried to increase its political power. Why did reformers—Catholic and Protestant—see this as a compromise of Christian values?
3. Some of the Protestant reformers emphasized the importance of the individual Christian rather than the church in matters of salvation and the interpretation of the Scriptures. What was attractive in this position? How is it clearly distinct from the medieval model?

The Reformation Continues: Christianity in the Sixteenth, Seventeenth, and Eighteenth Centuries

CHAPTER 6

The Reformation responded to and encouraged religious ferment. The original groups of the Reformation were confined to a small geographical area, new versions of a unified Christianity within a fairly uniform cultural context. As Christianity moved into the seventeenth and eighteenth centuries, the social and religious situation became much more complex. Religious reform continued but not in such a way that it could easily be classified as Lutheran or Calvinist. New religious groups formed, sometimes within a particular Reformation church and sometimes as a more generalized response to some secular attitude. In the eighteenth century especially—when the Enlightenment and new scientific discoveries threatened all religions—new Christian groups were formed on the basis of widespread religious response to a cultural development that was hostile to religion.

This chapter summarizes some significant developments within Christianity in the sixteenth, seventeenth, and eighteenth centuries. We review the European situation in the first two of these centuries briefly and then focus on Christian diversity in England. The English situation merits closer attention for two reasons: it was extraordinarily rich in new forms of Christianity, and it is the parent of the U.S. religious experience. After a brief description of the struggle between science and religion in the eighteenth century (which provides a context for the birth of Deism and Pietism and the growth of Methodism), we move to the American context, where we will concentrate throughout most of the rest of this book.

SIXTEENTH- AND SEVENTEENTH-CENTURY CHRISTIANITY: INCREASING DIVERSITY

The Reformation raised issues of polity, doctrine, and practice so wrenching that reverberations continued for centuries. In the sixteenth century, some divisions occurred within Protestant groups, and Protestants and Catholics continued to war with and often kill one another. The religious situation on the Continent stabilized with the Peace of Westphalia (1648): France and much of southern Europe were Catholic, northern Europe was Protestant, and Germany was a patchwork quilt of Catholicism and Protestantism depending on the religion of the regional ruler. Developments within Lutheranism, Catholicism, and the Radical Reformation on the Continent can be described briefly and simply. The Reformed (Calvinist) tradition, however, especially in England, was so prolific and so important in the religious history of early America that it will be of particular importance to us.

ROMAN CATHOLICISM

The reverberations of reform were felt in the Roman Catholic church in a proliferation of new religious orders but not in new liturgical or doctrinal forms. Church-state issues—the political power of the pope, the role of the church in the conquest of the New World, and relations between European nations and the Vatican—continued to play an important role in the history of Roman Catholicism. The Council of Trent strengthened the Roman Catholic church against the demands of the reformers and inspired a real reformation within the church. Roman Catholicism was defined by the teachings of the Council of Trent until the middle of the twentieth century. Because of its strong centralized model of ecclesiastical authority, Roman Catholicism did not foster or accept divisions within itself: one was either a loyal Roman Catholic or one left the church (by choice or through excommunication). By definition, a loyal Roman Catholic was one who followed the teachings of the church, accepted the hierarchical structure with the pope at its head, and participated in the specified liturgical and sacramental life of the church.

In many ways, Catholicism flourished after the Reformation by reaffirming some of the things Protestants denied and by attending to their legitimate complaints about corruption. Many of the abuses were eradicated. For example, training for the priesthood was regularized, which meant that the clergy was increasingly well educated and that men entering the priesthood were often more dedicated to the spiritual welfare of their people than they had been in the past. If Protestants were seeking a simplified Christianity, stripped of splendor and mystery, Catholics responded by emphasizing those very things: churches were lavishly decorated, especially in Rome, where artists gave Roman Catholicism a glorious baroque flavor; liturgy was celebrated with pomp and ceremony, often accompanied by elaborate orchestrations of the Mass; and new devotional forms were added to attract people to the everyday mystery of Catholic practice.

LUTHERANISM

Lutheranism spread throughout Germany and the Scandinavian countries without division. The Lutheran church was strongly congregational; issues of polity and practice were left up to the local congregation. Accordingly, Lutheranism developed in different but not divisive ways: in some places, one could find a liturgy that looked vaguely Roman Catholic—structured, formal celebration of the Eucharist—and in other places, services were more clearly Protestant—worship consisting mainly of hymns and Bible study. The primacy of the Gospel was the most important Lutheran principle; it was solidified in creeds like the Augsburg Confession, part of the Book of Concord (see Appendix 5).

Radical Reformation

Radical Reformation groups were strongly invested in the local congregation and were therefore able to support a variety of practical forms within the general framework of Anabaptist belief. Anabaptists were often victims of brutal persecution by both Catholics and Protestants and by both religious and secular authorities. Their strategy during this time was one of survival. The two main groups—Mennonites and Hutterites—continued to exist and to move from place to place to be free from harassment. One new Anabaptist group emerged at this time. The Amish were the conservative followers of Jacob Amman, about whom little is known. The Amish split from the Mennonites because they wished to see a strict enforcement of *Meidung*, the practice of shunning the excommunicated. They became a separate group at the end of the seventeenth century and migrated to America in the eighteenth century.

The Reformed Tradition in the Context of the Puritan Reformation

England was a Protestant country but with a much different history and a much more volatile political situation than Protestant countries on the Continent. Recall that the rationale for the Tudor Reformation was King Henry VIII's assertion than he (not the pope) was the head of the church in England. The key document, the Act of Supremacy (1534), stated that the monarch was the legitimate head of the church in England. The English Reformation, therefore, focused on the rights of the monarch versus the rights of the pope. The issues that galvanized the Continental Reformation—questions of polity, liturgical practice, and doctrine—were not pursued by Henry. The Church of England, therefore, continued to operate in a way that looked much like Catholicism: their institutional structure was hierarchical, they continued to celebrate the Eucharistic liturgy, and they continued to uphold ancient doctrinal formulations. Continental Protestants, on the other hand, had shifted to congregational or Presbyterian structures (see Appendix 6), had simplified their worship services, and had developed new doctrinal positions. In some senses, therefore, the Church of England under Henry VIII had not been reformed; it had simply been cut loose from Roman supremacy.

The English situation was a complex snarl of religion and politics, as England was the home of Catholics, Anglicans, and a growing body of Christians who longed for a more thoroughgoing reform. Each group tried to make its position dominant with no success. Let's review the situation briefly. Henry VIII (d. 1547) was succeeded by three of his children: his son, Edward, and his daughters, Mary and Elizabeth. During Edward's reign (he became king when he was ten years old and died when he was fifteen), regents with Continental Protestant sympathies tried to make the English church more Protestant. When the strongly Catholic Mary I came to the throne, however, she reversed Protestant measures, restored Catholicism, including allegiance to the pope, and began severely persecuting anyone who opposed her policies. During those persecutions, many reform-minded Christians fled to the Continent, where they nurtured a strong desire to make the church in England fully Protestant, a chance they hoped to have when Mary died (1558).

Elizabeth I (1533–1603), Mary's half-sister, grew up in the tangle of palace intrigue and religious uproar that characterized the early sixteenth century. Unlike her brother and sister, whose reigns had been short and ineffective, Elizabeth ruled England for 50 years. When she began her reign, Catholics favored by Mary were a significant part of the English population, Anglicans constituted the official church, and Puritans, who wanted a church "purified" of Roman practices and beliefs, were a growing religious group. Elizabeth, more interested in political stability than in the details of doctrinal disputes, was willing to live and let live, but she was in put into difficult positions by each group.

Although Elizabeth allowed Roman Catholics to practice their religion openly, she was never acceptable to the pope. Elizabeth was the daughter of Henry's second—illegitimate, according to Catholics—wife. The pope ruled that Elizabeth was a bastard with no genuine right to the English throne. His condemnation of Elizabeth forced English Catholics into a completely untenable position: if they professed their loyalty to Catholicism, they were in treasonous opposition to the crown. Indeed, there were various Catholic-inspired plots against Elizabeth's life, and she soon approved anti-Catholic legislation that effectively silenced the Catholic church and forced it underground.

Anglicans were the officially recognized church. Elizabeth was indebted to them because they upheld her legitimacy and so ensured her right to rule. In addition, the Church of England was a compromise group, one that attempted to find a *via media* (a middle way) between Roman Catholicism and the thoroughgoing reformation of Continental Protestantism. Elizabeth, like her father, asserted the independence of the Anglican church. Under her supervision, the church adopted the 1552 version of the Book of Common Prayer and revised and reduced the Forty-two Articles to the Thirty-nine Articles (see Appendix 5).

Puritans had wide-ranging possibilities in both religious and political terms. When they returned to England after Mary's reign, they hoped to find Elizabeth sympathetic to their desires to reform English Christianity along Continental lines: they wanted a church purged of anything Roman in practice, liturgy, or doctrine and were attracting many people to their movement. Elizabeth, however, did not encourage them, and neither did her immediate successors, because there had been an old and mutually advantageous relationship between the monarchy and the episcopal form of government found in the Anglican church.

When the cry for *religious* reform from Puritans was combined with a call for *political* reform from Parliamentarians, civil war broke out in England (1642–1648) followed by a dozen years of Puritan rule. During that time, the Church of England followed a presbyterian polity, and the government made it a crime to use the Book of Common Prayer. When the monarchy was restored in 1660, it was not merely a political victory; it was also a victory of the Church of England over the Puritans. In 1662, the Act of Uniformity required episcopal ordination of all ministers and declared that the Book of Common Prayer was the only legal worship book in England. In reaction to the Act of Uniformity, more than two thousand clergymen resigned from the Church of England to celebrate their worship in nonconformist *chapels* (the official Church of England was the only Christian body that was allowed to call itself a church).

There were two main groups of Puritan reformers: Presbyterians and Congregationalists—that is, groups divided not so much by belief but by the way they chose to organize their churches (see Appendix 6). Eventually, both groups became denominations: Presbyteriansim, the English and Scottish branch of Calvinism founded by John Knox (1513–72), was the dominant group in England. Congregationalism (Puritans who preferred a different type of government) separated itself to become its own church.

By the end of the seventeenth century, the Reformation in England had resulted in the establishment of Anglicanism as the official Church of England. Roman Catholics continued to live in England, but quietly, and were still suspected of disloyalty to the crown. They maintained a low profile and did not take a prominent place in English life until the end of the nineteenth century. Puritan groups, both Presbyterian and Congregationalist, existed alongside Anglicanism and continued to attract new members. In addition, two entirely new religious denominations were formed within this context: Baptists and Quakers.

BAPTISTS A new denomination with Congregationalist roots, the Baptist church shared the church polity views of the English Congregationalists but developed a distinctive teaching about baptism. Since 1644, the name Baptist has been applied to those who believe two things about baptism: that it must be done by immersion (not by pouring water over the head or sprinkling) and that it can be administered only to convinced believers—that is, to adults and not to babies. The first group of Baptists formed in Holland at the beginning of the seventeenth century. A group of Separatist Congregationalists led by John Smyth (1554–1612) migrated to Holland to live in an atmosphere of religious freedom; there, influenced by some Mennonites, they repudiated infant baptism and formed the first English Baptist congregation.

QUAKERS The Religious Society of Friends, or Quakers, was a new religious group founded by George Fox (1624–1691) that attracted many unattached nonconformists. Fox, disillusioned with the ferocious wars fought for Christian truth and frustrated with the disparate claims of the churches, sought a new religious understanding. In 1646, he had a religious experience that caused him to find peace within himself, an experience that led him to the doctrine of the Inner Light. According to Fox, all people have the voice of God within them; the Inner Light is the fundamental source of religious certainty and deep spiritual assurance. The Quakers presented a new religious alternative for people by opposing traditional Calvinist doctrines of human depravity and the preeminence of biblical revelation. A person with the Inner Light is not depraved but possesses the voice of God within; if God speaks directly to the heart, biblical revelation is less central. Since the Inner Light is so important, Fox believed, all outward forms of religion should be rejected: church institutions, sacraments, ritual, ministers, hymn singing—all outward signs of established institutional church life were dropped. Like the Anabaptists, Quakers refused to swear oaths or to participate in wars and were persecuted physically and legally.

Summary of Sixteenth- and Seventeenth-Century Christianity

By the end of the seventeenth century, there were many more religious groups than there had been at the beginning of the Reformation. Roman Catholics did not divide into separate churches but did continue to be touched by the reforming spirit of the times. Lutherans moved into Scandinavia, forming new congregations without any significant division, though the Pietist movement (see next section) was very important in Lutheranism at this time and beyond. The Anabaptists struggled to survive, and the main groups—Mennonites and Hutterites—continued to baptize members into their fellowship. The only significant division was the formation of the Amish church at the end of the seventeenth century. In England, the Reformed tradition inspired the Puritan movement, which eventually split into several different groups: Congregationalists, Presbyterians, Baptists, and Quakers. Ultimately, the Anglicans were the established Church of England, though non-Anglican chapels were permitted to exist in England and continued to attract new members throughout the country. Representatives from all these different religious groups emigrated to America and played an important role in American religious history.

THE EIGHTEENTH CENTURY: RESETTLEMENT AND REFORMATION

In the eighteenth century, religious arguments did not occur as frequently between one church and another, but most churches had members who began to challenge some of the fundamental assumptions of Christianity. New religious alternatives such as Deism and Pietism were generated in response to some of these challenges. Our purpose here is to summarize the eighteenth-century context briefly to describe Christianity in Europe and then in America. Part III of the book will deal with Christianity in the modern world and will review the impact of science and the Enlightenment as we expand on the challenges of modernity for Christianity in general. At this point, however, we take only a quick look at the context so that we can have some appreciation of the patterns of resettlement—Christianity in the New World—and continuing reformation up to the nineteenth century.

The Scientific Revolution

The church in the Middle Ages was the single most powerful institution in the West and claimed (as we have seen) to have jurisdiction over virtually everything. Conflicts arose when someone disputed that claim (as, for example, when political leaders challenged the church's political power). As scientists began to learn more about the world and its wonders, they began to disprove some long-held and religiously supported views. The Protestant Reformation gave an implicit impetus to the scientific revolution by questioning religious authority and thereby making it easier for scientists to question established patterns.

The discoveries of Copernicus (1473–1543) and Galileo (1564–1642) upset old notions of the order of the universe and undermined what some people believed to be an immutable view of the cosmos and our centrality therein. One of the most famous cases in which the church condemned a scientific view (one we all know today to be true) was the condemnation of Galileo. His support for the Copernican view that the sun is the central body in the universe and that the earth moves around it was not the officially sanctioned view. In 1633, he was called to Rome by the Inquisition and forced to retract his scientific findings.

René Descartes (1596–1650) and Francis Bacon (1561–1626) established the importance of the scientific method based on empirical observation and systematic doubt; Isaac Newton (1642–1727) brought the world to the threshold of modernity with his physical and mathematical discoveries. Very few people believed that science could really endanger religious beliefs, yet as the world was transformed by new discoveries, a great change came over the way educated people looked at the heavens and the earth. The discoveries of the scientific revolution suggested that the whole universe was not so mysterious and, indeed, might be subject to the control and domination of human ingenuity.

The Enlightenment and the Beginnings of Deism

The Enlightenment followed on the heels of the scientific revolution. People were called out of the darkness of religion (perceived as mystery or superstition) and into the "enlightened" world of reason: they were given light to see the world around them and encouraged to believe in an orderly universe. "Dare to know," the Enlightenment philosophers challenged, and their followers stretched toward a new individualism and a theory of human perfectibility. Immanuel Kant (1724–1802), perhaps the greatest of the Enlightenment philosophers, wrote *Religion Within the Limits of Reason Alone* to argue the need for moral consciousness without miracles. Old Christian doctrines like divine providence were seen as needless interference in the orderly lives of people.

The combination of scientific discoveries about the universe and Enlightenment philosophy challenged old and cherished Christian assumptions. During the next hundred years, Christians reacted in various ways to this challenge, as they still do today. Some grew defensive, spending their energy denying the legitimacy of the challenge; others tried to defend Christianity by using the skills and tools of post-Enlightenment scholarship. Still others, in the eighteenth century at least, tried to combine Enlightenment insights with religious impulses and so developed a new religion, Deism.

The old religion was criticized for being ponderous and superstitious, for weakening rather than enhancing human freedom. Deism was extolled for its simplicity and reasonableness and for its insistence on religious toleration and freedom. Deism is a religion of logic that believes God is sufficiently revealed in the natural world. There is, accordingly, no need for supernatural revelation. According to Deist belief, God created the world and filled it with reasonable people and discernible natural laws; one's task is to discover the laws of nature and to live according to one's reason. John Locke (1632–1704) wrote his essay "The Reasonableness of Christianity" to prove that the ethical injunctions of Christianity were in conformity with the dictates of reason: the excellence of Christianity lay precisely in its reasonableness.

The rationalism of the Enlightenment and Deism was a philosophical response to some of the confusion and distress present in Christianity in the sixteenth and seventeenth centuries. Wars fought in the name of Christianity, the systematic use

Controversy

Science and Religion: The Trial of Galileo

Protestant reformers were not the only persons to challenge the dominant authority the Roman Catholic church had possessed during the Middle Ages. Scientists did so as well, for they began to claim that they could describe the natural world based on their own observations rather than on the Bible and traditional church doctrine. The career of Galileo (1564–1642) may be the most famous example of the emerging conflict between science and the church.

Galileo was a promising young scientist at the University of Padua in Italy. He became world famous in 1610 when he published the astronomical observations he had made with a new scientific tool: the telescope. For example, Galileo discovered that the moon has a rocky, mountainous surface like earth's and that Jupiter has moons. Use of the telescope also convinced Galileo of something he had long suspected: that Copernicus (1473–1543) was correct to say that the sun is the central body in the solar system and that the earth moves around it. The traditional view, dating back to the ancient astronomer Ptolemy (100–170 C.E.), was that the sun went around the earth. When Galileo began to express his views publicly, he encountered fierce criticism.

Galileo was opposed by both theologians and other scientists. Some scientists resisted any new theories that did not rest on the fundamental ideas of Aristotle, and they found Galileo personally abrasive. Theologians were disturbed because certain passages of the Bible appeared to support the Ptolemaic view that the sun goes around the earth. For example, in Joshua 10:12–14, God makes the sun stand still in the sky: the phrasing makes clear that the biblical author believes that the sun moves, not the earth. Galileo correctly pointed out that for centuries Christian theologians had interpreted biblical passages symbolically or spiritually when historical or scientific investigation showed that they could not be understood literally. But Roman Catholic theologians rejected this argument. The Protestant emphasis on the authority of Scripture had made them extremely sensitive about seeming to be "soft" on the interpretation of the Bible. Moreover, science was now questioning so much that they felt the need to draw a line.

In 1616, Galileo met with a committee of the Inquisition, led by Cardinal Robert Bellarmine, to discuss his teachings. At this meeting, Galileo was apparently told that he could promote the Copernican view as a good mathematical model to chart the movement of the planets but not as the truth about how things really are. Then in 1632, with approval of religious censors, Galileo published *A Dialogue Concerning the Two Chief World Systems—Ptolemaic and Copernican,* in which the Copernican view was clearly favored. The next year, Galileo was put on trial for heresy. During this trial, a new document from the 1616 meeting was "discovered" in which Galileo was told not to teach the Copernican view in any way. Historians now believe that this new document was a forgery. In any event, Galileo was forced to reject his past errors, and he spent the remaining years of his life under house arrest. Three centuries later, Galileo gained a victory. In 1979, Pope John Paul II suggested that the church may have made a mistake in condemning Galileo, and he appointed a commission to investigate the matter. Four years later, the commission ruled that Galileo should not have been condemned and ordered that the records of his trial be released.

of torture by one group against another, and the leadership of the churches in identifying and burning witches caused many people to abandon organized religion altogether or to be less than enthusiastic in their religious devotion. A religious response to the rationalism of the Enlightenment and Deism and to a growing sense of moral laxity and confusion was evangelical Pietism. It not only regenerated some churches, but it also inspired new ones.

Pietism and the Emergence of New Christian Churches

The original impetus for Pietism arose during the seventeenth century in a new reformation within German Lutheranism. Associated with the teachings of Philipp Jakob Spener (1635–1705) and August Hermann Francke (1663–1727), this movement was a reaction to moral laxity, formalism, secularism, and religious indifference. Spener longed for a rebirth of religious seriousness within the Lutheran church. He organized Bible study groups in his home, which were known as the *collegia pietatis,* later the Pietists. Spener was more interested in a right feeling in the heart than he was in pure doctrinal formulation, and his teachings were ultimately condemned by the Lutherans, though they continued to have an effect on the Lutheran church. Francke, a professor at the University of Halle, built Pietism into the ministerial curriculum of the university. More than two hundred Lutheran ministers graduated from the university every year, each with some exposure to Pietistic doctrines. Pietism has some dominant characteristics: a Bible-centered faith, a keen sense of guilt and forgiveness felt in the heart, personal conversion, practical holiness in simple Christian living, and a concern for the needs of other people. All of these characteristics were thought to be manifested and supported by an emotional outpouring of one's feelings and aspirations. Pietism influenced members of many different churches and inspired the formation of new religious groups, including the Brethren and the Methodists.

Brethren Churches The Brethren were an Anabaptist group formed in Germany by Alexander Mack (1679–1735). Mack had been a member of the Reformed church, but he separated from it, along with some others, to find a more biblical expression of Christianity. His group was composed mostly of Pietists and Anabaptists; in 1708, they formed a new fellowship and elected Mack as their leader. Because of persecution, they migrated first to the Netherlands and then to Germantown, Pennsylvania; they had all come to America by 1735. They were sometimes called Dunkers or Dunkards, though their official name was the Fraternity of German Baptists. Brethren are distinguished in practice by a threefold immersion at baptism and a threefold Holy Communion service: footwashing, the Lord's Supper, and an *agape,* or fellowship meal, sometimes called a love feast.

Methodists Methodism was a revivalist movement within the Anglican church influenced by Moravian Pietists. John Wesley (1703–1791), his brother Charles (1707–1788), and their friend George Whitefield (1714–1770) were at Oxford University together when they experienced a religious awakening. They and a few other students were interested in a more heartfelt religious experience than they found among people in the Church of England, and they spent much time in prayer and spiritual discipline in search of it. Other students ridiculed them for trying to devise a

SPIRITUALITY

Searching for Sanctification

The numerous religious options that developed in the post-Reformation period occurred simultaneously with enormous changes in science, exploration, economics, politics, and philosophy. The fixed stars by which people navigated their spiritual lives were no longer always clear, and many people had anxious questions about their own salvation. Calvinists insisted that only a small number would be saved—that God's sovereign, saving will rests on a select few. Wesleyan Methodists, however, preached a saving grace available to everyone. God loves freely and gives freely: God's merciful love does not depend on human virtue, desire, merit, or works. Wesley believed that the doctrine of predestination destroyed holiness, happiness, and a zeal for good works, which are all attractive and biblically grounded aspects of Christianity.

John Wesley (1703–1791) was a religiously serious young man who led a small Bible study group in college. He prayed and fasted, visited prisons, and was drawn to the piety of those who found spiritual fulfillment in the experience of simple Christian living. Yet, when a fellow missionary in Georgia asked him how he knew that he was *saved,* Wesley had no answer. His heartwarming experience in London 3 years later assured him of forgiveness and reconciliation and impelled him to preach about God's love and call to holiness.

Methodist societies, which were open to everyone, were guided by three simple rules: those who joined were to do no harm (avoid evil), to do good (be kind and merciful to all), and to follow the laws of God (through worship, prayer, and Bible study).

Methodism choreographed the sinful nature of human beings and the merciful grace of God into a lifetime quest for perfection. Through *repentance,* they see themselves as sinful, deserving punishment, hopeless, and frozen, but through *faith,* they experience themselves as purified, protected, accepted, and empowered by the merciful goodness and grace of God. Justification is instant: a surprising break with the past and a rebirth into new possibilities. Through faith, one is cleansed from sin and given a power to resist evil, but this process is not magical. Sanctification takes a lifetime and may include backsliding. Indeed, Methodism attracted those who understood the sometimes circuitous path to perfection. Methodist hymns, which sang fervently of an ever-sustaining God, helped believers to perfect their holiness through a life of prayer, compassion (for self and others), and zealous good works.

method for religious experience, and the name Methodist stuck to Wesley and his work. John Wesley was influenced by Moravians in the American colony of Georgia (where he went as a missionary in 1735) and in England (where he returned dejected a year later). On a visit to a Moravian settlement at Aldersgate in 1738, Wesley had a religious experience in which he felt his heart "strangely warmed," when he knew that God took away all his sins. From that warm assurance, his acquaintance with Pietist doctrine through the Moravians, and his own early preoccupations with religious experience, Wesley built a significant religious movement.

Wesley called the world his parish: he rode more than 250,000 miles on horseback and delivered in excess of 40,000 outdoor sermons; he preached in slums and prisons, anywhere people would listen to his message of religious regeneration. The emphasis on personal conversion, warm fellowship, and fervent preaching made Methodism attractive to thousands of people inside and outside the Anglican church. One important factor in the spread of Methodism was the hymnody; the Methodist hymnal, said Wesley, was a "distinct and full account of scriptural Christianity." The hymns were comforting and easy to sing; they reassured people about God's love for them.

Methodism, as a revivalist movement within the Church of England, was never intended to become a separate religious group; Methodists were members of the Anglican church, and Methodism was their style of fellowship and religious revival. It was a means of regeneration within the church, as Methodists desired inner holiness and wanted to live lives of prayer, discipline, and fellowship. To maintain a disciplined prayer life for converts, Wesley established Methodist societies and classes and specified weekly prayer meetings and other means of communication and fellowship. All these disciplinary innovations made Methodists *feel* separate from the Church of England. They were not separate, however, as long as they were dependent on the Anglican church for sacraments and ordination. The English Methodists did not become a separate body until 1897.

While the scientific revolution and the Enlightenment inspired Deism and a reaction to it, the migration of various religious groups to America caused further religious changes in the seventeenth and eighteenth centuries. We look next at the American context and the changes it engendered.

THE AMERICAN CONTEXT

We have to step back for a moment to the seventeenth century to understand the American experience in the eighteenth century. Puritan Congregationalists and Presbyterians who did not stay in England fled to America in the early part of the seventeenth century; the Pilgrim colony at Plymouth was founded in 1620 by the first of such groups. In 1648, representatives of the Congregational churches of New England met in Cambridge, Massachusetts, where they adopted *A Platform of Church Discipline.* The statement, which quickly became known as the Cambridge Platform, was not a creed but a plan of action based on Congregational principles. One of the points stressed in the Cambridge Platform was *covenant theology*. Puritan New England was founded not on principles of religious toleration but on federal or covenant theology. The Puritans believed that God operated in history through covenants and was now forming a new covenant with them in this new land; interpretations of covenant theology had an important influence on the political and religious order in New England. Because the community was a covenanted one, each member of the community was to follow God's law as it was found in the Bible and enforced by local religious and civil magistrates. Puritanism in America's early years was a powerful religious force, a thriving community.

Nevertheless, by the middle of the eighteenth century, religion became less important in many people's lives, and the Puritan ideal was crumbling. Although preachers accused people of infidelity and called them to return to the principles of the covenant, they did not respond to the challenges of the Puritan ideal, perhaps because they were occupied with settling the new land. Puritanism lost much of its persuasive power. By the middle of the eighteenth century, survival was no longer the primary issue in people's lives; Puritan exhortations about fear of the Lord did not strike responsive chords in people. Ideas from the Enlightenment—a reasonable God

People

The Genius of the Great Awakening: Jonathan Edwards

Jonathan Edwards (1703–1758), a leading figure in the revival movement known as the First Great Awakening (1740s), was one of the greatest theologians America has ever produced. His life and character epitomized the diverse and sometimes conflicting strands that made up American evangelicalism: great learning and commitment to higher education combined with high moral standards and emphasis on the emotions. In a time when some believers thought one had to be either intellectually or emotionally inclined in their religious practice, Edwards proved that one could do both. Indeed, his preaching strongly affirmed the need to be both intellectually rigorous and emotionally vulnerable to God's grace.

Edwards was born in the colony of Connecticut well before the American Revolution. His father was a Puritan pastor who nurtured his son's genius. By the time he was thirteen, Jonathan Edwards was fluent in Latin, Greek, and Hebrew. When he graduated from the Collegiate School of Connecticut (known today as Yale University) in 1720, he was at the top of his class and had written a work of philosophical speculation on the nature of being. Like many of the great religious figures we have studied, Edwards one day had an unexpected, life-changing experience. While reading his Bible, he had a clear sense "of the glory of the Divine Being." He became acutely and joyously aware of God's absolute sovereignty and of his own dependence upon God.

As a preacher in Northampton, Massachusetts, Edwards worked to foster this intense feeling in the members of his church. His powerful preaching and obvious personal conviction led to the beginnings of a religious revival in America starting in 1735. We can find the narrative of this revival in his book *A Faithful Narrative of the Surprising Work of God*. If the revival was a good thing—as Edwards clearly believed it to be—it was also an event that disrupted his life. His rigorous standards of congregational purity divided his church and led to his dismissal in 1750. After a period of preaching to Native Americans and white settlers in Stockbridge, he became the president of Princeton (1758) but died shortly thereafter from a smallpox vaccine.

Edwards was able to combine critical study of the Bible, orthodox Calvinism, and emotional Pietism in his theology. He developed a highly elaborate apocalyptic theory (postmillennialism) that emphasized the need to prepare the elect for the coming kingdom of God. As a Puritan divine, he accepted and defended the Calvinist doctrines of human depravity and divine predestination (see the Calvinist TULIP on pp. 94–95). But his highly intellectual approach to theology never lost sight of the practical work of revival and pastoral care. God's grace, he said, bestows on the elect "a divine and spiritual light" that gives the soul "a true sense of the divine excellency of the things revealed in the word of God" and brings the soul into a "saving close [contact] with God."

---

and the advantages of religious toleration—undermined the Puritan system, which was built on a sovereign (not always reasonable or understandable) God and intolerance of other forms of religious expression. The lures of the modern world—mercantilism and commercialism—affected Americans as it had Europeans: they were often more interested in the adventure of making money than they were in the drama of salvation. Within this context, two different movements are worthy of attention: the revivalist impulse of the Great Awakening and the rationalist religion of Deism in its American form.

The Great Awakening

The eighteenth century began with a religious decline. It is not clear how many of the American colonists were church members: probably only a few. Religious indifference was as much a part of the American scene as it was in Europe. One of the revivifying factors for European Christianity was Pietism; American Christianity was regenerated by revivalism in a movement known as the Great Awakening, a series of revivals that spread throughout the American colonies from 1725 until the 1760s. The Great Awakening cut across denominational lines and engendered a spirit of religious cooperation based on shared religious feeling. The revivalist movement began in specific churches through the efforts of charismatic preachers. Theodorus Frelinghuysen (1692–1747), a member of the German Reformed church, was influenced by Pietism. He came to America in 1720 to preach personal repentance and a more emotional expression of religion to people of several Dutch Reformed churches. Gilbert Tennent (1703–1764), a Presbyterian minister influenced by Frelinghuysen, brought the revivalist message to Presbyterians and to Christians of the middle colonies. The most famous figure of the period was Jonathan Edwards (1703–1758), a Congregationalist theologian and preacher responsible for the New England phase of the Great Awakening. By the 1740s, these evangelical preachers had high hopes for a religious revival in America; there was, after all, a religious revival occurring in England under the impulse of Methodism, and American Christians were quite enthusiastic about a new awakening of religious fervor. About this time, George Whitefield, Wesley's friend and a phenomenally successful preacher, came to America. Whitefield was a strong Calvinist-Methodist who took the country by storm. In his zealous preaching, tireless travel, and contagious religious excitement, he set the pattern for roving revivalist preaching in the colonies for years to come.

American Evangelicalism was born in the Great Awakening: it emerged from the Reformed tradition and the Puritan experience, but it also stressed new forms and some new content in the Christian message. The religious strategy of Evangelicalism is designed to elicit a response: it stresses new birth, which is sudden and which determines whether one is or is not a Christian; the importance of the *emotions* to demonstrate that the conversion is of the heart and not just of the head; and the *sufficiency of God,* underlining the Calvinist preoccupations of the message. This last point underwent some rather profound changes in subsequent revivalist movements, but during the Great Awakening, God's sovereignty was a fundamental tenet; evangelists recognized that God glories in a person's absolute dependence, that God alone grants the conversion experience.

The Great Awakening regenerated American Christianity, but it also caused further divisions within it. Tennent's preaching about the dangers of an unconverted ministry caused a division within the Presbyterian church: New Side Presbyterians welcomed the revivalist message; Old Side Presbyterians repudiated it. The Congregational church split into New Lights and Old Lights. Charles Chauncy (1705–1787) was the outspoken opponent of revivalism within the Congregational church and the leader of the Old Lights. He was a spokesman for the rationalism of the Enlightenment and a forerunner of the Unitarian schism in the Congregational church in the nineteenth century. Even those who favored the message and tactics of the Great

Concept

Deism and the American Revolution

Deism is a form of natural (as opposed to supernatural) religion that made its appearance in history toward the end of the seventeenth century. In a cultural climate that welcomed political common sense and Newtonian physics, some philosophers thought it was time to imagine God in scientific terms. A God who worked miracles and interfered with the natural laws of the universe did not make sense to them. A church dominated by priests, dedicated to rituals or based on biblical principles, was not logical. They needed a concept of God to explain the order of the universe—but they did not need religion.

Many of America's founders were Deists (or influenced by Deism), who found in this new religion a way to believe in ultimate values and to support the American Revolution. According to Deists, the superstition and blind obedience required by traditional religion upheld monarchy. Deism, on the other hand, by upholding reason and tolerance of differences, promoted democracy. Thomas Jefferson actually created his own "Gospel" by collecting sayings of Jesus that taught traditional morality or condemned traditional religious practices; he omitted accounts of Jesus working miracles. The American patriot whose religious views were the most controversial was Thomas Paine (1737–1809), whose best-selling pamphlet *Common Sense* rallied the American colonists to the cause of independence.

Paine is a good exemplar of Deism because his views are so clear and sharp. In 1793, Paine was in France participating in their revolution. In that turbulent atmosphere, he wrote a pamphlet, *The Age of Reason,* that attacked both atheism (the position of radical revolutionaries) and traditional Christianity. On the one hand, Paine argued that the Bible was an incompetent history full of immoral tales and that traditional religion was profoundly undemocratic. As he saw it, priests were unnecessary and dangerous because they tried to stand between God and humanity and because they encouraged people to accept certain teachings without question. On the other hand, Paine argued that God's existence is evident in the beauty and order of the natural world. For him, reasonable, natural religion promotes morality, tolerance, and the critical thinking necessary for the flourishing of democracy.

Deism, especially as found in the works of Tom Paine, imagined a world at peace in which people of different faiths would emphasize their shared belief in God and would agree to disagree about other matters. However influential these views were in the political thinking of some of America's founders, they were also profoundly shocking to others. Paine's position—that rational belief in God as taught by Deism is fundamental to democracy—was misunderstood by later Americans. Theodore Roosevelt (president of the United States from 1901 to 1909) called Paine a "filthy little atheist." Deism has sometimes been called the "halfway house to atheism" because it limits the ways in which people can relate to God. By insisting on a religion whose tenets are wholly in harmony with reason and nature, Deism rejects revelation, miracles, mysticism, intercessory prayer, a good deal of the Bible, and a God who has a personal interest in human life—the very things that are foundational to Christianity.

Awakening argued about the place of the emotions: radicals said that the heart alone accounted for conversion; moderates recognized the importance of the heart but did not want to deny the importance of an intellectual understanding of Christianity as well.

Deism in America

Many of the founding fathers of America were Deists: Benjamin Franklin (1706–1790) and Thomas Jefferson (1743–1826) were both deeply affected by the rationalism of the Enlightenment; both believed that religion could be reduced to ethical consciousness and good moral conduct. Deism, remember, was a reasonable religion; doctrines not understandable through reason—miracles or the doctrine of the Trinity—were denied. Many of the accents of Deism are echoed in the Declaration of Independence: reason, religious toleration, optimism about the pursuit of happiness, and a trust in a reasonable God. Deism was able to attract people because it stood in judgment of many of the troublesome religious trends of the time: it was against dogmatism, sectarian infighting, enthusiasm, and clericalism. On those grounds, it appealed to many people who were formally connected with churches.

Growing Denominationalism

By the end of the eighteenth century, America was an independent nation with a highly diverse religious population. During the early years of settlement, there was reason to predict regional churches in America—different religious groups tended to settle together in different regions—but by the end of the eighteenth century, *denominationalism* was a fact of American religious life. Many different churches were allowed to coexist peacefully within the same region. As a consequence of the Enlightenment, the U.S. Constitution supported the "great experiment" of religious freedom and toleration. No church was supported by the state, nor did the state interfere with the internal life of the churches. The separation of church and state supported a relatively new religious idea—voluntarism—whereby church membership was understood to be purely a matter of personal choice.

The census of 1790 showed the following numbers of Protestant churches in America: Congregational, 749; Presbyterian, 495; Baptist, 457; Anglican, 406; Lutheran, 240; German Reformed (Calvinist), 201; Quaker, 200; and Dutch Reformed, 127. There were no figures in that census for Roman Catholics because Catholics were still not welcome in the English colonies: they were not allowed to live in some places and were not permitted to hold public office or own land in others. In 1785, there were fewer than 25,000 Roman Catholics in a population of 4 million; there were fifty-six churches.

Roman Catholics Though scarce in the English colonies, Roman Catholics were the dominant religious group in the Mississippi basin and large parts of the Southwest and California by the end of the eighteenth century. Catholics had come to the New World with the Spanish and French explorers and settled in French and Spanish territories. The city of New Orleans and the southern Louisiana territory were predominantly French Catholic, and Catholics of Spanish descent had established settlements and churches in New Mexico, California, and parts of Texas.

Quakers, Mennonites, and Amish The religious climate of Pennsylvania was unique in the American colonies and made it a haven for a variety of religious groups that were unwelcome or actively persecuted in other colonies. William Penn (1644–1718) was a convinced Quaker whose interest in founding an American colony was motivated by principles of religious freedom and liberty of conscience. The federal theology of the Puritan colonies did not allow religious toleration, and many of the other colonies had legislated restrictions against one religious group or another (usually Roman Catholics, Quakers, and Anabaptists). Penn founded his colony as a "holy experiment" and established it upon a constitution that permitted all forms of worship compatible with monotheism. Mennonites and Amish settled there and moved west from there in the nineteenth and twentieth centuries. The Quakers also settled in Pennsylvania. Their positions, especially their pacifism, made them victims of persecution. Their history in eighteenth-century America is a relatively quiet one; they separated themselves from the rest of the society by their plain dress, their obscure biblical forms of speech, and their avoidance of worldly ways.

BRETHREN The Brethren originally settled in Germantown, Pennsylvania. But they were persecuted during the Revolutionary War for their refusal to participate in it, and the geographical scattering of the Brethren occurred at this time. They experienced one minor schism but not over pacifist principles: the Ephrata Community advocated celibacy and mystical religious experience and formed as a separate group in 1728 but lasted as a society less than 100 years.

LUTHERANS As the Lutherans settled into the colonies, they maintained ties to the churches in their diverse homelands (Germany, the Netherlands) and did not form wider organizations in America until the late eighteenth century.

PURITANS (PRESBYTERIANS AND CONGREGATIONALISTS) The Puritans divided denominationally into Congregationalists and Presbyterians, the major religious groups within the colonies. Both groups were regenerated during the Great Awakening, and both groups experienced some division because of the revivalist nature of that regeneration, as we noted earlier.

BAPTISTS The Baptists, led by Roger Williams (1603–1683), had originally grown out of the Congregational church in England and continued to grow and to attract members of that church. During the Great Awakening, hundreds of people separated from the Congregational church to become Baptists. The decline of the Baptist religion during the first half of the eighteenth century was totally reversed during the Great Awakening; by the end of the eighteenth century, the Baptists were the largest single Christian denomination in the United States, with their greatest strength in the South.

ANGLICANS The Anglican church in America was supported by the British crown and suffered many of the vicissitudes of seventeenth-century English history. The early Anglican communities reflected the variety of opinion within the Church of England. The most pressing problem for the American Anglican church was the lack of native bishops; for complex political reasons, bishops were not sent to the American colonies. With the support of the English government, Anglicans established missionary societies, colleges, and influential churches. These gains, however, were outweighed by their liabilities: Anglicans were politically suspect during the Revolution, their ministers were forced to go back to England for ordination (by a bishop), they tended to attract mostly aristocratic people and had little common appeal, and they refused to participate in the Great Awakening. In 1789, the Anglican church in America reformed itself as a separate entity within the Church of England: it was in communion with the Church of England, but it established its own episcopacy and called itself by a new name, the Protestant Episcopal church.

METHODISTS The situation for Methodist societies in America changed the course of Methodist history. Once Anglican priests (who could administer the sacraments) began to return to England during the Revolution, American Methodists were left without access to the sacraments. In response to this situation, John Wesley ordained two lay leaders as deacons and elders and appointed a superintendent for the American group. Wesley was a minister in the Church of England and knew that ordinations could be valid only when performed by a bishop. By the end of the eighteenth century, however, he had become convinced that bishops and priests differed from each other in terms of function but not in terms of power. His ordination of the two lay leaders, therefore, was done in good faith and with no intention of forming a separate denomination. Thomas Coke (1747–1814) was the man appointed by Wesley to be the superintendent of American Methodists; he in turn ordained Francis Asbury (1745–1816) as a general superintendent at the Christmas conference of Methodist preachers held in Baltimore in 1784. At that conference, the American Methodists established themselves as a separate denominational group with the name Methodist Episcopal church. Asbury assumed the title of bishop and, despite severe remonstrances from Wesley, would not relinquish it. When Asbury first came to America in 1771, there were 1,200 Methodists in various Methodist societies and prayer groups; when he died, there were more than 214,000 members of the Methodist Episcopal church.

SUMMARY By the end of the eighteenth century, a wonderful and somewhat surprising arrangement had taken root in America: almost every conceivable variety of Christianity was practiced in relatively peaceful coexistence with other groups and even with professed Deists. The struggle for religious freedom was more complicated than we have indicated here. The Baptists, especially under the leadership of Roger Williams and John Leland, worked very hard to secure freedom of worship for all, including Jews. Still, some groups continued to feel the sting of religious persecution; sectarians and Roman Catholics encountered prejudicial laws and bigoted behavior from some of their neighbors well into the nineteenth century. For the most part, however, Christians in America were free to practice their religion without interference from the government and without hostility from other groups.

CONCLUSION

The Reformation continued in Europe, stimulated in part by a growing antagonism between science and religion. Although significant religious growth occurred throughout Europe, we have focused mainly on England, where the arguments between Anglicans and Puritans (and later, the influence of Pietism) produced a rich variety of religious responses. Representatives of nearly all Christian groups moved to America in the seventeenth and eighteenth centuries and settled in specific regions of the country. The Great Awakening regenerated much of Protestant Christianity in America and stimulated new growth in many churches. The American experience engendered two new denominations that had formerly been part of the Church of England: the Protestant Episcopal church remained in communion with the Church of England but acquired its own separate hierarchy; the Methodist Episcopal church separated from the Church of England—against Wesley's intentions and desires—to form a new religious body. By the end of the eighteenth century, the American religious climate was ready to foster the phenomenal growth that characterized nineteenth-century Christianity.

Focal Points for Discussion

1. The Enlightenment challenged Christians to base their religious beliefs on reason and logic. Deists tried to meet this challenge. In doing so, did they abandon the core beliefs of Christianity?
2. Another response to the Enlightenment was a renewed focus on the emotional elements of religion. Which groups were formed in this way? How are they similar and different as expressions of Christianity?
3. The American religious climate led to denominationalism: people could choose their religion and even whether or not to be religious. What are the benefits and shortcomings of this arrangement for both Christianity and America?

Christianity in the Modern World: Context and Creativity in the Nineteenth and Twentieth Centuries

PART III

The third part of this book situates Christianity within the modern world so that the growth and diversity from the nineteenth to the twenty-first century make contextual sense. It forms a bridge to the last part of the book, which looks at contemporary problems and challenges. We need to remember that our goal is not a comprehensive understanding of Christian history but a general sense of how and why so many different forms of Christianity developed. The purpose of this part is to sketch the problems offered to Christianity in the modern context.

The most perplexing question one faces when attempting to discuss the "modern world" is finding a date for its beginning. What constitutes modernity? Is it scientific discovery and the unsettling of the old notion that the earth is the center of the universe? Or is it geographical exploration, which opened up new frontiers for Christianity in the Far East and eventually in a whole New World? Is it new philosophical challenges, which raised vexing questions about the relationship between reason and revelation? Or is it the new political arrangements, national rulers in the seventeenth century giving way to various forms of republican and democratic governments throughout the eighteenth and nineteenth centuries?

In some ways, all of these things constitute the fabric of modernity and must act as a backdrop against which we can understand the major developments of Christianity. But what is at the bottom of all the newness? What caused Christians to continue to search for new expressions of their religion? What, in other words, is the modern challenge?

There is no simple explanation. Beginning with the attention to human achievement during the Renaissance and continuing through the scientific revolution and the Enlightenment, the focus of human life shifted from the supernatural to the natural realm. If you were to walk through an art gallery arranged historically, you would notice that medieval art featured religious themes—paintings of events in the life of Jesus, for example—and mythological figures, but Renaissance artists began to concentrate on human subjects and objects in the natural world. By the nineteenth century, religious subjects were only a small part of the artistic repertoire.

The medieval worldview divided reality into two realms, heaven and earth. The qualities of heaven were similar to the qualities of God: heaven was the realm of grace, eternity, absolute truth, and revelation; it was God's place and the "true home" of all creatures. The qualities of earth were quite different: earth was the created order, the realm of nature, time, change, and human reason; it was a temporary home, a testing place from which one hoped to escape. In this model, the church was the bridge between the two worlds, the institution that offered human beings the means to get from this world to the next.

Because God had intervened in human history—in the Bible and in the life and mission of Jesus—the church believed it had its mission, its laws, and its authority from God: it was the place where God's work on earth was done, and its dogmas, symbols, and authority were, like God, changeless, eternal, and absolute. Churches functioned on earth as Christ had during his lifetime, with utter authority. As such, the church could demand obedience, and it understood itself to be in an unassailable position. Modernity challenged this understanding by posing a series of difficult questions and developing a set of new structures over a 200- to 300-year period. The increasingly prominent role played by biblical criticism; the astonishing growth and diversity of religion (especially in America) in the nineteenth century; and the destabilizing effects of modern industrialism, science, urbanism, and so on, led to some remarkable new religious forms and ideas.

Chapter 7 deals with the challenges of modernity, an attempt to concentrate on the kinds of issues raised since the eighteenth century that many Christians have found threatening. We will talk in general terms about ways various forms of Christianity reacted to those challenges. Chapter 8 focuses on the proliferation of new Christian movements in the New World in the nineteenth and early twentieth centuries. Because the American context was so rich in new religious experiments, we will concentrate our energies there. Finally, in Chapter 9, we will look at the beginnings of the missionary movement to get a general understanding of the state of Christian cooperation in the world and to get some sense of Christianity as a worldwide religion, responsive to a complex set of challenges raised in increasingly diverse cultural contexts. All these chapters are meant to lead logically to the final part of the book, which deals with some contemporary issues as a set of different angles from which to appreciate the diversity of Christianity.

Again, it is important to remember that Christianity has survived partly because of its genius for both accommodation and resistance to trends in the world surrounding it. The early Christians adapted themselves to the realities of Greek and Roman culture even as they resisted some of the claims of those cultures. Medieval Christianity shaped itself in relation to the political realities of the time and imposed its own order on the world in ways that were both beautiful and dangerous. Christians during the Reformation looked back to the ancient church for models of interpretation and authority and also made realistic adaptations to the newly emerging modern world. Since the Reformation, Christianity in its many forms has had to define and redefine itself in relation to momentous new intellectual, political, and cultural movements. This part of the book explains the general terms of some of those movements and shows some of the ways Christians learned to cope with them to survive.

CHRISTIANITY AND MODERNITY

CHAPTER 7

We take the modern world for granted. Most of us have no experience of a world in which, as in medieval times, church and state were united in a single task. Most of us cannot fathom a world in which the church was "established"—that is to say, supported and sometimes governed by the state.

We have to begin, therefore, by remembering the experience of the very early church. Christianity was born into a Roman world where church and state were separate entities. Christianity was one religion among many, in no way favored by the empire and not thought to be any truer or worthier than any other religion. Constantine changed this system dramatically because, as we have seen, he perceived the power and usefulness of Christianity and sought to merge his political ambitions—the re-creation of the Roman Empire—with the missionary enthusiasm and attractiveness of early Christianity. The Christian empire, as Constantine understood it, was a felicitous blend of political power and religious energy. We have seen that this model led to centuries of controversy and to ingenious attempts to define the ultimate source of authority, and we have seen the emergence and triumph of medieval Christianity.

The Reformation did not challenge the basic model. The political assumptions of Luther, Calvin, Zwingli, the English monarchs, and the Puritans were similar to those of the Catholics: the state and church were linked in common cause and cooperated with one another for the general good of society. The only dissenting voice to this understanding of church-state relations was that of the radical reformers: Anabaptists were considered dangerous by both Catholics and Protestants precisely because they conceived of religion as a separate reality. Mennonites, Hutterites, Brethren, Amish, and Quakers understood their allegiances to be entirely defined by the Bible, and they used their interpretations of discipleship to resist the demands of the state to pay taxes, to swear oaths, and to fight in wars. Anabaptists were, therefore, troublesome to other Christians, but they were a small movement and their ideas did not reconstitute society.

The separation of church and state, which characterizes much of the modern world, was indebted to a series of political philosophies and revolutionary movements in the seventeenth and eighteenth centuries. The American Revolution and the French Revolution in particular—and later, the Russian Revolution—led to the disestablishment of the church and forced Christians to ask themselves what it meant to be a Christian in the modern world. If religion was no longer established, neither was it required. Modern people could choose not to be religious at all.

SECULARIZATION: THE NEW PHILOSOPHY AND POLITICS

From the seventeenth to the nineteenth century, people in general were faced with a new set of intellectual and social problems. Secularization, the shift from a theological to a humanistic worldview, was a slow, subtle, and pervasive process that occurred in an enormously complicated context. Scientific discoveries focused attention on the natural world and suggested that men and women could figure out the problems of their lives for themselves without recourse to the "mysterious" and intervening aspects of revealed religion.

Before the Enlightenment, people asked themselves difficult questions about life. What can I know? What must I do? What may I hope for? Christianity provided answers to those questions: Protestants and Catholics differed on the sources of authority for the answers, but they agreed that the questions had certain religious answers. Enlightenment thinkers and scientists, however, argued that the questions needed to be asked again and that there were probably no certain answers. Early modern philosophers did not so much question the *sources* of religious authority as they questioned the whole *idea* of religious authority. To their way of thinking, religious authority, with its reliance on revelation, providence, miracles, and other supernatural phenomena, was a kind of backward mentality that preferred superstition and ignorance to scientific inquiry and demonstration.

Enlightenment philosophers and scientists wanted people to use their reason and to think for themselves. They attempted to involve religious people in an adventure—some would say a crisis—of freedom. They themselves experienced the terror and delight of uncertainty: they were free from the fetters of faith and so had the exhilarating experience of figuring things out for themselves, but they were also hostile to faith and so could reap none of its rewards and assurances.

The spiritual odyssey of one of the eighteenth-century French philosophers, Denis Diderot (1713–1784), may help explain the general mood of the times. He was born a Catholic but found the superstition and unverifiability of some of the church's claims troublesome, so he became a theist; that is, he still believed in a personal God but without the institutional support and, to his mind, superstitious nonsense of the church.

As he explored the conclusions of the new science, he was led to questions and speculations about the place of religion in human life. If the universe was a realm in which the laws of cause and effect were operative, he reasoned, then divine providence was not necessary. Humanity did not need a God who breaks into the world to make things happen, Newton had said; events occur according to scientific laws, and human beings ought to question authority and to demand that "truth" have the certainty of mathematics. It was therefore reasonable to conclude that failure to prove something meant that it was not true.

You can see where this position leads: the Holy Spirit, inspiration, providence, and miracles—the mainstays of religious belief—could not be proved with mathematical certainty and so must be rejected. Still, the created order had a logic within it, and one could show that some cosmic intelligence must have made the world. There must be some kind of supreme being, Diderot reasoned, and so he became a Deist. He believed in an impersonal God who created the world and established a set of scientific laws to govern its events.

As a Deist, Diderot tried to live in harmony with the laws of the universe and to be reverent in his feelings for the Supreme Being, but he was not personally involved with God and found the God of the Bible to be a childish belief. Eventually, as Diderot continued to ask questions, he was led to skepticism and wondered what, if anything, could ever really be proved. Finally, he said, he was forced by the processes of his own quest to become an atheist, to believe formally that God did not exist at all. He found atheism unsatisfying but true, whereas he experienced Catholicism as emotionally attractive but false.

We have introduced Diderot here not to make a slippery-slope argument for religious belief but simply to suggest that the kinds of questions the early modern philosophers asked were not intended to provide *comfort.* Diderot was a pioneer. He looked backward in time and saw a medieval world that was dangerous and violent, where men and women were forced by circumstances to submit to things they could not understand, where nature dominated the human spirit. Diderot looked forward to a time when humanity could dominate nature, learn its secrets, and change the world. He imagined a future in which people could be safe, free, and in command of their own destinies. To his way of thinking, such a shift in the balance of power required a real revolution of spirit, a heroic resistance to fate. The Enlightenment, therefore, was not simply a quest for knowledge. It was an attempt to impose one's rational will on the environment, and it required self-reliance, daring, and a sense of adventure.

The political results of much of this new thinking led to the great revolutions of the eighteenth century. In an age of turmoil, new political leaders forged concepts of democracy and talked about rights and progress. By 1800, after the American and French Revolutions, the notion of equality had become a profound new political value. It is not easy to understand the momentous shifts that the revolutionary period brought to government unless we contrast them with the ideas of absolute monarchy that were advanced in the medieval world by the church and in the seventeenth century by monarchs like Louis XIV. Even without having much sense of political history, we can still understand these new political ideas when we compare them with what we already know about religion.

Let us remember for a moment what religion looked like in the period following the Reformation. Millions of people were killed, especially in Germany, in brutal religious wars. The Thirty Years War (1618–1648) was the last set of wars fought for purely religious reasons. The treaty that ended those bloody conflicts, the Peace of Westphalia, marked a significant military change from wars fought for and by churches to wars fought for reasons of state.

Besides igniting religious wars, the Protestant and Catholic Reformations extended medieval notions of religious intolerance to new levels. Religious persecution and torture of Catholics by Protestants and of Protestants by Catholics—not to mention the persistent persecution of Jews by Christians—were scandals that endured

Controversy

Creationism: Christianity and Science

Charles Darwin's discoveries concerning the age of the world, the process of natural selection, and the process of evolution scandalized many Christians. *The Origin of Species* (1859) questioned the Bible's picture of creation, in which God creates all forms of life, including the first human beings, Adam and Eve, just as they are, in 7 days. Christians disagreed sharply about evolutionary theory, one of the distinctive features of modernity. Those inclined to accept Darwin, at least in some form, saw in his work further testimony of God's majesty and inventiveness. Others saw Darwin's conclusions as a direct contradiction of the biblical story of creation and, therefore, a rejection of biblical authority and perhaps even of God. How Christians respond to Darwin illustrates the complexity of Christianity's relationship to modernity.

Darwin's theories had a wrenching impact on many Christian churches, and they forced a public debate of unprecedented importance in the United States in the early twentieth century when John Scopes, a science teacher in Dayton, Tennessee, was arrested for teaching evolution in his high school biology classes. A Tennessee law made it illegal to teach anything but creationism as found in the Bible. The Scopes trial—dubbed the "Monkey Trial" by reporters—attracted national attention in part because Clarence Darrow, America's most famous trial attorney, was the lawyer for the defense, while William Jennings Bryan (a political leader who had run for president of the United States) was the attorney for the prosecution. Although the trial held American fundamentalism up to national ridicule, Scopes was found guilty.

By the 1960s, however, most public schools taught the theory of evolution as the only scientifically recognized explanation for the origin and diversity of species. Conservative Christians sought to challenge this in two ways. On the one hand, in the *Mozert v. Hawkins* case in Tennessee in the mid-1980s, seven fundamentalist families sued their school board, claiming that the teaching of evolution undermined their religious values and so violated their constitutional right to free exercise of their religion. The courts disagreed, ruling that "mere exposure" to values such as tolerance, relativism, and evolution did not violate their right to believe otherwise.

On the other hand, conservative Christians increasingly present creationism not as opposed to science but as a kind of science. Proponents of creationism disagree on many points, such as the age of the earth and how literally to follow the Bible, but they all attribute creation to some supernatural agent rather than to the entirely natural process of evolution. Intelligent design theory, the most recent form of creationism, argues that the great complexity of certain life forms implies the existence of some designer.

In 2004, the school board of Dover, Pennsylvania, required teachers to read to students a statement that suggested that intelligent design was a scientifically valid alternative to evolution. In *Kitzmiller v. Dover Area School District,* a group of parents challenged this policy as an unconstitutional promotion of a religious view. The judge agreed, ruling that intelligent design is not science but a religious claim. In contrast, he said, the theory of evolution limits itself to natural explanations and is neutral as to whether there is a God.

Although creationism appears to resist modernity, in fact conservative Christians adapt to modern ways of thinking when they present their beliefs as scientific.

into the twentieth century. The frenzy of persecution against witches that began in the latter part of the fifteenth century lasted almost until the beginning of the nineteenth and found most of its support in the treatises and fears of religious writers. And the resistance to new scientific discoveries, like those of Galileo, came from religious authorities and appeared, by scientific standards, arbitrary and unreasonable. All these characteristics provided the immediate context for those Enlightenment thinkers who urged skepticism about religious authority, tolerance for different viewpoints, and a general sense of human equality.

Enlightenment thinkers and new politicians looked at the world around them and saw how old models of church and state had led to persecution and inequality. The Anglican church was established in England and barely tolerated dissenters. Colonial powers in the New World attempted to govern and tax the residents without their consent. Upper classes in France asserted their authority over commoners and gloried in their nobility. City folk felt superior to their country cousins, and believers fought with unbelievers, Christians with Jews, Catholics with Protestants. European immigrants to the New World exploited Native Americans and imported black people as slaves. The idea that "all men were created equal," while it did less for women and minority races than it did for white, Anglo-Saxon, Protestant men, still introduced a new idea into the New World. The constitutional guarantee for freedom of religion and the insistence on separation of church and state would have profound consequences for religion.

CHALLENGES TO SECULARIZATION

Secularization did not occur without resistance from religious institutions and individuals. By 1800, religion was only one interest among many and had to compete with science, industry, and new ideas. This very situation that put religious belief on a plane with atheism, skepticism, and other nonreligious systems was profoundly disconcerting to believers and led to a whole range of responses, as denominations attempted to defend themselves from or dialogue with these secular options. In the sixteenth century, Protestant and Catholic reformers relied on creeds and religious authority, but Christianity had suffered a general decline in the seventeenth century because the authority of reason offered an attractive alternative to many people. The idea of a world based on tolerance, reason, logic, and an ability to control one's destiny was a persuasive one.

The political independence of the New World and the notion that human beings were perfectible rather than naturally depraved gave a sense of adventure to emigration to and new life in a democratic New World. When millions of people migrated to the American colonies, they found that they had to rely on themselves, and they gloried in self-reliance. Old religious notions of predestination seemed obsolete in a land where, it was said, anyone could find work, prosper, and rise to undreamed levels of power and respect.

By 1800, the arts were removed from their primarily religious concerns: music, painting, and sculpture focused on human models, and thinkers talked more about ethical ideals than about religious mysteries. The age of reason challenged religion and set the stage for the battles that religious believers would carry into the twentieth century.

At the beginning of the nineteenth century, an attempt was made in Europe to restore the old regime, to reassert the claims of monarchy. By midcentury, however, a

SPIRITUALITY

God in a Scientific Age

In the thirteenth century, Thomas Aquinas responded to the scientific writings of Aristotle by creating a theological system that combined natural and supernatural theology. God was discoverable through reason and found in revelation. When modern experimental science came to dominate intellectual discourse in the eighteenth and nineteenth centuries, however, many thinkers concluded that they no longer needed the supernatural. Since God's attributes could be deduced from nature, they said, God was clearly evident in the laws of the universe, and religion need not be mysterious.

The physics and mathematics of Isaac Newton (1643–1727) allowed philosophers to derive the more or less mechanistic God of Deism, sometimes described as a "watchmaker God" (who winds up the universe and then lets it tick away). Newton and his contemporaries assumed that nature was reasonable and its laws clear. Subsequent generations, however, questioned the idea that the universe operated within the parameters of discernible and predictable laws. Whereas atoms were once described in fixed terms, new atomic models were dynamic and ruled by "uncertainty" principles.

Einstein and others opened a universe that was 300 billion, billion light years of expanding space and older than anyone could imagine. Some cosmologists speculate that there are an almost infinite number of universes and dimensions existing simultaneously with our own. New scientific explanations like chaos theory and superstring theory led some religious believers to deepen their suspicions and conclude that science and religion are enemies. Scientist Stephen Jay Gould (1941–2002) drew a less hostile but similar conclusion in *Rocks of Ages* (1999): science and religion are separate worlds that cannot and should not mix.

Some religious believers, however, were able to find a new sense of mystery in the face of scientific discoveries like evolution in the nineteenth century and new cosmologies in the twentieth. Jesuit paleontologist Teilhard de Chardin (1881–1955) was drawn to the wonder of the universe and saw evolution unfolding toward an "Omega Point." He hoped for a Christianity deeply connected to the evolving world, energized by the God of a dynamic, surprising, and spirit-drenched material world. John Haught, in *God After Darwin* (2000), welcomed evolution as a spiritual challenge that can stimulate a new concept of God as a creator who is the cosmic source of possibility, novelty, and beauty.

The sense of mystery that people can find in the subatomic world and the feelings of wonder and awe they have in relation to the heavens have encouraged millions who are alienated from traditional religious discourse to seek new forms of spiritual life.

new series of revolutions had unsettled most monarchical governments, and powerful new ideas threatened to shake the world at its foundations. Karl Marx (1818–1883) interpreted world history in terms of class warfare and delineated a theory of modern socialism. Charles Darwin (1809–1882) postulated his theory of organic evolution and argued that evolution proceeds by the basic rule of the survival of the fittest. In religious philosophy, Ludwig Feuerbach (1804–1872) argued that Christianity is not the decisive force in modern life and stated that his goals included what he called the humanization of religion. Toward the end of the century, Africa was "discovered" and divided among the world's great powers. Finally, the world inhabited by Christians had undergone a profound Industrial Revolution that changed the nature of the family and the economic value of certain kinds of work.

Throughout the century, all realms of life underwent progressive secularization, and religion was forced to reconstitute itself and determine new ways to attract believers. In this tumultuous period, religious institutions and thinkers set new boundaries in which to conduct religious inquiry. The Catholic church, for the most part, adopted a posture of resistance to the modern world. The internal battle within the Roman Catholic church was defined by papal opposition to modernity and by a series of movements that pitted "modernists" (those who hoped for accommodation to the modern world, its theories, and methods) against "ultramontanists" (those who supported strong papal authority). Protestants, because they were already divided on a number of issues, cannot be so easily labeled, but in general, the Protestant churches were also defined by their reactions to modernity, with liberals forging links with the modern world while conservatives resisted any such attempts to accept the terms of modernity.

We will see some of the creative responses to the modern world in the next chapter in the context of American Christianity. In this chapter, however, we need only understand some general characteristics and attitudes as well as some specific movements in the European context.

ROMAN CATHOLICISM AND MODERNITY

The Roman Catholic church reformed itself at the Council of Trent and in many ways was not prepared for the Enlightenment and the scientific and industrial revolutions. The French Revolution was a profound shock to Catholicism, and one place to begin our examination of modern Catholicism is with reactions to that revolution. Try to imagine a country where hierarchy and religious order had been fundamental characteristics of society. Remember the alliances between the early Frankish tribes and the papacy, the power of the pope during the medieval period in France, and then the power of the monarch from the Avignon papacy through the reign of Louis XIV. Then picture a revolution that culminated in the beheading of the king by the people, the overthrow of the notion of privilege based on wealth, and the persecution and dispossession of the Catholic church.

For some, the French Revolution was a great step forward: liberty, equality, and fraternity were meant to be slogans for a whole new order. Royalists and nobles fled or were killed, the church became a department of state without power of its own, and the new government claimed to reflect the power of the people. For others, however, the French Revolution was a tragedy, an end to any semblance of law and order, a descent to mob rule and a rejection of religion.

In November 1789, the National Assembly seized all the property of the Roman Catholic church, approximately one-fifth of the country! You can imagine that the church did not welcome the revolution, and perhaps you can understand why the church tended to greet Napoleon Bonaparte (1769–1821) as a savior. At first, it appeared as if Napoleon's empire would restore order and return Catholicism to its former position of power in France. The Catholic church was soon to find out that Napoleon was not its champion: he wanted to restore some semblance of religious order for his own aims, not for the sake of the church. Paradoxically, when Napoleon imprisoned Pope Pius VII for 5 years, he strengthened rather than weakened the power of Roman Catholicism. A frail pope in prison had the sympathy of Catholics and Protestants and inspired a romantic valorization of the papacy.

People

Unorthodox Humanitarian: Albert Schweitzer

Born in 1875, Albert Schweitzer was a theologian, physicist, musician (an authority on Bach and an accomplished organist), and medical missionary who based his life on his conviction that Christ's central teachings were eschatological in nature. This belief allowed him to postulate a universal concept of ethics that ultimately required total "reverence for life," a concept that suggested itself to him while he was on a river journey in Africa. He saw deep mystical connections in all life and believed that human beings, torn between selfishness (egoism) and generosity (altruism), could look to the spiritual example of Jesus, who laid down his life for his convictions.

Schweitzer was a brilliant man who earned a Ph.D. in philosophy (with a dissertation on Kant), a Ph.D. in theology, and finally, in 1913, a Ph.D. in medicine. His life was an attempt to balance his deep humanitarian principles with his love for science, music, and philosophy. Although Schweitzer was a deeply rooted Lutheran, he was more drawn to Jesus' spirituality than to his historical life. And he believed that the core of Jesus' spirituality was his conviction that the world was about to end. As early as his first published work, *The Mystery of the Kingdom of God* (1901), Schweitzer contended that at the heart of Jesus' teachings was an expectation of the imminent end of the world.

Like others in the then-powerful movement of biblical criticism, Schweitzer wanted to understand religious figures and texts not only from the standpoint of faith but in terms of their surrounding cultural context. In *The Quest of the Historical Jesus* (1906), he argued that Christ's eschatological expectations were like those of his contemporaries and that, when the world did not end, Christ decided that he himself must suffer to turn the wheel of history.

Despite his distinction in the fields of theology and biblical criticism, Schweitzer felt compelled to live a different life. After he earned his doctorate in medicine, he married a nurse and the two of them spent the rest of their lives caring for the sick in western Africa. In 1913, he established a hospital in Gabon (then French Equatorial Africa) and built it into an extensive medical facility, partly because his fame drew attention and financial support to his work. He received the Nobel Peace Prize in 1952.

Schweitzer continued to publish—memoirs, theological reflections, and philosophy—and remained a prominent figure until his death in 1965. His ability to accept the radical demands of the ethics of Jesus while resisting the historical claims of the Gospel make him an unusual man of his time: he was both liberal and radical, mystical and scientific, a scholar and an activist.

The experience of the Roman Catholic church during the revolutionary and Napoleonic years set the stage for Catholicism's battles with the modern world. In the beginning of the nineteenth century, great waves of support enveloped the papacy. As people tried to imagine a world that was free from the disruptions of revolution, some began to look "over the mountains" (hence the name *ultramontanists*) to Rome for a renewed sense of leadership and moral power. To their way of thinking, Enlightenment philosophy, with its rejection of revelation in favor of the power of human reason, had led to tragedy and anarchy. What was needed, they believed, was a strong reassertion of religious authority. The pope became a symbol of international religious order for ultramontanists, who hoped to reclaim the authority of revelation by upholding the power of the papacy to define the terms and limits of religious truth.

Although some of the early nineteenth-century popes were unable to assert their power rigorously—because they were occupied with complicated political problems involving the so-called papal states and various revolutionary moves in Italy—Pope Pius IX (1846–1878), the first of the modern popes, claimed his spiritual authority in no uncertain terms. He began his reign with some liberal reforms, but he quickly retreated to a conservative position in relation to the modern world.

In 1864, Pius IX issued the *Syllabus of Errors,* which summarized eighty modern errors and enjoined Catholics to avoid naturalism, socialism, communism, the conclusions of modern biblical scholarship, modern political arrangements like the separation of church and state, freedom of religion, ethical theories, and even the idea that the Roman Catholic church should reconcile itself with the modern world. In 1870, this pope called the First Vatican Council, which defined papal infallibility and appeared to make future councils unnecessary.

His successor, Pope Leo XIII (1878–1903), was somewhat more accepting of the inevitabilities of the modern world and attempted to define the ways that Catholics could be good citizens in modern liberal states, but he was essentially conservative and unbending about accommodations to modern thought. Leo XIII is remembered for his encyclicals about the narrow limits in which Catholics could pursue some of the conclusions of modern biblical criticism but also for his support of the working classes. In *Rerum Novarum* (1891), he supported both labor unions and private property, thus forging a middle ground between socialism and capitalism.

Pope Pius X (1903–1914) presided over the Catholic church during the modernist controversy, the most difficult crisis to face late nineteenth- and early twentieth-century Catholicism. The modernist controversy involved two uncongenial groups: a loosely connected collection of European scholars who hoped that the Catholic church could make some profound intellectual adjustments to modern biblical scholarship and a tightly organized group of religious authorities who refused to accept any such accommodations. That controversy is too complicated to describe here. Suffice it to say that the pope condemned "modernism" in terms that made it impossible for future Roman Catholic scholars to be anything but defensive in relation to the modern world, and he laid to rest any hope that Roman Catholicism would in any way be defined by the conclusions of modern scholarship.

Roman Catholics who hoped for modernization had to wait for the Second Vatican Council (1962–1965). That council was called to bring Catholicism up to date, but an institution as enormous as the Catholic church, with a history of resistance to the modern world, is not easily changed. Today, many Catholics are energetically involved in serious conflicts about the extent to which the documents of Vatican II can really be understood as an acceptance of modernity. Pope John Paul II (1978–2005) dampened the enthusiasm of postconciliar Catholics who looked for significant changes in Catholic teaching.

PROTESTANTISM AND MODERNITY

Protestantism, as we have seen, experienced phenomenal growth and development from the sixteenth to the nineteenth century. New expressions of Protestant Christianity were formulated, especially in England and in America, and became the soil out of which newer understandings of the Christian life would grow. Protestant

Christians, like their Catholic counterparts, had to respond to the challenges of modernity. And just as one can find liberal Catholics in the nineteenth century, one can find liberal Protestants as well.

The main difference between the two groups lay in the ways internal church controversies were settled. In the Roman Catholic church, liberals were condemned, and those who sought accommodation to the modern world were silenced or forced out of the church. The strong hierarchical model buttressed by clear assertions of papal infallibility in the nineteenth century ensured that Catholicism would have one particular profile, a conservative one that resisted the claims of modernity. In the Protestant churches, there was no such appeal to a single authority. Protestant liberals tended to take up the Enlightenment challenge in a quest for new values, whereas conservative Protestants reacted to modern questions with attempts to reassert traditional orthodoxy or to reclaim traditional values. We will see some of the ways these two groups emerged in the context of nineteenth-century America in the next chapter. Here we need only get a general understanding of differing religious climates and attitudes.

Protestants had to figure out what it meant to be a Christian in the modern world. How could they relate the claims of Christianity to the new conclusions of science? How could they understand the authority of the Bible in relation to new historical studies of biblical literature that threatened some of the traditional beliefs of Christianity? What could they say about divine authority, grace, and the will of God when confronted with theories of personal freedom and human perfectibility? And how could they relate the goals of the church to the goals of society?

We will look at four areas of concern as they affected different kinds of Protestant Christianity: Evangelical Pietism and the Oxford movement were two conservative attempts to respond to modernity, whereas the emergence of biblical criticism and the relation of the Gospel to the social conditions of the world were two liberal responses to the modern world. Because Protestantism is a fluid concept, these four areas have some natural overflow from one group to another and are not intended to be hard-and-fast categories. For example, the attempt to relate the Gospel to the real needs of people in depressed social conditions was a concern of both liberal and conservative Protestants. Still, these four areas can give us a preliminary understanding of some of the background and attitudes that shaped Protestantism throughout the nineteenth century.

Pietism and American Evangelicalism

Evangelicalism has its roots in Europe and its distinctive features from American religious history. The term *Evangelical* was used in sixteenth-century Germany to describe Christians who accepted Luther's principles of salvation through faith alone and the Bible alone as the source of religious authority. In the seventeenth century, German Pietism and English Puritanism both emphasized the importance of personal conversion and Bible-centered faith. Their emphasis on a deeply felt sense of guilt and forgiveness sustained by warm fellowship and community support inspired a new Anabaptist group (Brethren) and a new group within the Anglican church that became a new denomination (Methodists). Early Evangelical Christians emphasized life-transforming personal faith over rational arguments. Some Evangelical churches showed little interest in traditional liturgical expressions like the celebration of the Eucharist, and some thought that one could have an experience of God in one's life and also be drawn to sacramental life.

Pietism and Evangelicalism stressed feelings rather than arguments or dogmas. The Enlightenment claim that everything had to be proved with mathematical certainty led some people to the logical conclusion that religious truths had to be abandoned. For Diderot, as we have seen, atheism was cold comfort but necessary, given the presuppositions of rational philosophy. Diderot is interesting precisely because he kept an emotional longing for traditional religion even as he believed he had to reject its unprovable claims.

Evangelicalism was, in part, a response to this kind of longing. It reasserted Christianity's power to change the lives of men and women. Whether the claims of Christianity could be proved with mathematical certainty was, for Evangelicals, beside the point: a fervent emotional response can touch the human heart, lead to deeply held convictions, and stir religious sensibility. American Evangelicalism is rooted in this sense of a personal relationship with God as experienced in the Great Awakening, that set of enthusiastic revivals that occurred in eighteenth-century America.

Pietism and Evangelicalism had international appeal: Francke and Spener in Holland, Wesley in England, Count Zinzendorf and the Moravians in Bohemia, and Jonathan Edwards and George Whitfield in colonial America were all drawn to a religion based on feelings of absolute dependence on God. Christianity, therefore, was no longer limited to geographical arrangements and treaties, nor was it reduced to ineffectiveness by the hostile claims of the Enlightenment. On the contrary, the claims of Evangelicalism proved that religion was an intensely rich *experience* that could revivify Christianity in a variety of places and in a variety of forms.

Evangelical Pietism, therefore, rejected the demands of Enlightenment thinkers who wanted to force religious beliefs into proof categories. The Evangelical contribution to a worldwide revival of religious interest and to deeply felt religious experience proved to them that religion was stronger than rational philosophy and, in many ways, as compelling as it had been in the early days of the Christian movement, when people experienced the power of Jesus and the attraction of his calls for repentance and new life.

The Oxford Movement

The Oxford movement occurred in England in the early part of the nineteenth century as a reassertion of traditional orthodoxy in the face of what appeared to be a general decline of religious interest. In many ways, it was a return to certainty by way of acceptance of some traditional Roman Catholic doctrines, coupled with a new experience of religious fervor on the part of a small group of young Anglican divines at Oxford University.

The same horrified reactions the Catholic church experienced in the face of the French Revolution also stirred many Christians who were not Catholic: they, too, felt that the revolution threatened the order of the world, and they cried out for a reassertion of religious authority. In addition to revulsion at the French Revolution, the leaders of the Oxford movement shared the perception that the Church of England had grown lax in its religious commitment and that the very belief in God—theism—was threatened by modern industrial life. In July 1833, John Keble (1792–1866), a professor of poetry at Oxford, preached a sermon on "national apostasy" in which he accused the nation of moral laxity and insisted that the only road to salvation lay in a renewed devotion to sacramental Christianity.

The leaders of the Oxford movement—John Henry Newman (1801–1890), William George Ward (1812–1882), Edward B. Pusey (1800–1882)—were not Roman Catholic, nor did they intend to become Roman Catholic, but their appeal to tradition led them to accept and argue for positions that were both Catholic and classically Anglican. They called believers back to the Anglican Book of Common Prayer and extolled the importance of apostolic succession for the proper reception of the sacraments (a traditional Roman Catholic belief).

As the group veered closer to Roman Catholic belief, Newman attempted to restate the beauty of traditional Anglicanism with his book *Via Media* (showing how Anglicanism forged a middle way between Catholicism and traditional Protestantism). Finally, however, many of the Oxford movement thinkers were led to the conclusion that the Roman Catholic church was the true expression of Christianity, and many of them converted to Catholicism. Their actions led to their dismissal from Oxford and the rescinding of their academic degrees, but they also stimulated a renewal of interest in Christianity and in religious argument and practice in England.

The response of the Oxford thinkers to the modern world was similar to that of Catholics, a reassertion of traditional religious authority based on belief in the rightness of ancient Christian tradition and the office of the papacy. The effect of the Oxford movement, however, was to force a renewal of Christianity in England, both in the revival of Roman Catholicism and in the restimulation of Anglicanism. In the late twentieth century, a mostly Anglican movement called Radical Orthodoxy sought to renew theology by a return to classic texts like the church Fathers.

The Biblical Movement

We have seen that Enlightenment thinkers rejected traditional concepts like inspiration, providence, and miracles that were standard expressions of biblical faith, and we will see in the next chapter how the battle between American fundamentalists and liberals was shaped by their different understandings of the possibility of error in the sacred text. In addition to Enlightenment critics, Christians had to deal with the theories of evolutionists like Darwin, whose scientific conclusions directly contradicted the information in the Bible about the creation of the world and humankind.

In response to threats to biblical authority, and in relation to new methods of historical scholarship, a movement of biblical criticism began in the nineteenth century. A critic, remember, is an expert, not one who finds fault, and a biblical critic is one who applies linguistic, archaeological, or historical expertise to biblical texts.

Protestant Christians had long accepted one kind of biblical criticism: the search for the best *textual* edition of the Bible had motivated scholars during the Reformation period and led to a rejection of the Vulgate as the most acceptable Bible for Christians. We have seen how humanist scholars like Erasmus applied themselves to the problems of finding the best edition of the Greek New Testament, and we have noted that Luther's theological insights were indebted, in part, to his interpretation of the Greek text.

Nineteenth-century scholars did not limit themselves to discovering the proper wording of the text: they were interested in historical and literary matters and so asked questions about authorship, date of composition, relationship of biblical materials to other ancient texts, and intention. Though this kind of questioning was not completely new—recall the critical work of Valla, Reuchlin, Erasmus, and others (Chapter 5)—it made major strides in the nineteenth century and caused significant religious turmoil.

Many of the conclusions of nineteenth-century biblical scholars are accepted today by Christians, but they were often resisted at the time and were perceived to threaten the very foundations of biblical faith. For example, the traditional view of the Pentateuch (the first five books of the Old Testament) was relatively simple: Moses was the author and he recorded what God inspired him to write. Julius Wellhausen (1844–1918) showed how the Pentateuch developed historically by applying the science of textual comparison to those first five books. His work, along with that of other scholars, led to the conclusion that the Pentateuch was a composite work (not written by one author) that developed over a long period of time (not written at one time). In New Testament scholarship, critics looked at the synoptic Gospels in relation to the Gospel of John, and they concluded that most of John was not historically reliable and that the synoptics themselves were all written from particular, sometimes antagonistic, points of view.

These conclusions and others led to some serious conflicts as Christian scholars questioned the credibility of the biblical history and the reliability of the Gospels for an accurate picture of the life and words of Jesus. The anxiety early biblical criticism produced led conservative Protestants and Catholics to reject its conclusions. The modernist controversy in the Catholic church was precipitated by the work of Alfred Loisy (1857–1940), a Catholic biblical critic whose work was condemned by the Vatican. The rise of Protestant fundamentalism can be directly traced to its inflexible resistance to biblical criticism and its insistence on biblical inerrancy and inspiration.

At the same time, the biblical movement played a significant role in the development of liberal Protestantism by engendering a respect for the scientific method and a general spirit of open-mindedness and optimism about the future of Christianity. One of the most influential liberal Protestant thinkers of the nineteenth century, Anglican clergyman Frederick D. Maurice (1805–1872), argued that the real danger to Christianity was not biblical criticism—which allowed the Bible to continue to speak powerfully in a modern context—but *resistance* to criticism, which implied that the Bible is feeble and in need of protection.

Christianity and Social Concern

One of the insights of the Renaissance that won strong acceptance during the Enlightenment was the focus on this world. We have seen the emergence of monasticism in early Christianity and noted that medieval conceptions of the Christian life placed perfection in a rejection of "the world" in favor of a life totally dedicated to one's relationship with God. One of the insights of the reformers was that a life dedicated to God could be lived anywhere: one did not have to enter a monastery or

Concept

The Modern Economy: Christians and the Rights of Workers

In the late nineteenth century, the Industrial Revolution permanently changed the nature of work and had an enormous impact on the rhythms and structures of family life and social organization. Many Christians attempted to respond to the new modern economy—especially how industrial capitalism affected the lives of workers—in a variety of ways.

Some Christians believed that the principles of the Gospel could join with the spirit of Marxism to form a Christian socialism. Others believed that the best way to preserve traditional religious and family values was to restore the medieval guild system. Labor union activists like Leonora M. Barry (1849–1930) and "Mother" Jones (1830–1930) were inspired by religious values but were often reviled by their churches. Mother Jones, a Catholic, once said, "I don't go to church. I'm waiting for the fellows in there to come out and fight with me, and then I'll go in."

One Christian response to the problems created by industrialism was the Christian Labor Union, which attempted to bring religious values and practice into the struggle for workers' rights. The CLU was founded in 1872 in Boston by a group of Protestant workers who championed the Bible as the "chief labor reform book of the world." Through their pamphlets and direct action, CLU members supported the 8-hour workday and other workplace reforms. They emphasized cooperation over competition and worked to end class divisions.

Although many derided these reforms as socialism in disguise, leaders of the CLU criticized a Christianity that was too individualistic and otherworldly. In calling for the communal spirit and social justice emphasis of the biblical prophets and Jesus, the CLU can be seen as part of a general trend toward the politicization of American Christianity.

The massive influx of Catholic immigrants in the nineteenth century stimulated American Catholic priests and bishops to champion workers and to support the American labor movement. In defending the rights of workers to unionize, they were in line with the teaching of Pope Leo XIII. The allegiance of Catholics to labor-endorsed programs of the Democratic Party in the first half of the twentieth century is another indication of the ways in which modern social issues tend to blend religion and politics.

The complexities of modern economies require Christians to engage social issues in ways they have not done before. Worker priests in France in the 1940s, liberation theologians in Latin America in the 1970s, and conservative Christian responses that condemn such initiatives as "communist" reflect and continue these earlier attempts to bring Christian teachings to complex economic issues.

become a priest to be a perfect Christian. On the contrary, Christians were called to serve God in the world wherever they worked. Calvin's doctrine of election—that God chooses certain people for salvation before they are even born—carried with it the demand that Christians glorify God in their daily lives by their honesty, hard work, sobriety, and thrift. This general openness to life in the world characterized Protestantism from the beginning and made it clear that one could be a good Christian entrepreneur as long as one used wealth wisely and shared one's bounty with the less fortunate.

The nineteenth century offered a new challenge to Christian social responsibility, which was responded to in various ways. The Industrial Revolution tended to be better for the owners of industry than for the workers, and sectors of massive poverty in the nineteenth century led social critics like Karl Marx to interpret history as a continual struggle of the workers against social elites. Protestant and Catholic Christians had to strive to respond to issues of poverty and social welfare, and that effort continues to this day, as we shall see in Part IV of this book. The problem was a complicated one. On the one hand, Catholics and Protestants both had ways to accept the status quo: Catholics focused on this world as a preparation for eternal life and so did not tend to take positions that would define the mission of the church in terms of the restructuring of society. Protestants, with their sense of vocation and sharing, were able to interpret their duties to impoverished peoples in ways that did not threaten social structures. As the list of social ills grew more pressing during the nineteenth century, Christians began to reexamine the relationship of the Gospel to life in the world. Some looked for ways to change things, to use the Gospel as a blueprint for a more enlightened society, whereas others looked for ways to maintain the status quo. We will examine some modern interpretations of this conflict in Part IV of the book. For now, we need simply to understand some of the general positions that moved Christians to action on these issues in the nineteenth century.

Evangelical Christians, especially during the Second Great Awakening—as we shall see in the next chapter—believed that conversion to Christianity required a personal relationship with Jesus expressed in social awareness and concern. The Evangelical Alliance, formed in 1846 (which we will consider in Chapter 9), was a powerful advocate for a wide range of social causes from antislavery activism to Prohibition. Catholics began to take positions in support of the rights of workers in the late nineteenth century and have continued to struggle with social questions in a variety of forms to the present time. Let us focus here on the responses of English liberal Protestantism to the grave social ills of the nineteenth century.

The same Frederick D. Maurice who championed biblical criticism was also a pioneer in a movement known as Christian socialism. As he looked around in mid-century, he concluded that the churches were not responsive to the social realities of the times. Old Calvinist ideas about poverty as God's judgment or curse, coupled with new evolutionist notions about the survival of the fittest, were leading some preachers to conclude that Christians should not help the poor (understood as morally unfit) and should surely pursue wealth as a sign of God's favor. Maurice along with religious reformers like William Booth (1829–1912), founder of the Salvation Army, looked at the human suffering caused by the Industrial Revolution and indicted the churches for not being more responsible to those whose lives were ruined by industrial "progress." Poverty, they said, was not a curse but the result of exploitation, and the church's proper role in society was to make such exploitation impossible. Maurice hoped to make the Gospel relevant to social conditions, whereas Booth attacked the ravages of poverty with a series of practical solutions and attempted to prod the conscience of Christians so that they would be aroused to the pain of hidden human suffering.

We will look at American expressions of social concern later. For now, it is important only to perceive the emergence of a new Christian principle: the Gospel should be made relevant to human life in such a way that it can be used as a plan to restructure society and eliminate social ills. If Christianity had adopted some of the Renaissance and Enlightenment ideals about individual happiness, readings of the Social Gospel reminded Christians that sin and salvation could also be conceptualized in social terms. Contemporary Christians are still faced with these questions and have extended them to apply to arguments about the relation of Christianity to the political order (as we shall see in Part Four of this book). In that way, the question of Christian social concern in the nineteenth century has been one of the major contributions to the continuing diversity and unity of Christianity.

CONCLUSION

We have examined the Christian response to modernity in a variety of ways in order to make contextual sense of the remaining chapters of this book. No attempt has been made here to provide a comprehensive history of the nineteenth century or to outline the great theological and philosophical debates that characterize nineteenth-century Christianity. Rather, we have tried to get an appreciation for the modern spirit and the kinds of questions it raises. We have looked more closely at some of the ideas we take for granted in the modern world—separation of church and state and the secularization of society, for example. We have tried to understand the impact of the Enlightenment on political and religious life, and we have seen that there were various levels of resistance and acceptance of the modern spirit on the part of Catholics and Protestants. This chapter has been designed to make it easier to understand some of the movements described earlier (Pietism and revivalism, for example) and some of the controversies that will occupy Part IV of the book. This chapter should also serve to contextualize some of the highly creative responses of nineteenth-century American Christianity to the thrill and challenge of the New World.

Focal Points for Discussion

1. By the nineteenth century, it was increasingly clear that there are no simple answers to questions of human existence. How were secularization, industrialization, and scientific discovery unsettling for Christians?
2. Roman Catholics through authority, Anglicans through tradition, and Evangelicals through their emphasis on experience all tried to avoid the problems of modernity. Are these traditional Christian responses to wrenching social change? Or is there something distinctively new about them?
3. One way in which Christians attempted to combine modern critical methods with belief was through biblical criticism. Why is one more likely to find biblical critics in liberal Protestant groups than in Roman Catholic or Evangelical groups?

Modern American Christianity

CHAPTER 8

The American atmosphere in the nineteenth and early twentieth centuries was exuberant and expansive; American Christianity reflected that atmosphere. The nineteenth century gave rise to extraordinary religious diversity that continues into the present day. Many of the complex issues of worship, nondenominational churches, varieties in ecclesiastical structures, and Christian attitudes toward American cultural values will be explored in subsequent chapters. In this chapter, we explore the proliferation of religious groups in America in the nineteenth century and preview the next section by introducing the religious issues of the first decades of the twentieth century.

THE NINETEENTH CENTURY: AMERICAN RELIGIOUS DIVERSITY

The nineteenth century, like the eighteenth, began with a general religious decline in America. The enthusiasm of the Great Awakening had subsided, religion had become a purely voluntary matter, and people were moving away from the cities to settle the new frontier. The population of the United States, which was about 2.5 million in 1776, grew to 20 million by 1845, a dramatic rise that reinvigorated religion in America.

A new wave of Protestant revivalism, the Second Great Awakening (c. 1790–1830), added new accents to American Evangelicalism. Enlightenment philosophy continued to be felt in what came to be known as Liberal Protestantism, and in the climate of religious freedom at the turn of the new century, several communitarian groups and some new churches formed in expectation of the Second Coming of Christ. In addition to changes in existing churches, two entirely new American religions were founded in the nineteenth century: Mormonism and Christian Science. And some traditional denominations were still struggling with how to adapt to the customs and language of their new country. The Civil War divided almost every church over the issue of slavery and spawned specifically black churches within the established denominations. Not surprisingly, divisions continued within the churches over internal matters: new groups continued to form over disagreements about church discipline or doctrine.

For purposes of convenience and internal unity, this section on the nineteenth century covers some new religious movements and denominations up to the outbreak of World War I in 1914. Many churches that were divided over a number of issues in the nineteenth century, then attempted to reunite or to join with other churches to form a new denomination. We cover the continuation of these efforts into the twentieth century so that we can have a coherent idea of the general history of the group.

American Evangelicalism

The nineteenth century began with a new wave of revivalism that differed significantly from the First Great Awakening. The central figure of this new wave was Charles Grandison Finney (1792–1875), a lawyer whose religious experience transformed him into a preacher. Finney, inspired by methods used by politicians, understood revival as the controlled manipulation of religious phenomena. During the First Great Awakening, preachers tried to elicit a response and commended emotional conversions, but they did not pretend to understand the mysterious inner working of conversion itself; the work of conversion was God's. In the Second Great Awakening, however, conducted at raucous camp meetings in the Midwest and by revivalist preachers on the frontier, holiness was thought to be voluntary and conversion a matter of personal choice.

Revivalism that preached personal choice joined with the revolutionary spirit of the new American republic to form a new type of religious understanding. Common people rather than church leaders were the most significant actors in religious matters, and preachers were judged more by what was in their heart than what was in their head. Preaching and practice grew decidedly more democratic, especially in sparsely settled territories, as distinctions between a learned clergy and an ignorant laity began to break down. Virtue was rooted in popular piety and simple faith, and an inability to follow complex doctrinal arguments was no barrier to conversion. Denominational differences grew increasingly unimportant. Furthermore, new religious movements, including Evangelicalism, put a premium on the spiritual impulses of ordinary people, who were encouraged to define faith for themselves and to be enthusiastic about it.

After the Civil War, Dwight L. Moody (1837–1899) applied business and advertising techniques to religious revivalism and developed large interdenominational urban meetings similar to the large camp meetings of the first part of the century. He founded Moody Bible College to train evangelical ministers in a simple, often anti-intellectual revivalist message: it centered on the love of God in Jesus Christ and contained a strong call to repentance. Revivalism was designed to be an emotional experience leading the sinner to rebirth and to a healing experience of God's love. Many evangelicals expected conversion to be accompanied by a manifestation they called exercises, which might include crying, running, or some kind of physical tremors.

American Evangelicalism often promised and produced social as well as moral improvement, readying people for a life of Christian action. The Evangelical Alliance was formed in 1846 to concentrate evangelical energy in the service of scriptural

Christianity and against what were considered unscriptural religions (for example, Roman Catholicism). Societies were formed throughout the nineteenth century to spread the evangelical message (the American Bible Society and the American Tract Society) and to inspire moral improvement (the American Temperance Union). Paradoxically, the energy of women for these causes, and their training to be leaders in important social movements like abolition, would eventually inspire them to turn their enthusiasm to women's rights.

Evangelicalism has often been used to describe an emotional approach to religion. It describes those who stress religious experience and the importance of making a clear, definite decision for Jesus Christ. Evangelicals emphasize biblical authority and human sinfulness; they insist on the need for a new birth and a life of holiness and personal witness. Although there were specifically evangelical denominations (Evagelical Covenant Church of America, for example), evangelical groups often exist within mainline Protestant denominations: one can find Evangelical Mennonites, Evangelical Presbyterians, Evangelical Methodists, Evangelical Lutherans, and so on. Eventually, Evangelical would describe a Christian whose choice for Jesus as a personal savior was more important than a denominational location.

Liberal Protestantism

Inspired by the rationalist philosophy of the Enlightenment and Deism, and often in reaction to the emotionalism of revivalism, some groups of Christians became more liberal in their interpretation of Scripture. The clearest example of a new denomination with these characteristics is Unitarianism. Formed within American Congregationalism and associated with the work of William Ellery Channing (1780–1842), Unitarianism rejects the mysterious doctrine of the Trinity in favor of a belief in the unity of God. Unitarians base their positions on the Bible and refuse to accept some theological tenets of the Reformation, especially the Calvinist doctrine of total human depravity.

Liberalism sometimes means freedom from prejudice and a readiness to welcome new ideas and progress in religion. By these criteria, one can find liberals in all churches: Catholic, traditional Protestant, and Evangelical. *Liberal Protestantism* usually refers to an understanding of Christianity that emphasizes its humanitarian impulses rather than dogmatic propositions or emotional conversion. It is, accordingly, an often misunderstood term and is frequently used to criticize people for being insufficiently religious in a traditional sense.

Communitarian Groups

A variety of religious experiments flourished in the climate of religious freedom of nineteenth-century America. The communitarian impulse derived from the early Christian tradition of members sharing their goods and living a common life (see Acts 4:32–37). The monastic tradition (as we saw in Chapter 4) sprang from the desire to live a life of perfection and to do it in a community. Throughout history, communitarian groups have drawn together for these general reasons: for example, the Waldensians gathered around Peter Waldo (c. 1176) to live in apostolic poverty, and the Beguines were a group of pious laywomen who shared a common life to do good works in their communities.

Concept

Political Christianity: The Double Legacy of Reinhold Niebuhr

In the years before World War I, Christians were more divided than ever on the issue of political involvement. New social needs created new divisions within American Christianity so that (liberal) Social Gospel adherents were almost always in opposition to (conservative) fundamentalists. Liberal Christians tended to embrace social action, whereas conservative Christians fled the evils of the world. Reinhold Niebuhr (1892–1971), theologian and activist for various social causes, had a distinctive interpretation about these matters; he urged Christians to work for social justice, yet profoundly distrusted the human capacity for goodness.

Niebuhr was one of the towering intellectual figures of the twentieth century. As a young seminarian, he became known for his confrontational style, his fierce convictions (both biblical and political), and his distrust of dogmatic thinking. As a pastor in Detroit (1915–1928), he was deeply involved in social issues (a liberal tendency) and also wrestled with the problems of human wickedness (a conservative preoccupation).

When Niebuhr looked to Scripture for answers to his questions, he was struck by two things: the radical nature of biblical thought (that demands involvement in the real issues of the day) and the profound nature of human limitations (the recognition of the sinful nature of humanity). He devoted his early career to demonstrating that the fact of sinfulness was not an exhortation to retreat from the world but was, instead, a call to confront human injustice with a prophetic critique.

To most eyes, Niebuhr's involvement in social justice made him a liberal, and although he himself was uncomfortable with labels, he was clearly active throughout the 1920s and 1930s on behalf of liberal causes. At the same time, he was clearly not optimistic, as were the Progressive and the Social Gospel movements of his day. People in those movements believed that human nature was continually evolving toward higher planes of moral perfection. Niebuhr believed that these liberal movements were far too trusting of humanity's capacity to change and to do good.

Niebuhr's critique of social arrangements—racism, economic injustice, and unfair labor practices—was uncompromising. Christians had to be involved in movements to overcome those injustices. At the same time, his profound sense of human frailty led him to have only modest expectations of human activity. Were his views "realistic" or just pessimistic? Niebuhr eventually turned away from the liberal activism of his early career to focus on the threat of communism in the 1950s. His "realism" led him to see war and other seemingly brutal policies as tragically necessary at times.

The two sides of Niebuhr continue to influence how intellectual Christians approach politics. So-called neoconservative Christians draw on Niebuhr's realism to advocate an aggressive American foreign policy, including the 2003 invasion of Iraq. Liberal Christians point to Niebuhr's lifelong commitment to social justice as his more significant legacy.

We have already seen that groups can break off from a major Christian denomination to form a separate religious entity (the Amish splitting from the Mennonites, for example). Communitarian groups sometimes split from a parent group and sometimes were an entirely new creation. In America, many of them were drawn together by their belief in the Second Coming of Christ. Whatever their beliefs, they were usually founded by a strong leader and lived together in separate villages or communes, often with some distinguishing practice or belief. There were groups inspired by perfectionism and made up almost entirely of intellectuals and literary people (like the Brook Farm movement) and groups inspired by German Pietism who practiced celibacy and waited for the world to be restored to harmony (like the Rappites, also known as the Harmony Society). Some of the products we use today (or brand names we know) were originally associated with nineteenth-century communitarian groups, like Amana appliances, connected to Amana Church Society in Iowa, and Oneida silver, connected to the Oneida Community, founded in New York by John Humphrey Noyes (1816–1886). Let us look more closely at two of these groups.

THE HOPEDALE COMMUNITY This group was founded in Massachusetts in 1842 by Adin Ballou (1803–1890), an American Universalist preacher. Universalism is the doctrine that affirms the salvation of all people; God's love for everyone and desire for the salvation of all souls accomplish this universal saving action. Hopedale was a nonviolent utopian community that required no common beliefs but did require members to refrain from engaging in violence, taking oaths, and imbibing intoxicating drinks. It disintegrated as a community in 1857, but the Universalist movement—of which Adin and Hosea Ballou (1771–1852) were among its most important leaders—continued, became the Universalist Church of America, and merged with the American Unitarian Association in 1961 to form the Unitarian Universalist Association.

THE SHAKERS The United Society of Believers in Christ's Second Appearing is the official name of the Shakers, a group of "Shaking Quakers" led to New York by Mother Ann Lee (1736–1784) in 1774. Shakers believed that God was manifested in male form in the person of Jesus Christ and in female form in the person of Mother Ann Lee. In New York, they established a community of celibacy, pacifism, and cooperative living. Membership depended on conversion and tended to fluctuate dramatically. Because of long-lived members and modern conversions, some Shaker communities still exist, though most have disappeared. They were the largest of the communitarian groups and are remembered historically for their ritualized ecstatic dancing, their distinctive architecture and furniture, and their theological innovations, specifically for their belief in a female manifestation of God.

Most of these communitarian groups have ceased to exist, but many of their settlements are preserved as historical sites, and they continue to be remembered for their experiments in community living. Utopian groups, both religious and secular, continue to exist throughout the United States today.

MILLENNIALIST GROUPS

From the New Testament, we can see that Christians have, from the beginning, thought about the Second Coming of Christ. If we think about the return of Christ, certain questions occur to us: *When* will he return? *What* will *happen* when he does? Some Christians, reading Revelation 20:1–10, believe that Christ will establish a 1,000-year period of bliss and so wait joyfully for the millennium (millennium means a 1,000-year period). Most Christians believe that Christ will return to judge the living and the dead, but they do not all attempt to predict the time of the Second Coming. Millennialist groups in the nineteenth century were preoccupied with questions about the Second Coming and very much involved with interpreting the signs of the times so as to maintain a high level of expectation about the imminence of Christ's return. The three most significant groups of millennialist Christians formed in the nineteenth century are the Adventists (represented here by the Seventh-Day Adventists, though there are other adventist groups), the Jehovah's Witnesses, and the Dispensationalists.

SEVENTH-DAY ADVENTISTS Adventism as a movement originated with the prophecies of William Miller (1782–1849) about the end of the world. Miller, a lay preacher in the Baptist church, concentrated on the books of Daniel and Revelation and devised a way to tell when the end of the world was coming. In 1831, he began to preach that Christ's Second Coming was to be expected in 1843. His preaching was apparently convincing because more than seven hundred ministers of various denominations welcomed him to their pulpits and helped him spread the word. When Christ did not return in 1843, Miller recalculated and predicted two dates in 1844, by which time between fifty thousand and one million people had left their congregations to wait for the coming (advent) of Christ. When Christ did not return on the second set of dates, some of these people left their churches altogether, some returned to their own congregations, and still others formed splinter adventist groups.

In general, Adventism is the belief that Christ's Second Coming is at hand, that the wicked are soon to be punished and the good rewarded. The largest and most famous of the adventist groups is the Seventh-Day Adventist church founded by Joseph Bates, James White, and his wife, Ellen Gould White (1827–1915), who is considered the prophetess of the Seventh-Day Adventist church. The first conference of the new church was held in Battle Creek, Michigan, in 1863; Ellen White's numerous visions were crucial in resolving early questions of doctrine and practice.

Seventh-Day Adventists observe Saturday (not Sunday) as the proper day of Christian worship; they accept the Bible as the only authoritative rule of faith and interpret it literally. They also affirm the prophecies of Ellen White and believe that the spirit of prophecy is present in their church. They are strict sabbatarians and follow many Old Testament dietary laws; they wait for the Second Coming of Christ but do not attempt to predict an exact time for it. They believe Christ *began* his judgment in 1844 (the date Miller set for the Second Coming) and will finish it in his own time.

JEHOVAH'S WITNESSES The Jehovah's Witnesses were founded by Charles Taze Russell (1852–1916), who studied the Bible and became convinced by 1872 that Christ would return secretly in 1874 and that the world would end in 1914. His published opinions secured a large following, and from 1879, he established himself as pastor of an independent church in Pittsburgh, where he published *The Watchtower*. His followers were known by different names, including the Watchtower People. They were named Jehovah's Witnesses by their second leader, Joseph Franklin Rutherford (1869–1942). The sect grew from a few thousand to 106,000 during Rutherford's lifetime and today claims more than a million members in various countries.

Jehovah's Witnesses believe that only the elect of Jehovah (a form of the Hebrew name for God) will get into the kingdom of God. The present world, according to them, is ruled by Satan, and all government, business, and organized religion are in league with the devil and in conflict with the will of Jehovah. They consider themselves

People

Ellen Gould White: Prophet and Sabbatarian

Ellen Gould White, one of the founders of the Seventh-Day Adventist church, was given the President's Award by the National Health Federation in 1986, nearly 70 years after her death. One of her many functions within this new religion was prophecy, and several of the things she was "shown" by God related to health. Many of the recommendations of today's doctors—a vegetarian diet and the avoidance of tobacco or caffeine—were teachings of hers in the late nineteenth century. She spoke of "electrical currents in the brain" long before scientists described brain waves that way.

As a young girl, Ellen Gould was a Methodist, following its evangelical teaching. Her formal education stopped when she was nine, but her lively interest in issues of the day impelled her to be alive to things happening around her. As a teenager, she heard William Miller predict the end of the world, embraced this new apocalyptic movement, and eventually married one of its preachers, James White. Many years later, after her husband died, Ellen Gould White traveled extensively and lectured on the end of the world, especially on the conflict between two armies, one led by Christ and one by Satan.

She also lectured extensively on health issues. Besides having early insights into medical health, she can also be said to have raised environmental health issues long before anyone thought of them. She warned people of the dangers of a polluted planet and the healthy aspects of sunshine in the last part of the nineteenth century.

When Seventh-Day Adventists held their first national conference in 1863 in Battle Creek, Michigan, Ellen Gould White's numerous visions helped the young community resolve practical and theological issues. Those visions began in 1844 when she was seventeen years old: she saw a vision of people following Jesus and marching toward heaven. Her visions were quite often similar in nature: in a trance, she would almost stop breathing, become rigid or temporarily blind, and would be "shown things." One vision, depicting the commandment to "keep holy the Sabbath Day," appeared to her as words surrounded by a halo of light. Seventh-Day Adventists worship on Saturday, the Sabbath honored by the Jews.

White was an extraordinarily prolific writer. It is estimated that her life's output exceeded twenty-five million words. Besides pronouncements about health and diet that seem to be right on target today, she also predicted moves to change the U.S. Constitution to reflect Christian values, an idea that one can find in evangelical and Pentecostal preachers in the twentieth and twenty-first centuries.

part of a theocratic kingdom and, accordingly, will not serve in the armed forces, salute any flag, or hold political office. They avoid the ways of the world and traditional religious feasts, refusing to celebrate Christmas or Easter. Based on the books of Daniel and Revelation, they believe that only Christ and 144,000 elect have immortal souls and that everyone else has a mortal one, but they will be given a second chance during the millennium. The present world will end and be replaced by a new world. At that time, the just will reign and the wicked will perish, the 144,000 will go to heaven, and the rest will live forever on earth.

Dispensationalists Dispensationalism is a system of biblical interpretation that divides all time from the creation of the world into units called dispensations. In each dispensation, God is revealed in a new way and treats people differently. The first five dispensations refer to periods in the Old Testament, the sixth is the time of the Christian church, and the seventh is the coming of the kingdom. If Christians are now living within the sixth dispensation, they are, in a sense, living at the edge of the kingdom and should expect the return of Christ soon. Dispensationalists read the Bible from this perspective and interpret its prophecies to support their beliefs. Today's American Dispensationalists use the Scofield Reference Bible, edited by Cyrus I. Scofield (1841–1923), which offers a dispensationalist key to the interpretation of Scripture. Scofield's notes on the King James Version of the Bible gave people a way to understand the Bible for themselves, to find in it all the answers to their concerns.

New American Religions

Most "new" religious groups were formed from a particular established church or were established on the basis of a generalized belief—such as nineteenth-century Adventism—that swept through all churches. Two religious groups founded in the nineteenth century, however, were *really* new: they did not spring from established churches or movements, and they were specifically American, with distinct aspects growing out of the American context. These were the Mormons and the Christian Scientists.

Mormons The Church of Jesus Christ of Latter-Day Saints (the Mormons) was a restorationist movement founded in New York by Joseph Smith (1805–1844) in 1830. As a boy, Smith could not decide which church was the right one and eventually decided to ask God to help him. He had a revelation experience shortly thereafter in which God told him that none of the churches was the right one. He was then led by an angel to discover the Golden Plates, which contained "the fullness of the everlasting Gospel." According to Mormons, the Book of Mormon, a new Scripture, was translated by Smith from the Golden Plates: it is approximately five hundred pages long and is divided into books like the Bible. The Book of Mormon describes the lives of the "lost tribes of Israel" who migrated to America; it covers the years 600 B.C.E. to 421 C.E. According to the Book of Mormon, Jesus appeared to these people after the resurrection and established a church among them; it is this church that Smith claimed to revive. According to Smith, no other churches have divine authority; his authority came directly from God, and he was ordained by John the Baptist.

Smith and his followers moved to Kirtland, Ohio, where an entire congregation joined them. From there, they moved to Missouri and then to Illinois, where they prospered but aroused their neighbors' animosity. Smith was killed by a mob in Illinois in 1844. When he died, the church divided into several groups, two of which are particularly important. The largest group followed Brigham Young (1801–1877) to Salt Lake City, Utah. There they established a theocracy and openly practiced polygamy, one of the doctrines of their faith, from 1852 to 1890. According to Smith, marriage was important for salvation—singleness and celibacy were considered to be against God's will—and plural marriage was a revealed doctrine.

In Mormon theology, God was once a man, who later achieved divinity, as can any man. Mormons say, "What man is now, God once was; what God is now, man may become." A man becomes a god by successfully living through the testing period of mortality on earth; if he does well, he can become a god presiding over his own world; there are many worlds and many gods. In Mormon belief, God is the literal father of human souls; God is a polygamist who mates with female deities to produce an abundance of spirits or souls. For those souls to have an opportunity to become divine, they must become embodied—be born as human beings. Thus, Mormons regard it as a duty to have as many children as possible, to embody as many souls as possible. The practice of polygamy enabled more souls to become embodied.

The other significantly large group of Mormons is the Reorganized Church of Latter Day Saints (1852). It considers itself the legitimate successor of Smith's church and repudiates some of the later doctrines, especially polygamy and polytheism. Theologically, this body resembles traditional Protestantism. It is headquartered in Independence, Missouri. Joseph Smith Jr. (1832–1914) was the original president, and this group owns the original church in Kirtland, Ohio, and the original manuscript of the Book of Mormon. Millennialism is an important part of all Mormon belief.

CHRISTIAN SCIENTISTS The Church of Christ, Scientist was founded by Mary Baker Eddy (1821–1910) in 1875. Most of her life, she had been unhappily married and critically ill, but her life changed radically in the 1860s when she met Phineas Parkhurst Quimby (1802–1866), a mental healer. After a healing experience with him, she developed her own system; in 1866, when she was seriously ill, she read the account of Jesus raising the daughter of Jairus (Luke 8:40–56) and was cured. This decisive experience led her to discover the real meaning of the Gospels: that Christ healed by spiritual influence and that healing continued to the present time for those who believed in it.

According to Eddy, Jesus taught people the power of the mind to eliminate the illusions of sin, sickness, and death. All people, she taught, can be loving, confident, and well instead of hateful, fearful, and sick if they simply understand the spiritual nature of all reality: God is a spirit or *idea* and God is everything. Human beings, as a reflection of God, are also spiritual and good. The role of Christ is to bring people to this understanding. Eddy wrote *Science and Health* in 1875 and added to it "A Key to the Interpretation of Scripture"; this book, according to Christian Scientists, presents the *only* way to read the Bible. In following it, people find that the only reality is *ideas* and that matter does not exist; God is all-good and there is no room for sickness; the cure comes when one can perceive this fact. In 1877, Eddy opened the Massachusetts Metaphysical College, where she trained healers. By 1886, these healers were so successful that the National Christian Science Association was founded. By 1900, there were over 100,000 Christian Scientists.

Christian Science was one part of a larger intellectual and emotional movement known as New Thought. Mental healing was popular and influential in the late nineteenth century, and its teachings appealed to members of many different Christian denominations. According to the followers of New Thought, God is a life principle; salvation is happiness here and now; the absence of sin makes repentance unnecessary; and Jesus Christ is the symbol of the divine spark of goodness in everyone. New Thought promises secret inner power and a "real" understanding of Christianity to its followers. Although there are certain common beliefs in New Thought—spiritual healing and the creative power of thought, for example—it was never an organized denomination. At the same time, as a healing movement, it influenced people like Mary Baker Eddy, who did found organized churches.

Americanization and the Churches

English-speaking denominations in some ways set a pattern for American religious development. Non-English-speaking groups—especially German Lutherans and European Catholics—had some trouble determining how American to become. Catholics had the added difficulty of being perceived as a church dominated by a foreign power.

Lutheranism Lutherans from Germany, Austria, and the Netherlands began to immigrate to America in the seventeenth century, but they never were well organized as a confessional group. In the eighteenth century, a German missionary, Henry Melchior Muhlenberg (1711–1787), came to America to minister to and organize American Lutherans. He organized the first synod (group of Lutheran congregations), and by 1770, eighty-one Lutheran congregations existed in Pennsylvania alone. By the nineteenth century, many more Lutherans had come and were spread out over a wider territory. Many of them were German. One question that arose in the minds of many of these people concerned the relationship between their ethnic and their religious identity. They wondered whether to maintain their German heritage or to become more thoroughly American in language and custom; they wondered how much being Lutheran had to do with being German.

The dilemma of Americanization gave rise to three general solutions. The wholeheartedly pro-American option was defined by Samuel Simon Schmucker (1799–1873). He urged Lutherans to band together into one American Lutheran church and to dissociate themselves from ethnically defined churches; he hoped to build a church without ethnic barriers. Schmucker had been touched by American Evangelicalism, and his plan was based on some doctrinal compromise; he was willing to abandon some traditional Lutheran positions to become more American. The conservative reaction to Schmucker's position was led by Carl E. W. Walther (1811–1887), who supported strict confessional Lutheranism (giving nothing to American Evangelicalism) and German ethnic heritage. Walther's group formed a German Lutheran Synod in the 1840s, which eventually became the Lutheran Church–Missouri Synod. The middle-of-the-road alternative was defined by Charles Porterfield Krauth (1823–1883) and became the basis for the Lutheran Church of America. Krauth supported the traditional Lutheran confessionalism of the conservatives but also advocated an American Lutheran identity as urged by Schmucker; Krauth's group maintained its Lutheran doctrines and also abandoned Old World ways. As more Germans entered the country, these arguments continued; the three main branches of the Lutheran church in the United States reflected the divisions and arguments.

In 1974, there was a major schism within the Missouri Synod, which resulted in the Association of Evangelical Lutheran Churches. The dividing issue was the interpretation of Scripture; the new group adopted methods and positions often associated with more liberal viewpoints. In 1982, the Lutheran Church of America, the American Lutheran Church, and the Association of Evangelical Lutheran Churches voted to merge into a single new church. This merger, which was completed in 1987, marks an important step not only in Lutheranism (making it the third-largest Protestant denomination in the country, after Baptists and Methodists) but in American religious history.

ROMAN CATHOLICISM Roman Catholics encountered two problems related to their Americanization. Internally, there was a division between the more liberal Irish bishops who pushed for Americanization and the more conservative German bishops who wished to avoid Americanization in favor of preserving their ethnic identity. Externally, hostility from a variety of anti-Catholic nativist movements followed Catholics up to the second half of the twentieth century. The English colonies had never welcomed Roman Catholics or made them very comfortable; Catholics suffered from a variety of social and legal restrictions and a lack of religious freedom. During the colonial period, few Catholics came to the colonies, but from the 1820s to the 1870s, the Catholic population increased from 195,000 to 4,504,000, most of whom were immigrants. The rapid increase in the Catholic population and their foreign connections (by birth or church affiliation) inspired the rise of nativist movements.

Nativism is intense suspicion and dislike of any foreigner, especially a Roman Catholic. Revivalist preachers and nativist publications warned Americans against the "international conspiracy" of the Roman Catholic church under the domination of a foreign monarch (the pope). Catholics, they believed, were unable to support American freedoms. In the early part of the nineteenth century, people were easily convinced that Catholics were a menace, that convents were dens of iniquity, and that there was a Roman conspiracy led by the pope and managed by the Jesuits. In some anti-Catholic riots, people were killed and convents burned.

The Know-Nothing movement (so called because members always claimed to know nothing about their secret activities) was founded in the 1850s as a secret society. In 1854, they formed the American Party to combat foreign influence, popery, Jesuitism, and Catholicism. Their political aim was to exclude all Roman Catholics from public office, and in 1856, they gained 25 percent of the popular vote. The Know Nothings disappeared after the Civil War, partly because of their alliance with the proslavery movement, but nativism did not disappear. In the 1880s, new waves of eastern and southern Europeans, predominantly Catholic, immigrated, and the American Protective Association was formed in 1887 to limit the Catholic population with a stringent immigration quota system. By 1896, the American Protective Association had a million members; it lingered as an association until 1911. In the 1920s, the Ku Klux Klan was revived against blacks, Jews, and Roman Catholics; Klan policies against foreigners were supported by a systematic use of terrorism. The Klan gained political power and was able to support legislation that restricted immigration of eastern and southern Europeans. The revival of the Klan in the 1970s is a modern example of nativism as directed against foreigners, though contemporary targets tend to be Asians, illegal immigrants, and Muslims.

Catholics responded to nativism by sequestering themselves in ghettos and by fierce patriotism. On the one hand, they pulled back from the mainstream of American life, founded a separate, extensive private school system, and organized Catholic neighborhoods and social units. When necessary, however, they exhibited a patriotism intended to demonstrate that Catholics were especially good Americans.

The strife within American Catholicism was essentially a battle between those who wanted Catholics to embrace American life and values and those who wished to retain their ethnic particularities. The two predominant groups of Roman Catholics in nineteenth-century America were Irish and German, with church leadership predominantly in Irish hands. German Catholics settled into the so-called German Triangle, defined by Milwaukee, Cincinnati, and St. Louis, where they hoped to live quietly and continue to retain their ethnic identity and the German language and customs they believed to be so superior to American or Irish Catholicism. A group of liberal bishops—John Ireland (c. 1838–1918), John J. Keane (1839–1918), and John Lancaster Spalding (1840–1916)—who were enthusiastic about American pluralism, urged an American Catholicism without ethnic divisions. Through a series of conflicts and misunderstandings centered more in Europe than in the United States, the Irish/German conflict was reduced to a phantom heresy called "Americanism," condemned by the pope in 1899. The papal condemnation was based on an inaccurate understanding of the American situation, but it tended to dampen all efforts toward liberalization within the American Catholic church. The American Catholic experience in the 1890s set the tone for the conservative and isolated Catholicism of the first 60 years of the twentieth century.

All Catholics opposed the tactics and theological positions of American Evangelicalism. Catholicism stressed the importance of the organized church and the sacraments as opposed to emotional conversions and reliance on subjective religious experience. At the same time, Catholics had a form of revivalism within their own churches. Specially trained priests moved from parish to parish, preaching missions that were intended to strengthen Catholic identity and renew religious experience. Although their style was not the same as that of revivalist preachers, the desired goal was similar. Revivalist preachers aimed at conversion as manifested in response to an altar call; Catholic mission preachers sought to engender deep feelings of repentance manifested by an increased use of the sacrament of penance and a marked increase in devotional fervor.

Growth and Division Within Christian Churches

The ethnic and ideological complexity of America inspired an enormous growth and division within the churches. Nearly every Christian church divided over slavery during the Civil War, and most churches suffered some division over the evangelical impulse. As happened during the Reformation, divisions continued over internal church polity. The melting pot image of America never quite took hold of the ethnic imagination—at least not during the nineteenth century—and many specifically ethnic churches and church groups remained. The so-called Restoration movement attempted to unify like-minded people into one "Christian" church.

Roman Catholics remained united as a single church, though often divided into ethnic neighborhoods in urban settings. Most other Christian groups experienced major schisms. Some of those divisions were over what were considered innovations (Sunday school or a paid professional ministry), some over major national conflicts (slavery), and some were continuations of earlier arguments (the appropriateness of evangelical preaching). In many churches, most members were willing to accept a particular progressive teaching or arrangement, and a small group split from them to be faithful to their understanding of the original vision of the group. Many churches split along North-South lines during the Civil War—American Baptists and Southern Baptists, the United Presbyterian Church (northern) and the Presbyterian Church in the United States of America (southern), the Methodist Episcopal Church (northern) and the Methodist Episcopal Church of the South—and reunited in the twentieth century (though some groups are still attempting reunification).

Spirituality

Religion at Home and at Work: Jesus the Friend and Businessman

Industrialization in the nineteenth century helped to separate work from family, as men (more than women) went off to work in factories and offices. Americans increasingly saw religion as belonging to the home, where the wife and mother was the central figure, and thus as "women's work." Mothers taught Christian faith to children in Sunday school classes and at home. The resulting feminization of religion had important effects on spirituality and later prompted a backlash.

As Christianity became associated with domestic life and raising children, it took on a moralizing tone that seemed to restrain the more aggressive interests of men. Drinking and gambling received particular disapproval from such groups as the Women's Christian Temperance Union. In turn, home-based religion became for men a refuge from work, offering them shelter from the competition and stress of the outside world.

In this domestic spirituality, Jesus became a teacher of morality and a loving companion. A popular hymn exclaimed, "What a friend we have in Jesus!" and urged Christians to take all their problems to him in prayer. Other hymns called Jesus "beautiful" to express his tender, concerned nature, and they romanticized the Christian's personal relationship with Jesus. The singer of "In the Garden" walks alone with Jesus in a garden of roses, talking with him and sharing a private joy.

As the twentieth century dawned, Christian leaders became concerned that this romantic spirituality feminized men and that a moralizing Christianity appeared to men and boys as prudish and no fun. They encouraged a more "muscular Christianity" that would help boys to take on traditional masculine characteristics and encourage men to see work, recreation, and other activities outside the home as religious. For example, the Young Men's Christian Association (YMCA) and the Boy Scouts combined outdoor and athletic activities with Christian morals. Evangelist Billy Sunday (1863–1935), a former baseball player, claimed "weak" and "effeminate" doctrines failed to build strong, moral men. During his energetic sermons, he leapt around on stages, lunged into audiences, and even shadow-boxed with the devil.

In his 1925 book *The Man Nobody Knows,* Bruce Barton (1886–1967), an advertising executive, presented Jesus as a man's man who lived outdoors and enjoyed parties; his self-confidence and physical strength attracted women and intimidated weaker men. As someone who took twelve humble men and formed the most successful organization in world history, Barton's Jesus was the ideal executive and a model for the American businessman. Barton's spirituality encountered God not in the quiet and reflection of the home but in the activity and productivity of the workplace.

African American Christianity A significant development in American Christianity was the formation of African American churches. Slave owners in the South along with preachers from various Protestant denominations worked to convert black people to Christianity, and the Christian religion appears to have served many of the psychological and social needs of the slave population. We can, of course, find fault with a religion that tolerated slavery at all, and we may judge those sectors of American Christianity that were unable to see beyond the limitations of their own racial prejudices, but for now, let us concentrate on the ways African American Christianity developed.

Christian slaves in the South developed a set of hymns and spirituals that still speak powerfully to the black religious experience. The black preacher, who eventually emerged as a political as well as a religious figure, was a special kind of community genius. Since congregations of black Methodists and Baptists were almost always supervised, black preachers had to find ways to become strong community leaders without attracting hostile suspicion, yet at the same time gaining the confidence of the local black congregation. Black churches were not granted independence until after the Civil War.

Besides Christian churches made up of slave populations, there were institutional churches made up of free blacks. The need for distinct black churches arose from the fact of second-class citizenship experienced by blacks in white churches. Methodists, Baptists, and others segregated black members of their own churches, forcing them to sit in balconies or to worship in separate buildings. In response to this situation, some blacks formed their own denominations. Black Methodists, for example, formed the African Methodist Episcopal Zion church in 1776. Richard Allen (1760–1831), born a slave in Philadelphia, founded the African Methodist Episcopal church in 1816. These two churches, though not the only black denominations, compose the congregations that serve a majority of African American Christians today.

Within the variety of Christian responses to the challenges of the late nineteenth century, three significant movements occurred: the Holiness movement; its lineal descendant, Pentecostalism; and the so-called Restoration movement. We will look at each of these movements briefly before drawing conclusions about religious diversity in nineteenth-century America.

THE HOLINESS MOVEMENT After the Civil War, a series of Methodist revivals were preached stressing a return to holiness and emphasizing "entire sanctification." Wesley believed that there were two distinct blessings in the Christian life: justification (which changes the condition of one's life because God forgives one's sins and restores fellowship) and sanctification (which changes one's nature and helps one live a life of perfect love). Sanctification or Christian perfection does not mean freedom from mistakes or illness, according to Wesley, but freedom from sin. The grace of God enables a person to love God so wholeheartedly that all that person's actions, thoughts, and words will be directed by love. The pivotal question is how sanctification is interpreted with regard to *time:* for the Methodists, sanctification is a gradual process attained throughout the Christian life. Those who became part of the Holiness movement, however, believed sanctification was a sudden acquisition by the action of the Holy Spirit. Within the Holiness movement, people expected to receive entire sanctification—instantaneous holiness at revival meetings. In 1867, a group of like-minded individuals formed the National Camp Meeting Association for the Promotion of Holiness. From this came an interdenominational movement and the formation of separate Holiness churches.

The two most widely known Holiness churches are specific branches of the Church of God (Anderson, Indiana, for example) and the Church of the Nazarene. The Church of God of Anderson, Indiana, is the oldest Holiness church, whereas the Church of the Nazarene is the largest. Holiness churches are usually grass-roots movements that are evangelistic and fundamentalist. They stand for what is known as the Four-Square Gospel: Jesus is the savior, the sanctifier, the healer, and the coming Lord.

PENTECOSTALISM The lineal descendant of the Holiness movement was the Pentecostal movement. Pentecostals believe in entire sanctification but as a gradual—not instantaneous—process initiated by baptism in the Holy Spirit (often referred to as the Holy Ghost). Baptism with the Holy Ghost is manifested in the gift of *glossolalia,* according to Pentecostals: those who receive the Holy Ghost will speak in tongues. Pentecostals believe the Christian experience at Pentecost—the coming of the Holy Ghost, the gifts of glossolalia, healing, and prophecy—should be a continuing and normal experience within Christianity.

Pentecostalism began in Kansas in the early part of the twentieth century. Charles Fox Parham (1873–1937), a preacher in the Holiness movement, convinced his followers that the baptism in the Holy Spirit required for salvation was essentially connected with speaking in tongues. One could determine whether or not one had received the Holy Ghost on the basis of a particular gift: only if the person spoke in tongues was it certain that he or she had received Spirit baptism. The most important source of Pentecostalism was the Azusa Street Revival held in Los Angeles, California, in 1906 by W. J. Seymour, a Holiness preacher.

Pentecostals are united in their belief that baptism in the Spirit and speaking in tongues are necessary signs of holiness; they are fundamentalist in their interpretation of Scripture, have strong dispensationalist leanings, and are strong believers in the imminent Second Coming of Christ. Pentecostals differ on matters of doctrine (some of them do not believe in the Trinity but see the Father, Son, and Holy Ghost as different manifestations of God in history), polity, and practice. The largest Pentecostal group is the Assemblies of God, an organization established in 1914. The United Pentecostal church is the largest "Jesus name" (non-Trinitarian) group; baptism is administered in the name of Jesus Christ, not in the name of the Father, Son, and Holy Ghost.

A movement that has touched most other Christian churches and that is in some ways associated with Pentecostalism is Neopentecostalism, or Charismatic Renewal. Christians in nearly all denominations, including Roman Catholics, have sought to experience the gifts of the Holy Spirit outside the context of classical Pentecostalism. These people are not usually motivated by a desire for the sign of glossolalia, but they do hope to have some tangible experience of God, some manifestation of the Holy Spirit in their lives, without separating themselves from their particular churches. They do not agree with some of the doctrinal and behavioral principles of classical Pentecostals, but they do share with them a desire for an experience of the Holy Spirit.

THE RESTORATION OR "CHRISTIAN CHURCH" MOVEMENT The Restoration movement, or New Reformation, of the nineteenth century was an attempt to combine efforts for Christian unity with a return to simple New Testament Christianity. Some people believed that Christians were unnecessarily divided over issues of polity, practice, and creeds, so they espoused a noncredal New Testament–based Christianity. One leader of this movement was Barton Stone (1772–1844), who participated in the Cane Ridge Camp Meeting (1801) and was led to dissolve his Presbyterian congregation so that they could be "simple Christians"; James O'Kelly (c. 1735–1826) led a group of congregational Methodists to accept the Bible as their only creed. Other leaders were Thomas Campbell (1763–1854) and his son Alexander (1788–1866). Thomas Campbell left the Presbyterian church to found the Christian Association to promote unity among Christians. His son Alexander worked within Baptist associations and then founded a separate community that supported a rational, biblical, practical approach to Christianity. He avoided theological disputation and subtlety, on the one hand, and emotional revivalism, on the other. All of these efforts aimed to restore ancient, primitive Christianity to bring the New Testament church to life in the contemporary world. Furthermore, Restoration leaders hoped to appeal to simple New Testament piety and free Christians from the scandalous divisions that so many options appeared to foster. Their aim was to heal all conflicts.

Ironically, however, this Restoration movement experienced a division within itself almost immediately. Alexander Campbell called his followers the Disciples of Christ, and their churches were known as Churches of Christ. A conservative splinter group opposing non–New Testament innovations like Sunday school, instrumental music in worship, and missionary activity took the name Church of Christ for itself and was recognized as a separate body in 1906. The hoped-for single "Church of Christ," therefore, was not to be. Disciples of Christ belong to the Christian Church, a different denomination from the Church of Christ.

Summary of Nineteenth-Century Christianity

The nineteenth century saw enormous growth and diversity within the Christian churches of America; by the end of the century, a widespread spectrum of belief and practice was manifested in a multitude of American Christian groups. Throughout this time and into the twentieth century, groups of Christians split and regrouped under different banners, a tendency that may attest to the dynamism within Christianity and the human need to join like-minded groups. By the middle of the twentieth century, many of the divided clusters had joined with others and merged to form large united churches like the United Church of Christ and the United Methodist church. Some groups continued to maintain themselves as small churches. For the most part, however, the growth and diversity experienced in the nineteenth century gave way to movements of unity and cooperation in the twentieth century.

THE TWENTIETH CENTURY PREVIEWED

Optimism and a belief in human progress characterized the first part of the twentieth century. American Protestants entered into the spirit of the times with plans to improve themselves (by way of the temperance movement, for example), while Roman Catholics put an enormous amount of energy into building and maintaining their own school system and network of hospitals, newspapers, and charitable and religious institutions. The feeling of manifest destiny, which supported the idea of American democracy as capable of saving the world, was often given religious formulation by the churches, and a broad-based missionary movement was designed by the evangelical center of American Protestantism. All these noble adventures, begun in the enthusiasm of the new century, had been abandoned by the 1930s: the Eighteenth Amendment (Prohibition—passed to stop the consumption of alcohol) was repealed in 1934 because it had been a massive failure; American nationalistic fervor cooled when World War I ("the war to end all wars") did not end human warfare; and the worldwide missionary movement, begun in the nineteenth century, collapsed for lack of cooperation.

The 1940s focused the nation's attention on World War II and its aftermath. There was a resurgence of monastic life in the Roman Catholic church right after the war and a renewed interest in religion in general. The 1950s were times of extraordinary success for almost all churches: more than 70 percent of the American population considered themselves religious, and almost all Christian groups were busy building new churches, schools, fellowship centers, and other structures. If the 1950s were a boom time for religions, the 1960s were a down time. For a number of reasons (related to the war in Vietnam and its attendant unrest, both personal and social), church attendance declined markedly, fewer people supported their churches financially, and most churches went into debt. Most Protestant churches went into a decline, the Roman Catholic church began to experience the unsettling reform attempts of the Second Vatican Council, and some of the newer Christian churches (Mormons and Pentecostals, for example) were growing at enormous rates. The closing decades of the twentieth century cannot be easily characterized, nor should they be at this point of insufficient historical distance, though we can relate some of the contemporary issues within American Christianity to older and perhaps deeper issues. But for background, we step back again to the beginning of the century and to the battle between two distinctly different religious views.

Fundamentalism Versus Liberalism: The Battle of the Century

As we have seen, Christians in the modern period did not divide neatly along denominational lines but were inclined to group together on the basis of shared beliefs or theological convictions. Many of the beliefs and practices in nineteenth-century American Christianity had repercussions in most of the churches; Adventism, Evangelicalism, and Pentecostalism all inspired the formation of separate churches, but they also precipitated groups within churches that did not split from those churches. The contemporary context, therefore, is genuinely pluralistic, and modern Christian churches often have a surprisingly wide range of opinions represented within them.

One of the main dividing issues in twentieth-century Christianity is *orthodoxy*. What are the "right" beliefs for Christians? As you can imagine, there are many answers to that question, all of them grounded on specific denominational histories. But for the moment, let us make a broad generalization and divide Christians into two main groups: those who have welcomed the discoveries of the age and sought to use scientific insights and methods within Christianity and those who have scorned or shunned new ideas to stay deeply in touch with the "old-time religion." Neither of these groups can be adequately described, but they stand at the limits of the argument: fundamentalists on the one hand and liberals on the other. Both words have been used as terms of derision and as badges of righteousness.

Orthodoxy is a question of right belief, and a certain theological orthodoxy had developed over many centuries. If we looked at Christians in the context of their long history, we could outline some basic shared positions that define right thinking. Christians believe in the resurrection, in Christ as Savior and Lord of the world, in grace as a power of forgiveness and enablement (the power to do good), in the Trinity (three persons in one God, as defined by the ancient church), in the statements of the Apostles' Creed (see Appendix 5), and in Original Sin and inherent spiritual weakness. To these central doctrines of Christianity in the first 1,500 years, Protestants added

Controversy

Politicized Preaching: The Stirring Vision of Aimee Semple McPherson

Canadian-born Pentecostal Aimee Semple McPherson (1890–1944) defied gender roles, adopted a Hollywood style to make her preaching dramatic, was a pioneer in the use of new technology to spread the Gospel, and urged Evangelicals and Pentecostals to adopt a new sense of their mission on earth. While liberal and conservative Protestants were fighting over the right way to understand Christianity, McPherson combined old-time religion, dramatic personal preaching, and patriotism into a movement designed to make America a Christian nation.

After a call from God, she embarked on a preaching tour in her "Gospel car" (a 1912 Packard with the words "Jesus is coming soon—get ready" painted on the side), spending 4 years on the road before settling in Los Angeles. She preached three times every day to a capacity crowd (5,300 people) in her church, Angelus Temple (opened in 1923). Although earlier evangelists had spoken to large crowds, used marketing techniques, or preached in a provocative manner, none were as famous and compelling as Sister Aimee. She traveled widely and created a huge international religious operation, the Foursquare Gospel church. Wearing makeup and jewelry, dressed in white and carrying red roses, she preached a Gospel that was more about love and healing than about fire and brimstone. With a press agent, her own newspaper and magazine, and eventually her own radio station (KFSG), she was the first woman to preach on the radio, a genius at fundraising, and able to attract millions of followers.

Sister Aimee was not inhibited by racial barriers, often preaching in black neighborhoods or helping Hispanic missions in Los Angeles. Although she did not call herself a Pentecostal, her services were marked by speaking in tongues and healings. After a scandalous episode in her life, she learned how quickly media can turn against one of its darlings. Nevertheless, she had a new and significant impact on American evangelical religion. Her sermon "America, Awake!" linked nationalism and old-time religion: Christians, she said, should unite to defeat secularism. She urged people to defend the faith of the founding fathers and spoke of Jesus in terms of patriotism: had he lived in her time, he would have been a valiant and patriotic American. Her hostility toward church-state separation and her drive to Christianize America galvanized Pentecostals and Evangelicals and brought them more squarely into mainstream American life, including politics.

---

some of the insights of the reformers: the priesthood of all believers, the salvation in Christ through faith alone, the sufficiency of Scripture as a religious authority, the sovereignty of God, and predestination. Catholics denied the Protestant insights and added instead the positions of the Council of Trent. The argument we are now describing, however, is a Protestant one for the most part, and what we say here relates to a debate within the Protestant church.

Important for Christian orthodoxy was the theory of the atonement. The orthodox Protestant position up to the nineteenth century was that of substitutionary atonement. This doctrine says simply that human sinfulness demanded a payment; Jesus paid the price (substituted for humanity), which satisfied the demands of divine justice, and because of his work, death, and resurrection, people can be saved. All these points of orthodoxy derive from the Bible.

The orthodox view, however, did not endure without challenges (in the Enlightenment, for example). Modern scientific discoveries were often at odds with established religious beliefs, and in the nineteenth century, a whole new scientific method of textual analysis presented Christianity with its most difficult modern challenge. For a number of reasons, scholars became interested in biblical texts. As we have seen, some wanted to find the most accurate version of the Bible (the earliest translation or the one least tampered with) and to revise the Bible people used in the light of new discoveries. Some wanted to read the Bible differently. They were interested not so much in its devotional message as in trying to discover what the biblical authors really meant in the text. They studied the history and archaeology of the biblical period to see what they could learn about those people and were able, they thought, to shed new light on biblical stories and figures. Some of the conclusions of these scholars were threatening to traditional Christian beliefs. Most Christians had always believed that Moses wrote the first five books of the Bible, that the Gospel of John was a historically accurate picture of Jesus, and that no matter what else one could find in Scripture, there were no mistakes.

You can imagine how threatening it was (and still is to some Christians) to see these beliefs challenged. If Moses did not write the first five books of the Bible, then who did? What did one do with the theory of inspiration that said God dictated those first five books to Moses? If the Gospel of John was not a historically accurate picture of Jesus, what was? Who was the *historical* Jesus? Did he really work miracles? Did he know he was the Messiah? Did he really think the end of the world was coming? Are his ethics really meant to be lived by people now, or were they meant to be an interim ethic based on his belief that the world would soon end? Finally, if there were mistakes in the Bible, what happened to the whole concept of revelation, of God's authorship of Scripture? Surely, God did not make mistakes.

All these questions—originally posed by scholars in Europe—made their way into American Christianity and became the backbone of American Christian liberalism. The American context provided a congenial atmosphere for such questions: people were much readier to believe in natural human goodness than in theories of human depravity and predestination, and perhaps this new scientific method could provide a new way to understand and embrace the Christian faith.

The pivotal issue was the *authority of the Bible*. Let us review this issue a little bit. Before the Reformation, there were profound differences of opinion about the Bible. Some parts of it were valued more highly than others. Luther judged the books of the Bible with reference to the norm of salvation by grace through faith and so had little good to say about the Epistle of James with its emphasis on good works. He was not worried about the infallibility of the Bible. Later, however, people wanted to place more authority in Scripture, to cite the authority of God (as written down in Scripture) against the competing authority of kings or popes or new religious views. In the seventeenth and eighteenth centuries, some people went to extremes in their defense of biblical authority, arguing that even the *punctuation* of the Bible could not be questioned or changed.

Fundamentalists inherited these conservative views about biblical authority. Although there is no single list of fundamentals, the most common set of beliefs recognized by them include biblical inerrancy, substitutionary atonement, the future Second Coming of Christ, full face value of biblical miracles, and the divinity of Christ, including his resurrection from the dead. A series of twelve paperback pamphlets published between 1910 and 1915, called *The Fundamentals,* probably gave the movement its name. Scholars disagree about the essential characteristics of fundamentalists—whether, for example, they are dominated by an interest in the end of the world or whether they are predominantly opposed to modernity and anything related to it. Although they believe in the inerrancy of Scripture, it is not fair to characterize all of them as extreme literalists or to picture them as closed minded. The term *fundamentalist* comes from their belief that there is an irreducible minimum of beliefs without which one cannot claim to be a Christian, and one of those beliefs is in the inerrancy of the Bible.

The heart of fundamentalism is a concern for salvation. The key question for them is simple and direct: "Have you been saved?" But how is one saved? According to orthodox Christian beliefs, a person cannot save himself or herself; God must act to do it. And God has done it in Christ, who atoned for human sinfulness, but that atonement cannot work for a person unless she or he accepts Christ. Once one accepts Christ as the Son of God and Savior, one is assured of heaven and receives the grace of God as a power to overcome sin. How does a person know this message or scenario to be true? Because God has said so: because it can be found in the Bible, which is God's word and so gives assurance to this position. Fundamentalists are concerned, therefore, to assert the inerrancy of Scripture to protect what they see as the essential message of the Gospel. They often link Christianity to conservative ideologies.

A few *extreme fundamentalists* believe that there are no mistakes in the Bible and that every word means exactly what it says: the Bible is to be read as fully and literally true. Some *extreme liberals* admit that there are mistakes in the Bible, see much of it as metaphor, and argue that the Bible should be read as an ethical guide for human life. Most of the people who tend to one or the other end of this spectrum are not extremists, and that makes the problem of interpretation more difficult. Conservatives or *neoevangelicals* are descended from the fundamentalist position but have moved away from it to meet scientific and biblical criticism partway: they support their traditional views by way of scientific methods. They do not condemn biblical criticism as the work of the devil (as some extreme fundamentalists do), but neither do they accept the basic presuppositions of liberals. Neoevangelicals accept the supernatural world as a reality and are not constrained to explain divine intervention in the world; at the same time, they are willing to defend their views with reason and logic. They combine traditional orthodoxy with social activism and scholarship.

After a stormy period in the early part of the twentieth century, *neoliberalism* emerged in the 1940s. Harry Emerson Fosdick (1878–1969) elaborated some key tenets of it in a 1935 sermon: it is necessary to adapt Christianity to the modern world but not by diluting the concept of God. Neoliberals are not overly optimistic about human nature (as earlier liberals, especially before World War I, may have been); they are willing to admit that the human situation is a predicament. People, they say, are sinful and there are no simple solutions. People need more than ethics: they need to find themselves driven to God. Neoliberals affirm the importance of the church as a living society and a divine institution (old liberals often looked at the church as no more than a social institution), and they affirm the necessity of repentance (some old liberals were not convinced of the reality of sin).

A tradition with some of its roots in liberalism but at the same time essentially convinced about the Protestant reformers' primary insights about God, human nature, and the Bible is *neo-orthodoxy.* Most neo-orthodox theologians have been suspicious of fundamentalism yet convinced of the sovereignty of God, the power of sin, and the importance of the Bible for a realistic appraisal of human nature. The most important proponent of neo-orthodoxy was Karl Barth (1886–1968), a Swiss theologian who made a major impact on twentieth-century Protestant theology. The strongest American advocate of neo-orthodoxy was Reinhold Niebuhr (1892–1971). Neo-orthodoxy is socially and politically liberal yet theologically conservative. It requires a special social activism based on a committed Christian life. Neo-orthodox theologians have a renewed appreciation of the church as a collective group or community, and they support the concept of a worldwide church and the ecumenical movement.

CONCLUSION

We hope that from this chapter you have seen that the complexity of the arguments and the peculiarities of denominational history, even in American culture, make it nearly impossible to offer simple characterizations of particular groups. Today, Christians face similar issues of biblical authority, orthodoxy, fundamentalism, and social activism, and they do so in a pluralistic context, often as part of larger social or political movements. Religious positions or controversies are no longer confined to denominational arguments or even theological arguments: many of the ways Christians respond to their religious impulses today have worldwide consequences or roots. Add to this the vast size of some of these contemporary issues, and we hope you will see how much caution needs to be exercised before making sweeping statements about any Christian group.

Christianity—in America and in the world—is not simply made up of a variety of churches or denominations; it is also characterized by specific beliefs, questions, and actions. The purpose of this chapter has been to show how difficult it is to know exactly what we mean when we say that someone is a Methodist or a Catholic: there are wide differences of opinion within single denominations. It is also extremely hard to know what we mean when we say evangelical or liberal or fundamentalist. The words have been used by one group to dismiss the importance of another group. We should be careful and generous, therefore, when using the terms descriptively. When we move to contemporary issues (in Chapter 12), we may be inclined to see either fractionalization or richness, depending on our proclivities and our background. Whatever we see, we have seen it coming: the early church began in variety and diversity, it was politically involved as soon as it was able to be in a power position, it responded to serious controversy and reform from within, it survived some challenges and reformed on the basis of others, and it has demonstrated extraordinary adaptability.

Focal Points for Discussion

1. Revivalism began in America with the First Great Awakening and developed new methods and new vitality in the Second Great Awakening. What were the essential differences between them? Do they preach a different God?
2. One remarkable fact about American religious history is the great diversity of religious expression and the founding of new religious groups. How do new

religions like Mormonism, Adventism, or Christian Science adapt the Christian story to their own experience?

3. The Civil War raised questions that are still important in American Christianity in terms of both politics and race relations. What impact did the war have on major American denominations? Why did black Christians believe they needed to found their own churches to have an authentic experience of Christianity?

Worldwide Christianity: Missions, Ecumenism, and Globalization

CHAPTER 9

In Chapter 7, we reviewed some of the challenges of modernity and noted the responses of various Christian groups, and in Chapter 8, we looked at the extraordinary creativity of Christian development in nineteenth-century America. From both chapters, we have become more aware of Christian diversity. We can no longer talk about Catholics, Orthodox Christians, and Protestants but must now add territorial adjectives—Russian Orthodox and Greek Orthodox, for example—and words describing general intellectual postures like *liberal* and *fundamentalist.* In addition, we have seen the emergence of evangelical and Pentecostal Christianity not only as new communities or denominations but as important dimensions of mainline churches. Finally, we know that America was the soil for experimentation, division, and regrouping. Communitarian movements and new religions like Mormonism and Christian Science flourished, established churches like the Methodists and Presbyterians divided over painful issues raised during the Civil War, and general impulses to restore Christian unity inspired a regrouping of like-minded Christians into new denominations such as the Churches of Christ.

New life and change show that Christianity is a growing and dynamic religion. In this chapter, we will examine the cooperative adventure of missionary activity, especially in the nineteenth century, and the extraordinary growth of renewalist—Pentecostal and charismatic—Christianity in Africa and Latin America. We will also notice some aspects of interfaith cooperation—the ecumenical movement and the World Council of Churches—all of this in the context of increasing globalization.

UNDERSTANDING THE MISSIONARY IMPULSE

From the earliest days of the Christian movement, evangelization was important. Jesus' words in Matthew 28:19–20 were interpreted as a clear command: believers were to "make disciples of all nations" with the confidence that Jesus would be with them always, even "to the close of the age." The very idea that the "close of the age" or end of the world might be near inspired some of the earliest Christians to extend their message throughout the known world in an effort to gather as many as possible into the new community. When it became clear that the world was not going to end soon, Christians still took the words of Jesus as a command and continued to spread their new faith wherever they went.

We have seen how hard Paul worked to make Christianity available to Gentiles and to preach the Gospel throughout the Roman world. Paul was the consummate missionary, partly because of his zeal and partly because of his mission strategy. When Paul was in Athens (Acts 17:16–34) and was asked to explain his new teaching, he accommodated himself to his audience. He told his listeners that he had seen in their marketplace an altar "to an unknown god," and he proceeded to explain that Jesus was that unknown God. Today, we might say that Paul understood missionary adaptation, the notion that a missionary first needs to know and respect the cultural values of those to whom he or she is preaching. Paul's zeal inspired missionaries throughout Christian history, even if his strategy of adaptation came to be forgotten.

The Christian empire under Constantine was distinguished by its power and beauty, as well as by its attention to philosophical debate and doctrinal definition. Another important feature of Constantine's patronage of Christianity was his support for missionaries, a practice continued by Orthodox Christianity. For example, Cyril and Methodius (d. 869 and 885), two brothers supported by the Eastern Orthodox empire, were known as the "apostles to the Slavs." Cyril gave up his post at the imperial university at Constantinople and Methodius relinquished his position as a provincial governor so that both could become priests and spread Christianity to the people of Moravia. They were able to succeed because they learned the Slavonic language. Their work on that alphabet enabled them to translate the Bible and the liturgy into Slavonic and to lay the groundwork for what would later become a flowering of Slavonic literature. For many Orthodox Christians today, Slavonic is the official liturgical language.

The missionary history of the western part of the empire reflected its political situation. We saw in Chapter 4 that missionaries were sent to the farthest reaches of the Roman world to bring Christianity to various peoples: Patrick in Ireland, Boniface in Germany, and Augustine of Canterbury in England were effective missionaries, able to adapt their message to the needs of their audiences. When Western Christianity fell on hard times in the Dark Ages, the peoples of Europe were "re-Christianized" by Irish and English monks who had kept the faith alive on their islands. The labor force for missionary activity available to Western Christianity through monasticism should not be underestimated. In addition to monks, new religious groups were formed to work outside monastic enclaves, and some of them did missionary work but in a much different context. The Dominicans, for example, were founded by Dominic (c. 1170–1221) in 1216 for the express purpose of preaching and teaching in territories threatened by heretical interpretations of Christianity.

In the medieval period, the missionary success of the Roman Catholic church and its political dominance led to the conclusion that Christianity had been made available to everyone in the known world. Muslims and Jews, increasingly perceived as rival religions and defined as infidels, were either driven from western Europe or forced into ghettos. Christians in western Europe tended to think of their world as the center of the universe and their religion as the most perfect expression of religious consciousness in the world. When groups deviated from Catholic belief or practice, they were prosecuted and punished. A missionary thus became someone who preached and taught in heretical territories to bring the people there under submission to church teaching as approved by the pope. The structure that solidified in the thirteenth century to deal with heresy was the Inquisition; Dominican priests, commissioned by the pope as inquisitors, tortured and executed heretics.

When new territories opened up outside western Europe, missionaries sent to win new peoples for Christ were often more like inquisitors than they were like St. Paul. The two new mission fields that opened in the late medieval period give us a way to explore opposing practices of missionary work: Jesuits in China were models of missionary adaptation (the New Testament model), and missionaries in the New World pursued an imperialist strategy willing to create new Christians by force.

A Jesuit in China

Marco Polo (1254–1324), an explorer from Venice, reached the magnificent court of Kublai Kahn in 1275. He made other trips to China accompanied by missionaries, and their work was impressive as they reached what is now known as Beijing, but this early attempt to evangelize China did not flourish. Once Marco Polo "discovered" China, European missionary and economic interests in the Orient were stimulated, and the stage was set for later missionaries, notably for the work of the Jesuits in the seventeenth century led by Matteo Ricci (1552–1610). Ricci had a marvelous facility for languages and made progress in China because, as he put it, he tried to "become Chinese in order to win the Chinese." Ricci let his hair grow into a traditional braid, dressed in local garb, spoke fluent Mandarin Chinese, and secured his place in the hearts of his audience by developing an interest in local literary classics. As a missionary, he pursued a strategy that was both ancient (Pauline) and, at the same time, innovative precisely because his first goal was to adapt to the culture rather than to impose European ideals on it.

Ricci spent years in China talking more about Western inventions—like the clock—than about the life and death of Jesus. As he understood the situation, only patience would work as a missionary strategy. He was careful to gain the confidence of his audience before slowly introducing them to Christian stories, and he realized that Christianity could make progress in China only to the extent that it was adapted to Chinese cultural realities.

Typical of his pioneering spirit, he asked for permission to celebrate the liturgy in the vernacular—remember that the official liturgical language for Catholics was Latin—and he worked to translate the Bible into Mandarin Chinese. He hoped that Vatican officials would permit a translation of Christian documents and liturgy into Chinese and that they would make some accommodations to Chinese cultural expectations. Unfortunately, those hopes were misplaced. Ricci's mission to China was, finally, a dismal failure because Roman Catholic officials could not understand the need to make any accommodations. The story of the collapse of the Chinese mission in the seventeenth and eighteenth centuries is a sad one and too complicated to repeat here, but it is instructive because it helps us define one of the problems of the missionary movement.

Ricci's instincts and methods are accepted practice today: missionaries from all branches of Christianity first adapt themselves to the culture and only later begin to draw their listeners into Christianity. Missionaries encourage people to maintain their cultural identity so that their possible conversions to Christianity do not force them to abandon their heritage to become Christians. In Ricci's time, however, such missionary adaptation was not possible. Roman officials were nervous about translating the Bible into Chinese because they feared that Christianity would become tainted with pagan Chinese beliefs. Vatican officials in charge of foreign missions insisted that new converts learn Latin to become priests and that native clergy follow the Western rules of celibacy, a practice that made no sense to the Chinese.

The whole situation was further complicated by competition from non-Jesuit missionaries who did not subscribe to the wisdom of missionary adaptation. Franciscans and Dominicans, for example, did not adapt themselves to the Chinese and so attempted to make Chinese converts into Europeans. Their strategies deeply offended Chinese officials, who perceived them as culturally imperialistic and as having no respect for the people to whom they ministered. The missionary movement in China, therefore, was closed and not opened again until the nineteenth century, when it flourished until political realities in the mid–twentieth century forced another dismissal of Christian missionaries from the territory.

The New World

The second great discovery that opened mission fields for European Christians was the "New World" discovered by Christopher Columbus and other explorers in the fifteenth and sixteenth centuries. When Pope Alexander VI "divided" the New World between Spain and Portugal in 1493, he split the responsibility for missionary activity between the two countries. Explorers went to the New World to "conquer it for the greater glory of God" *and* to bring its treasures—gold, silver, precious stones—back to Europe. The story of missionaries in the New World—in present-day Mexico, Central America, South America, California, Canada, and the Mississippi Valley—is not a simple one. The missionaries had little respect for native culture and were determined to destroy it while they saved its peoples. They sometimes treated native peoples as children or, worse, as slaves, forcing them into a new religion and into slave labor camps for Spain or Portugal.

Some missionaries, vehement advocates of Indian rights, protested the harsh treatment of native people. Their voices were not the dominant ones, however, and the same attitudes that led to the dissolution of the Chinese mission characterized the activity of many missionaries in the New World: most attempted to make Europeans out of Native Americans, forcing them to change their names, their dress, their places of residence, and their practices. The difference between the two settings was power: the Chinese empire was able to resist Christianity and to expel its missionaries, whereas the Native American tribes were easily conquered by the explorers. Native cultures and religions were often simply wiped out as Christianity was forced on the people under threat of harsh punishment and as missionaries and conquerors brought epidemic diseases with them to the New World.

The history of Christian missions in the New World, as in China, is not a simple one: we can find stories of great heroism and compassion on the part of missionaries—the work of the Jesuits among the Hurons, for example—and we can find stories of exploitation and cruelty. The only point we wish to make about this early modern period of Christian missionary activity is this: missionaries did not believe that they should adapt themselves to native cultures or respect native beliefs; in alliance with the explorers, their goal was often to *conquer* new peoples for Christ. However well meant the ultimate goal—the belief that they were bringing the true faith to new peoples—the methods were often brutal. However successful the outcome—the overwhelming presence of Christianity in the Western Hemisphere—the price of that success can still raise questions for us.

Protestant Missionaries in the Nineteenth Century

For reasons that may be obvious, Protestants did not rush into missionary activity during the sixteenth, seventeenth, and eighteenth centuries. Besides being entirely taken up with establishing their new religious visions, their rejection of monasticism as an option for Christian life meant that they did not have the labor force for missionary conquest. Furthermore, the belief that God elected those who would be "saved" often enabled Protestants to see conversion as "God's problem," in no need of help from human agents. They tended to read the passage in the Gospel of Matthew as a directive of Jesus to the apostles rather than as a mandate for Christians at all times.

There were, of course, some notable exceptions. The Pietist movement had a strong missionary impulse, and the Moravians in the eighteenth century were distinguished by their missionary zeal, especially with Native Americans in the New World. John Wesley's rejection of predestination and his emphasis on salvation available to all who could respond to the invitation of Jesus tended to stir a missionary fervor in Methodism. We can also find historical evidence for Puritan missionary activity, but the real heyday for missionary work in Protestant churches began in the nineteenth century.

The first great hero of the Protestant missionary movement was an Englishman, William Carey (1761–1834), a self-educated shoemaker and linguistic genius who converted to the Anglican church and later became a Baptist. Carey changed the typical Protestant attitude toward missionary activity at a time when the British empire was conquering new peoples in India and Africa. His book *Enquiry into the Obligations of Christians to Use Means for the Conversion of the Heathens* (1792) supported his understanding of the words of Jesus as a modern Christian duty. Jesus was not speaking only to the apostles, he argued; he was speaking to all Christians and sending them forth to bring the message of the Gospel to the world. Carey inspired the Baptists to get interested in mission fields. He raised money to finance a trip to India, where he translated the Bible into Bengali and attracted converts to Christianity because he was able to speak to them in their own languages. Years later, he became a professor of languages in Calcutta and produced important grammars in a variety of Indian languages.

Missionary enthusiasm characterized Protestant churches in general in the nineteenth century, notably in England and America. Young people especially were interested in the challenges of bringing God's word to peoples in the far corners of the globe, and like Carey, they heard Jesus' word directed to them. Hymns and tracts produced at the time inspired them to proclaim "the joyful sound of salvation" to the remotest regions of the world. The lyrics of Reginald Herber's hymn "From Greenland's Icy Mountains" (1819) show the paternalistic aspect of missionary zeal describing the "heathen in his blindness" bowing down to wood and stone and urging those "whose souls are lighted with wisdom from on high" to minister to benighted peoples in foreign lands. The attraction of missionary work, therefore, was strong: missionaries, like St. Paul in the Acts of the Apostles (16:9), had a sense of people calling to "come and help us." Some believed that enlightening those in darkness would hasten the Second Coming of Christ.

Evangelical Christians in particular believed that the best response they could make in thanksgiving for their own Christian faith was to bring the revelation of Christ to everyone. If Reformation Christians understood their lives as dedicated to love of neighbor, revivalist Christians in the aftermath of the Second Great Awakening understood that love of neighbor now extended everywhere. The hope that stirred them was that the world could be totally won for Christ, and they aimed to bring a moral revolution to the entire globe. Enthusiasm and optimism abounded and blended well with American ideas of manifest destiny: America was destined by God, many believed, to bring democracy to the world, just as Christians were enjoined to preach the Gospel to all nations.

Carey's success, coupled with a general expansionary enthusiasm in the nineteenth century, led to the formation of a number of supportive societies. For example, the London Missionary Society was founded in 1795 as the first interdenominational missionary group, famous for sending David Livingstone (1813–1873), a Scottish missionary and explorer, to Africa. Because missionaries needed materials for their work, they established societies to produce Bibles and religious tracts. In many ways, the work of these groups was the first adventure in interdenominational cooperation.

The American Board of Commissioners of Foreign Missions was organized in 1810 to send Congregationalist missionaries to Southeast Asia. Its founding was stimulated by the interest of some remarkable young people at Williams College, notably Adoniram Judson (1788–1850), who felt that his call to ministry was, in fact, a vocation to carry the Gospel to Burma. When he and his friends were commissioned, great enthusiasm spread to other groups. When Judson, stopping in India to see Carey, became convinced that the Baptist form of Christianity was more representative of New Testament practice, he became a Baptist and stimulated the formation of the American Baptist Missionary Union (1814). Like Carey, Judson was a linguistic pioneer who spent his early years in the mission fields translating the Bible into Burmese. Like Matteo Ricci in seventeenth-century China, he did not attempt to preach the Gospel until he established cultural and linguistic links with the people.

During the nineteenth century, missionary societies were formed throughout Europe and the United States in all denominations. Mission boards and mission societies attracted many zealous Christians and helped spread the Gospel to Southeast Asia, the Pacific, China, Japan, and Africa. In many ways, Christian missions came of age in the nineteenth century. They were not supported by the government and so were forced to rely on the devotion and financial sacrifices of believers. Missions were staffed and supported by laypeople who saw their Christian destinies bound up with the conversion of the world.

Furthermore, mission activities tended to involve much more than the Gospel: missionaries founded churches, schools, hospitals, and other institutions as they worked to understand the languages and grammars of new cultures. Much of what we know today about foreign languages and practices was first recorded by Catholic and Protestant missionaries in the field. Missionaries developed native leadership and introduced some innovations to native agricultural and trading practices.

Modern Missionaries and Liberation Theology

For the most part, until the middle of the twentieth century, Christian missionaries worked for countries pursuing colonial expansion: their efforts were aligned with and supported by imperialism. Missionaries, therefore, preached Christian discipleship within a political context of exploitation and conquest. In the second half of the twentieth century, however, that situation changed dramatically. The control of large territories in Africa and Asia by the British empire gave way to movements of independence as people fought to gain control over their own political and religious lives. Mohandas Gandhi (1869–1948) invented a nonviolent form of political action to confront the "Christian" government of India and to inspire a movement for independence. Countries in Africa and in Latin America became independent, sometimes through peaceful negotiation and sometimes through violent revolution. Gradually, indigenous people were able to shape Christianity in their own idiom. For example, when the Second Vatican Council in the Roman Catholic church (1962–1965) encouraged liturgical experimentation, African masses were accompanied by native drummers and dancers, native priests in tribal costumes, and forms of preaching that were more indebted to African culture than to traditional forms of worship.

By far the most dramatic change in the ways missionaries understand themselves has occurred in Latin America, where a new theology was born in the early 1970s. Liberation theology is a particular application of political theology to the poverty and oppression found in Latin America. Its special method, *praxis,* developed by Brazilian educator Paulo Friere, focused on actions rather than on words. Based on a reading of the Bible in which God's special concern rests with the poor and the oppressed peoples of the world, liberation theology holds that God's most significant actions in the Bible are those involved with deliverance or liberation (from oppression, slavery, exile, sin). According to this view, God has a special relationship with the poor and marginalized members of any society.

Liberation theology, therefore, starts with a commitment to the poor and to their struggle and finds its primary example in the life of Jesus, who called all Christians to work for the elimination of all forms of oppression. Liberation theologians claim that their commitment to the poor gives them a new perspective from which to read the Bible, and it gives their theology an edge that is both critical and prophetic. Far from being an isolated view of Christian social action relevant to Latin America, liberation theology claims to be a whole new way to understand Christianity and its doctrines. This new theology articulates an experience of God as involved in the human problems of the world. The Bible with its covenant theology, according to them, is a history of deliverance. When people in bondage cried out, God liberated them and made them responsible for establishing peace and justice on the earth. When the Israelites forgot this mission, God reminded them of it through the prophets.

For liberation theologians, the mission of Jesus was to the poor. His life was spent trying to counteract human selfishness. God is deeply implicated in human history in

CONCEPT

Mission in Reverse

When Tissa Balasuriya described a mission in reverse in his book *Planetary Theology* (1984), he was asking Christians in powerful Western nations to reexamine Gospel values in relation to Christians in the Two-Thirds World. These Christians, often wrenchingly poor and powerless, are numerically dominant but economically peripheral. They are young, more drawn to practice than to theory, and experience God actively involved in their lives. They see the Gospel as good news not only for their ultimate salvation but for their situation on earth.

Some Christians in the Two-Thirds World see the West as a challenging new mission field where the Gospel has been distorted and are surprised that American Christians do not understand their own marginal status (a minority among the world's Christians). Since at least a quarter of the world's two billion Christians are members of Pentecostal or charismatic churches, non-Western Christians often bring a worship style marked by the "gifts of the Spirit" (speaking in tongues, prophesying, and divine healing). In such a context, traditional forms of prayer, sacrifice, mystical experience, asceticism, worship, leadership, and social justice are being explored in new ways in a theological framework that is dynamic and changing.

Non-Western churches are now the primary force in the spread of the Gospel in the world. For example, in 1986, a young Nigerian, Sunday Adelaja, experienced a call from God similar to the one received by Abraham (Gen. 12:1) to leave his country and go to a new land. Today, his church in Kiev has established more than one hundred churches outside the Ukraine and has developed a number of social ministries (for example, soup kitchens, drug rehabilitation centers). The *Sunday Times* (London) reported in July 2000 that Latin American and African evangelists were emigrating to "pagan Britain" because, like American missionaries in the nineteenth century, they heard the words from the Acts of the Apostles (16:9), "Come and help us." Missionaries from African countries have established a presence in North America as well. For example, the Church of Pentecost, founded in Ghana in 1937, has 1,700 churches worldwide, 70 of which are in the United States.

Two-Thirds World churches, relatively poor and politically powerless, are intensely spiritual. They often have at least one all-night prayer meeting each month, most have large attendance at their midweek meetings, and all of them emphasize the power of prayer and fasting. Their intense witness, sense of community, and confidence that God will bless their lives have made their message attractive to millions of Christians in the Western world.

---

the liberation perspective: Jesus is God's dramatic reminder that believers are required to work for justice, to lay down their lives for their neighbors if need be. Like the Anabaptists, liberation theologians believe that the ethics of Jesus are meant to be followed in the lives of ordinary Christians. Liberation theology grew in predominantly Catholic soil and was inspired in part by some of the modern social teachings of the Roman Catholic church. Pope John XXIII's encyclicals, *Mater et Magistra* (1961) and *Pacem in Terris* (1963), focused on Christianity and social progress: the pope criticized economic disparity and the arms race and urged universal peace established in truth, justice, charity, and liberty.

Many of the themes of liberation theology have been found in Protestant Christianity as well, especially in the meetings of the World Council of Churches (see below and Appendix 7). The 1961 meeting of the WCC in New Delhi dramatized the problems of world hunger and poverty, and a 1966 meeting of church leaders of the

WCC in Geneva concluded that the Gospel is revolutionary by nature and that Christians ought to be involved on the side of social revolutions. A meeting between Roman Catholic and WCC leaders in Beirut (1968) discussed Pope Paul VI's encyclical *Populorum Progressio* (1967) and urged Christians to be politically active on behalf of peace and world development. The WCC meeting in Uppsala in 1968 was also geared to the needs of the world and concluded that those who were complacent in the face of vast social injustice were guilty of heresy.

The liberationist perspective can be applied to any group that has experienced oppression. Black theology, for example, reads the Bible from the perspective of racist oppression, and James Cone has argued that the only authentic understanding of Scripture and faith is a black one. Women's groups have also identified with liberation perspectives. Two-Thirds World peoples in general tend to take the exodus motif in the Old Testament as a metaphor for their relationship to God. To their way of thinking, God is involved in their suffering and active with them in the struggle to overcome oppression.

In Christian churches today, liberation theology has the potential to build up and to divide communities. This volatile capacity is especially evident in responses to Christian missionary activity and reminds us that most denominations are made up of Christians from both liberal and conservative perspectives. Most congregations are going to have differences of opinion about whether the Gospel is meant to change individual hearts or to alter social policy, and those congregations may quarrel bitterly on the goals of their missionaries. At the present time, several Protestant churches are sharply divided over the proper role for their missionaries in Latin America. Are they there to identify with the poor and help them to build a more just society? Or are they sent primarily to preach the Gospel and to move their hearers to personal conversion? Does a Christian have to choose between these two possibilities? Can a missionary fulfill the intentions of Jesus by simply asking people to change their hearts? Or must missionaries also involve themselves in helping to change the circumstances of their lives?

The Roman Catholic church is also divided on this issue. Participation of missionary priests and sisters in some Latin American struggles—notably the Nicaraguan revolution in 1979—was based on a liberationist reading of Scripture as supported by the Latin American bishops. Yet, the Vatican has sharply criticized active political involvement by its clergy and has attempted to frame social justice issues in less partisan ways. Are the issues at stake for Catholics different from those raised by Protestants? What kinds of work should priests and nuns be doing in Africa, Asia, and Latin America?

What are the connections between the work of Christian missionaries and the ways Christianity is perceived by Two-Thirds World peoples? One of the sharpest criticisms of contemporary Christianity comes from Tissa Balasuriya, a Sri Lankan Catholic priest who argues that modern Christianity is morally bankrupt and in need of what he calls a "mission in reverse." Two-Thirds World Christians, who understand how to live the Gospel—its values of poverty, nonviolence, and sharing—should now go as missionaries to industrialized countries where Christians have abandoned the teachings of the Gospel in favor of policies of exploitation.

Christians in Europe and America took seriously Jesus' words to carry the Gospel to all nations. Their missionary zeal was compromised, however, by their desire to

PEOPLE

Modern Missionaries in Danger: Four Women in El Salvador

Liberation theology and missionary adaptation have changed the missionary strategy of both Catholics and Protestants working in foreign countries. Those who minister to the poor and marginalized in these societies generally live with them in solidarity (sharing their poverty and frustrations) and also work to empower them toward their own self-determination. As we have seen, this combination of religious and political values has split some churches on the question of missionary goals. It has also sometimes led to violence against the missionaries themselves.

In December of 1980, four Catholic women were murdered in El Salvador, probably by soldiers acting under orders from the government. Although political assassinations of religious leaders were not new—Archbishop Oscar Romero was killed while he was saying Mass in March of 1980 because he had been speaking out against military violence—the murder of Americans and women caused a sensation. Three of the women were nuns: Ita Ford and Maura Clarke were Maryknoll sisters; Dorothy Kazel was an Ursuline.

The fourth victim, Jean Donovan, was a young woman who grew up in the protected suburbs of Connecticut and felt called to make something of her life. As a wealthy young socialite, she was used to country club dances, horseback riding, and the kind of life that goes with privilege. As a young Republican and a successful accountant, she astonished her friends when she announced that she intended to leave that life behind to become a lay missionary working with Maryknoll sisters in Latin America. When she met her death in the jungles of Latin America, Jean Donovan had become a different person, one who discarded the badges of American success to embrace the poverty and violence-torn world of Salvadoran peasants. Donovan's story has been the subject of television specials and a movie, *Roses in December*.

Before her death, Maura Clarke wrote a letter home saying, "My fear of death is being challenged constantly as children, lovely young girls, old people, are being shot and cut up with machetes . . . a loving God must have a new life of unimaginable joy and peace prepared for these precious, unknown, uncelebrated martyrs."

When these women were killed, some conservative Christians said that they were not religious workers at all but were engaging in guerrilla politics in a foreign country. Their story is the missionary goal conflict writ large.

preach their culture and politics as well as their religion. This policy was disastrous in seventeenth-century China and successful in the Americas only at murderous cost to native religions and cultures. In the nineteenth century, Christianity was linked with the expansion of the British Empire in Africa and India and with American manifest destiny in the Pacific. Many of the people in those places have struggled throughout the twentieth century to establish their political independence. It should not be surprising that they hope to find and articulate a religious independence as well.

Christianity is no longer a religion with an essentially European or American character. On the contrary, Christians throughout the world are bringing their own perspectives, their own forms of celebration, their own music and styles of preaching, and their own evaluations of the proper roles for Christians in the pressing social questions of the day. Global Christianity in the twenty-first century is full of explosive new energy whose transnational connections have led to more cooperation and more divisiveness.

GLOBALIZATION AND THE RISE OF WORLD CHRISTIANITY

We have seen that the missionaries from Europe and North America shifted their goals and methods to meet new international situations. Nineteenth-century missionaries, who came from colonizing countries like the United Kingdom, saw themselves as bringing "civilization" as well as the Gospel to "natives" who needed both. As nations in Asia and Africa gained their independence in the twentieth century, however, missionaries from the north had to reexamine their role and increasingly worked with local people to alleviate social and economic problems and to achieve justice. Even in this new situation, however, European and North American Christians continued to see themselves as the center of the Christian world: they lived in Christian lands, and other regions needed their message and help.

The story we have told so far has focused on Europe and on Christians of European heritage in the United States. In geographical terms, we first saw how a religion that began in Palestine ("the Middle East" today) spread through the Mediterranean empire that the Romans ruled. With the fall of large areas of the former Roman Empire to the Muslims, we followed Roman Catholicism into Western Europe and noticed how Orthodox Christianity moved into Eastern Europe and western Asia. We then studied how Christianity came to North America and diversified, and now we have seen that European and North American missionaries took the Christian message to other areas of the globe. This story has helped us to understand the varieties of Christianity in the United States, where the authors and most of the readers of this book live.

Neither the vision of missionaries nor the basic story, however, accounts for Christianity as it exists at the dawn of the twenty-first century. Globalization has transformed and continues to shape Christianity, just as it has profoundly changed the social, political, and economic world in which we live. *Globalization* refers to the increasingly interconnected nature of the world: events and practices in one part of the world affect and are affected by what happens in other regions. In the decades after World War II, political and economic differences divided the world into clear blocs—a communist world dominated by the Soviet Union and China, a democratic capitalist world dominated by the United States and its European allies, and a "Third World" of less developed countries and nations that were not aligned with either of the major powers. Especially since the mid-1980s, these divisions have broken down in favor of both smaller regional and political groups and a greater sense of one world.

Globalization is an ongoing process that began in the nineteenth century, but it accelerated rapidly in the late twentieth century and continues to do so. The growth of the airline industry in the 1950s and 1960s enabled rapid, comfortable, and increasingly less expensive travel across great distances, and television and radio allowed people to learn about other cultures and events in foreign lands quickly. The rise of the Internet, cell phones, and e-mail in the 1990s simplified and expanded communication across the globe. Workers, products, and technology now move back and forth across national borders. An American consumer who calls a company's customer service department may well talk to a representative based in India, who after work will watch an American music video that she has downloaded from the Internet. Problems such as climate change and terrorism do not affect single countries but require cooperation on a global scale. So, too, we can no longer think of Christianity as a European religion or even as a world religion centered around Europe; rather, it is a global religion with no single center.

It is helpful to remind ourselves that global Christianity is really not so new. Although we may have focused our attention on Europe and North America, forms of Christianity existed from ancient times in such areas as Asia and Africa. The controversies of the fourth and fifth centuries over Christ (see Chapter 4) resulted in churches in the Middle East, Egypt, and Ethiopia that were separate from the Roman Catholic and the Greek Orthodox churches. These churches flourished on their own, many under Muslim rulers, through the Middle Ages into the modern period. When Roman Catholic missionaries from Portugal arrived in India in the sixteenth century, they found an already existing community of Christians, who claimed that their church had been founded by Jesus' disciple Thomas in the first century. Although it is possible but not certain that Christianity has existed in India since apostolic times, we know for certain that Christians came to India from Persia in the sixth century. The church in Ethiopia is as ancient as any in northern Europe: it got its first bishop around 340, developed its own distinctive traditions over centuries, and now has over thirty million members.

So there have long been Christians in different regions of the world, but only since the nineteenth century have these Christians multiplied, diversified, and come into increasing contact with one another. Today, there are more Christians in Africa than there are in North America, and most new Roman Catholics in the United States are Spanish-speaking immigrants from Latin America. Globalization has accelerated certain trends that have characterized Christianity for centuries, particularly tendencies to perceive a particular form of Christianity as the only right one and desires by different forms of Christianity to seek greater unity and cooperation. The global character of Christianity is increasingly found in Africa, Latin America, and Asia rather than in Europe and North America. And forms of Christianity now travel more quickly and easily across traditional boundaries, creating both innovative transnational connections and new tension-filled divisions.

The Ecumenical Movement

Christians who seek dialogue and cooperation with other groups are part of the ecumenical movement. *Ecumenism* comes from the Greek word *oikoumene,* which means "the whole inhabited world." You may recall that some early church councils were called "ecumenical" because they aimed to include Christian bishops from the entire known world. The ecumenical movement is usually defined as the attempt of Christian churches to recover the unity of all believers. Ideally, ecumenism should enable Christians to rise above differences in doctrine and practice to achieve the unity that the New Testament imagines when it speaks of "one body of Christ." We have seen that Christians have been always diverse and almost always divided, but they have continued to believe that there can and should be only one church.

Christianity has not often been characterized by tolerance for diverse views. Medieval Catholicism perceived different expressions of Christianity as heresies and worked hard to uproot and destroy them. Protestant and Catholic Reformations resulted in religious warfare, and in the modern period, divisions among Christians multiplied as groups put a premium on their own particular understandings of Christian truth and perceived efforts at unity as a dilution of the truth.

Globalizing trends of the nineteenth and twentieth centuries did not stop the proliferation of new Christian denominations—in fact, they increased it—but they did encourage new efforts to find some unity of practice or, at the very least, unity of project. The ecumenical movement illustrates a shift from a missionary paradigm originating in Europe to a global paradigm with no center, but it was born in the experience of those earlier missionaries. In the nineteenth century, missionaries from different churches began to realize that their individual efforts might not be as effective as cooperative ventures could be. Idealistic Christian students in Britain who formed the Student Christian Movement to encourage Bible study and missions and an American student active in the YMCA movement, John R. Mott (1865–1955), worked together to found the World Student Christian Federation in 1895. These young people hoped to win the world for Christ in their lifetimes, and their enthusiasm culminated in the Edinburgh World Missionary Conference of 1910. Their belief that "service unites but doctrine divides" and the formation of the International Missionary Council united diverse Christians around missionary cooperation.

Other early ecumenical ventures likewise emphasized common projects rather than doctrinal agreement. The Evangelical Alliance, formed in London in 1846, was a coalition of interested individuals with no official connections to organized churches. It expanded into the United States after the Civil War and published a journal, *Evangelical Christendom*. The Evangelical Alliance, formed by people who had been shaped by the Second Great Awakening's emphasis on Christian social justice, encouraged evangelical Christians to unite to address social ills such as alcoholism and slavery.

The ecumenical potential of the Evangelical Alliance was limited because it included only evangelical Protestants and was a union of individuals, not churches. Still, its example inspired other efforts such as the Federal Council of Churches of Christ in America, which formally convened in 1908, and was made up of over thirty separate churches. In 1950, it merged with another group to form the National Council of the Churches of Christ in the USA (NCC), which includes Protestant and Orthodox churches that total over forty-five million members. Roman Catholics and many Pentecostal churches are not members of the NCC but cooperate in some of its work. The NCC has concentrated on biblical translation, theological dialogue, publications, and social advocacy. It sponsored the widely used New Revised Standard Version of the Bible. Conservative Christians have sometimes criticized the NCC for its commitment to such social issues as environmentalism and affirmative action.

The most important expression of the ecumenical movement is the World Council of Churches (WCC), founded in 1948 at a conference in Amsterdam. The roots of the WCC in earlier missionary cooperation can be seen in its naming of John Mott as an honorary president and its merger with the International Missionary Council in 1961. The members of the WCC include most of the Orthodox churches and many Protestant and independent churches. The Roman Catholic church is not a member but sends observers to meetings and works with the WCC on individual projects. The WCC does not seek to create an actual new united church body; rather, it promotes dialogue and mutual understanding and works for peace and justice.

The World Council of Churches illustrates both the promises and difficulties of the ecumenical movement. For example, constructive theological dialogue led to the publication in 1982 of the pamphlet *Baptism, Eucharist, and Ministry,* which prompted discussion throughout the world and inspired many churches to reform some of their rituals and offices along similar lines. On the other hand, when a WCC program designed to fight racism in the 1970s gave money to liberationist movements, some critics accused them of supporting terrorists. The generally liberal theology and politics of the WCC eventually made Orthodox Christians so uncomfortable that a special commission was formed to discuss WCC theology and to encourage more Orthodox participation in decision making.

The history of the World Council of Churches reflects the changes associated with globalization. Its roots were in missionary efforts led by Europeans, and it has sought unity in social action more than in shared theology. By 2007, the WCC was much less centered around Europe: its general secretary was a Methodist from Kenya; it supported a major initiative to combat AIDS in Africa and dedicated the decade 2001–2010 to overcoming violence in the world.

The Rise of Christianity in the Southern Hemisphere

When the World Council of Churches was formed in the 1940s, it held its first meeting in Amsterdam and located its headquarters in Geneva, Switzerland. Christianity may have been a world religion, but Europe was understood to be its heart, and Western Christians thought of themselves as constituting a majority of the world's Christians. Sixty years later, the situation was quite different. According to one estimate, of the 2 billion Christians who were alive in 2000, Europe still had the most, around 560 million, and North America had 260 million. But there were estimated to be 480 million Christians in Latin America, 360 million in Africa, and 313 million in Asia. Already by 2000, then, more than half of Christians lived outside Europe and North America, and it is possible that by 2050 Africa and Latin America together will account for more than half. It is already dubious to call Christianity a European religion, but soon it will make no sense whatsoever. The weight of Christianity is shifting to the Southern Hemisphere and becoming even more diverse.

To some extent, these statistics reflect larger population trends, as birthrates fall in Europe and North America and rise elsewhere. But there is also an undeniable shift in religious energy. Although the United States remains one of the most religiously active nations in the world, a large number of the 560 million European Christians attend church only once or twice a year, and many do not attend at all. As Europeans try to find greater political unity and avoid a renewal of conflicts based on religion, they have turned to the secular values of tolerance and human rights as their foundation. In the early 2000s, politicians worked on a new constitution for the European Union, and most resisted any reference to God or Christianity as central to the shared European heritage, dismaying religious leaders. When Joseph Ratzinger of Germany was elected pope in 2005, he took the name Benedict XVI and explained that his choice honored Benedict of Nursia and thus "the Christian roots of Europe." The new pope believed that he must revive Christianity in Europe.

In contrast, growth and enthusiasm characterize the southern forms of Christianity, as the example of Africa illustrates. When European countries gave up control over their colonies in Africa in the decades after World War II, it might have seemed that Christianity too would leave with its European supporters. Indeed, some African nationalist leaders were openly hostile to Christianity, and African Christians themselves often told missionaries from the north to leave. But Christianity itself made a major contribution to the establishment of independent African countries by spreading ideas of human rights and self-determination and by educating even women and girls in mission schools. As foreign missionaries departed, local Christian leaders could take over existing Christian institutions like schools and hospitals and make Christianity more suited to local traditions. Just as medieval Europeans after the collapse of the Roman Empire looked to the church for stability and moral authority, so too did many Africans in the turmoil that followed decolonization.

As African Christians began to preach the Gospel and lead their own churches, Christianity grew rapidly and took on more characteristics of local cultures. By the 1980s, Africans had started seven thousand new denominations, often called African Initiated Churches (AICs), even as mission churches like the Anglicans and the Lutherans continued to grow under African leadership. Most AICs and even traditional churches exhibit signs of charismatic spirituality, such as speaking in tongues, exorcisms, and visions, and many have allowed traditional local practices such as polygamy. These distinctive practices grow out of the contact between Christianity as it came to Africa from missionaries and traditional African ways of being religious. For example, the translation of the Bible into vernacular languages enabled some African Christians to see their traditional polygamy in the lives of the Old Testament patriarchs. Exorcisms and dream visions may look like they come from North American Pentecostalism, but their real roots may lie in the New Testament example of Holy Spirit–filled Christianity and in a long history of prophets in African religions. Latin American Christianity has made its significant marks on Christianity as well: Our Lady of Guadalupe is an example of a specifically Latin American way of being Christian.

The characteristics of Christianity in Asia, Africa, and Latin America are diverse and highly dependent on local conditions, but generally, Christians on these continents expect to experience God and the Holy Spirit in their daily lives much more than Christians in Europe and North America. By one estimate, Pentecostal and other charismatic Christians make up over half of the entire populations (not just Christians) of Kenya and Guatemala and nearly half that of the Philippines. A 2006 survey by the Pew Forum on Religion and Public Life found that only 29 percent of Christians in the United States had witnessed divine healings, but 62 percent of Christians in Nigeria and 44 percent in India had done so. In the United States, 11 percent of Christians reported experiencing or witnessing exorcisms in contrast to 28 percent in the Philippines, 34 percent in Brazil, and 61 percent in Kenya. We have seen that the presence of the Holy Spirit, evidenced in speaking in tongues, healings, and exorcisms, characterized early Christianity as it spread through the Roman Empire. Today, as Christianity grows in the Southern Hemisphere, we see similar practices. This renewal of spirit-filled religion is not limited to the Southern Hemisphere, however; in the United States, about one-fourth of all Christians identify themselves as Pentecostal or charismatic.

Christians in the Southern Hemisphere also tend to be more conservative in doctrine and morals than their counterparts in Europe and North America. According to the Pew poll, 35 percent of U.S. Christians think that the Bible is the word of God, to be taken literally, in contrast to 50 percent in India, 77 percent in Guatemala, and 88 percent in Nigeria. Likewise, on such moral and social issues as homosexuality, drinking alcohol, and divorce, Christians in Asia, Africa, and Latin America are markedly more conservative. We shall see in Chapter 12 that this strong difference

Spirituality

Our Lady of Guadalupe

Born in the meeting of Spanish Catholicism and indigenous Aztec religion, the Virgin of Guadalupe became a distinct feature of Mexican Christianity. Seventeenth-century documents tell the story of the Virgin Mary appearing to a Christian Indian, Juan Diego Cuauhtlatoatzin, in early December 1531. As he was walking on the hill of Tepeyac (near Mexico City), Mary materialized in front of him, addressed him in his own language (Nahuatl), and told him to tell his Spanish bishop that she wished a shrine to be built on that hill. When the bishop, Juan de Zumárraga, was skeptical, Juan Diego sadly returned to the Virgin. Undaunted by ecclesiastical doubt, she told him to gather flowers from the hillside, put them in his cloak, and return to the bishop. When Juan Diego opened his cloak in the bishop's office, the flowers fell out and a highly colorful icon of the Virgin of Guadalupe remained imprinted on it. The shrine of Our Lady of Guadalupe at Tepeyac contains the original cloth with the image on it.

Decades before this event, Spaniards had conquered the Aztecs and imposed Roman Catholicism on them. The story of Our Lady of Guadalupe enabled local people to embrace Christianity on their own terms. The Virgin resembles Tonantzin, an Aztec earth goddess who had a shrine at Tepeyac, and when she chose to appear in Mexico, it was not to the Spanish rulers but to a poor Indian. She empowered Juan Diego to confront a Spanish bishop and to persuade him to honor her. Devotion to Our Lady of Guadalupe, who bestows special favor on the lowly people of Mexico, thus provided a connection between traditional native culture and the new Catholicism of the Spanish rulers. In 2002, Pope John Paul II declared Juan Diego a saint.

Our Lady of Guadalupe has been many things to Mexican peoples. She is a comforting presence and a heavenly mother, but she also became a symbol of Mexican nationalism. In 1810, when Miguel Hidalgo y Costilla began his fight for Mexican independence, he cried out, "Death to the Spaniards and long live the Virgin of Guadalupe!" Praying to Guadalupe expresses one's identity as both Mexican and Catholic. Mexican and Mexican American women often feel empowered by this heavenly figure that looks like a relative.

As some Mexicans, like other Latinos, leave Catholicism for Pentecostal and other Protestant churches, they take their devotion to the Virgin with them, introducing into Protestantism a form of spirituality that was once distinctly Catholic.

The history of Our Lady of Guadalupe thus reflects the story this chapter tells. She originated in colonization by a European power, but she became a symbol of Mexican Catholicism and now receives devotion even from Protestants in the United States.

causes conflict within churches like the Anglicans, which maintain a worldwide structure. Recall that one appeal of Christianity in formerly colonized areas has been its moral authority and stability: it can support steady families and communities in times of great change.

The global shifts in Christianity make the history of Christianity more complicated than the story we have told so far. Modernity, with its emphasis on science and reason, pushed many Christians in Europe and North America to interpret the Bible less literally and to be open to changes in doctrine and morals; they emphasized rational thought more than spirit-filled experiences. We have also seen many exceptions to this trend even in Europe and North America, but the global Christianity of the early twenty-first century is much more diverse and moving in complex directions. It is impossible to predict the future and not clear that the spirit-filled, conservative nature of Asian, African, and Latin American Christianities will persist. For example, in South Korea, Christians tend to be closer to U.S. Christians in character. Furthermore, influence does not run in only one direction: Christianity in North America is changing as immigrants and even missionaries from other regions of the globe now come to the United States.

Transnational Connections and New Conflicts

As a wider trend, globalization fosters both diversity and connections. On the one hand, the decentralization of media and the freedom of the Internet enable countless groups and individuals to develop their own subcultures. In the 1960s, television viewers in the United States could watch four national networks and sometimes a few local channels, but in 2000, television networks number in the hundreds, many aimed at small communities such as golf enthusiasts, history buffs, and gay and lesbian people. On the other hand, the world is more connected, and ideas and cultural elements cross borders with lightning speed. Thanks to the Internet, a teenager in Brazil can watch a video made at home by a teenager in Japan, and people on different continents can form virtual communities. This same paradox characterizes Christianity in the global era. New transnational communities bring together like-minded Christians from across the world apart from traditional church structures, and Christianity in individual regions has become more diverse, sometimes leading to new conflicts between Christians.

An example of the new transnational ties created by globalization is a movement called Global Awakening. In 1994, when Pastor Randy Clark from St. Louis, Missouri, preached at the Toronto Airport Christian Fellowship, congregation members interpreted the laughing, shaking, and healings that they experienced as manifestations of the Holy Spirit. Christians from throughout the world began to visit Toronto for spiritual renewal, and an estimated three million have done so. Clark and his colleagues travel the globe preaching and healing people, and Clark integrated exorcisms into his ministry after he witnessed them in Latin America. The North American Christians who travel south with Global Awakening do not go primarily as missionaries but to participate in what they see as a renewal of Christianity in Africa and Latin America. They believe that they are getting in touch with more "authentic" Christianity. Global Awakening did not develop out of any traditional church structure: it began and developed as a transnational, independent movement.

The stream of immigrants from Latin America, both legal and illegal, has created another new transnational network that is transforming religion in the United States. Most obviously, the Roman Catholic church in the United States is changing dramatically. In 2007, about one-third of U.S. Catholics were Latinos, and it is estimated that by around 2030 Latinos will make up one-half. Much Catholic worship is now in Spanish, and Latinos have brought with them to the United States their more enthusiastic style, reviving the charismatic movement in Catholic churches. However, many Latinos who come to the United States do not remain Catholic but convert to Protestant, especially Pentecostal, churches: one-quarter of Latinos in the United States

CONTROVERSY

Word of Faith: Holy Spirit or Holy Fraud?

Although healing was enshrined in the New Testament as a gift of the Holy Spirit and was experienced in early Christian communities, it eventually gave way to the official structures of sacramental theology in the Catholic church. Still, many Christians looked for healing in other ways: stories of miraculous cures have been associated with shrines and specific saints from medieval times until the present day (for example, Our Lady of Lourdes in France). The Order of St. Luke, founded in California in 1932 by an Anglican priest, is now an international ecumenical group that promotes the practice of healing ministry.

Word of Faith, a controversial new movement that uses healing texts and practices of the Bible to offer physical, mental, emotional, and spiritual restoration, emerged from Pentecostalism in the late twentieth century. Word of Faith, one example from a wide array of divine healing movements, is a global movement with a fervent following and passionate critics: its use of modern media, especially television and Internet sites, makes it highly visible.

Word of Faith has some affinities with nineteenth-century mental healing movements in America, but its modern expression was founded by Kenneth Hagin (1917–2003), whose worldwide ministries are promulgated under the name *rhema,* Greek for "word" or "utterance." Pentecostals understand *rhema* as the voice of the Holy Spirit speaking to believers in the present moment through dreams, experiences, preaching, and so on. Hagin's most visible American disciples are Kenneth Copeland, Joyce Meyers, Joel Osteen, and Frederick Price.

Word of Faith or divine healing ministries are fast-growing churches and organizations like Living Faith Ministries, also known as Winners Chapel, founded in Nigeria by David Oyedepo, and boasting a church with a seating capacity of fifty thousand. In Sweden, one can find Word of Faith at Livits Ord (Living Word) church and university founded by Ulk Eckman and claiming to have preached the Gospel to nearly a half a million people worldwide.

Word of Faith teaches that physical healing is available today through the atoning work of Jesus Christ. Sickness is the devil's way to rob believers of their right to total health. Some of its preachers include financial prosperity in the atoning work of Jesus and claim that Jesus and the apostles were rich. Word of Faith preaches that Jesus restored human dominion over nature (lost by Adam) and that redeemed Christians, speaking in the name of Jesus, can make things happen. Partly because of teachings like these, which are easily misunderstood, Word of Faith has been criticized as an arrogant and misguided cult.

are now Protestant. Latino immigrants retain close ties to families in their original countries, and these connections serve as a means for worship styles and religious ideas and practices to travel between north and south. If and when Protestant Latinos return to their homelands, they contribute to the changing character of Christianity in Latin America.

Once solidly Roman Catholic, Latin America is becoming increasingly diverse in religious affiliation thanks to the forces of globalization. We have seen that in the 1960s and 1970s, liberation theology became a powerful force in Latin American Catholicism. In what were called base Christian communities, groups of laypeople read the Scriptures or their own and applied them to their own circumstances. As political regimes became more repressive in the 1980s and the official Catholic church became more conservative under Pope John Paul II, many of these Latin American Catholics became disillusioned. Some simply left the church, but others sought new ways of expressing their more engaged Christian spirituality. Protestant groups, especially charismatic ones, have grown rapidly in the last 25 years, especially in Guatemala, Puerto Rico, El Salvador, Brazil, and Honduras. It is possible that by 2010, one-third of the population of Latin America will be Protestant. Latin America remains predominately Roman Catholic, but it is now more religiously diverse, which is a new situation for this part of the world.

The easy movement of ideas across borders has facilitated the spread of Pentecostal and other Protestant groups throughout the region and beyond. A good example is the Universal Church of the Kingdom of God, the Igreja Universal do Reino de Deus (IURD). Founded in 1977 by Edir Macedo de Bezerra in Brazil, the IURD by 1990 had around two million members in as many as ninety countries, including the United States. The church spread in part by purchasing media (radio and television stations and newspapers) and later through websites in English and Portuguese. The IURD resembles Global Awakening as a transnational movement, but it originated in Latin America and then moved to Europe, the United States, and Africa. It promises healing through liberation from demonic forces and encourages members to give generously to the church so that they can receive material benefits. The teachings and financial wealth of the IURD dismay many other Christians, but in 1995, traditional Brazilians were even more shocked when on television an IURD bishop kicked a statue of Our Lady of Aparecida, the patron saint of Brazilian Catholics, to show that it was only a statue. Offices of the IURD were attacked, and the bishop had to leave for Africa.

As this incident demonstrates, the new religious pluralism of Latin America is causing tensions and conflicts. In countries like Peru and Guatemala, Pentecostals have emerged as important voting blocs, posing a challenge to traditional Roman Catholic elites, both military and civilian. Roman Catholic leaders have responded to the growth of Pentecostalism with alarm: in 1992, Pope John Paul II warned Latin American bishops of "ravenous wolves," and he once called evangelicals "an oil stain" spreading through the area. In 2007, Pope Benedict XVI traveled to Brazil, hoping to revive a Catholic church that in 1980 claimed 90 percent of Brazilians but in 2007 had less than 70 percent. Some Catholic leaders in Brazil have adopted the charismatic style of Pentecostals: Father Marcelo Rossi, "The Singing Priest," preaches to large crowds in soccer stadiums in worship services that feature intense music and charismatic experiences. The rivalry between Catholics and Protestants has turned violent in the Mexican province of Chiapas and other regions, but fortunately, such incidents remain rare.

The complex connections between and among Christians in Latin and North America demonstrate that globalization has not created a single, more inclusive Christianity. Rather, forms of Christianity continue to multiply, creating new networks between distant regions and fostering new diversity within previously more uniform areas. The new world Christianity that is emerging may be defined less in terms of the traditional sectarian divisions that we traced earlier in this book and more in terms of shared worship styles, social and economic status, political goals, and transnational ethnic ties. It becomes increasingly difficult to say what all or even most Christians practice and believe in a world without a center.

CONCLUSION

Chapters 7, 8, and 9 have suggested patterns of growth and diversity for Christianity in the modern global world. We have looked briefly at the nature of modernity to see the various ways Christians responded to the pressures of the Enlightenment, and we have seen that some religious groups greeted modernity in a welcoming fashion, whereas others reacted in a resisting way. We have characterized those positions as liberal and conservative and will continue to use those terms but with more complicated examples. So far, we have noted that these general postures sometimes characterize entire churches: Southern Baptists tend to be conservative, for example, while Unitarians are understood to be religious liberals. Often, we can find both liberal and conservative Christians within particular denominations.

We have also seen what can happen to Christianity in a totally new environment. The American context in the nineteenth century, with its millions of immigrants in a setting of church-state separation, led to experimentation and diversity. We have seen that Christianity refused to be defined by its European parameters and blossomed into a remarkable number of different expressions, including two new religions with their own Scriptures. Finally, we have noticed moves toward cooperation along with divisive trends in an increasingly global Christianity.

The final part of this book is devoted to contemporary Christianity. As we might expect, Christians in today's world continue to find ways to resist dialogue with one another. We will examine contemporary Christianity mostly within the context of the United States to examine the ways Christian adaptation to or resistance to cultural challenges has stimulated a redrawing of boundaries among American Christians. We have already seen that modernity tended to divide Christians not by denominations but by patterns of resistance (conservative) and moves toward adaptation (liberal). In the next part, we will see that even in the United States, Christianity is extraordinarily diverse not only in its historical roots but also in its responses to contemporary challenges.

One conclusion we might draw from this part is that Christianity will not be forced out of existence by modern political and scientific theories. On the contrary, Christians have shown themselves to be creatively adaptive to the modern world in some cases and stubbornly resistant to it in others. All the developments that we have noted in this part—in response to modernity, in relation to the American adventure, and in light of calls for "cooperation and unity"—continue in the next as we attempt to understand Christianity within a framework of internal volatility, global expansion, and increased political involvement on the part of most Christians.

Focal Points for Discussion

1. In the new global age, Christians use the Internet to spread their messages across the world. Explore the websites of organizations we have met in this chapter (for example, World Council of Churches, Rhema, Universal Church of the Kingdom of God, etc.). Do you see similar themes in these groups with worldwide missions? How does each group present itself as distinct? You may also want to examine websites of critics of these groups and notice the concerns they express.

2. The Faith and Order Commission observed that "service unites but doctrine divides." Is this insight naive? Since people have different doctrines with regard to their approaches to other cultures, are they really going to be able to work together harmoniously even when not discussing doctrine?
3. Some Two-Thirds World Christians have suggested that American Christians have become callous to Gospel values and would profit from a "mission in reverse," where Two-Thirds World peoples would evangelize First World Christians. To what extent is this mission in reverse a political strategy? To what extent does it evoke early Christian values?

Contemporary Christian Life

PART IV

Now that we have dealt with some aspects of the biblical background for Christianity, its history, and its general responses to the challenges of modernity, we will look at some of the ways Christians relate to the world and to their culture. We will also outline some of the contemporary problems Christians face in relation to general postures of liberal and conservative Christianity.

Chapters 10 and 11 focus on some typical Christian responses to the world, particularly in modern American culture, by showing variations of accommodation and resistance. The alternatives can be visualized as shown on the accompanying diagram, which, though not perfect, is meant to suggest some of the differences among Christians in their attitudes toward the world and their culture. Many Christians experience a tension between the lure of the world on the one hand and the attractions of the church on the other. Let the jagged line between church and world define the field of interaction. How do modern Christians place themselves on this field?

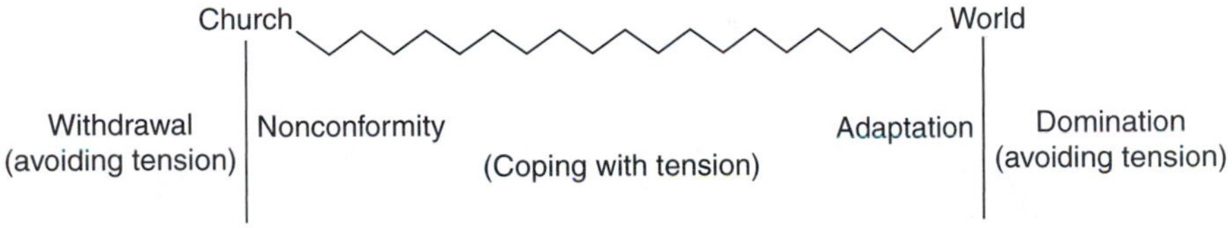

We have already seen that the challenges of modernity generated responses that were sometimes positive and sometimes negative. In this part of the book, we will characterize these postures as those of resistance and accommodation and make some further distinctions. Some Christians resist the attractions of the modern world by withdrawing from contact with that world wherever possible. We will see that this attitude characterizes groups of Christians who may have nothing in common historically or doctrinally but who *do* share some common assumptions about the ways Christians ought to relate to the surrounding culture.

Other Christians resist accommodation to modernity in a more active way: they take the field as combatants ready to assert what they understand to be essential Christian truths against the values of the modern world. We have called their position *nonconformity* because it is an attempt to define the field by way of the Gospel rather than in the terms offered to it by the modern world. These groups are often linked by their beliefs that the words of Jesus about Christian behavior are to be taken literally. Accordingly, they tend to uphold nonviolent resistance to war, a simplified lifestyle, and racial harmony.

As we have seen, many Christians saw the challenges of modernity as calls for accommodation. Many Christians have adapted themselves to the modern world and do not see a great tension between the values of the Gospel and the values of American culture. We have characterized their posture as *adaptation* because these groups tend to blend into the culture and find ways for the church to work within the American pluralistic system. Some adapted Christians are liberal and some are biblically conservative, but all share the conviction that Christian life does not require withdrawal from the world or active resistance to its principles.

Other Christians tend to adapt to the modern world in a different way. Like withdrawn Christians, they hope to avoid the tensions created by relations between the church and the world, but their preferred mode of action is different. We have characterized their position as that of *domination* because they attempt to resolve the tension by denying American pluralism and trying to dominate the society with their particular understanding of Christian life. Like withdrawn Christians, those in the position of domination hope to avoid the field of tension: withdrawn Christians flee from this tension, whereas domination Christians hope to obliterate it by imposing their religious values on the whole culture.

We will discuss those who resist the tension in Chapter 10 and those who cope with it in Chapter 11. We hope you will see that these categories are fluid and that one can just as well compare any set of postures. Our purpose in arranging them as we have is simply to raise a series of rhetorical questions about the nature of the Christian life and the relation of that life to modern political problems. The diagram will be explained more fully in Chapters 10 and 11. Chapter 12 will introduce a whole new set of contemporary questions and invite you to imagine how different groups of Christians respond to them.

CHRISTIANS AND THE WORLD

CHAPTER 10

The Bible and history reflect a tension believers have often experienced between the demands of faith and the demands of life in the world. From early Christianity to modern television evangelists, Christians have been warned to avoid the temptations of "the world, the flesh, and the devil." The meaning of these words—*world, flesh, devil*—has not always been clear, although people often have had more trouble describing the world than the other two. Sometimes, the world is understood to include sinful enticements of the flesh and devilish preoccupations of pride as well as temptations of power and greed. In this framework, a major tension exists between the values of the Christian faith or church and the values of the world, between the sacred and the secular. Some Christians regard the tension between the church and the world as no more than a reflection of the Christian belief in Original Sin; it simply points to an internal individual battle between good and evil desires. Whatever the understanding of the tension, it has figured prominently in Christian experience.

A simple way of diagraming this idea is:

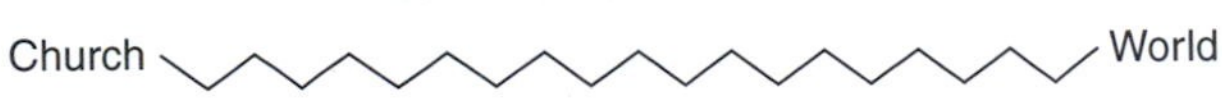

The jagged line represents tension. There are many different ideas about the nature of the church and the world. For purposes of our discussion, *church* is linked to the values of the Bible or Christian tradition, and *world* refers to the values of the surrounding culture. Individual denominations feel a pull from both sides just as individual believers do; different religious denominations take significantly different positions within the tension. Because religion exists not in isolation but within a community of believers who live in the world, the community feels the tension between the attractions of the church (spiritual values, love of God and neighbor, specific moral demands, and the hope of future happiness) on the one hand and the lures of the world (worldly values, material goods and power, love of oneself or one's culture, and satisfaction with the here and now) on the other. If the two poles of the tension can be said to set limits, the diagram of possibilities might look like this:

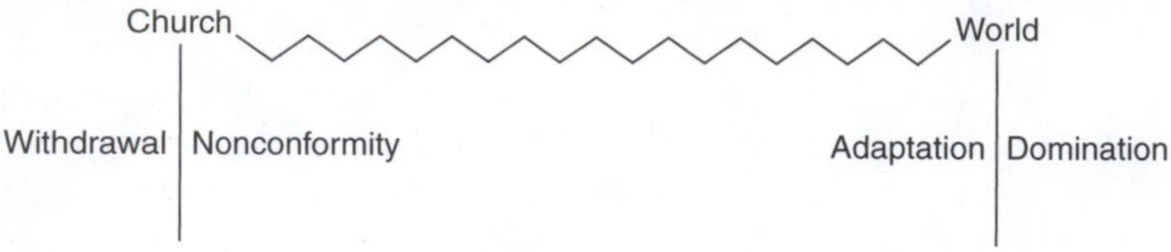

Here *church* is idealized and never perfectly realized and *world* encompasses a wide range of meanings, some positive and some odious. Most religious denominations work out their existence within the boundaries of the tension and take different positions within the middle area of the diagram. But this chapter describes two attitudes toward the world that support positions—radically different from one another—outside the limits of the tension. Each wants to avoid the tension, one by withdrawing from the field of conflict and the other by conquering it.

The withdrawn position is placed on the *Church* end of the scale because the motivation for it usually derives from religious purity or perfection and a longing to achieve the ideal; domination is placed on the *World* end of the spectrum because its tactics and strategies often derive from worldly or political power. Both groups have definite attitudes toward the world—usually negative ones—and both seek to avoid the tension between competing values. Those who withdraw from the tension usually create their own worlds within the church and therefore widen the space between the limits of church and world. They respond to the tension by pushing the world far away. Those who take a position of domination usually extol the values of the world insofar as those values can be controlled by the church. They reduce the space between the church and the world—may even obliterate it—by imposing church values on the world. In modern terms, they may seek to obliterate the separation between church and state to create a Christian nation.

WITHDRAWN COMMUNITIES

Groups that withdraw from the tension often want little or nothing to do with the world; they think of themselves as removed from the world or as standing entirely against its values. At least three forms of withdrawal are possible: physical, cultural, and psychological. Any of them may allow for some interaction with the world, but that interaction is perceived as an unwelcome necessity. Members of these groups, who may have nothing in common historically, are united in their belief that the secular world interferes with their religious lives.

Why would a religious group choose to withdraw from the world? There are at least two general aims: purity and perfection. Purity here means seeking to defend one's values and culture from the harmful ways of the world. Some believers, to keep their beliefs, practices, and lives free from taint, separate themselves from those who do not share their convictions and concerns. The less contact they have with people in the world, the more likely their religious life is to remain constant and pure. Others perceive the world as an evil place, a den of iniquity and a hotbed of temptation. According to them, the world is the place of the flesh and the devil; it feeds on vice, narcotics, gambling, and prostitution; one keeps pure and out of the reach of temptation by staying away from it.

A second aim of withdrawal is perfection. Some groups feel called to live a more rigorous, more communitarian, or more "perfect" life than can be lived in the world. Jesus commanded people to love one another but also added these challenging words: "If you would be *perfect*" (Matt. 19:21) then sell all you own, give the money to the poor, and follow me. Some people have believed that following Jesus means retreating from the world. The monastic vows of poverty, chastity, and obedience (discussed in Chapter 4) have been called counsels of *perfection,* and they have been built on a strategy of isolation from the world. Some withdrawn communities have been separate religious entities and have been physically, culturally, and psychologically withdrawn from the world. Nineteenth-century communitarian groups (discussed in Chapter 8) often lived out their interpretations of the Christian life as separate, intentional communities.

Physical Withdrawal: Monastic Communities

Withdrawn groups are often parts of larger communities of faith. Monastic communities represent a specific vocation within a particular kind of Christianity and are usually a small part of the larger religious group. They are separated from the larger group not by differing beliefs but as a special way of life within that larger community. Monks and nuns are a significant part of Orthodox Christianity, Roman Catholicism, and Anglicanism. The monastic vision has been discussed already (in Chapter 4) and need not be repeated here. Monastic life is an example of physical withdrawal from the world. Monks and cloistered nuns live in self-contained communities apart from the world and often in isolated places. Monasteries and convents have existed from very ancient times, and some contemporary monasteries provide a way of life that has not changed much in centuries. Some modern monasteries are a blend of the old and the new: they trace their origins to ancient religious communities but also accept some contemporary ideas. In today's world, one can find ecumenical monastic experiments like Taize (France) and Iona (Scotland) that welcome people from many different traditions. Monasteries are a world unto themselves and are supported by nonmonastic believers in the same denomination.

Cultural Withdrawal: The Amish

Sometimes, a withdrawn community expresses the pure extreme of a particular religious viewpoint, which itself has undergone some significant changes; it is separated from the world and, in some senses, from its parent group. The Amish are an example of cultural withdrawal: they share a sectarian viewpoint with other Radical Reformation groups but have separated from those groups precisely over the issue of involvement in the world.

A word about sectarianism. Sociologist of religion Ernst Troeltsch (1865–1923) distinguished between church and sect and characterized sect-type Christianity as emphasizing an individual religious experience, voluntary membership, and radical obedience to Christian ethics as specified in the words of Jesus. It appeals to the life and beliefs of the primitive church and specific attitudes toward the world. Sectarians

Concept

An Alternative to Vengeance: The Amish School Shooting

On an early October morning in 2006, a heavily armed gunman broke into a one-room Amish schoolhouse in West Nickel Mines, Pennsylvania. He allowed the boys and the teachers to leave but took the girls hostage. By noon, he had killed five of them (aged 7–13) and himself. Before supper that night, the parents and relatives of the slain children sent words of forgiveness to the family of the killer, and the Amish set up a charitable fund for them. One mother invited the killer's family to her little girl's funeral.

These acts of forgiveness stunned the world but did not surprise those who know the Amish. Their refusal to think evil of the killer and their willingness to extend help to his family in no way deny the devastation and grief they experienced. Nor does their desire to live apart from the world take them beyond human emotion. Their confidence in divine providence and their historic practice of mutual aid surely helped them to move beyond the tragedy, but their swift forgiveness seemed inexplicable to most observers outside the peace church tradition.

In an article on "Forgiveness," Mennonite Conflict Studies Professor Joe Liechty says that while forgiveness and reconciliation can bring personal benefits, those benefits cannot be the reason one forgives a wrong. Neither can forgiveness be tied to a desired outcome: in fact, not every wound can be healed, and effectiveness cannot be a measure of one's practice. Forgiveness is, at bottom, a letting go of the right to vengeance, the first step in a process of coming to terms with injury.

Relinquishing vengeance does not paper over a serious wrong: the murder of one's children cries out for vengeance. Is vengeance an integral part of human nature? If it is, then Amish forgiveness is incongruous and goes beyond human experience. Amish witness, however, offers another suggestion: it asks people to question whether vengeance is necessary to human flourishing. In Amish society, forgiveness is normative, as deep a human need as vengeance is to others. The Amish response to the Nickel Mines shooting, therefore, shows more than a tender face of religion. It calls attention to the possibility that radical forgiveness is a viable alternative in a tragic situation.

---

aim at personal fellowship and inward perfection and have no desire to dominate the world; they are indifferent or even hostile to the world and tend to be suspicious of worldly ways. Troeltsch's distinctions cannot adequately describe the American religious situation, but they do serve to describe the Amish viewpoint.

In some senses, the Amish have built a world of their own, but not for monastic reasons. Monks and nuns are often willing to adopt some of the conveniences of the modern world; their isolation does not necessarily reflect a negative judgment of surrounding culture, though their lives are decidedly simple. The Amish refuse to be part of the general society—the world—and they refuse to conform to cultural values or adopt modern conveniences. To their way of thinking, God's law has a specific rhythm that cannot be interrupted by the contrivances of the modern world. They do not drive cars but continue to use horses and buggies. They have nothing against the gasoline engine—indeed, they will ride in other people's cars, and one can sometimes see an Amish farmer using a horse-drawn wagon and a gasoline-powered cutting machine—but have a sense of life's pace that will not be hurried or overwhelmed by modern gadgets. They have no electricity, except in places where Amish bishops have deemed it acceptable as a way to cool milk and comply with state dairy laws, and are not disturbed by television and radio. The values of the world are resisted, and their cultural and religious ways—styles of life, patterns of worship, language, and dress—have remained much the same for centuries.

The Amish are a small group; they have definite and rigorous qualifications for admission. Their idea of community is intimate and physical: they believe that one must identify with a concrete local group. They are, accordingly, perfectly sectarian but have also chosen to remain culturally withdrawn. Some groups that were originally sectarian—Mormons in their early years in Utah, for example—were slow to change and to adapt to new ways but have adapted to the society in which they live. The Amish, on the other hand, are bound to their withdrawn position by their understanding of the world and its culture as inherently destructive to their religious life.

Psychological Withdrawal: Millennialist Christians

Many Christian groups, especially those with highly developed eschatological consciousness (those anticipating the end of the world in their lifetime), are withdrawn from the world in mind and heart only. They live and work in the world, do not establish themselves as isolated communities (like monks and nuns), and are not hostile to modernity; yet they create worlds of their own in such a way that they exemplify psychological withdrawal. Some Adventists, Pentecostals, Jehovah's Witnesses, and fundamentalist Christians share a perception about the world as an evil or dangerous place and often see others as outsiders in relation to their own world in the church.

Most of the individuals in these groups take a dim view of the world; it is a place of seduction by alcohol, drugs, or sex. They work in the world but are mentally and behaviorally removed from it. A rousing old hymn states the theme: "Take the world but give me Jesus, I won't go back [to the world and its vices], I won't go back." Testimony during religious services often takes a world-disparaging form: "When I was in the world I drank [or gambled or was unfaithful], but now that I am here [in the church] I am free from those things." Preaching compares those in the church with those in the world in such a way that the worldly ones are invariably wicked, misguided, and not worthy to be part of God's entourage when Jesus comes again.

Most of these millennialist Christians live their lives within the framework of their organization: Bible study meetings, working for church concerns, social events within the churches, and various missionary enterprises (in the case of Jehovah's Witnesses, going door to door with a religious message) take up much of their lives outside work and family time. Their friends and family are (ideally) church members, and their reading and interests are very much defined by their religious preoccupations. Often, television and movies are forbidden along with drinking, smoking, and dancing.

The groups mentioned here are united primarily by their millennialist views. They eagerly await the end of the world and interpret political events and worldly happenings predictively as part of God's plan. They build upon an apocalyptic scenario culled from the Bible, especially from some chapters in Daniel and from the book of Revelation. In the apocalyptic vision set forth in those books, one can find a general plan: the world is dominated by a godless evil power (often shown as a beast or a tyrannical ruler); that evil power persecutes the saints and treats them shamefully; suddenly, the saints are able to rise up and overthrow the beast or evil potentate; and

Spirituality

The Fear and Reassurance of Judgment

Judgment and damnation have always been prominent themes in American Protestant preaching. Jonathan Edwards's frightening sermon "Sinners in the Hands of an Angry God" (1741) encouraged Christians to repent and prepare for the coming kingdom of God. Interest in the end of the world has also been a popular theme from ancient times (see Chapter 2) to the present. Hal Lindsay's novel about the end of the world, *The Late Great Planet Earth* (1970), sold millions of copies. In the 1990s, as the millennial year of 2000 approached and Americans grew increasingly anxious about massive computer crashes, vivid depictions of the end of the world, divine judgment, and the reality of hell were written to frighten and to reassure Christians worried about their future.

In 1995, Tim LaHaye and Jerry B. Jenkins published *Left Behind: A Novel of the Earth's Last Days,* the first in a projected series of sixteen books. All are based on a belief that Christ will reign on earth for a thousand years after a period of intense trial and suffering (the Tribulation), and all support a conservative Christian belief that some Christians will escape this period of suffering by being transported instantly to heaven (the Rapture). The first book opens with an account of millions of believing Christians disappearing from earth and then relates the turmoil faced by those "left behind." The United Nations and other advocates of international cooperation turn out to be tools of the Antichrist, and leading Jews begin to advocate conversion to Christianity. The massive popularity of the book led to a feature film, a video game, a comic book, and even a parody episode on *The Simpsons.*

There have been other conservative Christian uses of popular culture to frighten and reassure believers. Hell houses, for example, available around Halloween, invite people to walk through a "haunted house" where they can see actors depicting gay men dying of AIDS, adulterers burning in hell, and grisly scenes of abortion. Graphic depictions of hell and novels about end-time judgment and suffering offer a spirituality that both frightens and reassures. The explicit horrors of hell and apocalyptic tribulation encourage people to accept and remain faithful to conservative Christianity as they reassure believers that they are saved and will not suffer these horrible fates. Readers of the *Left Behind* books say that they are great stories and that they "confirm their beliefs and strengthen their faith." This spirituality increases the distance between believers and the damned while it motivates conservative Christians to work against the trends in morality and globalization that it demonizes.

the saints inherit the earth or reign in heaven. In that vision, no one wants to be on the side of the world. *All* Christians are enjoined to remember that no one knows the day or the hour when Jesus will return, and they are, accordingly, supposed to be always ready. In many millennialist groups, however, the readiness goes hand in hand with fear and/or assurance; in both cases, the world figures heavily as an evil place.

Summary of Withdrawn Communities

All these various religious groups—monks and nuns, the Amish, Adventists, Pentecostals, Jehovah's Witnesses, dispensationalist Christians, and some fundamentalist Christians—differ from one another theologically, historically, and in terms of doctrine and practice. But they are bound together by their relationship to the tension between the world and the church; they all seek to avoid that tension by withdrawing from the world. All see the necessity of being in some way separated from the world, but they differ about how and why that separation should occur. They are united in believing that the world interferes with their goals of purity or perfection, but they have different attitudes toward that interference and toward the world itself.

Monastic life is built on the notion of withdrawal from a *distracting* world. Monks and nuns do not hate the world, but they choose to withdraw from it to "pray without ceasing" (1 Thess. 5:17)—to pray for the world and the people in it even while they pursue their own spiritual journeys. The religious traditions that support monastic life—Orthodox Christianity, Roman Catholicism, and Anglicanism—all believe that the world, created by God, is good and not evil. They may quarrel with specific worldly positions, but they do not, by definition, hate the world. Monasteries stand as a witness to a specific way of Christian life. The desire to leave the world, monks and nuns believe, is the result of a distinct and special call by God to an individual; other individuals are called to life in the world.

The Amish withdraw from the world because the world is a *threatening* place, where the time-honored ways of their ancestors are not respected. The world is a place of change—not fundamentally motivated by religious concerns—and their policy of cultural isolation is based on their own needs for preservation; they hope to conserve their culture and way of life, which they believe is better suited to the commands of Scripture. Many of them have a hostility toward the world and tend to see it as irredeemable and not worth bothering with; in that way, they reflect something of the spirit of sectarianism. There is no need, in a sectarian model, to get involved with politics or other worldly preoccupations. The life that matters is the life of the church, and the church exists in the small group that lives out its convictions without reference to the world. The Amish do not make much of an attempt to draw others into their life, despite the active missionary stance of their Anabaptist predecessors. To a great extent, one is born into an Amish way of life and then is asked to choose whether or not to accept it when one becomes an adult. Often, those who reject it must leave farm, family, and the whole way of life.

Millennialist Christians view the world under the influence of their apocalyptic understanding as an *evil* place dominated by evil powers. By virtue of their hopes and beliefs, they tend to hate the world and to denounce its ways. The world is not simply distracting or threatening to a specific way of life; it is evil and predatory and to be avoided at all costs. Unlike the Amish and monastic communities, many millennialist Christians proselytize with vigor. Withdrawal from the world is not a matter of vocation or of birth but a matter of perceiving the state of things and asking for admission into the group that stands ready and waiting for the return of the Lord. Jehovah's Witnesses, especially, are tireless in their door-to-door ministry, and many other groups, such as Pentecostals, support a wide network of local and foreign missionary activity. Assurance of salvation and methods of increasing church membership differ among them, but they are all zealous to draw as many as possible into the church and away from the world.

All these groups build their own worlds in some ways. Monks and nuns build a physical world of their own to pursue their relationships with God apart from the distractions of the world. The Amish live in their own cultural world and live on their own terms and at their own pace so that their religious beliefs are not threatened by modern conveniences, language, and ideas. Millennialist Christians build their own worlds psychologically in their churches; the church is the social and religious center of their lives, a place safe from the dangers of the outside world.

DOMINATING POSTURES

Another way to avoid the tension between the church and the world is to obliterate it by making one's religious views predominant in a society. In the United States, those who want a Christian nation seek to master the tension by conquering the world with their religious point of view, attempting to shape the life and values of the culture to match their own. A society dominated by Christian values has no tension with the world because the sacred so imposes itself on the secular that they become as one. Theocratic states operate on this principle: they are governments by God administered through a church or one of God's special agents. Calvin's experiment in Geneva is one historical example of domination; the medieval papacy of the Catholic church is another.

Why would a religious group seek to avoid the tension by dominating the general society? There are probably many reasons, and most of them combine negative views of the world, optimistic evaluations of human potential, and a thirst for power to ensure their vision of life. The medieval popes saw worldly princes as dangerous to the aims of religion and so sought to dominate the state. The church-state arguments that plagued the Catholic church from the eleventh through the nineteenth centuries in some ways reflected papal hope to dominate opposing rulers to safeguard the lives of religious believers and protect the Gospel.

Some modern religious leaders were so enamored of human progress and the power of the Gospel that they hoped to build the kingdom of God on earth. This plan presupposes that the general society ought to be shaped into that kingdom, to be dominated by a particular religious view whether the society is willing to be shaped to that vision or not. Some groups want to assume political power for themselves to establish what they perceive as a more Christian society.

No one Christian group can dominate American society, and there is little point in worrying about the renewal of medieval papal policies or Calvinist theocracies in the contemporary world. The *mentality* of domination, however, does survive in at least two ways: politically and financially. Since these ways take in a broad range of activity, they cannot be primarily associated with particular Christian groups and will be discussed here as *attitudes* present in many different Christian communities and embodied in certain plans or movements. Like the discussion of the withdrawal mentality, this one gathers disparate groups together that otherwise would not be discussed in the same chapter in an attempt to look at a range of Christian groups with a different lens.

Political Domination

Political domination as a religious strategy uses the political process to impose a religious viewpoint on everyone. Historically, it was adopted by the Roman Catholic church and, later, by Calvinists, Anglicans, and Lutherans. One of the wrenching arguments of the Reformation was over the appropriateness of the Christian desire for political power to support its positions. Groups that strive for political domination usually want some sector of the government or the society at large to conform to their particular religious interpretations; they hope to link a religious position to a political one and to pursue them as a single (usually religious) entity. We will look at three contemporary manifestations of the religious strategy of political domination here: liberation theology, the antiabortion amendment, and "Christian politics."

LIBERATION THEOLOGY The theology of liberation, as we have seen, is based on a reading of the Bible in which God is perceived as a liberator of captives and Jesus is identified with the poor. According to this view, God's primary interest lies with the poor: they are the objects of divine concern in the writings of the prophets and the ones to whom Jesus brings the message of salvation. Liberation theologians argue that Christians who want to imitate Jesus should work for the elimination of oppression, a task that may mean working to overthrow corrupt and exploitive political structures. Liberation theology is not entirely clear on its relation to violence: some who accept the premise that God has a preferential option for the poor also believe that nonviolent means are the only appropriate ones for a Christian; others believe that the abuse perpetrated by economic or political systems on the poor cannot be changed except through violent revolution. Whatever its position on violence, liberation theology is often revolutionary: its adherents seek to replace an existing regime with a different, more "Christian" one. Liberation theology has found its most fervent adherents in Latin America, where totalitarian governments and multinational corporations are regarded as exploitive institutions that undermine "Christian" social models. The aim of liberation theology is consistent and clear: to bring what is perceived to be God's love for the poor into the political realm to disempower those who do not follow the Gospel. Their ideal society is based on biblical models of shared wealth and power.

THE ANTIABORTION AMENDMENT Some religious groups use *constitutional* power to promote their views to dominate the entire society. The campaign of conservative Christians from all denominations to secure a constitutional amendment against abortion is an example of this strategy. The campaign for an antiabortion amendment is on the dominating end of the spectrum not because its supporters believe that abortion is a sin but because they use political means to make it illegal. Other Christians may perceive abortion as wrong but also see it as the proper concern of the church rather than the state. The purpose of the amendment strategy is to make abortion a crime and to put the state in a position to punish those who commit what these Christians perceive as a grave sin.

"CHRISTIAN POLITICS" Religious groups on both the right and left wings of the political spectrum seek to enforce their religious views *politically* in the belief that society will be better if all people live according to their ethic—willingly or unwillingly. Right-wing Christians often identify their religious beliefs with conservative political views and link Christianity itself with a specifically conservative political agenda. They take political positions—against communism, against welfare, in support of capital punishment and conservative fiscal policy—and tie them to God's will or to the Bible. Their reading of the Old Testament and the words of Jesus leads them to a political-religious viewpoint that is politically conservative.

People

Jim Wallis: Left-Wing Evangelical Politics

Jim Wallis has long been on the front lines of evangelical politics but much closer to the left than many of his fellow religionists. Growing up in suburban Detroit, Wallis claims to have been dissatisfied with the social teachings of his church. In the heated controversies of the 1960s, when Wallis was looking for new ways to be both religious and political, he was inspired by Martin Luther King Jr. and by the iconoclastic war protests of Daniel and Philip Berrigan. Yet, he yearned for a voice within his own evangelical tradition.

In 1971, he and a group of like-minded seminary students in Chicago founded *Sojourners,* a magazine to serve as a political forum for Christians. In 1975, the group that had become affiliated with the magazine moved to Washington, D.C., in search of a place where they could fully live the Christian life as they understood it. They moved into a poor neighborhood near the riot corridor in Washington, choosing to live in solidarity with the poor.

Wallis came to special prominence in 1979 when he organized Sojourners—also the name of the community—and the local neighborhood to protect a young mother who had been evicted from her house. Wallis used the attention given to him by media to proclaim his views on Christian charity and obligations to the poor, the themes of his career as an activist.

Throughout the 1980s, Wallis began to take on political issues. He built alliances with Christian peace activists and created a national network of contacts through the magazine. He also continued his activism in the local area, lobbying for housing rights, increased funding for health clinics, and improved education. In 1995, Wallis issued a statement calling for Christians to reject the traditional political distinctions between right and left. Although he takes it for granted that Christians should be involved in the political process, he condemns ideologically aligned Christianity as "false religion." He formed a new organization, Call to Renewal, to focus on poverty, but in 2006, his two groups merged to become Sojourners/Call to Renewal.

In the 2000s, as spokesmen for the Christian right like Jerry Falwell and Pat Robertson faded and some conservative evangelicals began to worry about poverty and climate change, Wallis saw an opportunity to increase the presence of the Christian left in the media and to encourage Democratic politicians to address religious voters more directly. In 2007, Wallis wrote an essay for *Time* magazine proclaiming the era of the Christian right at an end, and Sojourners/Call to Renewal invited the leading Democratic candidates for president to a forum to speak about faith and politics. Like conservative Christian activists, Wallis does not believe that religion and politics should be separate; unlike them, he believes that Christian values lead to more liberal views on issues like poverty, war, and the environment. The continuing activism of Wallis is also an effort to impose a particular Christian view of life on the social order.

On the other end of the spectrum, some large church organizations—the World Council of Churches, for example—have sometimes supported left-wing political viewpoints. In certain circumstances, they have identified their religious beliefs with select revolutionary movements and have given financial support to aid victims of "liberation movements." Their reading of the Bible and the Gospels leads them to liberal political positions on welfare, war, capital punishment, and other issues. In both cases—from the right and from the left—churches and church members have been asked to endorse political viewpoints as if they were God's will. Both groups see their positions as the clearest readings of the Gospel and the best course for worldly governments. Many Christians today see political engagement as an aspect of living the Gospel.

Financial Domination

Financial domination is the propensity to tie the Christian message to money in such a way as to control the society. What does one find in the Gospels about money? In the synoptic Gospels, we find a story about a rich man who wished to follow Jesus. He had kept all the commandments and wondered what else he should do. Jesus told him to sell everything, give the money to the poor, and follow him, whereupon the rich man changed his mind and went away. His inability or unwillingness to do as Jesus asked inspired Jesus to say, "It is easier for a camel to go through the eye of a needle than for a rich man to enter the kingdom of God" (Mark 10:25). What do these words mean? If fidelity to God's law is bound up with justice, sharing, and concern for the poor—there is also Old Testament evidence for this—then does Jesus means that it is virtually impossible to have much money and be faithful to God? From the earliest Christian communities to today, some interpret these words on a literal level: being rich is dangerous and keeps one away from the kingdom of God. Historically, Christians have also given this text an allegorical reading, saying that Jesus asked the rich man to get rid of his *attachment* to money. In other words, one can be rich but cannot be obsessed with riches, and one has an obligation to share with others.

The question turns, to some extent, on what one thinks about poverty. On a practical level, people cannot "feed the hungry" if they are poor themselves; on the other hand, Jesus seemed sometimes to have a particular concern for the poor. The Beatitudes reflect Christian ambivalence: in the Gospel of Luke, Jesus says, "Blessed are the poor" (6:20); in Matthew's Gospel, Jesus says, "Blessed are the poor in spirit" (5:3).

We have already seen that poverty was embraced in monastic life and understood as one of the counsels of perfection. In the Middle Ages, the Franciscans valued poverty for its own sake as a way of following Christ, and church laws protected the poor and reminded the rich of their obligations to all people who lived in poverty. Poverty became a pressing religious issue during the Industrial Revolution from the mid-eighteenth to mid-nineteenth centuries. As we have seen, the Salvation Army, founded by William Booth (1829–1912), was a specifically religious response to poverty in England.

American Christianity in the nineteenth and twentieth centuries took two fundamentally different positions on poverty: the Social Gospel and the Gospel of Wealth. One extolled collective responsibility and the other advocated self-help; both based their views on the Bible. The Social Gospel, a theory associated with the teachings of Walter Rauschenbusch (1861–1918), offered a theological justification for collective responsibility for the poor. Poverty, Rauschenbusch believed, was a disgrace, a blight on the Christian conscience that ought to be addressed by Christians in terms of building the kingdom of God on earth. The Gospel of Wealth, rooted in American self-confidence and the work ethic, offered a theological justification for self-help: the poor were exhorted to change their lives and to pull themselves up by their bootstraps, and well-to-do Christians were absolved of obligations to change society or to work for the elimination of poverty.

The Social Gospel and the Gospel of Wealth both rejected the idea that there is some inherent virtue in poverty. As religious responses to the social conditions of the nineteenth century, they engaged issues of poverty in different ways. Social Gospel adherents tended to follow the ethical teachings of Jesus about caring for the poor, whereas Gospel of Wealth advocates cited texts like 3 John 1:2 ("I wish above all things that thou mayest prosper") and Deuteronomy 28:13 ("The Lord will make you the head and not the tail; you shall be only at the top, not at the bottom"). Both had strong feelings (in different directions) toward the rise of American capitalism. In some ways, this argument about poverty and social ills reflected a fundamental argument in Christianity between personal salvation and the regeneration of society. Are Christians bound to look after the society in which they live, or are their efforts to be primarily directed at their own personal salvation? The conflict between the Social Gospel and the Gospel of Wealth did not settle that controversy: it continues down to our own day.

THE SOCIAL GOSPEL Rauschenbusch argued, in a series of books and articles, that capitalism and individualism had numbed the Christian conscience. Poverty was not a divine curse (as some had suggested) but was a result of human exploitation. The poor, said Rauschenbusch, were victims, and Christian men and women had an obligation to care for them. He believed that the church was the vehicle to be used for spreading the kingdom of God on earth, and he perceived the kingdom of God to be concerned primarily with social justice. Rauschenbusch tried to combine both sides of the argument: he did not think that external improvements by themselves were sufficient but believed that social or collective concern was related to personal regeneration as well. A person was truly Christian only insofar as he or she was concerned both for personal salvation and for changing the societal structures of oppressed peoples.

The Social Gospel, as espoused by most of its adherents, can be placed in the category of domination because it was a justification for imposing a specific vision of God's will on the churches and, through them, to "Christianize" American society. Rauschenbusch's followers hoped to establish the kingdom of God on this earth, by which they meant they wanted the churches to change the social order by supporting a specific political programs. The Social Gospel understanding of Christianity was essentially collective: it hoped to use the churches and the political structure to put this view (with its economic ideas) into practice in the general society, to create the kingdom of God on earth.

THE GOSPEL OF WEALTH Many Christians, however, had quite a different idea about responding to poverty. Led by their belief in individual salvation, they argued that one did not change social structures but tried, instead, to change human hearts. The Gospel of Wealth also reflected some other theories current in the nineteenth century, though its basic belief was in the primacy of individual salvation. The doctrine of predestination led them to believe that God was interested only in the elect and that poverty was a sign that a person or a family was not part of God's chosen few. The work of Charles Darwin on the evolution of the species and the popular slogan about the survival of the fittest led many people to look upon the poor as morally unfit, a position known as Social Darwinism. Sociologists linked poverty with crime as surely as some church members associated it with sinfulness. Some Christians saw poverty as a divine curse or punishment for sin, and if poverty was a divine curse, then it was the will of God, and working to eliminate poverty was tantamount to opposing God's will. These Christians took the words of Jesus, "The poor you will always have with you" (Matt. 26:11), as a mandate to leave the structures of poverty in place, while at the same time exhorting the poor to move up out of them. Some Christian preachers saw riches as a sign of God's favor and the kingdom of God as a kingdom of wealth, as a place where the morally fit should be allowed to make money. Rich Christians acknowledged their great wealth as a sign of approval by divine providence.

In contemporary terms, a version of the Gospel of Wealth is supported by some conservative Christians who think Jesus would have supported the American Dream had he known about it. According to them, the economic system of America is God's plan, and they say that one needs wealth to aid the poor. Some evangelists assure their members that God wants them to be rich, and many poorer Christians in the United States and in the Two-Thirds World believe that Jesus and his apostles were prosperous. The sign of salvation for these preachers—who can be seen regularly on television—is prosperity. The Gospel of Wealth belongs in the category of domination because it adopts the financial values of the culture and equates them with the values of religion: it avoids the tension between the secular and the sacred by imposing religious approval on a particular economic system.

Financial perspectives from the left (collective) and from the right (individualist) both tend to associate economic positions with God's will and thus raise some important questions. Does God wish believers to prosper spiritually at the expense of physical prosperity, or are spiritual and physical riches two aspects of God's concern for the whole person or society? Is the kingdom of God to be sought in the future or in the present? Both groups base their beliefs in a reading of Scripture and believe that they have correctly interpreted the divine will. Both want the society at large to conform to an economic stance they regard as "more Christian."

Summary of Dominating Postures

All these religious attitudes—liberation theology, support of a constitutional amendment against abortion, varieties of "Christian politics," the Social Gospel, and the Gospel of Wealth—differ from one another radically in terms of religious interpretation and ultimate goals. And each is comprised of members from churches that historically may have nothing in common, but they are bound together by their desire to eliminate the tension between the church and the world by imposing a specific religious perspective on the general society. All of them consider it appropriate for Christians to impose a particular viewpoint on all members of a society, though they employ different strategies in pursuit of that imposition. Most of them can be classified on either the right or the left wing of the political spectrum, and in that way, they reflect perennial arguments within the society and show us that contemporary Christians often from coalitions based on political goals rather than on doctrinal disputes.

Liberation theologians from many denominations have been active mostly in Two-Thirds World countries. Liberation theology is usually a left-wing, socialist movement working on social justice issues in repressive political climates. The coalition that supports a constitutional amendment against abortion is made up of conservative church members from a number of denominations that are fundamentally conservative in their religious and political views. Specifically, "Christian" political

CONTROVERSY

Gender Divisions and Promise Keepers

We saw in Chapter 8 that late nineteenth-century economic and social changes left religious education and practice in the hands of women, making Christianity appear "feminized." Some Christian evangelists responded with a "muscular Christianity" that combined religion with manliness. In the late twentieth century, as women gained greater equality in the workplace, at home, and in church, conservative Christians feared that men were failing to assert their proper moral leadership.

Promise Keepers is a Christian group that takes special aim at gender equality, which it associates with corrosive social forces like sexual promiscuity, pornography, abortion, gay and lesbian rights, profanity in the arts, and sex education in the schools. Promise Keepers was founded in 1990 by Bill McCartney, former football coach at the University of Colorado, who was one day struck with the idea of filling the football stadium with Christian men. His organization provides them with a place to discuss their responsibilities as husbands and fathers. Promise Keepers held multiday "conferences" in arenas and civic centers throughout the United States in the 1990s, reaching its greatest popularity in 1998, when its assembly "Stand in the Gap" gathered an estimated one million men in Washington, D.C. Lack of financial support in the following years reduced the number of conferences; in the 2000s, there were sixteen to eighteen each year.

Promise Keepers assumed a place in the growing network of grassroots organizations and private associations that make up the New Christian Right. The meetings—which call Christian men from lives of promiscuity, drunkenness, and heedlessness of family to fidelity and patriarchal supervision of the family—bear surface similarities to the tent revivals of old. They attract crowds through promotional spots on Christian radio and television and by word of mouth. The organization has been criticized from the left (by feminists) and the right (for not being doctrinally strict).

All Promise Keepers must assent to seven promises they believe are embodied in Jesus, the archetypal male figure. Thus, their message is similar to that of nineteenth-century muscular Christianity: they make appeals to manliness along with arguments for male integration into family life as leaders—men who exercise "headship" over their wives (whose roles, according to the Bible, are submissive ones). In the words of speaker Tony Evans, men must "resist forces like feminism that have created sissified men who abdicate their role as spiritually pure leaders, thus forcing women to fill the vacuum." Men should embrace their manly roles as spiritual leaders.

ideologies manifest themselves as right-wing political attitudes in some sectors of the evangelical and fundamentalist churches and have been active to some extent in the attempted politicization of such organizations as the Campus Crusade for Christ. They have taken on left-wing or radical political embodiments in the World Council of Churches. One of the results of this overt political activity among Christians has been a new wedge of divisiveness among Christians: they are no longer defined solely along denominational lines but work together on specific political agendas. Some conservative or right-wing evangelical Christians tend to adopt the attitude of the Gospel of Wealth. Modern adherents of the Social Gospel theory tend to be left-wing or socialist Christians. All of them perceive their position as the one sanctioned and supported by the Gospels. Their strategies are those of domination: all hope society (or the political structure) will be run according to their reading of the Gospels.

QUESTIONS RAISED BY THE POSTURES OF WITHDRAWAL AND DOMINATION

The reason for making these general interpretations of some Christian attitudes about the world is to see what kinds of questions can be raised by such radically different attitudes and ideas. All these groups, whether they adopt a strategy of withdrawal or domination, take their positions on the basis of their readings of Scripture. The life and words of Jesus provide the support they need for their positions. The very notion that such different attitudes are legitimate embodiments of the Christian vision, however, raises interesting questions.

Consider the question of the church and the world, especially in terms of political action. If the church is made up of members who believe that they in some way understand God's will and corporately reflect God's intentions, words, and actions, then we must first speculate a moment about God. According to the Bible and traditional Christian belief, God is perfect, eternal, invisible, and the source of absolute truth. How do these attributes correspond with the political order of the world? God is perfect, yet societies are imperfect; does an attempt to raise them to perfection—to an embodiment of divine will—invite frustration and violence? Or is it a real possibility that Christians have an obligation to pursue? God is eternal and invisible, yet societies are visible and continually changing; does a Christian political vision deny the necessity of change to societies? God possesses absolute truth, yet societies can reflect only relative truths; does a Christian approach to the situation obviate the room for disagreement that has historically been a part of all societies? These are general questions, but there are more specifically religious questions as well.

In What Sense Is Christianity Political?

The first question within this question is definitional: What does *political* mean? If it means "worldly" politics, some Christians would answer that Christianity is not at all political and should not be. These believers might cite the words of Jesus, "Render therefore to Caesar the things that are Caesar's and to God the things that are God's" (Matt. 22:21), and argue that Jesus was more interested in changing people's minds and hearts than he was in changing political structures. Others might wonder how it is so clear what things belong to Caesar and what things belong to God, and they argue from the Bible that God loves the weak, clothes the naked, visits the sick, comforts the afflicted, cares for widows and orphans, feeds the hungry, and buries the dead and that Christians must work toward those ends—even politically—within the society.

If politics can be described broadly as the way people deal with the structures and affairs of the government (or state), then some people might argue that "Christian" politics do not correspond to the aims and tactics of traditional politics. The politics of Jesus, they might say, are revolutionary because they attempt to deal with political questions in fundamentally new ways. Christians, according to this view, are enjoined to behave differently from everyone else: they are to follow Jesus' words and example by turning the other cheek, doing good to those who persecute them, and loving their enemies. If this is the case, then the political action of Christians becomes a way of life inherently different from and in some ways hostile to the political action of the state; the ethic of the church is an alternative to the ethic of surrounding society. On these grounds, some Christians refuse to support wars and violence, and they manifest their political consciousness precisely by embodying a different sort of society from the one embodied in the surrounding culture.

What Is the Church?

The same sorts of arguments arise with this question. Is the church an agent to promote societal change and to create a better life for all? Or is it the kingdom of the saved, the fellowship of personal regeneration, with no obligations to the larger society? Is the church a small body of believers who embody the kingdom of God and invite other people to become a part of it? Or is it a large organization that uses its power as an aggressive social agency? Does the church transcend the world in such a way that it must refuse to become involved in secular values and questions? Or is it necessarily involved in the world and somehow responsible for its values?

Is the church a prophetic fellowship that speaks out on injustice but leaves the remedy of injustice to secular agencies? Or are church members to take a prophetic stand within the secular world by working for specific political goals? Is the church a moral educator responsible for raising the consciousness of its members and other people by working for a better world? Or is the church the kingdom of God already come and yet still waiting to become the kingdom, the place in which one should be born again and wait for the coming of the Lord? Is the kingdom of God within the individual believer? Or is it a possible model for the general society? How does the kingdom come? Do believers create the kingdom on earth by virtue of their own works and political vision? Or is it entirely an act of God that makes human efforts worthless?

What Is the Christian Vision of Jesus?

We have already seen that presuppositions about Jesus color the way one interprets the Christian vision. The questions of who Jesus was and what he hoped for are crucial to this issue. Was Jesus primarily a man of prayer who inspired people to withdraw from the world to pray for it? Was Jesus a revolutionary interested in the political order? Was he concerned primarily with the individual believer? Or was his concern primarily for the future of his movement and not for the general society? Did Jesus speak as a political figure and imply that Christians are competent to speak out on political issues? Or was Jesus manifestly not interested in political values, implying that Christians should only be interested in their personal relationships to God through him?

If believers take a purely social reform approach to Christian life, do they ignore the underlying issues of temptation, greed, and evil in the human heart? Is a purely political approach naive, acting as if the elimination of poverty and injustice also eliminates people's grasping and selfish interests? Must one also seek spiritual elevation and moral earnestness? If believers take a purely evangelical approach to Christian life, is that enough? Is there a valid point in the historical example of converted Christians with good hearts and good intentions who continued to own slaves and to participate in the sweatshop abuse of women and children? Is there a way to be both personally converted to Jesus *and* to work toward a better society? Was

Jesus socially conscious—eager for the welfare of the weak—as well as interested in the personal conversion of his followers? Does faith in Jesus require service in the world?

CONCLUSION

None of the questions this chapter raises about the relationship of Christians to the world can be answered simply. Those Christians who take a position of withdrawal or a position of domination have different answers, all of which are based on a careful reading of the Gospels and a thoughtful understanding of Jesus and his desires. How people can read the Gospels so differently is one of the continually perplexing questions in Christianity. The questions have been raised here not to confuse you but as an attempt to broaden your understanding of the complexity of Christian belief and behavior. Other questions could also be raised, but there are enough here to indicate that there is no single Christian position on these issues and that the arguments within the Christian community are worthy of consideration.

Focal Points for Discussion

1. Withdrawn communities—like monks or the Amish—see themselves as living the most authentic Christian life. If this view were correct, how could they attract modern Christians to their position?
2. A number of conservative Protestants and Roman Catholics have formed a political coalition to urge a constitutional amendment prohibiting abortion in the United States. Is this goal—an example of Christians compelled to follow God's law rather than those of the state—a new one or basic to the way Christianity has been followed since Constantine?
3. The Gospel of Wealth and Social Darwinism were prominent in the nineteenth century but have not disappeared from American Christianity. Where do you think you would be most likely to find current examples of each of these ideologies?

CHAPTER 11

Christians and Their Culture

This chapter deals with two options Christian groups have chosen to live with the tension between the world and the church rather than outside it. The two groups may be represented on the diagram like this:

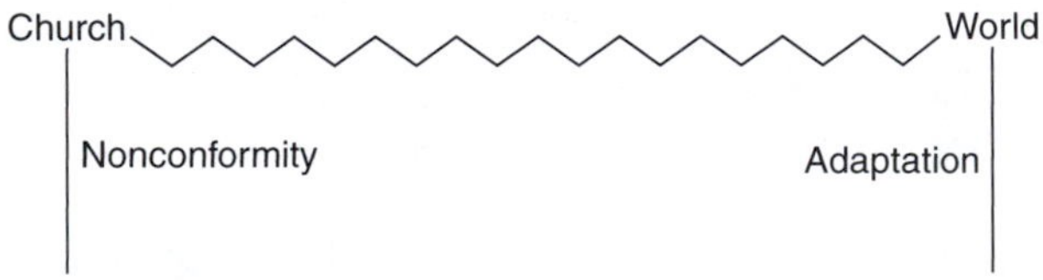

Recall that the jagged line represents tension between the values of the church and the values of the world and that these interpretive descriptions allow us to raise some religious issues in ways that would not be possible if we were content simply to understand Christian groups in denominational terms. Since the culture and values described here are American, the issues and examples have a particularly American flavor in most instances. The postures themselves, however, could be used to describe the varieties of Christian response to the world and church within other cultures as well.

Nonconformists consciously resist some of the values of the culture they live in but are not so alienated that they withdraw from the tension. They understand themselves as embodying a small but persistent witness to the values of the Gospel insofar as those values are at odds with the values of the society. Those who believe in adaptation tend to be part of large, established churches who have, for a number of reasons, accommodated themselves to the values of the society. They are not so identified with the general society that they wish to impose their values on everybody (the position of domination). They may lobby for a particular religious position—the abolition of the death penalty, for example—but they tend to do it in the framework of American pluralism, as in appealing to humanitarian values through a Washington-based lobby supported by a coalition of people who share similar views.

THE POSTURE OF ADAPTATION

Christians usually adjust to their environment. They conform or modify themselves to be more intimately a part of the culture. In America, a pluralistic environment, one is free to adopt any religion and to practice it freely. That has not always been the case, however, in America or in Christian history. The early Christians had a chance to adapt themselves to Roman culture—to be free to pursue their own religious pre-occupations as long as they occasionally offered sacrifice to the pagan gods—but they refused. Their understanding of Jesus and the Gospel made them radical monotheists who would not offer sacrifice to pagan gods. They would not conform, adjust, or adapt. The response of the government to their intransigence was persecution; Christians were burned, maimed, tortured, and harassed, and the Romans made periodic efforts to destroy the movement altogether.

With Constantine, the situation changed dramatically; his reign marked the end of persecution and the beginning of a state-supported church. As we have seen, the contested issues after Constantine were conflicts between church and state about the limits of their relative authority. In the West, the culture was eventually dominated by the church, and nonconformists were identified and persecuted as heretics. During the Reformation, though there were great and practical disagreements between Catholics and Protestants, both continued to identify religion and culture, to assume that the aims of the state could be supported by the church, and to count on the state to protect the church when necessary. The nonconformists of the Reformation period were the Anabaptists who believed that Christian faith and the culture should not be identified; their sectarian assumptions were offensive to both Roman Catholics and Protestants precisely because they divided religion from culture.

We saw that one of the results of the Reformation was a series of religious wars in which Catholics and Protestants fought each other in the name of Christianity. Those wars and the peace that followed them raised questions about adaptation. What should a Roman Catholic in a Protestant country do? Or a Protestant in a Roman Catholic country? Should one withdraw and hide away or be a public witness to a particular religious view? Openly advocating a religious view different from the officially sanctioned one often ended in a gruesome public execution for the preacher. Should one move to a more congenial place? Thus, during the Reformation, people began to find ways to adjust or adapt to their situation if they could not move away from it. Various religious undergrounds came into being, and some groups had to hide to survive: in the mountain area of Switzerland and Italy, the Anabaptists took refuge from persecution from all sides.

In America, different religious groups might have wanted to reproduce the pattern of established churches they had known in Europe, and some would have liked to dominate the country with their particular religious view. But the American landscape, the revolution, the gradual demise of Puritan influence in New England, and the strong Deist flavor of the founding documents all conspired to create a new situation. In America, separation of church and state meant that religious pluralism eventually prevailed.

Still, in some areas, religious persecution persisted. For example, non-English-speaking Christians, Roman Catholics, and new religious groups like Mormons were all persecuted for their religious beliefs and practices. For a while, most of

Concept

A Matter of Inclusion: César Chávez and Mexican American Catholicism

Although the Catholic Church embraced European immigrants to the United States and helped with their assimilation, it struggled with the question of inclusion of Hispanic and Latino peoples. One of the most visible struggles for recognition by the government and the church came from César Estrada Chávez (1927–1993). He became an important civil rights leader by his use of nonviolent techniques to promote the cause of Mexican American farm workers.

Born in Arizona to a family who lost their land during the Depression, Chávez attended nearly thirty schools before graduating from the eighth grade. The poverty of his family forced him into farm labor like many others from immigrant families. Though this life offered steady employment, Chávez and others still suffered from economic and cultural discrimination—in the Catholic church as well as in the general culture. He became an organizer in a Latino civil rights group in the 1950s. In 1962, inspired both by Catholic social teachings and by his sense of being neglected by the institutional church, Chávez and Dolores Huerta (b. 1930) founded the National Farm Workers Association to strike and lobby for better working conditions and greater benefits.

The Catholic church and the agricultural industry were profoundly uncomfortable with this activism, but La Causa, as the farm worker movement came to be called, eventually succeeded because of three factors. First, Mexican Americans in the postwar period had experienced a resurgence of their cultural identity, due in part to the lasting influence of the pro-Mexican intellectuals known as the Pensadores. Second, the type of direct action and grassroots politics Chávez orchestrated had proved hugely effective in the hands of Martin Luther King Jr. and others. Finally, Chávez had been trained as an organizer in Saul Alinsky's Industrial Areas Foundation, which emphasized using local and cultural attachments like religious affiliation as a basis for political action.

From his first organized strike in Delano, California, through the 1970s, Chávez used his Catholicism to appeal to immigrant workers and to couch his claims for social and economic justice in a commonly recognized religious idiom. Like King and Gandhi, he insisted that La Causa participate only in nonviolent activism, and Chávez himself was said to possess an authentic and deep Catholic faith that helped strengthen his appeal to everyday workers and his demands on the church. After nearly a decade of struggle, La Causa finally gained wide support, including that of the Catholic church, which recognized that Latinos shared the labor experience and desire for inclusion of earlier Roman Catholic immigrants.

---

them drew back into their own communities, separated from the mainstream of American culture, and created enclaves for themselves. As time went on, however, and people were no longer barred by language or education from participation in the American experiment, more and more formerly isolated groups joined the mainstream.

Roman Catholics adapted to American culture partly because persecuted groups often labor to prove that the surrounding culture is unjustified in discriminating against them. Other religious groups are increasingly adapting to American cultural values because they are losing their ethnic distinctiveness. Some Radical Reformation groups like the Mennonites are no longer simple rural folk; many have become professionals and have moved to urban areas, where they have lost the trappings of their ethnic distinctiveness.

Adaptation is the posture most groups throughout Christian history have adopted. In the American context of religious pluralism, adaptation involves taking on an attitude of religious toleration: groups recognize that people of other beliefs may possess no less truth and may in fact be just as likely to be "saved." In the context of the American Dream of upward social mobility, these Christians live comfortably within the culture. Finally, adapted church groups cooperate with the government and often perceive their own aims as compatible with those of the government.

THE POSTURE OF NONCONFORMITY

Nonconformity is a failure or refusal to conform or adapt to the established order. Nonconformists believe that the church must often witness against the policies of a government. Sometimes, they believe, the values of the church are in conflict with those of the world, and they cannot conform to the surrounding culture. They share some of the assumptions of the adapted Christians. They may recognize that people in other religions can be "saved" (endorsing religious pluralism), and they may be active in political matters, sometimes cooperating with government agencies in pursuit of a specific goal. Their main point of difference lies in their willingness to criticize the policies and pursuits of the establishment, whether that establishment is political or religious or both.

Unlike adapted groups, nonconformists do not assume that their religious beliefs are compatible with the values of the general society or the policies of the government. Unlike withdrawn groups, they are not so pessimistic or apolitical as to write the culture off as entirely evil or irrelevant to their belief. Rather, they accept and adopt some aspects of the culture but maintain the importance of some critical distance from it, emphasizing the need to discern between what suits their convictions and what undermines or runs counter to them.

These postures are easier to describe in terms of specific issues than they are in isolation. Nonconformity changes as the society changes: in the second century, it might have meant sure martyrdom; in the seventh, it might have inspired a monastic life; in the thirteenth century, nonconformists might have joined the communities of Francis of Assisi to live in "holy poverty"; and in the sixteenth century, nonconformity might have meant risking one's life in pursuit of the Anabaptist vision. In the twenty-first century, nonconformity means a number of different things depending on the cultural context and the religious alternatives available.

RELATIONSHIP OF THE TWO POSTURES TO VITAL ISSUES

The positions of adaptation and nonconformity are clearer when understood in relation to specific issues within the culture. No more than a sampling of groups and their responses to issues can be presented here; this treatment is not intended to be complete. Here we discuss these two different attitudes as they relate to concrete problems of war, poverty, and racism.

Controversy

Iconoclastic Antiwar Protests

When Jesus told his followers to "turn the other check," did that mean that Christians must be pacifists? Some early Christians thought so, but thinkers from Augustine to Reinhold Niebuhr have argued that Christians are under obligations to protect their neighbors as well as to love them, a task that sometimes requires violent means.

Antiwar protests have become increasingly ecumenical in the twenty-first century. Christians who actively promote peace—members of traditional peace churches or part of ecumenical coalitions—have opposed all forms of coercive activity, including torture, as inherently un-Christian. An American Catholic, Dorothy Day, was one of the most influential peace activists in the twentieth century. She was opposed by some priests and bishops and revered by others, including Daniel Berrigan (b. 1921) and Philip Berrigan (1923–2002), priests who devoted themselves to a brand of activism that disturbed many people.

By seizing files from the Catonsville, Maryland, draft board and burning them with homemade napalm—a horrific chemical substance that was being dropped on villages in Vietnam—and later by pouring their blood on nuclear warheads and going to prison, the Berrigan brothers and other peace activists called dramatic attention to American policies they considered inhuman and un-Christian.

A contemporary contested form of peace activism occurs annually outside Fort Benning, Georgia, site of the Western Hemisphere Institute for Security Cooperation, formerly School of the Americas (SOA). SOA trains soldiers from Latin and South America in military techniques and human rights, but critics point to the number of SOA graduates who have been implicated in assassination and murder in places like El Salvador. For example, three of the five soldiers arrested for the deaths of four American women in El Salvador (Chapter 9) were trained at SOA.

SOA Watch was founded by Maryknoll priest Roy Bourgeois (b. 1938) in 1990. Bourgeois, inspired by slain archbishop of El Salvador Oscar Romero (1917–1980), had been participating in creative nonviolence at SOA since 1983. When six Jesuit priests along with their housekeeper and her daughter were killed in El Salvador by SOA graduates, he founded his organization to sponsor an annual memorial protest. In 2006, more than twenty thousand Christians from all traditions, joined by Buddhists, Jews, and pagans, came to Fort Benning to be part of this action. This kind of peace activism does not get a neutral response: on the one hand, church officials from all traditions have distanced themselves from this group; on the other hand, priests, ministers, nuns, and laypeople have supported it, some saying that activism of this kind is precisely "what Jesus would do" if he were here today.

Problems of War and Peace

War has historically been part of the human experience; hostility and violence seem to be part of the human condition. How might one think about war? On the one hand, one could hold that every war that serves someone's legitimate interests is acceptable: war is simply another way of doing politics, and if the cause is justified, then the means used to pursue that cause are necessarily justified as well. On the other side of the question, one could say that all wars are wrong: every war, even a war of self-defense, is unacceptable because bloodshed is always evil. The two extremes of the argument are these: war is always right and war is always wrong.

Most Christian churches have adopted a position somewhere between these opinions. Peace, they say, is to be preferred but is not always possible. Because we live in a sinful world, sinful, unscrupulous people will attempt to involve a society in dangerous criminal ventures. Experience shows, the argument continues, that only violence can stop violence. Here Christian participation in war is permitted, but only under certain circumstances. The theory of just war specifies the conditions under which Christians may wage war. To be justified in waging war, a group:

1. Must have just cause (one side must persist in unjust aggression).
2. Must exhaust all peaceful means first (so war is a matter of legitimate self-defense regretfully taken up when negotiations have failed).
3. Must have reasonable hope of success (a tiny country should not sacrifice its people in a hopeless war against a superpower).
4. Must use proportionate means (one side cannot use guns when the other side is just using swords and spears).
5. Must observe noncombatant immunity (violence may not be directed against civilians).

Almost all American Christian groups have adopted this theory in some form, and members have distinguished themselves in every American war as soldiers, chaplains, nurses, and so on. Adoption of just war theory is a form of adaptation because it enables Christians to sanction warfare.

The nonconformist position on this issue is taken by the "peace churches," which consider pacifism and nonresistance a Christian obligation. The historic peace churches have been Anabaptist groups (Mennonites, Amish, Hutterites), the Religious Society of Friends (Quakers), and Churches of the Brethren. In recent years, they have been joined by Christians from other churches who are convinced that the peace churches have a valid reading of the Bible and a valuable position of witness on this question. Peace churches are opposed to Christian participation in all war, no matter what the circumstances. They argue that experience does *not* teach us about the efficacy of violence but about its uselessness; violence, they argue, breeds violence. Jesus meant what he said about loving one's enemies and turning the other cheek. They say that nonviolent means have never really been tried and taken seriously. More important, the peace churches argue that Christians must be nonviolent whether nonviolence works or not: their position is not based on a pragmatic judgment about the possible good outcomes of the position but is based on Jesus' words and his way of dealing with violence. These people believe that being faithful is more important than determining by violent means what kind of government they will live under.

Many members of the peace churches are absolute pacifists: they will not fight in a war, nor will they contribute to the war effort in any way (for example, they will not take a desk job in the army, which then frees someone else to carry a gun). Some may help the wounded, but they are as willing to nurse the "enemy" as their compatriots. Some peace church agencies were severely criticized for providing vitamins and medicine to children in North Vietnam during the Vietnam War. Peace church members have been involved in relief work in the aftermath of war: Mennonites, Quakers, and Brethren poured into Europe after World War II to clean up the rubble, distribute food and clothing, and tend to the wounded and homeless. Quakers won the 1947 Nobel Peace Prize for their work in relief, reconstruction, and international services during the war.

Christians from almost all denominations are drawn to the witness and activity of traditional peace churches, and one can now find peace initiatives in a number of different churches. For example, the international Catholic peace movement, Pax Christi, founded an American branch in 1972 (the movement began in France in 1945 and spread throughout Europe). Pax Christi encourages people to take their "Vow of Nonviolence" promising, among other things, to refuse to retaliate in the face of provocation. Friends, Mennonites, and Brethren founded A New Call to Peacemaking movement in 1972 to strengthen the commitment to nonviolence and to recover the Christian understanding of power as love, compassion, and forgiveness. Each of the historic peace churches sponsors extensive training and support for nonviolence and peaceful interaction, work that has attracted members of other churches to the dynamics of peacemaking. Two new peace initiatives that respond particularly to modern war and conflict are Christian Peacemaker Teams and the National Religious Campaign Against Torture. The first is an international organization that trains and sends teams of peace workers to conflict areas throughout the world (for example, Iraq, the West Bank, the United States–Mexico border). The second works through churches in the United States to raise awareness about torture: they sponsor films, workshops, and a national campaign to sign a statement of conscience called "Torture Is a Moral Issue."

In these ways, the peace churches do not conform to the cultural assumption that war is sometimes necessary. Rather, they witness against government policy and against those churches that accept and support that policy. Christians with a pacifist position have not always been welcome in American culture, especially in times of war. Their position assumes a willingness to spend time in jail, and during every American war, some members of peace churches have spent time in prison and some have been harassed by their neighbors. Because of the efforts of the historic peace churches, the American government made a legal provision for alternative service and conscientious objection.

Problems of Poverty and Lifestyle

The poverty issue surfaced in the last chapter in the discussion about financial domination. Scripture focuses on two concerns: the needs of the poor and the appropriateness of accumulating personal wealth. Some Christians have tied the message of Scripture to prosperity, whereas others have linked it with a distribution of goods and properties. Christians use Scripture to justify both extremes. But what about poverty itself? If one maintains that feeding the poor is a primary New Testament value, then one can argue that some private wealth is necessary to perform this service. Christian churches can have money and individual Christians can accumulate wealth as long as they attend to their obligations to the poor. Nonconformists see the issue not simply as one of caring for the poor; they regard accumulating personal wealth as contrary to their calling. The questions, from their perspective, cannot be separated: Christians have an obligation to help the poor by identifying with their state; Christians should stand as a witness against the American values of accumulation and upward social mobility. Nonconformist Christians identify with the poor, move into their neighborhoods, and live at their standard of living.

One Christian denomination founded specifically to minister to the poor is the Salvation Army (discussed in Chapter 7). Two other groups that illustrate this position are both affiliated with larger Christian groups. The People's Christian Coalition, sometimes called the Sojourners Fellowship because the magazine they publish is called *Sojourners* (see the box on Jim Wallis on page 194), is rooted in the American evangelical tradition. The Catholic Worker Movement comes out of American Catholicism. The Sojourners group is relatively young; it began in the early 1970s and moved to Washington, D.C., in 1975. The Catholic Worker Movement was founded in 1934, enjoyed considerable success at one time, and is still quite active in some parts of the country. Both groups read the Gospels, and conclude that it is necessary to identify with the poor, not just provide food for them. Both groups have been active in peace movements and serve as advocates for causes of social justice.

The Sojourners Fellowship began when a small group of young evangelical seminarians in Chicago prayed together and began to look for a place to live according to their interpretations of the Gospel about poverty, helping the poor, widows, orphans, and other disenfranchised peoples. After some initial experiments in the Chicago area, they moved to Washington, D.C., found a large house in a depressed neighborhood (mostly black and very poor), and moved in there as a group. They did not immediately design programs or enlist government aid but simply went out into the street each evening and invited people without places to go to come in for dinner and a place to sleep. Their community has grown, as has their magazine's circulation. Members live in several households in one neighborhood in a conscious attempt to offer an alternative to American values of consumption, accumulation, and upward social mobility. Accordingly, they feel called to demonstrate and write against the arms race and American defense policies. In addition to spirituality and Christian nurture, their magazine deals with poverty, peace, the arms race, political repression, and so on. The publication has become a forum for other like-minded groups; their movement is not unique but exemplifies one type of nonconformity in the area of poverty and lifestyle.

The Catholic Worker Movement was founded by a young, well-educated Roman Catholic convert and a French peasant with ideas about agrarian reform and Christian poverty. Dorothy Day (1897–1980) had been a young socialist at the University of Illinois who rejected religion as poppycock even as she continued to read evangelical sermons. She was drawn to the Roman Catholic church because of its teachings about poverty—the social encyclicals of the late nineteenth century—but found those teachings were not often implemented within the church. She could not understand piety that did not help poor people. Peter Maurin (1877–1949), a French agrarian anarchist disdainful of modern technology and urban middle-class values, gave her the impetus she needed; together they founded the Catholic Worker Movement.

They set out to practice a self-consciously nonconformist Catholicism: they were socialists when most Catholics were staunchly anticommunist, pacifists when Catholics were strong supporters of the just war theory, and they opposed big government when some of the principles of the New Deal echoed modern Roman Catholic social theory. Their fundamental principle, derived from their reading of the New Testament, was subsidiarity: what a small group can do, it should do; people ought to do what they can to look after one another, however small the scale. Catholic Workers perceive government policies like Social Security as an indictment against churches, which are not fulfilling their obligations to the poor, widows, orphans, and the elderly. With headquarters in New York City, they operate a soup kitchen and shelter in the Bowery. They publish a newspaper, the *Catholic Worker,* that has sold for a penny per copy since its beginnings.

Both Sojourners and the Catholic Worker Movement are examples of nonconformity around questions of poverty and lifestyle. Both have moved into poor neighborhoods to identify with the people to whom they are ministering. For both groups, community life and prayer are important parts of their Christian self-understanding. That prayer life takes evangelical form in the Sojourners community and traditional Roman Catholic form with the Catholic Workers. The communities themselves, however, are increasingly ecumenical, staffed by Christians who share their views about helping the poor.

Mainline churches have addressed the issues of poverty in a different way. They set aside a portion of their budget to give to the poor, unite in groups to establish programs for the forgotten members of society, and support missions in poor neighborhoods to care for and preach to the poor. They do not feel compelled, however, to move into those neighborhoods or to identify with the poor by living at the same income level. Ecumenical groups have funded organizations to lobby for legislation for the poor and the powerless; their organizations in Washington try to influence congressional decisions on the one hand and raise the consciousness of Christians within their constituent churches on the other.

Problems of Racism

The belief that one race is inherently inferior to another has sometimes led Christians to violent exploitation of other peoples. Racism, especially white discrimination against blacks, has been a continuing problem in the United States because of slavery. From the seventeenth through the nineteenth centuries, black Africans were systematically uprooted from their own civilizations and religions and sold into slavery. Their culture was destroyed and their religion was replaced with a form of Christianity used as a means of social control. The New Testament injunction, "Slaves, obey... your earthly masters" (Col. 3:22), was used to justify slavery. Nevertheless, people began to ask, "If slaves have been baptized into the body of Christ, does that mean they must be set free?" Christian approaches to slavery vividly illustrate the postures of adaptation and nonconformity, as does the Civil Rights movement of the 1950s and 1960s. Immigration in the global context makes Christianity's relationship to race much more complicated.

Only one group made a concerted protest against slavery in early America: nonconformist Quakers, united and firm in their protest, condemned slavery consistently. When Thomas Jefferson and George Washington still owned slaves, Quaker preacher John Woolman (1720–1772) traveled up and down the colonies speaking against it. Later, Quakers formed an important part of the Underground Railroad, which provided an escape route to the North for runaway slaves. Apart from the Quakers, the abolitionist cause had few advocates in the eighteenth century. The American principle that all men are created equal did not apply to slaves: each slave counted as only three-fifths of a human being under the Constitution. The liberal positions of the time, though opposed to slavery, were shaped by antiblack stereotypes. Liberals wanted to find a cure for blackness (as if it were a disease) or a way to surmount the problems of black genetic "inferiority." The religious viewpoint was shaped in part by acceptance of slavery as part of God's plan: God created black people for a reason—to be slaves. Many ministers argued that blacks could not be set free because freedom would violate a divine design. (This argument, as we have seen, was later extended to the problem of poverty.)

We have already seen that one product of the Second Great Awakening was an informal coalition of evangelical Christians united by their conversion experience and prepared for a life of action. The American Bible Society and the American Temperance Union were two projects supported by the evangelical alliance. The American Anti-Slavery Society was also part of the evangelical alliance, but it did not succeed in uniting all evangelical Christians for the abolitionist cause. Theodore Dwight Weld (1803–1895) became a leader of the antislavery movement and a founder of the Anti-Slavery Society, which spread abolitionist views along with evangelical Christianity. Weld influenced politicians in the North and shaped public opinion on the issue. His book *Slavery As It Is* (1839) inspired Harriet Beecher Stowe's novel *Uncle Tom's Cabin* (1852), and those two books became the most important antislavery works written in the United States. Stowe's novel opposes slavery more than racism in general. She assumes racism will continue: freed blacks will want to be *separate*. In this view, neither the Gospel nor abolition requires fellowship with blacks. Stowe could, therefore, imaginatively enlist white evangelical preachers in the cause of abolition without challenging them to speak for integration.

A swelling tide of humanitarian reform inspired solutions to the slavery problem: some people thought blacks ought to be free to emigrate elsewhere to form their own colonies; others joined in the abolitionist movement and hoped to free all slaves and so destroy the institution of slavery. The Nat Turner rebellion in 1831 unleashed latent fears in the South and precipitated a tightening of the slave code. William Lloyd Garrison (1805–1879), a strong abolitionist, founded the *Liberator,* a proabolition newspaper whose editorial policy led to increased hostility between North and South. By the end of the 1830s, the South had rallied to support slavery both theologically and with its own distinct form of revivalism. The Methodist, Baptist, and Presbyterian churches split into northern and southern churches, reflecting the division within society as a whole.

Both pro- and antislavery Christians looked to the Bible for support of their views and sometimes made use of the new biblical criticism (see Chapter 7). By the standards of scholarship, southern Christians had the better case: both the Old and New Testaments assume that slavery is a normal part of society and express no opposition to it. Proslavery Christians argued that baptism meant only that slaves were set free in the Lord (Gal. 3:28). Their freedom consisted in the ability to obey their masters willingly and cheerfully to secure a place for themselves in heaven (Col. 3:22–25). Segregation was extolled as a sensible arrangement and projected into the future. One white minister told a slave congregation they would reach heaven if they were docile and obedient, but even in heaven, they would not mingle with the master and mistress; they could look forward to a heaven with a dividing wall. Northern Christians also supported their abolitionist views with the Bible, arguing that the Bible's emphasis on

People

Martin Luther King Jr.: Nonconformity and Social Change

Few issues illustrate the conflict between adaptation and nonconformity better than U.S. Christians and race. Most American churches followed society's racial patterns by supporting slavery, forming separate churches for whites and blacks, and later counseling Christians to stay out of the struggle for civil rights. The Reverend Martin Luther King Jr. (1929–1968) famously said that 11 A.M. on Sunday was the most segregated hour in America. King decided to challenge segregation directly and so defied the Christian tendency to adaptation.

King was the son and grandson of ministers of the Ebenezer Baptist Church in Atlanta where he learned the black church's emphasis on justice and love for others. In his theological and doctoral studies, King studied theologians like Reinhold Niebuhr (see Chapter 8), who argued that Christians must engage the world. King was ready to put these ideas into practice when in 1955, as a young pastor in Montgomery, Alabama, he led a boycott of city buses to protest segregation.

King combined his Christian ideals with the tactics of nonviolent resistance that Mohandas Gandhi and his followers used against British rule in India. The nonviolent resister disobeys unjust laws after a period of prayer and reflection but accepts the consequences of doing so (prison, attacks, and so on) and refuses to retaliate against persecutors. In 1963, King led a large protest in Birmingham, Alabama, and was thrown in jail. Some Christian leaders expressed sympathy for King's goal of desegregation and equal rights but criticized his direct action as "unwise and untimely."

King responded to his Christian critics in *Letter from Birmingham Jail,* a classic statement of Christian nonconformity. King admitted that his sit-ins and marches increased social tension, but he said that "there is a type of constructive, nonviolent tension which is necessary for growth." God would judge the church for being "an archdefender of the status quo," whether passively or actively. Christians have "blemished and scarred" the body of Christ, he said, "through social neglect and through fear of being nonconformists." King looked to the examples of Jesus, Paul, and the early Christian martyrs and called on Christians to "recapture the sacrificial spirit of the early church," when Christians resisted the society in which they lived. Christians must not accept human-made laws that violate God's justice.

When King was murdered in 1968, many Christians called him a martyr like those of the ancient church. Since his death, both conservative and liberal Christians have cited him as a precedent for directly challenging the values of society in the name of Christian principles.

justice and the participation of slaves in the early churches anticipated a later time when slaves would be free. The theological stances of both northern and southern Christians reflected their differing cultural and political beliefs.

During the century between the Civil War and the Civil Rights movement of the 1950s and 1960s, American Christians—North or South—did not lead the way in integrating U.S. society. To be sure, only very few white Christians participated in such groups as the Ku Klux Klan, which presented itself as a Christian movement, but most adapted to the country's division between blacks and whites. A number of specifically black churches were formed in the eighteenth and nineteenth centuries within mainline Protestant Christianity. Black churches often existed as segregated adjuncts, represented as such. Catholics, too, supported a policy of separation by a set of parallel institutions, black seminaries, church organizations, convents, and schools. For most Christians, no obvious "Christian" alternative to segregation presented itself until blacks themselves began to work for change in the 1950s.

Christian leaders took a prominent role in the movement for civil rights that began in the late 1950s. Despite the end of slavery, black citizens were still second-class citizens, especially in southern states, where laws and taxes prevented blacks from voting and facilities from restaurants to city buses were segregated. Black pastors like Martin Luther King Jr. (1929–1968) led nonviolent resistance to segregation, and in 1957, he and others founded the Southern Christian Leadership Conference (SCLC) to coordinate civil rights activities. Most members and leaders of the SCLC were Baptists, but it relied on a network of diverse black churches. King's speeches drew heavily from the Bible, especially the prophets.

Some white Christian leaders criticized this political activism and urged a more cautious approach, but many others saw racial discrimination as immoral and became active participants in the movement. The struggle to pass the Civil Rights Act of 1964 engaged the energies of many mainline Protestant churches, for which direct political action like lobbying members of Congress was a new activity. Numerous Roman Catholic priests and nuns were also moved by racial injustice to become active protesters in campaigns for fair housing as well as in civil rights marches.

The effects of Christian involvement in the Civil Rights movement were large and long-lasting. It hastened changes in Roman Catholic religious orders as nuns came out of their cloisters and engaged the world. The leaders of mainline Protestant churches became more politicized and liberal than many of the people in the pews, a gap that contributed to a decline in membership. Since both liberal and conservative Christians saw that they could and should work to change society, the activism of the Christian Right of the 1980s can also be seen as a legacy of the Civil Rights movement.

By no means did the passage of civil rights legislation in the 1960s bring an end to racial discrimination, and controversies over practices like affirmative action (giving preference in hiring and other decisions to racial minorities) continued through the following decades. Globalization and immigration have complicated the racial picture in the United States, especially since the rapidly growing Hispanic population means that the United States is no longer a nation of simply black and white. Immigration, whether legal or illegal, is an issue that may be primarily economic, connected to the availability of jobs and inexpensive labor, but it has a racial dimension as well. In 2004, the U.S. Census Bureau projected that by 2010, Hispanics of any race would represent a larger share of the population than blacks and that by 2050, non-Hispanic whites would make up only 50 percent of the total population (as opposed to about 70 percent in 2000). As in the past, fears of racial change have spawned fringe Christian groups, like the Christian Identity movement, which claims that only people of European descent are God's chosen people, the descendants of the lost tribes of Israel.

In the 2000s, as politicians struggled to balance control of the nation's borders with the economic role played by an estimated twelve million illegal, mostly Hispanic immigrants, Christians divided along multiple lines. Roman Catholic bishops, led by the archbishop of Los Angeles, strongly endorsed compassion and support for all immigrants and formed the Justice for Immigrants Campaign to advocate for their rights. Proposals to reform immigration and to integrate illegal immigrants sharply divided evangelical Christians: the large and growing Hispanic evangelical community supported such efforts, but many white evangelicals opposed them. Hispanic evangelicals cited the biblical mandate to care for the foreigner, while a spokesman for the Christian Coalition called protection of national boundaries "a biblical principle." Polls showed that two-thirds of white evangelicals considered immigrants a burden to society, compared to only half of all Americans.

On racial issues, the postures of *adaptation* and *nonconformity* help us to see how a primarily white Christian community, found in the mainline Protestant and Roman Catholic churches, accepted or challenged the racial discrimination of slavery and segregation. But the U.S. Christianity of the 2000s, like the United States as a whole, is much more racially diverse, and the mainline Protestants have lost their dominant position. In this situation, alliances among Christians shift along theological, political, and racial lines.

QUESTIONS RAISED BY THE POSTURES OF NONCONFORMITY AND ADAPTATION

Although these brief glimpses into the problems of war, poverty, and racism do not shed light on the issues as such, they clarify the distinction between nonconformist and adapted Christianity. Examining the postures within the context of specific cultural issues permits a view of their interconnectedness with society. Some of the general questions raised in the last chapter are important here as well; the same questions about the churches and the political order are raised within the framework of these alternatives of nonconformity and adaptation.

In What Sense Is Christianity Political?

Christian understanding of the church's role in the political order varies according to the definition of politics different groups adopt. Nonconformist Christians take politics to be broader than the accepted life of the society, its government, and public institutions. Their political stance rests on the assumption that the Christian community is inherently different from the state; in some cases, the church provides an alternative to the established order. Christians in this group limit their cooperation with the state on the grounds that its values and policies are sometimes different from and even hostile to the values of the church. Their loyalty to the distinctive witness of the church, they believe, prevents them from fully endorsing the values of the culture. Christians in churches that are more adapted accept more of the values of the culture; they tend to see the aims of the state as coextensive with the aims of the church. Adapted Christians usually see no reason, in *principle,* to oppose the goals and policies of the state; they minimize areas of possible conflict between the aims of the society and those of Christian truth.

Whether Christianity is concerned primarily with personal regeneration or with restructuring the society is not the fundamental issue between nonconformity and adaptation. The argument, to some extent, is part of Christianity in whatever form it takes; both nonconformist and adapted Christians would see need for both personal regeneration and efforts for social change. The difference between the positions lies in the way they conceptualize the church and its role in society. Nonconformists tend to see the church as fulfilling an important prophetic function in society; they regard the church as the locus of strong social critique and as a witness to a radical alternative. Adapted Christians tend to see the church as moral educator and helper; they are often more willing to proceed slowly toward change because they regard the church as an institution in fundamental cooperation with the state. Their confidence in social structures is manifested in their willingness to change society through their votes and through participation as candidates for public office.

What Is the Church?

Sociologists of religion sometimes distinguish between "church-type" and "sect-type" Christianity. According to this distinction, sectarian Christians identify the church as a small group of believers whose values differ from those of their culture; their lifestyle is often rigorous and they do not expect to attract many followers or to see their views adopted by the society in general. Christians with a nonsectarian perspective see the church as a large institution whose values contribute to the stability of the society as a whole. They expect the church to be socially acceptable, with many followers, and to exert a positive influence on society. They expect to see their views sanctioned by the culture in which they live.

Were the words of Jesus, which are taken seriously by many sectarians—about loving one's enemies, for example—meant to apply for all times? Or were Jesus' ethics meant to be for the interim: did Jesus expect the world to end so soon that he formulated positions to be adhered to only for the short period between his death and the end of the world? These serious theological questions and issues of scriptural interpretation are reflected in the differences between the nonconformist and adapted positions on some of the issues outlined above.

The questions raised by an argument between sectarian and nonsectarian perspectives often lead to self-righteous judgments on the part of one group or the other. Both groups can perceive themselves as the locus of true Christian conviction. Sectarians often see themselves as more righteous or more faithful to the commands of Jesus; they may condemn the nonsectarian position as secular and perceive the churches as interested in the salvation of the world on the world's terms. Nonsectarians may see the church as no longer motivated by divine ideals but by the business of the world, whereas sectarians provide the witness of the faithful remnant. Nonsectarians often understand themselves as more realistic interpreters of the Gospel because they do not present the message of Jesus in such stark terms; they may condemn sectarians for being socially ineffective and alienating. Church-type Christians may see sectarians as narrow and unnecessarily hostile to the world, while the churches provide an effective Christianity attractive to modern society. Church-type Christianity can be universal, reach out to large numbers of people, and bring its influence to bear on social and political problems. Sectarian Christianity can remind people of the demand for personal commitment. Together they reflect the range of opportunities within the Christian experience.

SPIRITUALITY

Redefining the Boundaries of Faith

When Anselm of Canterbury (d. 1109) defined theology as "faith seeking understanding," faith meant a set of truths revealed by God and defined by the church. When Luther (d. 1546) declared that one is saved by faith alone, he understood faith as a living, bold trust in God's grace. Millions of people today who talk about themselves as "spiritual but not religious" are not so sure one can define faith and tend to seek God in eclectic ways.

In their search for meaning, they may be drawn to meditation techniques from Eastern religions or back to practices at the roots of their own traditions. They might find holiness in a deep reverence for the earth and Native American attitudes toward it or in megachurches where preaching, programs, and music are entertaining. Nondenominational megachurches like Willow Creek (Bill Hybels, pastor), near Chicago, minister to twenty thousand people each weekend and offer something for everyone (small groups, volunteer opportunities, self-help workshops, Bible study, counseling, effective parenting classes). Other megachurches include the Potter's House in Dallas (T. D. Jakes, pastor), and the Saddleback Church in Lake Forest, California (Rick Warren, pastor).

People with new religious ideas are often lumped together and ridiculed by established groups. Methodist was once a word used to make fun of followers of John Wesley; Quakers was a word meant to make people laugh at the practices of George Fox's followers. Words used to describe three different groups of those searching for new religious meaning are "Seeker sensitive," "Emerging," and "Emergent." Critics say that they are untraditional in their preaching, unbiblical in their teaching, and more interested in entertainment than in worship. Those who attend such groups, however, say that their unconventional journeys have led them to deeper, more expressive understanding of the divine. They often find God more readily in their own stories than in biblical narrative, may relate to God in feminine terms, or find meaning in Catholic devotional practices. Many are unchurched, but curious about the varieties of religious experience available in the modern world. Religious bookstores sell more books on angels, aliens, Native American chants, religiously inflected self-help techniques, Buddhist mediations, and medieval mystics than books on traditional Christian topics.

The Seeker sensitive network includes megachurches and small communities throughout the world. Emergent churches often position themselves between mainline churches and conservative Evangelicalism. Their cousins in the Emerging church movement may identify with the life of Jesus, but they remain skeptical about truth claims and believe that the church needs to reinvent itself for the twenty-first century. For many of those redefining the boundaries of faith, theology is a continuing and sometimes surprising conversation.

HOW SHOULD THE BIBLE BE INTERPRETED?

As with the options described in the last chapter, adapted and nonconformist Christians support their positions with their reading of the New Testament. Does their use of the New Testament to support fundamentally differing views mean that the message of the New Testament is not clear with regard to racism, violence, and poverty? Does the New Testament itself reflect differences or disagreements already present in the early Christian community? Or is the New Testament perfectly clear on every issue and do some Christians willfully misunderstand it? Did the cultural context in which the Bible was written shape its message? Does their cultural context shape the way North Americans read the Bible?

Most Christian groups agree that Scripture is normative, but how, exactly, does it bind people? Are only the general principles found in Scripture—for example, to love God wholeheartedly and one's neighbor as oneself—binding? Or are specific injunctions addressed to a particular cultural context—"A woman ought to have a veil on her head" (1 Cor. 11:10)—equally binding? How does one discriminate? Should Christians conform their behavior to descriptive statements in the Bible—for example, that Abraham had slaves? Or are they bound only by prescriptive statements like the Ten Commandments? How do they decide about these matters? Must Christians do only what the Bible commands? Or may they do anything not specifically forbidden: for example, since Jesus said nothing about slavery, can one assume owning slaves is acceptable?

Are some parts of the Bible more important than others? In the Old Testament, God urges people to go to war and often supports their efforts to conquer another nation; in the New Testament, Jesus enjoins his followers to love their enemies and to put away their swords. How do Christians decide which texts are more important in times of war? Most Christians use the New Testament as an interpretive key to the Old Testament: they see God's words and actions in the lives of the Jewish people as pointing directly toward Jesus. Does that mean that the words of the New Testament must always supersede those of the Old Testament? Within the New Testament, how does one resolve differences in wording, as between being poor and being poor "in spirit"? Are some parts of the New Testament more important than others? Are the words of Jesus more binding than the teachings of Paul?

All these questions occur in the differences between nonconformist and adapted perspectives on particular issues. They are usually answered within the context of the believing community's historical experience and tradition. Can those answers change? Will textual criticism and biblical scholarship help people answer these questions more clearly? Or does biblical scholarship threaten the inerrancy of the Bible? Will cultural attitudes be the major interpretive framework in which such questions are answered? Or is it possible to read the text purely, without being influenced by the cultural context? Does a literal reading of the New Testament lead to clear interpretations? Or does that reading tend to reduce issues to a simplicity they do not have?

CONCLUSION

None of the questions raised in this chapter or the previous one can be answered simply; they reflect ancient disagreements and contemporary problems of interpretation. The four postures outlined—withdrawal, domination, nonconformity, and adaptation—do not describe particular groups in an ironclad way but suggest some pressing theological issues underlying a wide range of Christian belief and behavior. As Christians continue to be challenged by problems within the world and their culture—nuclear power and weapons, sexism, multinational corporations in Two-Thirds World countries, worldwide poverty, the emergence of new nations in Asia and Africa—most will not find simple solutions. They will continue to seek answers within the tension between the church and the world and beyond its bounds.

Focal Points for Discussion

1. Compare the peace programs of any of the historic peace churches (Friends, Mennonites, Brethren) with peace programs in any mainline Protestant or Catholic church. What are the essential differences? Are there any similarities?
2. The Bible does not condemn slavery, yet all Christians today agree that slavery is immoral. What arguments have Christians offered and what arguments might they offer to disagree with the Bible in this way?
3. Twentieth-century Christians like Martin Luther King Jr, César Chávez, and peace activists advocated nonviolence and pacifism as Christian positions. What precedents in the Bible and Christian history might they point to for their position? Are there biblical and historical precedents that argue against nonviolence and pacifism?

Contemporary Christianity

CHAPTER 12

Our understanding of Christianity began with a look at the religious experience of the ancient Hebrews, noticing that their beliefs about God's personality and desire encompassed two different concepts. On the one hand, God was the transcendent creator, remote, powerful, and resplendent, a God who came with fire and thunder to deliver commandments and to instill feelings of awe. On the other hand, God was the immanent partner, close, protective, and involved, a God who came with compassion to offer a covenant relationship and engender feelings of friendship. We noted that throughout the Hebrew Bible, God acted both to judge and to uphold the people. We can see, therefore, that there is room for different points of emphasis when one attempts to interpret God's will in today's world.

In the New Testament, Jesus had harsh things to say to those who exploited the poor and the weak, and he had comforting words for the afflicted. Furthermore, as we have seen, the wording of the New Testament allows for different interpretations of the divine design in relation to specific social problems. Although the early Christians understood themselves to be in partnership with the Holy Spirit, they were continually involved in a struggle to define themselves in relation to the world around them. Christian history, as we have seen, has been marked by a continual adjustment to new circumstances and has been informed at various times by particular readings of Scripture. We should not be surprised, therefore, that contemporary Christianity is also defined by its struggles to relate to the world and to culture. Nor should we be astonished to find that widely variant interpretations of Christianity can all be based on the Bible.

Our goal in this last chapter is to show how Christians can disagree on fundamental issues in good faith. We do not attempt to prove that one group is right and another wrong but to suggest that the bases for disagreement have long historical roots and proceed from dearly held assumptions about the nature of God, the power of biblical authority, and the definition of the church. When we looked at the challenges of modernity (Chapter 7), we noted two general reactions that define a wide spectrum of response: welcoming the insights of modernity and resisting them.

Contemporary Christianity is distinguished, in part, by new articulations of these two postures in response to a set of new challenges raised by Christians themselves in the latter part of the twentieth century. This chapter examines the general distinction between liberal and conservative Christianity (which we examined as the liberal-fundamentalist debate in Chapter 8) and looks at some particularly vexing issues and opportunities offered to Christianity from the women's movement, religious uses of electronic technology from radio to cyberspace, and the challenges to biblical interpretation offered by homosexuality. By the end of the chapter, we hope you will be better equipped to make some judgments for yourself about the future of Christianity.

LIBERAL AND CONSERVATIVE CHRISTIANITY

As we have seen, modernity engendered at least two widely different responses on the part of Christians. In broad terms, we can define these positions in relation to one another, knowing, as we do, that they come from the different experiences of both groups in the nineteenth and twentieth centuries. Both liberals and conservatives are dedicated to the preservation of Christian truth as they understand it, but that understanding is shaped by their relation to the modern world.

We are using intentionally general terminology in this section as a caution against assigning labels to particular groups of Christians. Liberal Christianity can mean a number of things in practical terms, and one can find liberal Christians in mainline Protestantism, Roman Catholicism, Evangelicalism, Orthodox Christianity, and Anglicanism. The kinds of concerns—for the elimination of racism, world hunger, injustice—that inform the World Council of Churches, along with that body's desire for ecumenical dialogue, characterize many of the desires of liberal Christians. Conservative Christianity can also mean a number of things in practical terms: some conservative Christians are fundamentalists and some are not. One can find conservative Christians in most mainline Protestant churches as well as in Roman Catholic, Orthodox, and Anglican churches. Evangelical Christians are usually considered conservative, but as we saw in the last chapter, one can identify left-wing evangelicals as well. The kinds of concerns taken up by the World Council of Churches are generally not embraced by conservative Christians, and many prefer to associate with the National Association of Evangelicals (NAE). Some members of the National Council of Churches also serve as official observes at the NAE, thus complicating easy description. We advise you to use caution when attempting to assign labels.

LIBERAL CHRISTIANITY

In general, liberals welcome pluralism, are comfortable with ambiguity, and understand Christian life as complex and their conclusions as tentative. They are influenced by the principle of continuity or development and tend to be optimistic, or at least open-minded, in relation to the world around them. The central authority for their faith is their relation to Christ, but that relationship is often rooted in experience and some trust in reason. Liberals, in general, are often attracted to the immanent images of God in the Bible and tend to blur classical distinctions between the natural and supernatural worlds. Accordingly, they see no need for extraordinary interventions of the divine into human life. Miracles for them are not necessarily proofs of God's existence and power. On the contrary, a person's experience of Christ shapes a belief in God, and a person's belief in God enables him or her to see the miraculous power of God displayed in ordinary life. According to them, revelation is contained in a special way in the Bible, but it is also available in the stuff of everyday life. Human experience and human existence provide clues about the nature of God, and revelation is considered a dynamic, ongoing event in the unfolding of human history.

One of the ways liberals have opened themselves to new theologies and pluralism is through the environmental movement. Since the 1960s, people across the globe concerned about the state of the natural world have organized the environmental movement to pressure governments and businesses to assume responsibility for caring for the earth. This cause, generally associated with the political left, has been increasingly embraced by Evangelical Christians along with more liberal-identified Christians. Since all Christians strive to read the Bible in a discerning way, we can expect most communities to at least consider ecology and the environment in biblical terms. One textual snarl is the seeming contradiction between two passages in Genesis: one urges humans to "have dominion" over the earth (Gen. 1:28), and another urges us to "till the ground" and to care for the earth (Gen. 3:23). Christian environmentalists argue that the first passage has been destructive and has contributed to the despoiling of nature because it separates humanity from nature in a way contrary to God's intentions.

Christians who support environmental responsibility have emphasized biblical themes of stewardship and reverence for nature. For example, the Evangelical Environmental Network (EEN) was formed because its leaders perceived environmental issues as spiritual problems. If Christians are to "declare the Lordship of Christ over all creation" (Col. 1:15–20), they say, then it is imperative to care for all creation in ecologically sound ways. According to this view, there is a divine plan for the earth and its creatures: as God's handiwork, they are to be cared for in a responsible and protective way. Many Christians—professional theologians and ordinary laypeople—have become active in the Green movement, an international environmental coalition, because they believe that their religious obligations to God and to their neighbors entail a responsibility for the natural world and a duty to preserve it for future generations. In other words, attitudes toward the natural world reflect dispositions toward others in general. In this sense, disregard for nature is seen by some commentators as a form of sin. Christian environmentalists sometimes claim that dependence on technology makes believers forget their dependence on God and that environmental sins, like pollution, place human comfort before religious obligations. What is at stake, they claim, is not only material resources or a pleasant environment but a world full of religious significance that has been desacralized through human actions.

Prior to the 1980s, many socially active Christians tended not to regard the environmental movement with much concern. Most of them were dealing with issues like poverty, women's rights, and racism. But in recent years, more Christians have seen environmental activism as a way to understand God's creation and human interaction on the planet. The National Council of Churches has endorsed concern for the environment. World Council of Churches conferences since 1979 have affirmed a commitment to care for the natural world, and the National Conference of Catholic

Bishops displayed similar ideas in their 1991 statement "Renewing the Earth." In 2006, leaders in the National Association of Evangelicals tried to put their political power to use to fight global warming but were opposed by a significant part of their membership. Despite that opposition, however, nearly ninety evangelical leaders—college presidents and leaders of megachurches like Rick Warren—supported an evangelical initiative to fight global warming.

Many Christian environmentalists affirm that God's created order is dynamic and continually unfolding. Because the natural world is sustained through human care and people's ability to work together, Christian environmentalists have been willing to share space with other religious traditions and with diverse groups of people. These Christians are willing, therefore, to commit to social action and to subject their beliefs to changing circumstances that can shed new light on the Gospel.

The world is therefore not perceived as a hostile environment for Christians. Liberals tend to be open to new theologies, new understandings about God, and they tend to welcome dialogue and pluralism. Convinced by nineteenth-century theologians that Christianity is a communal experience, liberals often perceive the nature of the Christian life in social terms and tend to see the mission of the church as connected with the regeneration of society.

American liberal Christians are not always comfortable with the language of America as the new promised land. If America has a mission to the world, they say, it is because the country has many problems of its own and is also blessed with resources that could be used to help the distressed peoples and situations of the earth. In terms of their political agenda, liberals can sound like secular humanists: they appeal to human rights and are convinced that the problems of the world need to be solved by human ingenuity. Some critics today say that liberal Christianity is declining in America precisely because it cannot differentiate itself from secular humanism, but we wonder whether that is a fair judgment. Liberals distinguish themselves from their secular counterparts primarily by virtue of their religious belief. Their Christian faith, they say, is a primary motivating power for them and gives them the strength to act creatively in the world. When they stress goals of social justice for the world, they are moved by the words of the biblical prophets and the example of Jesus. The Bible, for them, galvanizes social reform, and they cite the influence of biblical power on reformers like Martin Luther King Jr.

Liberal Christians tend to be social activists with an agenda that leans to the left. Issues of nuclear power and disarmament, along with ecological concerns, and a general support for the goals of the World Council of Churches define many of their fields of interaction. In terms of the diagram introduced in this part of the book, liberal Christians might be found in nonconformist or adapted positions. At the same time, a prayerful concern for liberal social agendas can be found in withdrawn monastic communities. Finally, specific groups, like the American Catholic bishops, who take the posture of domination on the issue of abortion, have a long history of creative response to issues of social justice. The bishops released a pastoral letter on nuclear war in 1983 and one on the economy in 1986. Both of these documents, while not ultimately grounded in the principles of liberal Christianity, do take positions that are attractive to liberal Christians. Where one can find liberals, therefore, is not easily predictable and sometimes needs to be addressed on a case-by-case basis. Still, the general outlines of this position should give you some basis for determining the general attitude.

SPIRITUALITY

Prayer: Something Understood

Clearly, Christians believe and practice their religion in many different ways, including distinctive forms of prayer. When metaphysical poet George Herbert (1593–1633) wrote his poem "Prayer," he used twenty-six wildly different phrases in fourteen lines. The last two words might be the best, "something understood." Whether Christians pray aloud or silently, in church or at home, with others or alone, using formal phrases or spontaneous words, with gestures or without, they want to be understood by God.

Prayer is an opening or lifting of the mind and heart toward the divine. Usually, people pray to adore God, to express sorrow for sins and failings, to thank God for the blessings of this life or the beauties of the world, and to ask for God's continued help. Christians are drawn to the transcendent, powerful lord of the universe and to a God who is personal and deeply interested in them. In intimate terms, prayer is a conversation driven by a need to understand oneself before God.

The Christian tradition has a rich vein of private prayer. Mystics seek union with God; contemplatives still their minds and hearts to a communication that needs no words or images; and those skilled in meditation concentrate on a particular image or word and let it fill up their whole consciousness. The hesychast tradition in Orthodox Christianity recommends the "Jesus prayer" ("Lord Jesus Christ, have mercy on me"). When people coordinate the words with their heartbeats and breath, they can "pray without ceasing" (1 Thess. 5:17) and eventually embody the compassionate nature of Jesus. Many Christians practice private devotions, including Bible reading, to let Christ take form within their lives.

Christians have myriad types of public prayer as well, at worship services, prayer groups, healing services, peace vigils, antiabortion rallies, and fellowship groups. They may pray at set times (morning, evening, before meals) with other members of their families or communities or sit meditatively with others in quiet communal prayer. They pray standing, sitting, kneeling, and sometimes lying down. They praise God, bless one another, and ask for help. Spiritual writers suggest that specific needs in prayer are symptoms of an infinite need for God and that prayer sets change in motion by putting people in touch with their own inner poverty (needs), which, in turn, puts them at the heart of the world's suffering. Prayer, therefore, is how Christians hold the world's pain up to God's mercy.

CONSERVATIVE CHRISTIANITY

In contrast to liberals, conservative Christians prefer certainty and understand Christian life to be clear, its conclusions fixed. They are influenced by the principle of a divine plan for humanity and tend to be pessimistic about and sometimes suspicious of the world around them. The central authority for their faith is their relation to Christ, a bond that is rooted in God's invitation in the Bible. According to them, God disclosed a plan of salvation to the peoples and authors of the Bible and guaranteed its essential rightness through divine inspiration. One can trust the Bible to be free from error and so only has to trust in God's word as found in the Bible.

Conservatives who are suspicious of the modern world sometimes focus on public education. One of the ways modern societies have transformed education is in broadening curricula to include sex education, new scientific theories, and ideas illustrating non-Christian cultures. Many conservative Christians object to the inclusion of such teachings in public schools because it is biased against their beliefs. Modern education leaves no opportunity for school prayer and often teaches "values" that conservative Christians think are relativistic or antireligious. They claim that not only are modern topics like sex education inappropriate for children's schooling but also that many of the ideas—Darwin's theories, for example—pose an implicit challenge to Christian belief. In response to this crisis, some Christians have opted out of the public school system and have chosen to educate their children at home.

The homeschooling movement, as this impulse has come to be called, has proved to be a highly effective cause for mobilizing Christian conservatives. The United States has seen the incorporation of thousands of Christian schools, especially since the 1960s, partly as a response to the above concerns. But many parents have increasingly sought to establish a more direct link with their children's education, choosing instead to withdraw from all educational initiatives outside the home. Homeschoolers resent having to pay taxes for a public education they find troublesome or having to pay extra for private education. The tax relief that home education provides for families is another reason for its attraction.

There are homeschooling movements in most states, with organizations to link families together. Michael Farris, a prominent lawyer for Christian causes, founded the Home School Legal Defense Association (HSLDA) to provide a national support organization and to help defend the legality of homeschooling. Central to the legal defense of homeschoolers is Farris's claim that public education actually endorses the "religion" of secular humanism and therefore can violate the First Amendment rights of conservative Christians who believe otherwise. The rise of homeschooling represents an important dimension of conservative Christianity, for it is testimony to the growing political skills of this group and to their politicization of new areas of social life.

Conservatives, in general, are often attracted to images of divine transcendence, and they tend to highlight the classical distinction between the natural and supernatural worlds. Accordingly, they expect extraordinary interventions of the divine into human life. Miracles, indeed, are a proof of God's existence and can be defined as extraordinary: everyday life may have glimmers of the divine in it, but God's power is especially evident in the miracles recorded in the Bible and, for some, in miraculous healings and manifestations in the lives of Christians today. According to them, revelation is contained in the Bible and is not to be found in contemporary history or ordinary events.

Human experience, far from providing clues to divine attributes, proves the constant need for God by its continual manifestations of sinfulness. The world is, in many ways, an alien environment for the Christian. Conservatives tend to resist any new theology, preferring what they sometimes call "the old-time religion." They may be open to dialogue with others, and they live in a pluralistic society, but they often regard their position as the only true one and see no need to absorb the insights of other religions. Convinced by reformers and revivalists that Christianity is a matter of individual conversion, conservatives often perceive the Christian life in individual terms and tend to understand the mission of the church as connected with the evangelical impulse to draw all people into a personal relationship with Jesus.

American conservative Christians may adopt the rhetoric of America as the new promised land, the new Eden where God has given humanity a chance to gather everyone into the kingdom. America is the home of God's chosen people and God's preferred way of life; the task set for the country is the evangelization of the world, an event that will hasten the Second Coming of Christ at the end of the world.

In terms of their political agendas, religious conservatives often sound like political conservatives: they appeal to capitalism, strong defense initiatives, and low taxes. They also may believe that the problems of this world will eventually be solved by God's intervention. Critics sometimes say that fundamentalist Christians who support conservative political positions are more interested in preserving the status quo than they are in religion, but we wonder whether that is a fair judgment. Conservative Christians distinguish themselves from conservative secular politics primarily by virtue of their religious belief. Their Christian faith, they say, inspires them to act and gives them the strength and wisdom to oppose the directions of the modern world. When they stress goals of individual salvation and preservation of the American way of life, they are moved by God's covenant with them and their belief in America as a new promised land.

Conservative Christians can sometimes be social isolationists, preferring to put their energies into the work of personal salvation, and sometimes they are political activists. As activists, they tend to gather around issues of American military superiority, antiamnesty for immigrants, and a general contempt for the goals of the World Council of Churches. In terms of the diagram introduced at the beginning of this part of the book, some conservative Christians can be found in the withdrawn position, while one would expect them to be interested primarily in personal regeneration and opposed to social activism. Some, whose biblical theology is conservative while their social justice initiatives are not, might be placed in the nonconformist position: Evangelicals for Social Action, for example, have taken strong positions both on the biblical basis of their lives and against poverty and world hunger. One can find conservative Christians in the adapted groups of American Christianity, and there are televangelists (like Jim and Tammy Bakker), who have exploited a Gospel of Wealth reading of the Old Testament to support their own personal financial gain.

Finally, one can find conservatives in the position of domination. When Jerry Falwell (d. 2007) founded the Moral Majority in the 1980s, it was a marriage of fundamentalist Christianity and a dominating political perspective. Pat Robertson's use of *The 700 Club* as a launching pad for his political ambitions is an example of the ways fundamentalist Christianity can take on the political goals of the new right. Falwell, Robertson, and other fundamentalists used fear of same-sex marriage to galvanize voters in the 2004 election. As was the case with liberal Christians, one cannot always predict where conservatives will line up on the diagram, but this general description should provide you with some clues for identification and rationale.

CONTEMPORARY ISSUES

Christians today, like their counterparts in other times, face issues of biblical authority, ministry, mission, and the definition of the church itself. As you can imagine, liberal and conservative Christians respond quite differently to challenges raised in these areas, and we can now trust you to predict how various groups will react and to explain why they react as they do.

A simple listing of contemporary moral problems that demand Christian consideration will show us that questions about gay marriage, the ordination of women, the

Controversy
Jesus in the Culture Wars

In 1966, John Lennon of The Beatles said, "We're more popular than Jesus now." He may have been wrong, but Lennon pointed out that, thanks to the modern global media, The Beatles were more widely known in their lifetimes than Jesus was in his. But Jesus soon entered the media age of celebrity: the rock opera *Jesus Christ Superstar* became a multimedia phenomenon in the early 1970s as a Broadway play, best-selling album, and major motion picture.

Popular depictions of Jesus soon reflected the diverse identities and theologies of global Christianity, often shocking and offending conservative Christians. The Reverend Albert Cleage claimed that Jesus was black in his book *Black Messiah* (1969), an idea given life in the 2006 film *Color of the Cross.* Edwina Sandys depicted Jesus as a crucified woman in her sculpture *Christa* (1984). Terence McNally's 1998 play *Corpus Christi* tells the story of a young Texan named Joshua who must accept both that he is gay and that he is the Son of God who must die. These artists understand racism, sexism, and homophobia as similar to the persecution that Jesus suffered.

Two presentations of Jesus provoked strong conflict in the United States, where conservatives and liberals battled over depictions of sex, gender, and religion in the media. Andres Serrano's 1988 photograph *Piss Christ* showed a crucifix suspended in urine. Serrano, a Catholic, may have hoped to communicate the sheer physicality of the incarnation and to show Christ's identification with people with AIDS, whose body fluids carried the dangerous virus. The image, however, enraged conservative Christians, who cited it as a reason to cut funding to the National Endowment for the Arts, which had given Serrano a grant.

In 2004, another Catholic, Mel Gibson, released his film *The Passion of the Christ.* Its painstaking and gory depiction of the crucifixion, with dialogue in Aramaic and Latin, reflected Gibson's traditionalist Catholic spirituality, but critics, especially biblical scholars, charged that it misrepresented the Gospels and portrayed Jewish leaders too negatively. Gibson asserted that he was being persecuted by cultural elites for his religious beliefs, and soon his film and its bloody, defiant Jesus became a rallying point for conservative Christians. Evangelical Protestants and others flocked to the movie, making it a huge success. As of 2007, it was the highest grossing R-rated film ever.

legitimacy of a pro-choice position on abortion, and the campaign to eliminate nuclear weapons make the practical realities of Christian life highly volatile in the twenty-first century. Our purpose in this chapter, however, is not to engage in extensive discussion of complex moral issues. We prefer to draw your attention to the kinds of issues we have been discussing throughout the book, which present perennial challenges to Christians by raising questions about ministry, church, and mission.

We will look at three complex issues and connect each with a specific kind of definitional problem. They have long, complicated histories, which we can only allude to in this book. We hope, however, that they will interest you enough that you will do some further study and try to grasp the nuances involved. We will discuss ministry in terms of the women's movement by focusing on questions of women's ordination. We will discuss the nature of the church in terms of media evangelism, and we will raise questions of biblical interpretation by showing how homosexuality has raised questions that have divided Christians denominationally and globally. By the end, perhaps you will have what we have hoped for throughout this book: a sense of the great dynamism of Christianity and its continuing bustle of life in the contemporary world.

The Women's Movement and Questions of Ministry

Any organization that exists within a particular culture is usually impelled to deal with the challenges and questions of that culture. Since the nineteenth century, women's rights activists have been raising critical questions that have enormous consequences for the Christian churches. Sexism, the systematic cultural and institutional denial of opportunity to women simply because of their gender, is an especially difficult problem because discussions and competing biblical interpretations often engender strong resistance. Some deny that there is a problem at all, and others, though recognizing the cry for justice, are often shocked at some of the directions taken by feminist critics.

At the heart of the matter for Christian women is the issue of biblical authority that we have encountered many times throughout this book. If women are treated as second-class citizens by religious denominations *on the basis of the Bible,* what does that say about biblical authority? Does God intend for women to be secondary? Did God create women as helpmates for men with no opportunities beyond motherhood or (in Catholic teaching) the convent?

Some church leaders (mostly male) would say that, indeed, God did create women with natures and attributes that are different from those of men: men are strong, rational, naturally inclined toward philosophical speculation, and meant to rule, whereas women are weak, emotional, naturally inclined toward bodily life (motherhood), and meant to be ruled. This division pleases some women and many men, and it has the advantage of being consistent with the kinds of opinions one can find in the Bible. At the same time, feminist interpreters in the churches point out that we can find a rather different perspective in the words and behavior of Jesus toward women. Jesus invited women into discipleship, appeared to have a special understanding of their lives, treated them with unusual dignity, and made his first postresurrection appearance to a woman. It appears, therefore, as if a tension is present even in the New Testament about the proper role and place of women: the example of Jesus tends to lead to the conclusion that the new community is a discipleship of equals. However, *some* of the other writings in the New Testament, including some of those attributed to Paul, lead to the conclusion that women may not speak in public, hold any office in the church, or have any life of their own apart from the protection and direction of their husbands. The fact that the New Testament can be read in different ways on this issue should not surprise us.

Feminists have challenged the male God-language of the Bible, attempted to create new theologies meant to reinterpret traditional Christian doctrines like the Trinity, and tried to find new ways to imagine their interaction with the divine in symbolic and practical terms. One issue that continually challenges the churches is that of women's ordination.

Women have always been the major practitioners of Christianity, but they have only recently taken some role in the leadership of the church. Eighty-four denominations now ordain women, and nearly as many do not. Whether women should be ordained is a question that divides Christians even within denominations: fundamentalist Southern

Concept

God-Talk: Language About God

Although language seems to be a neutral means of communication, it can be an ideological vehicle that shapes thinking and values. Racial epithets, abusive language, and name calling are examples of the ways language reflects and shapes attitudes. In recent years, Jewish and Christian feminists have raised language issues as a modern challenge to traditional religious authority. They have argued that the ways believers talk about God affect the ways gender is conceived and modeled in society.

In the texts and traditions of Christianity, God has been represented as a supreme being who created the world and governs it. This powerful, transcendent figure, with omniscient qualities, is usually described in male language and is usually associated with "masculine" jobs in the world, like fatherhood, kingship, judge, and warrior. The linkage between divine power and male authority has also been underwritten by biblical stories— like Eve's creation from one of Adam's ribs—that depict women as naturally inferior to men and in need of male guidance. Even in ancient pagan societies, divine qualities like power, reason, and an aptitude for governance have been claimed by men, while human qualities like weakness, emotion, and a need for direction have been said to be womanly traits.

Feminist theologians like Elizabeth Johnson, in her book *She Who Is: The Mystery of God in Feminist Theological Discourse* (1993), argue that the search for God is grounded on divine incomprehensibility: the mystery of God makes it impossible to talk about God in exclusive language. If *female* language about God is inadequate and ambiguous and requires a negative critique by other terms lest we think of God as a *woman,* then so also does *male* language about God. According to Johnson, the biblical and traditional language used to talk about God in the past is no longer adequate.

In suggesting an identity between masculinity and divinity, male God-language supports structures and practices that devalue and discriminate against women. Exclusively male God-language also reduces the incomprehensibility of the divine personality to a single concept, imposing limits on what is without limits. In thinking about the place of women in the world and in the church, authors like Johnson claim that we must rethink the way we speak about God. Both God-language and the practical language of the church should become more inclusive and more representative of the dignity given women in creation. The use of other metaphors and images of God—divine wisdom, mother, beloved—can help to restore the mystery of God and rescue it from the limitations of human language. It can be a base upon which discriminatory social practices can be redressed.

Baptists forbid it, moderate Southern Baptists allow it, and the American Baptist church ordains women as a matter of policy. Although women were not admitted to divinity schools in any significant way until the 1950s, by the 2000s, they accounted for nearly 40 percent of all seminary students. It appears, therefore, that many Christian churches have met the criticisms of the women's movement and now welcome the leadership of women as well as men. For example, in 2006, the Episcopal church in America elected a woman as its presiding bishop for the first time. Katherine Jefferts Schori, a former oceanographer and airplane pilot, had been consecrated as the ninth bishop of Nevada in 2001.

Appearances of women's advancement in churches, however, can still be deceiving. One of the problems faced by churches that ordain women is the placement of those women. Many of them are *not* called as the primary ministers of churches but are relegated to secondary positions as hospital chaplains, as assistant ministers, and as ministers of education. The mere fact of ordination, therefore, does not eliminate the challenge. In fact, many ordained Protestant women talk about a "stained glass ceiling" that prevents them from being called to large influential churches.

The problems faced by the churches that do *not* ordain women are different. Roman Catholicism is a case in point. The refusal of Catholics to ordain women is based on the idea that the priest represents Christ and so must resemble him physically, an argument that has been denied and criticized by Catholic feminists and theologians. The desire for reunion between Roman Catholic and Anglican churches, a process that has absorbed great time and energy in both churches for the last hundred years, is now in jeopardy because of the Anglican practice of ordaining women. That practice has also divided Anglicans globally: Bishop Peter Akinola, the presiding bishop of Nigeria, would not participate in a Eucharistic celebration with Bishop Katherine Schori. Finally, the appeal to "tradition" made on the part of Roman Catholic officials, an appeal shared by Orthodox Christians, raises the whole question of the validity of tradition and introduces questions about the ways tradition has been used to support the power structures of the church rather than to enhance the life of the faithful. The question of women's ordination, therefore, raises challenges about the authority of the Bible, the role of tradition, the credibility of church leadership, and the need for new attitudes toward women in the churches.

It also raises the question of *ministry*. What is a minister or priest supposed to do in a congregation? If the minister represents God, then is the presence of women ministers an invitation to find and use images for divine-human interaction that stress female images of the divine? If the minister is the authority figure in the community, does the presence of women in the ministry contradict Paul's injunctions about women not having power over men? Does it mean that Paul was wrong about this issue? Or might it suggest that Christians need new ways to understand and exercise power? How will the participation of women ministers affect the ways congregations think about God? Will the presence of more women in church leadership change the nature of the church in some way?

If you think women in ministry will change patterns of worship and articulations of religious language, how do you envision such a change? If you think such a change might "ruin" Christianity as we have known it, *how* do you think it might have that outcome? If you think such a change might "improve" Christianity as we have known it, *how* do you think it might do so? The questions are not simple because they touch the very core of Christian worship and challenge Christians to think more deeply about the ways they pray, sing, preach, and in general, relate to God. The questions will not disappear: in many ways, the challenge of the women's movement in Christianity sets part of the agenda for the churches in the twenty-first century.

Media Technology and the Nature of the Church

When we consider the challenges of modern technology, it appears that we cannot appeal to the Bible. Jesus had nothing to say about radio, television, or the Internet, nor did ancient Christian writers. They did, however, give the church a task to preach the Gospel to all nations, to make disciples out of all peoples. Has modern media technology made that task possible in new ways? Is the church a community of believers united in fellowship in a particular place, associated with a larger institutional structure, or is it a collection of those who have a personal relationship with Jesus whether they gather together in a local congregation or not?

In the early 1920s, an innovative program manager at KDKA, Pittsburgh, invited a local minister to broadcast a short message over the radio. The minister and the idea were both highly successful: by 1926, nearly all of the six-hundred-plus radio stations in America supported some kind of religious broadcasting. In the competitive radio market, program directors began to look for preachers with "personality" who could draw large audiences and build national reputations. Catholic audiences tuned in to two priests, the controversial Charles Coughlin and the man who would later become a television personality as well, Fulton Sheen; mainline Protestant churches had special shows like *The Lutheran Hour*. The real supporters of this new form of ministry, however, were Pentecostals, like Aimee Semple McPherson (see sidebar on page 156) and fundamentalists.

Radio appeared to be a great medium for preaching the Gospel to all nations and a perfect way to disseminate the work of independent churches and Bible institutes. For example, the Moody Bible Institute in Chicago had its own radio station and was the strongest fundamentalist voice in the Chicago area in the 1930s. A young, powerful new preacher from North Carolina, Billy Graham, was clearly a man who was going places and who knew how to use the media for an evangelical advantage. Finally, Charles Fuller, whose program *The Old-Fashioned Revival Hour* was carried nationally on the Mutual Radio network, was reputed to have the largest audience of any preacher on the airwaves.

Fuller's success was amazing: he began with a local program in Los Angeles, pioneered the use of audience participation with a weekly phone-in segment, and finally entered into radio ministry full-time, supported by his listeners' contributions. You should know that he managed to do this during the Depression: people who had little hope and less money made donations that financed expensive airtime and finally resulted in the capital necessary for founding the Fuller Evangelical Seminary.

In the mid-1950s, the strategies of radio evangelism were transferred to television. Preachers began to build national audiences with a blend of "old-time religion" and commercial appeals. Oral Roberts, Rex Humbard, and Billy Graham, all with different styles, became phenomenally successful and began to change the ways people looked at the church. People were no longer confined to local congregations but could now participate in a kind of national evangelical consciousness by way of their contributions and support for these new ministries.

The freewheeling intensity of televangelism reached a high point in the 1970s and 1980s with such stars as Jimmy Swaggart and Jim and Tammy Faye Bakker. Swaggart preached with incendiary rhetoric against homosexuality (the worst sin in the world) and against rock and roll (demonically inspired). His daily contributions were estimated at a half a million dollars, and Swaggart claimed at one point to be saving 100,000 souls each week. Jim and Tammy Faye Bakker's *PTL Club* (Praise the Lord) celebrated material as well as spiritual blessings, as the Bakkers wore expensive clothing, displayed their opulent home, and built a Christian theme park called Heritage USA. In the late 1980s, sexual and financial scandals humiliated Swaggart and Jim Bakker and brought an end to the era of excess and spectacle in televangelism.

Televangelists of the 2000s tend to be less confrontational, more affirming, and less crass in their pleas for money. Joyce Meyer, although charismatic, preaches in a low-key style and emphasizes overcoming difficulties in one's everyday life. She blunts criticism of her personal wealth by drawing a modest salary from her ministry and instead making her money through book royalties. Joel Osteen, pastor of the Lakewood Church in Houston, emphasizes God's love and personal fulfillment on his popular television show and his best selling-book, *Your Best Life Now: 7 Steps to Living at Your Full Potential* (2004). The positive, nonjudgmental messages of current televangelists do not differ radically from other self-help programs in contemporary American culture.

In the mid-1960s, computer technology added new dimensions to media evangelism. At first, computers were used to store names, addresses, and personal information so that television preachers, like smart advertisers, could appeal to the American public by way of "personalized" letters. Preachers began to hire writers and to use combinations of religious entertainment and the Gospel to increase their audiences. They found that they could get massive financial support for building projects and began to appeal for funds to build hospitals and colleges (such as Oral Roberts University and Jerry Falwell's Liberty Baptist College).

The political possibilities of religion were enhanced by the computer sophistication of televangelists. Conservative political advisers like Richard Vigeurie, head of the largest political mailing organization in the United States; Tim LaHaye, president of the American Coalition for Traditional Values; Morton Blackwell, head of the Leadership Institute; and others began to steer some television evangelists into politics. Increasingly, a new generation of television evangelists called for Christians to get involved in politics. Jerry Falwell founded the Moral Majority as a means of gathering support for conservative political causes. Pat Robertson, the founder of the popular television program *The 700 Club,* ran for president of the United States. Predictably, the political issues held dear by television evangelists assumed religious dimensions. A strong national defense, support of the death penalty, and strict immigration quotas, for example, are said to be "Christian" causes.

There is nothing new about the claim that one's political position is endorsed by God or the Bible. During the civil rights campaign in the 1960s and during actions against the Vietnam War, liberal Christians claimed that their views best represented Christian principles. The question of who speaks for American values and who speaks for Christianity is not one that we need to solve. We need only realize that the question has become increasingly complicated by the emergence of the conservative Christians as political activists. At this point, we will leave the political issues aside and focus on the challenges raised to the concept of church.

Today, the Internet is yet another way to spread the Gospel and to invite people to be part of the church. New groups like the Emergent or Emerging church make significant use of cyberspace as do megachurches, mainline denominations, and others. Presbyterian minister Charles Henderson founded the First Church of Cyberspace in 1994 to bring Christianity online and to address questions often avoided in traditional church services. Many Internet users access information about their own traditions but, increasingly, look into other faiths. Interdenominational chat rooms and websites were apparently sources of comfort for many people after the terrorist attacks of September 11, 2001.

Television and the Internet in service of the Gospel raise some questions. For example, do such initiatives draw people away from local congregational participation, or do they inspire Christians to become more active at the local level? Has the use of the Internet and television to connect religion with political causes challenged other churches to be clearer in their own political agendas? Does the survival of Christianity depend on increased use of television and the Internet by other groups? Can we expect Christianity to change dramatically because of the stimulation of television evangelism? Will cyberspace religion change the nature of the church as a local community?

Homosexuality and the Authority of Scripture

In the last decades of the twentieth century, European and North American societies became increasingly tolerant of sexual diversity and made enormous strides in recognizing the rights of lesbians and gay men. Many governments, universities, and businesses no longer discriminate on the basis of sexual orientation and offer spousal benefits to same-sex partners of employees. Gay themes and characters appear frequently in movies and television programs, and celebrities like Ellen DeGeneres and Elton John live openly gay lives without damage to their careers. In 2003, the U.S. Supreme Court declared antisodomy laws targeted at consenting adults of the same sex unconstitutional. By 2008, same-sex couples could legally marry in seven countries, including Canada, Spain, and South Africa, and in one state in the United States (Massachusetts), and they could enter civil unions or other forms of legal partnership in numerous other countries and in several U.S. states, including Connecticut, Hawaii, and New Hampshire. Polls show that young people, even those who identify themselves as conservative Christians, are more accepting of homosexuality and gay marriage than their elders, and thus, the trend toward greater tolerance in these countries appears unlikely to change.

As in the case of women's roles, this dramatic and far-reaching social change has put enormous pressure on the Christian churches in Europe and North America. Gay and lesbian Christians, who may once have chosen to remain "in the closet" and even to marry persons of the opposite sex, now expect to participate as openly and freely in their churches as they do in the wider society. They challenge a long tradition in which churches allowed homosexual persons to be members, music leaders, and even ordained clergy as long as their homosexuality was not acknowledged. Most conservative Christian churches have refused to alter their view that homosexuality is a sin, and thus, gay Christians must repent and make every effort to change their behavior. More liberal churches have accepted and acknowledged their gay members as they are. Two issues, however, have emerged as controversial even among liberal churches that accept gay and lesbian members. Should gays and lesbians be eligible for ordination, particularly if they do not agree to be celibate? Should the church bless same-sex marriages?

Churches in the United States have responded to these questions in every conceivable way. Many congregations of the United Church of Christ ordain gay men and lesbians, and in 2005, the UCC's General Synod voted to support marriage rights for same-sex couples. But most mainline Protestant churches, even if they welcome homosexual members, face grave conflicts over ordination and gay marriage. The Roman Catholic church has recognized that homosexuality is an orientation, but a "disordered" one; traditionally, it has ordained some homosexually inclined men because all priests are required to be celibate. A major scandal over the sexual abuse of children (boys and girls) in the 2000s, however, led the Vatican to consider refusing to ordain gay men at all. Conservative evangelical Christians not only have refused to bless same-sex marriages but have worked actively to prevent the legal recognition of same-sex couples as marriages or civil unions by state governments. In the U.S. elections of 2002 and 2004, leaders of the Christian right sponsored several proposed amendments to state constitutions that banned gay marriages or unions and even outlawed benefits for domestic partners. On the other hand, liberal Christians in Massachusetts formed the Religious Coalition for the Freedom to Marry to defend gay marriage there.

The Anglican church provides a good example of church division over homosexuality, especially in the age of globalization. In 2003, the Episcopal church in the United States consecrated openly gay Gene Robinson as the bishop of New Hampshire. For decades before this event, liberal bishops in the Episcopal church had been ordaining gay men and lesbians as priests, even though a church convention in 1979 said that such ordinations were "not appropriate." Likewise, sympathetic priests performed formal blessings of same-sex unions between church members, whether in homes or in churches. Liberals and conservatives within the church debated these issues, while respecting the independence of individual bishops and priests. But the election of Bishop Robinson forced the issue to a point of crisis. When his election was affirmed at the church's General Convention, twenty conservative bishops denounced the decision and walked out of the meeting. A network of conservative congregations, which formed originally in opposition to the ordination of women, gained new members and sought to have its own hierarchy of bishops, separate from the national one, which they considered too liberal.

Because the Anglicans maintain a worldwide communion, led by the Archbishop of Canterbury, the controversy became an international crisis. As we saw in Chapter 9, Christians in the rapidly growing Southern Hemisphere tend to be more conservative in doctrines and morals than Christians in Europe and North America. One 2006 poll indicated that 50 percent of U.S. Christians thought that homosexuality is always wrong, but 98 percent of Christians in Kenya and Nigeria thought so. At that time, there were 3 million Anglicans in Kenya and nearly 20 million in Nigeria, compared to 2.2 million in the United States. Anglican bishops from these countries called the election of Bishop Robinson unacceptable, and Bishop Akinola of Nigeria came to the United States and consecrated a new bishop to oversee conservative Episcopalians. In 2007, Anglican bishops from other countries issued an ultimatum to the U.S. Episcopal church: stop blessing same-sex unions, and do not consecrate another gay bishop. But Episcopal leaders initially rejected this demand as an intrusion into their community, and Anglicans faced the possibility of a schism not only between members within the U.S. church but also between the U.S. church and other churches in the world.

The Christian debates about homosexuality in part reflect cultural differences that are not completely religious. Unlike European culture, which from antiquity has sometimes tolerated and even celebrated same-sex desire, Africa has always considered homosexuality taboo. Since Christian churches in Africa compete for converts with Islam, which makes homosexuality punishable by death in Muslim areas of Nigeria, Christian churches there do not wish to be less morally rigorous than Muslims. African Christians, recall, have looked to Christianity for stability and predictability during a period of rapid change. Within the United States, Christians in large urban areas tend to be more accepting of gays and lesbians than those in rural areas, reflecting the greater diversity of city life. Despite these cultural factors, however, Christians tend to see the debate as one about the interpretation and authority of Scripture.

Conservative Christians argue that the Bible plainly condemns homosexuality and that Christians cannot claim that the Bible is the word of God and then oppose it on so important an issue. They point to Leviticus 20:13, which prescribes the death penalty "if a man lies with a male as with a woman," and Romans 1:26–27, in which Paul cites both male and female homoerotic behavior as a graphic sign of Gentile sinfulness. Besides such specific condemnations, conservatives say that the Genesis creation story, in which God creates a man and a woman and commands them to multiply, indicates that it is God's will that only men and women marry and have sex for procreation. Having seen the authority of the Bible eroded by evolutionary theory and historical scholarship, conservatives consider acceptance of homosexuality a clear demonstration of preferring one's own moral relativism to the certainty of God's word. They see the Bible as clear on this point: to reject the unambiguous view of the Bible is to reject the Bible's authority and thus the truth of Christianity.

Liberals defend their acceptance of gay and lesbian Christians in several ways. They challenge the relevance of the condemnations in Leviticus and Romans: the biblical authors had no concept of sexual orientation and so could not imagine people who are unchangeably homosexual and enter committed, loving relationships. Instead, these condemnations reflect ancient gender roles, in which men could only be active or dominant in sexual activity and women only passive or submissive. They point out that there are many ways in which even conservative Christians do not follow the plain teaching of the Bible. For example, Jesus said nothing about homosexuality, but he did condemn lending money at interest (Luke 6:34–35), and so did the church for centuries; nevertheless, Christians now participate fully in the interest-based banking system as lenders and borrowers. The Bible clearly accepts the morality of slavery, which no Christians defend today. Liberals sometimes cite the decision of the early church to accept Gentiles, whom Jews considered immoral, based on the manifestation of the Holy Spirit among Gentile believers (Acts 10–11). Who is to say that the Spirit is not acting again to lead Christians to be more inclusive?

Homosexuality raises important questions about church fellowship and the authority of the Bible. Christians have divided and formed separate churches many times over issues of doctrine, like the Trinity, and of practice, like slavery. Is the question of homosexuality serious enough that Christians should be prepared to divide their churches? In this age of globalization, should an Anglican bishop in Nigeria be able to tell Episcopalians in New Hampshire who they can and cannot choose to be their bishop? Should liberal Christians give up or delay their acceptance of gays and lesbians to preserve unity? Are the moral teachings of the Bible timeless and unchanging, or must they be understood in the historical contexts in which they were made? How do Christians determine which teachings of the Bible are eternal and absolute (for example, the centrality of Jesus) and which can be changed in light of new insights (for example, slavery)? Does the Holy Spirit reveal new truths to Christians even today, and if so, how can these be identified? Does the truth of Christianity depend on the absolute truth of the Bible?

People

Eboo Patel: Deliberate Engagement with Difference

Eboo Patel (b. 1975), a Muslim American whose parents immigrated from India, founded the Interfaith Youth Core in 1998 to create a generation of religiously inspired activists who can change the climate of interreligious conflict and hatred to one of cooperation and understanding. He calls them social entrepreneurs.

When Patel read *The Souls of Black Folk* (1903), he was struck by the way W. E. B. DuBois identified "the color line" as the problem of the twentieth century. Patel believes that the problem of the twenty-first century is the faith line, the attitudinal divide between totalitarians and pluralists. He puts Osama bin Laden and Pat Robertson together on the side of religious totalitarianism, each of them so zealous for his own way of believing that he concludes that all others are the enemy, someone to be converted, condemned, or killed. Religious pluralists are on the other side: they are those of different creeds, communities, and practice who choose to live and work together not by way of forced consensus or passive coexistence but by way of proactive cooperation that affirms identity and respects difference.

As Patel sees it, religious extremists in all traditions appeal to young people and recruit them into battalions of intolerance and hatred. At the same time, those who are interested in interfaith cooperation tend to be older people whose endless meetings and discussions have no appeal for youth. College students and young adults do have service options: they can work for a faith-based organization or a civic one. The first has little or no diversity; the second has no religious dimension. The Interfaith Youth Core (ifyc.org) is therefore a new idea: it engages young people in intercultural encounter, social action, and interfaith reflection.

In April 2006, IFYC sponsored community actions in thirty sites worldwide, attracting four thousand young leaders. They were Christians, Jews, Muslims, Hindus, Buddhists, Baha'is, Jains, and Sikhs, willingly engaged in interfaith conversation and cooperative service. IFYC points to deep and significant social values of hospitality, compassion, and stewardship for the environment at the core of all religions, values that can provide common ground for action and reflection.

Patel recounts his own struggle for coherent identity among conflicting options—Indian, Muslim, American—in *Acts of Faith* (2007). His organization works against the religious isolation that happens when one feels religiously comfortable only among others like oneself. Since most of one's life in the twenty-first century will be lived in interaction with others unlike oneself, engaging creatively with difference is the best way to preserve one of America's greatest strengths, its pluralism.

Like the challenges raised by the women's movement and problems associated with the religious interaction with new media technology, questions raised about the ordination and marriages of gay people will not disappear. The questions we have posed here are, in many ways, only the beginning and should alert you to areas of debate that promise to have continuing impacts on the churches. The issues are now global, and modern communication makes them accessible to almost everyone.

CONCLUSION

Christianity is an extraordinarily rich religion, rooted in ancient texts and traditions that continue to be upheld and followed. We have seen throughout this book that Christianity has always understood its obligations to be "faithful" to the life, work, and words of Jesus, while at the same time attempting to adjust itself to new circumstances, cultures, and peoples. As we have mentioned several times in this book, conflict and controversy characterize any living religion: Christians have always argued heatedly over important issues as they attempted to figure things out in ways that they believed would preserve the integrity of the early church even as they responded creatively to new situations.

The general distinction we have made between liberal and conservative Christians is not a modern one. From the beginning, there have been those whose energies have been primarily invested in guarding the tradition from the encroachment of new ideas, just as there have been those who have been inspired to seek new articulations and open new possibilities. In the New Testament, the church in Jerusalem presided over by James represented a dedicated following of traditional patterns, whereas the new churches founded by Paul were examples of a radically different way of interpreting the intentions of Jesus. Throughout Christian history, we can locate these two different modes of operation: conservatives cling to traditional understandings, whereas liberals press for adaptations and adjustments. Both groups are necessary for the creative survival of Christianity and will continue to set the parameters of argument within the Christian churches.

This chapter has been an attempt to recapitulate these two governing attitudes within the churches, while raising some of the vexing issues that, we believe, will remain under discussion by Christians well into the century. The women's movement, media technology, and issues of sexuality will continue to raise challenges for Christianity that involve practical matters like ministry and church membership. At the same time, underneath those practical matters will be important conceptual issues like the personality of God, the authority of the Bible, and the understanding of a faithful Christian life. The questions should not surprise us, and the arguments they will inspire should not disturb us. If there is one thing to take away from our study of Christianity, it is this: Christianity unfolds in history like a great story, full of passion and promise, intrigue and integrity, and still capable, after all this time, of astonishing itself.

Focal Points for Discussion

1. Look back through this book at references to women and their roles in the churches. How might the historical examples you find provide support for both the supporters and the opponents of women's ordination?
2. A variety of movies about Jesus have appeared since the beginning of cinema: for example, *The King of Kings* (1929), *King of Kings* (1961), *Jesus Christ Superstar* (1973), *The Last Temptation of Christ* (1988), *Jesus of Montreal* (1989), *The Passion of the Christ* (2004), and *Color of the Cross* (2006). View one or more of these films and consider how they reflect the themes we have explored in Chapters 8 through 12.
3. In this book, we have taken two approaches to understanding Christianity: the historical rendering of Christianity on the one hand and the political rendering of contemporary religious issues on the other. Could a good introduction to Christianity leave one of them out?

The Order of the Books in the Old Testament

APPENDIX I

The Christian Old Testament is a reordering of the books in the Hebrew Bible. The Tanakh is divided into three parts: the Law (Torah), the Prophets, and the Writings. The Christian Old Testament eliminates the distinction between the Prophets and the Writings and puts the Prophets at the end to serve as an introduction to the New Testament. Notice that the order of the books changes the tone and emphasis. Because of the differences in intention and theological signification, it is not correct to say that the Old Testament is the same as the Hebrew Bible.

Roman Catholics and Eastern Orthodox Christians use Old Testaments that contain more books than are in the Hebrew Bible or the Protestant Old Testament. Why? Because, like the early church, these Christians base their Old Testaments on the Greek translations of the Hebrew Scriptures, whereas Protestant reformers chose to base their Old Testament on the Hebrew version used by the Jews. Some Protestants call the ancient Jewish writings not included in their Old Testament (for example, Tobit and Maccabees; see Appendix 2) "the Apocrypha," and some Roman Catholics and Orthodox Christians call such books "deuterocanonical." Many modern editions of the Bible, such as the New Revised Standard Version, include the Hebrew Bible (Protestant Old Testament), the Apocrypha/Deuterocanonical books, and the New Testament.

Hebrew Bible		Protestant Old Testament	Roman Catholic Old Testament
Genesis	the Law	Genesis	Genesis
Exodus		Exodus	Exodus
Leviticus		Leviticus	Leviticus
Numbers		Numbers	Numbers
Deuteronomy		Deuteronomy	Deuteronomy
Joshua	the Prophets	Joshua	Joshua
Judges		Judges	Judges
Samuel (1 & 2)		Ruth	Ruth
Kings (1 & 2)		1 Samuel	1 Samuel
Isaiah		2 Samuel	2 Samuel
Jeremiah		1 Kings	1 Kings
Ezekiel		2 Kings	2 Kings
The Twelve:		1 Chronicles	1 Chronicles
Hosea		2 Chronicles	2 Chronicles
Joel		Ezra	Ezra
Amos		Nehemiah	Nehemiah
Obadiah		Esther	Tobit*
Jonah		Job	Judith*
Micah		Psalms	Esther†
Nahum		Proverbs	1 Maccabees*
Habakkuk		Ecclesiastes	2 Maccabees*
Zephaniah		Song of Solomon	Job
Haggai		Isaiah	Psalms
Zechariah		Jeremiah	Proverbs
Malachi		Lamentations	Ecclesiastes
Psalms	the Writings	Ezekiel	Song of Solomon
Proverbs		Daniel	Wisdom of Solomon*
Job		Hosea	Sirach*
Song of Solomon		Joel	Isaiah
Ruth		Amos	Jeremiah
Lamentations		Obadiah	Lamentations
Ecclesiastes		Jonah	Baruch*
Esther		Micah	Ezekiel
Daniel		Nahum	†Daniel
Ezra-Nehemiah		Habakkuk	Hosea
Chronicles (1 & 2)		Zephaniah	Joel
		Haggai	Amos
		Zechariah	Obadiah
		Malachi	Jonah
			Micah
			Nahum
			Habakkuk
			Zephaniah
			Haggai
			Zechariah
			Malachi

*Books not included in the Hebrew Bible or the Protestant Old Testament.

†Books that include sections not found in the corresponding books of the Hebrew Bible and Protestant Old Testament.

Synopsis of the Books of the Old and New Testaments

APPENDIX 2

The following list is a synopsis of the *content* of the books of the Old and New Testaments. Scholars debate the authorship and dating of many biblical books. Students who want more precise information should refer to a wide variety of reference works and recent scholarship and should, in any case, be advised that the system adopted here is a starting point, not a final word.

THE OLD TESTAMENT

GENESIS ("origins"): The first of the Five Books of Moses, recounting the beginnings of the world and the creation of humanity, the story of Noah and of the patriarchs—Abraham, Isaac, and Jacob—ending with the death of Joseph.

EXODUS ("a way out"): The second of the Five Books of Moses, recounting the oppression of the Jews in Egypt, their deliverance by Moses, the covenant at Sinai, and the establishment of the Tabernacle, the movable community shrine.

LEVITICUS (Levites = assistants to the priests): The third of the Five Books of Moses, containing the legislation dictated to Moses by God after the establishment of the Tabernacle, dealing primarily with ritual purity.

NUMBERS: The fourth of the Five Books of Moses, relating the history of the Jews in the desert from the second to the fortieth year of their wanderings.

DEUTERONOMY ("repetition of the Law"): The last of the Five Books of Moses, containing Moses' review of the events since Sinai, a repetition of the Ten Commandments, and Moses' final admonitions to Israel.

JOSHUA: An account of the history of the Israelites in their conquest and division of Canaan from the death of Moses to the death of Joshua, his successor (c. 1220 B.C.E.).

JUDGES: Describes the acts of ancient heroes and heroines of Israel from the death of Joshua until the time of Samuel (c. 1050 B.C.E.); it includes the stories of Samson, Deborah, and Gideon.

RUTH: Story of a non-Israelite woman, Ruth, married to a Hebrew. After his death, she returns to Judah with her mother-in-law to live with the Israelites. Through her marriage to Boaz, Ruth becomes great-grandmother of King David.

1 and 2 SAMUEL: Relate the history of the Jews from the end of the period of Judges to the last days of King David (972 B.C.E.), focusing on the biographies of Samuel, Saul, and David. These books depict the Davidic monarchy as a divine institution, established to represent God's rule on earth.

1 and 2 KINGS: Contain the history of the Jews from the reign of Solomon (c. 970 B.C.E.) to the fall of Jerusalem (587 B.C.E.) and can be seen as a continuation of the books of Samuel. Kings recount a period of Israel's glory, division, decline, and fall.

1 and 2 CHRONICLES: Contain genealogical lists of Israelite tribes, a history of David's rule, and an account of Solomon's rule, emphasizing the building of the temple and ending with the destruction of the temple and the Exile to Babylon. Chronicles picture the events in Israel's history as divine judgments.

EZRA: Relates the events after the return from the Babylonian Exile (538 B.C.E.), including the beginning of the rebuilding of the temple.

NEHEMIAH: A continuation of the book of Ezra, recounting the reconstruction of Jerusalem.

ESTHER: A story of the deliverance of the Jews of Persia through the influence of Esther on the king of Persia, her husband.

JOB: Relates the story of a righteous man who suffers as a result of God's testing his faith. It points to the mystery of human suffering and the inadequacy of human knowledge in things pertaining to the purposes of God.

PSALMS ("poems sung to stringed instruments"): A collection of Hebrew poetry (150 psalms) that contains deep religious feeling and conviction. Many of the psalms are attributed to King David. This book contains some of the most beautiful poetry in the Bible.

PROVERBS: A collection of maxims on how an individual can survive and prosper.

ECCLESIASTES ("members of the assembly"): A somewhat pessimistic book that concludes that "all is vanity" and that one should resign oneself to suffering and injustice. It claims that there is no correlation between righteousness and happiness.

SONG OF SOLOMON: Contains love poems written in dialogue form that have been read as describing love between persons, love between God and Israel, or love between Jesus and the church.

ISAIAH: First of the major prophets, who protested strongly against moral laxity. Isaiah emphasizes that God will punish but not exterminate Israel for its sins and that there will come times of redemption and comfort.

JEREMIAH: Second of the major prophets, containing bitter prophecies addressed to foreign nations and some biographical material on the prophet himself. Jeremiah's ministry began around 627 B.C.E. and ended sometime around 580 B.C.E.

LAMENTATIONS: Contains elegies and mournings over the destruction of Jerusalem and the temple by the Babylonians.

EZEKIEL: Third of the major prophets, who prophesied at the time of the destruction of the temple (587 B.C.E.). Ezekiel contains rebukes spoken before the destruction of Jerusalem and prophecies of disasters, consolation, and the coming of the new kingdom.

DANIEL: Contains two parts, the first of which recounts the miraculous experiences that happen to Daniel and his pious friends during the Babylonian Exile; the second contains apocalyptic visions.

HOSEA: First of the minor prophets (so called because of the brevity of the books compared to Isaiah, Jeremiah, and Ezekiel), containing comments on the relationship between God and Israel and oracles rebuking Israel, followed by promises of salvation.

JOEL: Second of the minor prophets; describes a locust plague and the "Day of the Lord," when Israel will be restored to God.

AMOS: Third of the minor prophets, focusing on social morality as the determining factor in the history of Israel.

OBADIAH: Fourth of the minor prophets, consisting of one chapter condemning Edom (a country in southeast Palestine) for refusing to help Jerusalem in its hour of need.

JONAH: Fifth of the minor prophets, relating episodes in Jonah's life illustrating the power of repentance and divine mercy for all creatures.

MICAH: Sixth of the minor prophets, containing prophecies against the oppression by the ruling classes and speaking of a future king of Israel who will bring peace.

NAHUM: Seventh of the minor prophets, containing a masterful foretelling of the fall of Nineveh, the capital of Assyria.

HABAKKUK: Eighth of the minor prophets, consisting of an outcry against the evil in the world, God's reply, a prayer, and a description of the "Day of the Lord."

ZEPHANIAH: Ninth of the minor prophets, containing mainly prophecies dealing with the last days, declaring the coming of the "Day of the Lord," when the wicked will disappear and the poor will inherit the land.

HAGGAI: Tenth of the minor prophets, calling for a rebuilding of the temple.

ZECHARIAH: A contemporary of Haggai, Zechariah shares his zeal for the rebuilding of the temple.

MALACHI ("my messenger"): Twelfth and last of the minor prophets, rebuking Israel for its sinfulness, complaining of mixed and broken marriages, and envisioning the "Day of the Lord," to be preceded by Elijah's coming.

APOCRYPHAL/DEUTEROCANONICAL BOOKS INCLUDED IN THE ROMAN CATHOLIC OLD TESTAMENT

TOBIT: A story about the sufferings and healing of a pious Israelite and his family living in exile in Assyria. It assures Jews in exile that righteous suffering will be rewarded.

JUDITH: A story of how the beautiful Judith saves the Israelite town of Bethulia from an invading Assyrian army by beguiling and then murdering the Assyrian general Holofernes.

WISDOM OF SOLOMON: Encourages Jews in exile to remain faithful to their ancestral faith by following Wisdom in study of the Law and by rejecting pagan idolatry and immorality.

SIRACH OR ECCLESIASTICUS: A collection of maxims and poetry that urges Jews to follow Wisdom in study of the Law and to support the worship of God in the Jerusalem Temple.

BARUCH: Claims to be a letter sent by Baruch, the secretary and friend of the prophet Jeremiah, from exile in Babylon to the priests and people in Jerusalem. Encourages the people to trust in God in the midst of their suffering.

1 MACCABEES: Contains the history of Jews from the revolt led by Judas Maccabeas and his family against the Hellenistic king Antiochus IV Epiphanes (175–164 B.C.E.) to 134 B.C.E.

2 MACCABEES: Describes the events leading up to the Maccabean revolt and narrates the achievements of Judas Maccabeas up to 161 B.C.E.

THE NEW TESTAMENT

GOSPEL OF MATTHEW (written between 70 and 90 C.E.): A synoptic Gospel, regarding Jesus as the new Moses, emphasizing Jesus as the fulfillment of the Hebrew Bible and as the bringer of the new law or covenant.

GOSPEL OF MARK (written around 70 C.E.): Likely the earliest synoptic Gospel, viewing Jesus as the Son of God who must suffer and die. Mark emphasizes Jesus as a man of action and focuses little attention on Jesus' teachings.

GOSPEL OF LUKE (written between 70 and 90 C.E.): Synoptic Gospel emphasizing the universality of Jesus' work and message. Here Jesus is the merciful one who forgives all humanity. The first of a two-volume work including the Acts of the Apostles.

GOSPEL OF JOHN (written between 80 and 100 C.E.): John emphasizes the mystery and divinity of Jesus more than the synoptics do. God's love for humanity is a central theme of this Gospel.

THE ACTS OF THE APOSTLES (written between 70 and 90 C.E.): The first history of the movement of Christianity, recording outstanding events in the spread of the Gospels from Jerusalem to Rome. It pictures the apostles as guided and empowered by the Holy Spirit. Written by the author of the Gospel of Luke as the second of a two-volume work.

THE EPISTLE TO THE ROMANS: Written by Paul around 57 C.E. and considered the first work of Christian theology. The intention of this letter is to announce Paul's coming to Rome and to prepare the Christians there for his arrival. In Romans more than in any other letter, Paul discusses the meaning of Christian salvation, the inclusion of the Gentiles, and the fullness of God's redeeming work.

THE FIRST EPISTLE TO THE CORINTHIANS: Also written by Paul around 55 C.E. to the church at Corinth, dealing with the Eucharist, love *(agape)* as the highest of spiritual gifts, and the meaning of the resurrection.

THE SECOND EPISTLE TO THE CORINTHIANS (written c. 56 C.E.): Dealing principally with Paul's personal position as an apostle in relation to the activities of the church at Corinth.

THE EPISTLE TO THE GALATIANS: Written by Paul around 54 C.E., emphasizing that Gentile believers need not get circumcised and follow the Jewish Law but that people require only faith in Jesus to be saved.

THE EPISTLE TO THE EPHESIANS: Attributed to Paul, emphasizing the universality of salvation for Jews and Gentiles alike, probably written between 70 and 90 C.E.

THE EPISTLE TO THE PHILIPPIANS: Written by Paul while in prison (c. 52–55 C.E.), thanking the Philippians for their assistance during his imprisonment and asking them to continue to follow Christ's example of charity and humility.

THE EPISTLE TO THE COLOSSIANS: Attributed to Paul (70–90 C.E.), stressing faith in Christ as all-sufficient redeemer.

THE FIRST EPISTLE TO THE THESSALONIANS: One of the earliest letters written by Paul (c. 51 C.E.), assuring the Thessalonians that both the living and the dead will partake in the glory of the Second Coming of Christ.

THE SECOND EPISTLE TO THE THESSALONIANS: Written either by Paul shortly after First Thessalonians or by a follower later (70–90 C.E.). Warns the Thessalonians not to neglect their everyday duties while they await the Second Coming.

THE FIRST EPISTLE TO TIMOTHY: The first of the pastoral Epistles, discussing the practices of false teachers and methods of combating these practices; probably written between 90 and 140 C.E.

THE SECOND EPISTLE TO TIMOTHY: The second of the pastoral Epistles, again concerning false teachers and reminding Timothy of the fidelity to tradition and the patience required of all apostles; probably written between 90 and 140 C.E.

THE EPISTLE TO TITUS: The third and last of the pastoral Epistles, discussing the duties of apostles and the need to struggle against false teachings; probably written between 90 and 140 C.E.

THE EPISTLE TO PHILEMON: Written by Paul while under house arrest (61–63 C.E.), asking Philemon to accept his slave Onesimus as a brother in Christ.

The Epistle to the Hebrews: Written before 96 C.E., it focuses on the idea that Christianity is the final and absolute religion because Jesus is the true high priest and the final mediation between God and humanity. Hebrews emphasizes that the Jewish Law points to Jesus.

The Epistle of James: Written between 90 and 140 C.E., this is the first of the general Epistles (not written to a specific church or person but to Christians in general) and deals with the superiority of deeds over theory, just treatment of the poor, the danger of evil speech, and the value of humility and sincerity.

The First Epistle of Peter: The second of the general Epistles, written between 90 and 140 C.E., emphasizing a life of hope in Christ, which entails faith in the redemptive work of Christ and submitting to the will of God.

The Second Epistle of Peter: The third general Epistle (written between 90 and 140 C.E.), warning Christians against false teachings, exhorting them to hold fast to their faith, and assuring them of salvation.

The Epistles of John: Three short letters written between 80 and 100 C.E., emphasizing that "God is Love," that morality, fellowship, and charity are extremely important in the Christian life, and that all false teachings are to be avoided. Associated with the same community that produced the Gospel of John but probably not by the same author.

The Epistle of Jude: The last of the general Epistles (written between 90 and 140 C.E.), reminding Christians that God's forgiveness of sins is not an excuse for immoral actions, that God does punish disobedience, and that Christians have duties of prayer, faith, and love for God.

Revelation or the Apocalypse: The last book of the New Testament (written between 90 and 100 C.E.), it describes the final struggle between good and evil and the eventual triumph of Christ and the church; it is written in highly symbolic language.

EARLY CHRISTIAN WRITERS

APPENDIX 3

Bishops and theologians in the early Christian community whose opinions on matters of doctrine and practice carried great weight are often referred to as "the Fathers." Because this designation makes it appear as if women made no contributions to the development of tradition in the early church, a point disputed by feminist theologians, we use the terminology *early Christian writers* here instead.[1] Little by little, there came to be an appeal to tradition, especially to these early writers, for a consensus on disputed questions within Christianity. When the New Testament did not provide enough of an answer on an issue, people consulted the opinions that had been developing in the church in the works of these great theologians. According to a commonly accepted notion, these respected writers were those characterized by orthodoxy in doctrine, holiness in life, and approval of the ancient church. This last point is important: their authority is ancient. There are several groupings of early Christian writers, the most important of which are Greek, Latin, and Syrian.

The tasks of these writers varied according to the place and time in which they were working. In the early church, they functioned mostly as apologists: as those who *explained* Christianity to a hostile world or to an emperor who was considering persecution of the Christians. As the church grew in numbers and power and in problems, they wrote on various disciplinary matters—marriage, divorce, paying taxes, fighting in wars—and on theological questions—the divinity of Christ, the place of Mary in the Christian church, and so on. When the church became the

[1]"It is not easy to find church "Mothers," as it is not easy to find women in any historical period. Nevertheless, one can name a few: Egeria, Perpetua, Proba, and Eudokia. For translations of their works, critical commentary, and an introduction to the issue of early Christian literature by women, see Patricia Wilson-Kastner et al., *A Lost Tradition: Women Writers of the Early Church* (Washington, D.C.: University Press of America, 1981).

dominant institution in the Western and Eastern worlds, they devised elaborate systems of theology—the doctrine of the Trinity, for example.

One can read them for an understanding of a particular period or for some introduction to the customs and beliefs of a particular region at a particular time. One can also find in them rich sources of spiritual writing and prayer. They provide the Christian church with much of its ancient history on several levels: cultural, religious, political, and moral.

The following brief outline mentions some of the important names and issues. An outline as sketchy as this is not meant to teach so much as to entice. Some people think that the only Christian writing from the ancient world is the New Testament. We hope this list of topics and writers will show you that there was extraordinarily energetic argument, speculation, and writing going on in the early church.

A SELECTIVE OUTLINE OF THE LITERATURE

I. **Primitive Ecclesiastical Literature**

A. Creeds developed in the period after the death of the apostles, the most famous of which is the *Apostles' Creed.*

B. Teachings about discipline and behavior, the most famous of which is the *Didache.*

C. Early writings associated with particular people that stressed the Christian philosophy of martyrdom, attitudes toward marriage, sin, penance, and so on. Some of the most famous writers were *Clement of Rome, Ignatius of Antioch,* and *Polycarp of Smyrna;* the most famous document was a work on penance and the forgiveness of sins called *The Shepherd of Hermas.*

II. **Apologetic Literature of the Second Century**

A. Works that were written to an emperor precisely to show that Christians were not dangerous to the state and should therefore not be persecuted. Some of the most important literature of this type was written by *Aristedes of Athens, Justin Martyr, Tatian, Athenagoras of Athens, Minucius Felix,* and *Theophilus of Antioch,* all of whom wrote toward the end of the second century.

B. Works that explained Christianity in philosophical terms and tried to make a case for Christianity that was philosophically respectable: good examples of this type of literature can be found in *Justin* and *Athenagoras.*

C. Some apologetic literature was cast in the form of a dialogue. The most famous dialogues were written by *Justin* (a Greek) and *Minucius Felix* (a Roman).

III. **Heretical and Antiheretical Literature of the Second Century**

Various types of what was later judged to be heretical literature were written during the second century.

A. Philosophical or religious works dealing with particular interpretations of Christianity. The most famous literature of this kind is *Gnostic literature.*
B. Stories about Jesus and his life that were not judged to be apostolic and therefore were not included in the canon of the New Testament. These are called *apocryphal Gospels.*
C. Works dealing with the final age, the end of the world: *apocalyptic literature.*

The Christian church, as a whole, opposed much of this writing. The theologian remembered especially for his writings against Gnosticism is *Irenaeus of Lyons.*

IV. **The Beginnings of Christian Theology**

A much more elaborate Christian theology developed during the second and third centuries. The church moved into various philosophical cultures and interacted with them, writers were exposed to different ideas (especially to Stoicism and Neoplatonism), and problems were raised not only by heretics but by the faithful—problems about Jesus, the way to live a Christian life, immortality, and so on. Early theologians tried to develop theological positions working mostly from the Bible and their own experience. This writing has great richness, a variety of opinions and solutions to problems. It is important to see that there was no single Christian answer to a problem but a variety of creative responses.

A. Writing in Greek were the famous theologians of the Alexandrian school, *Clement of Alexandria* and *Origen.*
B. Writing in Latin were apologists and controversialists like *Tertullian,* writers on church-state politics like *Cyprian,* and writers concerned with the internal matters of the Christian church like *Hippolytus.*

V. **The Golden Age of Christian Literature**

As problems of doctrine and discipline became more difficult, the writings became more complex. When Christianity was no longer a persecuted religion, Christian writers were able to pursue their theological preoccupations more directly. Much of the writing was more overtly philosophical and specific to particular controversies or problems: the person and nature of Christ, the foundations of a theology of grace, the doctrine of Original Sin and justification, the development of a sacramental system, and so on. In the writings of this period, one can find catechists (those who devised systems to teach people about Christianity), mystical writers (those who attempted to discern and articulate a theology of religious experience), preachers, theologians, and bishops, all interested in specific ecclesiastical problems.

A. Writing in Greek were *Eusebius of Caesarea* (a church historian), *Cyril of Jerusalem* (a catechist), *Gregory of Nyssa* (a spiritual writer), *John Chrysostom* (a renowned preacher), *Basil* (an ecclesiastical writer), and theologians like *Athanasius, Theodore of Mopsuestia,* and *Cyril of Alexandria.*

B. Writing in Latin were those interested in political questions like *Ambrose* and theologians like *Hilary of Poitiers* and *Augustine.* Some of the writers of the Latin church were also popes, notably *Leo I* and *Gregory I.*

VI. **Additional Sources**

It sometimes appears that there were no significant Christian writers after the death of Pope Gregory I (604). The "Dark Ages" were indeed centuries of decline and political instability, and it makes sense to pick up the story of great Christian literature after the reforms of Pope Gregory VII in the eleventh century. Still, there are some writers in those dark times whose work was significant and worthy of attention. All of them wrote in Latin.

A. Historians: Venerable Bede (c. 672–735) a Benedictine monk in Northumbria, wrote *The Ecclesiastical History of the English People* and was later known as "the father of English history." Einhard (c. 775–840), a Frankish monk at the court of Charlemagne, wrote *The Life of Charlemagne.*

B. Philosophers: Johannes Scotus Eriugena (c. 815–877), an Irish Neoplatonist, translated the works of Pseudo-Dionysius (see Spirituality sidebar on page 70) and wrote commentaries on them. Anicius Manlius Severinus Boethius (480–524 or 525) wrote his most popular work, *The Consolation of Philosophy,* in prison awaiting execution. His translations of Aristotle's works on logic were the only texts of Aristotle available in Latin until the twelfth century.

Ecumenical Councils

Appendix 4

A council is a formal meeting of bishops and representatives of the Christian churches convened for the purpose of regulating doctrine and discipline. Councils can be held on a local or regional level (sometimes called *synods*) as well as on a worldwide, universal level. The great councils in the history of Christianity have been the *ecumenical* (from the Greek word meaning "universal") councils, meetings that include bishops from the whole, universal church. Decrees of a council are considered the highest authority the Christian church can give. Roman Catholics and Eastern Orthodox Christians recognize the dogmatic decrees of ecumenical councils as truly authoritative, authentic interpretations of the Gospel; for them, the dogmatic decrees of the council represent the mind of the whole church.

Some Christians do not recognize any councils; they believe Christianity is a matter of New Testament faithfulness alone or base their Christianity on an experience of Jesus that does not need doctrinal definitions. Thus, not all Christians recognize a need for or the importance of councils. Those Christians who *do* accept ecumenical councils are divided into two groups: some Protestants and Eastern Orthodox Christians accept the first seven ecumenical councils as authoritative and have some interest in the Second Vatican Council; they reject the rest of the councils on the grounds that they were not truly ecumenical but were only local Roman synods. Roman Catholics accept twenty-one ecumenical councils and reject the Council of Pisa on the grounds that it was not authentic; many scholars accept the validity of the Council of Pisa, and it has been included in the following chart.

Council and Year Held	Problem	Which Means	Council's Resolution
1 Nicaea I 325	Arianism	There is only one God, so Jesus is not God (creator) but a creature.	Jesus is the son of God and is God, of the same divine essence as the Father.
2 Constantinople I 381	Apollinarianism	The Logos takes the place of the human mind in Jesus; he is not then fully human.	Jesus is divine, as Nicaea said, but also fully human. Also, the Holy Spirit is divine.
3 Ephesus 431	Nestorianism	If Jesus is human and divine, then there are two persons in Christ, and Mary is mother of Jesus, not mother of God.	There are two natures (in hypostatic union) but only one person in Christ. Mary is the Mother of *God.*
4 Chalcedon 451	Monophysitism	The hypostatic union taken to an extreme so that there is only one nature *(mono physis)* in Christ.	There are *two* natures, as Ephesus said, and they are unmixed and unconfused.
5 Constantinople II 553	Three Chapters	Emperor issued a condemnation of three positions; pope refused to go along with this interference.	Council accepted the edict of the emperor, implicitly going against the pope.
6 Constantinople III 680	Monothelitism	Emperor attempts to win back the monophysites with the theory that Christ had only one will.	There are two wills and two energies in Christ, fully coordinated, divine and human.
7 Nicaea II 787	Iconoclasm	Emperor issued edict (726) against images and icons in churches.	Iconoclasm is condemned; veneration of images is permitted.

These first seven councils are accepted as authoritative by Orthodox Christians, Roman Catholics, and some Protestants.

8 Constantinople IV 870	Photian Schism	Complicated political problem involving papal authority in patriarchal appointments. Photius was the patriarch of Constantinople.	A council, actually held in Rome, deposed Photius and restored Ignatius as the patriarch of Constantinople.
Greeks do not recognize the Roman solution so held their own council in Constantinople in 880, which favored Photius as patriarch.			
9 Lateran I 1123	Investiture	Can an emperor choose and invest a bishop or an abbot with symbols of office? A struggle for power in the West between pope and emperor.	Settled by the Concordat of Worms (1122) and council called to confirm it.
10 Lateran II 1139	Arnold Brescia	Arnold was an early reformer, against worldly popes and sinful priests; argued that sinful priests cannot administer sacraments.	Arnold and his views condemned.
11 Lateran III 1179	Papal elections	Emperor Frederick I, in a political struggle with the pope, had supported an antipope and caused a schism.	Schism ended; principle from now on was that the College of Cardinals would always elect pope.
12 Lateran IV 1215	Doctrine and discipline	Church in high point of its power was plagued with questions and problems of doctrine and discipline.	Most important of Lateran councils; defined doctrine of the Eucharist and transubstantiation.
13 Lyons I 1245	Frederick II	Emperor in contest with the pope for supreme political power in Europe.	Council deposed emperor; a complicated chapter in history of church-state relations.
14 Lyons II 1274	Reunion with Greeks	Greek Orthodox church thought it politically wise to ask for reunion with Roman church.	Greeks pledged obedience to the pope, ended old schism; the peace lasted until 1289.
15 Vienne 1311–1312	Templars	A twelfth-century military-religious order, highly influential and wealthy; Philip IV of France wanted their lands.	Convened during Avignon papacy; Templars condemned; Philip took their land.

(*Continued*)

(Continued)

Council and Year Held	Problem	Which Means	Council's Resolution
16 Pisa 1409	Schism	Two men claimed to be the legitimate pope; church had been divided on the issue from 1378.	Healed the schism (temporarily) by deposing both popes and electing new one.
17 Constance 1414–1418	Schism	Three men all claimed to be the rightful pope; European Christendom completely split on issue.	Ended the schism and declared that councils are superior to popes and councils ought to meet often.
18 Florence 1438–1439	Reunion	Greek Orthodox church sought support of West against the Turks; also sought to discuss theological differences.	Reunion voted for but not ratified by Orthodox synods; important council for theology of the Trinity.
19 Lateran V 1512–1517	Reform	Convoked by pope to invalidate the decrees of the Council of Pisa (1409), which was an antipapal power council but not recognized by Roman Catholic church as ecumenical.	Touched on some minor areas of needed reform, but main causes of the Reformation were left untouched.
20 Trent 1545–1563	Protestants	Called to respond to reformers, to define Roman Catholic doctrine, and to tighten up teaching and theology.	Very important for Roman Catholics as it defined most doctrine and discipline that would hold up to twentieth century.
21 Vatican I 1870	Infallibility	Called to deal with various issues of doctrine and discipline but also to define the limits of papal power.	Pope declared primate of the universal church and infallible in matters of faith and morals when speaking *ex cathedra*.
22 Vatican II 1962–1965	Renewal	Called by John XXIII to evaluate contemporary church and to bring the Roman Catholic church up to date.	Issued documents for modernization of doctrine and practice; accepted ecumenism and principle of religious freedom.

Creeds and Confessions

APPENDIX 5

The word *creed* comes from the Latin word *credo*, which means "I believe." A creed summarizes the beliefs or lists the doctrines agreed upon by a particular church. For a number of reasons, Christians have developed statements that outline their doctrinal positions. Some heretical groups in the early church claimed that Christians could, in good conscience, believe almost anything: some groups said that Jesus did not really rise from the dead but just "seemed" to die and rise; others denied any link between Jesus and the God of the Bible. In response to the confusion created by heretical groups, Christians developed a systematic list of official beliefs. Creeds helped them clarify their own positions and oppose heretical teachings with an official statement. Early creeds were used for religious instruction and often were used in liturgical celebration as well. When new churches emerged during the Reformation, a variety of new creeds were written, many of which were called *confessions* rather than creeds. Christian churches generally have some agreed-upon principles of behavior or practice; most have some way to define the membership requirements of their church. Not all churches have creeds, however, nor do they desire to have them.

One early summary of beliefs is the Apostles' Creed, so called because it contains the essential Christian doctrines as they were understood and believed in the apostolic church. The Apostles' Creed was not written by the apostles (as legend has it) but dates back to the old Roman Creed. In its present form, it probably did not exist before the middle of the seventh century, though there is evidence that it developed from the baptismal creed used in the Roman church in the second century. The Apostles' Creed is short and was apparently easy to learn; it summarizes early belief about the Father, Son, and Holy Spirit, the life and mission of Jesus, and the life of the church.

THE APOSTLES' CREED

I believe in God, the Father almighty, creator of heaven and earth.
I believe in Jesus Christ, his only son, our Lord.
He was conceived by the power of the Holy Spirit and born to the Virgin Mary.
He suffered under Pontius Pilate, was crucified, died and was buried.
He descended to the dead.
On the third day he rose again.
He ascended into heaven and is seated at the right hand of the Father.
He will come again to judge the living and the dead.
I believe in the Holy Spirit, the holy catholic church, the communion of saints, the forgiveness of sins, the resurrection of the body, and the life everlasting.

Creeds have been important in history as a means of further refining the basic beliefs of Christians. The following list describes some of the more important creeds in the history of Christianity; they are specific to certain groups of Christians.

THE NICENE CREED (325; revised at the Council of Constantinople, 381): The official creed of Roman Catholics and Orthodox Christians and accepted by some Protestant churches. It is often used during the liturgy as a common expression of beliefs. In the eleventh century, the word *filioque* ("and the Son") was officially added to the creed by Christians in the West; this addition has long been a source of dispute between Roman Catholics and Orthodox Christians.

THE ATHANASIAN CREED (written between 381 and 428): Attributed to but probably not written by St. Athanasius, it sets forth the doctrines of the Trinity and the Incarnation. It was used until recent times only in Western Christian churches.

THE SCHLEITHEIM CONFESSION (1527): Lists points of agreement among Radical Reformation groups that fixed the direction of the Anabaptist movement. It includes insistence on adult baptism, separation from the world, refusal to swear oaths, and pacifism.

THE AUGSBURG CONFESSION (1530): The Lutheran confession of faith written, for the most part, by Philip Melanchthon. The first part lists essential Lutheran doctrines; the second part lists the abuses in the Roman church that needed to be remedied.

THE HELVETIC CONFESSIONS (1536 and 1562): Confessions of faith written in the Swiss Reformed church. The first contained twenty-seven articles that embodied many of Zwingli's teachings yet, at the same time, sought reconciliation with Luther's positions. The second is a long discourse on the main Reformed teachings and expresses disagreement with Roman Catholicism and Lutheranism.

THE HEIDELBERG CATECHISM (1563): A Reformed confession of faith that is more concerned with Christian life than with theological formulations. It was accepted by the Reformed churches in Europe and approved by the Synod of Dort (1618–1619). The catechism was designed to correspond to Paul's

Epistle to the Romans: human misery in sin, redemption, and new life were key themes.

THE THIRTY-NINE ARTICLES (1563): A set of doctrinal formulas accepted by the Church of England. It is not so much a creed as a brief summary of acceptable doctrines. Royal supremacy over the church is clearly enunciated.

THE BOOK OF CONCORD (1580): The assembled confessions of the Lutheran church. It is a doctrinal standard that defines Lutheranism and its norms. It includes the accepted creeds (Nicene, Athanasian, and Apostles'), the Augsburg Confession, some of Luther's writings, and the Formula of Concord (drawn up in 1577 to restore unity among German Lutherans).

THE WESTMINSTER CONFESSION (1648): Profession of Presbyterian faith as set forth by the Westminster assembly. It is thoroughly Calvinist in its theology and expounds leading articles of the Christian faith from the creation to the last judgment.

THE CAMBRIDGE PLATFORM (1648): Not a doctrinal confession but a plan for organization and practice in American Congregational churches; it includes provisions for the autonomy of local churches, covenanted membership, and the obligation to foster fellowship with other congregations.

MORMON ARTICLES OF FAITH (1842): In response to a question by a Chicago newspaper editor about Mormon beliefs, Joseph Smith listed thirteen articles of Mormon doctrine, including belief in the inspiration of the Bible and the Book of Mormon, continuing revelation, and the literal gathering of Israel in the restoration of the ten tribes on the American continent.

CONFESSION OF 1967 (Presbyterian): A contemporary statement of faith designed for the union of American Presbyterian churches that represents a major doctrinal shift within Presbyterianism.

APPENDIX

6 A Summary of Structural Arrangements

Christians believe that the Holy Spirit is present in the church, but they differ about the locus of that presence and its implications for church authority. They also differ in their interpretations of New Testament passages on issues of organizational structure and authority: some believe that Jesus intended to entrust the church to one chief apostle who would govern the community with the cooperation of the other apostles; others believe that the early church, in fact, operated in local, autonomous groups, where leadership was found within the congregation; still others noted that many of the early communities were organized along the lines of the old Jewish synagogue, where a group of elders administered the daily life of the church.

One of the key arguments during the Reformation concerned the nature of the church: for Catholics, the church is a highly organized institution founded by Christ with definite patterns of authority modeled on Peter, whereas for Protestants, the church is a more loosely structured community of believers who share salvation through faith. For the most part, Christian groups have adapted to three polities: episcopal, congregational, and presbyterian. Some communities, including many nineteenth-century communitarian groups, were founded by a single charismatic individual and often disbanded when that leader died. Others have created unique structures for themselves. Mormons, for example, follow early church organization by including apostles, prophets, and elders in their leadership. For the most part, however, Christians follow one of these three organizational models.

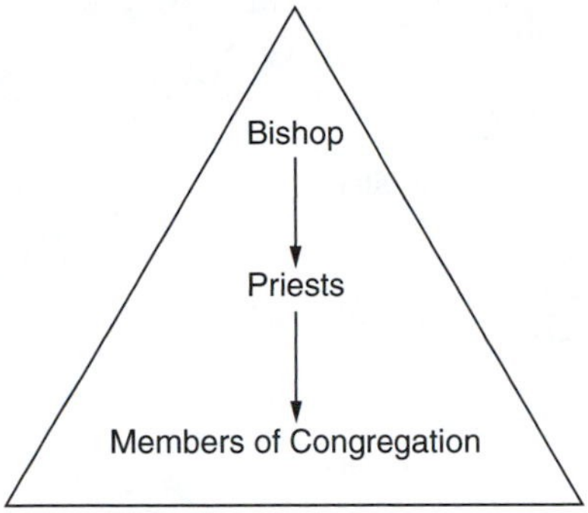

The Episcopal Polity

THE EPISCOPAL STRUCTURE

Episcopal comes from the Greek word for "overseer" and is translated into English as *bishop*. The episcopal system, therefore, is church government by bishops. The episcopal structure is hierarchical and looks like a pyramid. According to the underlying assumptions of this model, authority in the church flows from the top down, from the bishop to the priests to the members of the congregation at the bottom of the pyramid.

Traditional episcopal churches—Roman Catholic, Orthodox, Anglican, and Old Catholic—are based on apostolic succession. They believe that their bishops are successors of the apostles and share in the power and authority Christ bestowed on the apostles. In this system, the clergy are divided into a hierarchy of order and powers: bishops possess the fullness of sacramental power (they can celebrate *all* the sacraments) and usually preside over extended territories (dioceses) made up of many local parishes. Priests share in the sacramental power of the bishop in a *limited* way (they cannot ordain new priests, for example) and preside over local congregations (parishes) within the diocese. Because of priest shortages, some parishes are administered by *deacons*, who have very limited powers (they can preach and baptize) and work cooperatively with a supervising priest. For the most part, however, the traditional episcopal system is defined by the shared powers of bishops and priests.

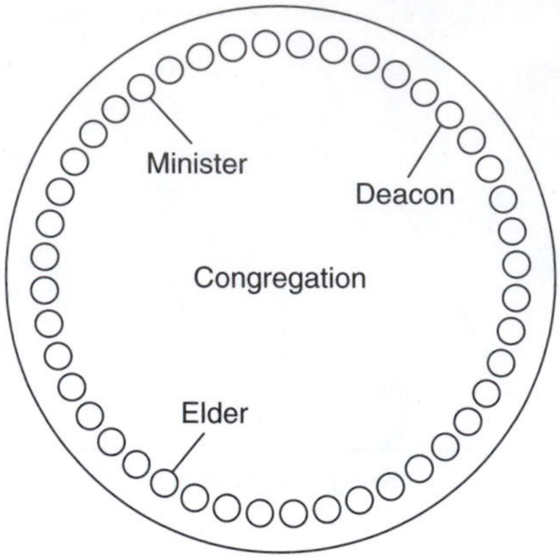

The Congregational Polity

THE CONGREGATIONAL STRUCTURE

The congregational polity, modeled on the New Testament concept of a house church (a small local group of believers gathered together in a home in the name of Jesus), makes the local community supreme. The ministers, deacons, elders, and other officers all come from within the congregation. The gathered group of believers is the church and as such is guided by the Holy Spirit. Those who espouse congregational polity often defend private judgment and interpretation of Scripture, but they believe that the gathered body of believers is a place where matters of worship, belief, and practice are discussed and decided.

The congregational structure is circular. According to this model, Jesus sent the Holy Spirit to the church, to the gathered Christian believers, not to a few leaders and administrators. The Holy Spirit guides the local church, and authority flows throughout the congregation. The local church does not need external or hierarchical authority, since the power of the Spirit is present in all and since the word of God in the Bible is equally accessible to everyone. Although congregations may appoint pastors, deacons, elders, or teachers, those offices designate people's differing functions and gifts; they do not create differences of status within the community.

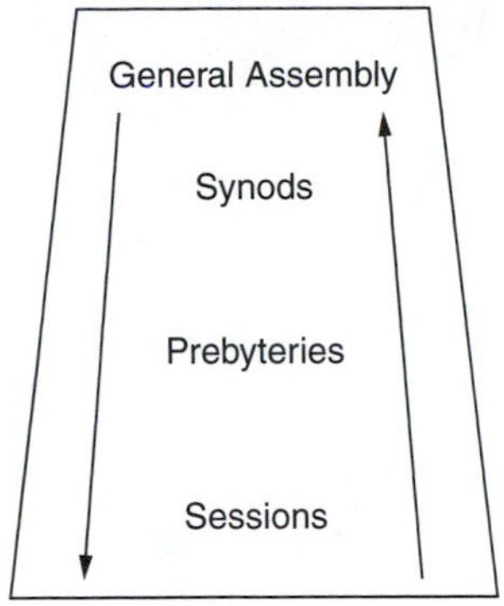

The Presbyterian Polity

THE PRESBYTERIAN STRUCTURE

According to the model followed by Presbyterian and Reformed churches, authority rests with a group of elected elders (the Greek word for elder is *presbyter*), not with a single authority (a bishop) or with a local congregation. The presbyterian model, based on New Testament offices like elder and deacon, combines some characteristics of both episcopal and congregational structures in an attempt to reflect the organization of the early Christian community. According to Calvin, the genius behind the presbyterian model, the church possesses divine authority but is also *semper reformanda,* always needing to be reformed. Accordingly, the church has no final and perfect form, no structure presented to it by divine design. One can, however, work out from the New Testament a set of offices and functions within the church.

The presbyterian model, which is basically an elected constitutional government, is best represented by a trapezoidal figure. It has an authoritative body at the top (like the episcopal structure) but also provides for local initiative and governance (like the congregational model). Authority circulates within the structure and moves from the bottom up (by way of suggested agenda) and from the top down (by means of decisions of the general assembly agreed upon by the presbyteries).

Not all Christians are comfortable with these models and may experiment with new ones. Some Christians display an anti-institutional bias, and others have a strong desire for interdenominational fellowship and worship; some form groups around specific issues of social justice. Within this mixture of discontent and desire, some Christians have abandoned old structures altogether in favor of new ones or modified ones, and others have supplemented old polities with new experiments in Christian living. New experimental structures include small groups that meet weekly for worship and fellowship; house churches that gather members together for worship and sharing in homes rather than the more formal atmosphere of church buildings; "floating parishes" where people meet to celebrate the Eucharist in smaller, more informal settings; and small Christian groups within megachurches. Any of these might be interdenominational; most have some form of congregational polity.

APPENDIX 7

Ecumenism and the World Council of Churches

Whereas the Roman Catholic church had the Vatican as a central organizing office, Protestant churches had bureaus: the Life and Work Bureau and the Faith and Order Bureau in Protestant churches handled matters of practical Christianity and worked out new expressions of Christian doctrine. Although each of these bureaus held international conferences, they did not meet in the same year until 1937. It was at those meetings (in London and in Edinburgh) that calls began to be heard for a World Council of Churches, an idea interrupted by World War II.

The World Council of Churches, which today has its headquarters in Geneva, formally began in 1948 with the cooperation of 144 church groups from 44 countries. Eastern Orthodox churches joined the council in 1961, but Roman Catholics and most Evangelical Christians have not yet joined this endeavor. In fact, many conservative Christians actively oppose the organization. Some of them, who believe that the WCC is insufficiently attuned to Bible-based Christianity and too eager to adapt to the modern world, even identify the WCC with the anti-Christ. Most Evangelical Christian groups belong to the World Evangelical Fellowship, an alternative to the WCC.

The ecumenical movement (Chapter 9) began in 1910 and took shape as a worldwide movement in 1948 with the founding of the World Council of Churches. Although Roman Catholics were not active members of theWCC, the Second Vatican Council's *Decree on Ecumenism* (1964) stimulated Catholic participation, inter faith dialogue, and cooperation. The World Council of Churches continues to work for interfaith cooperation and unity among the churches. At the same time, ecumenism has changed shape during the twentieth century, especially in the context of worldwide Christianity.

Globalization (Chapter 9) has not created a single, more inclusive Christianity (the dream of the early ecumenical movement) but has fostered new diversity. The new world Christianity cannot be defined by way of sectarian divisions and doctrinal disputes. World Christianity in the future will likely be defined by shared worship styles, social and economic status, political agendas, and transnational ethnic ties. The following table compares ecumenism in its heyday (1960s) and today.

Time	1960s	2000s
Metaphors	Global and uniting: we live in a global village; we are in this together	Particular and divisive: we are all different in background, nationality, race, class, and social issues
Dream	One church, one huge denomination for all	There are five new denominations formed each week
Location	Most attention on North America and Europe	Southern Hemisphere, Africa, and Latin America
Activities	Orderly discussion and cautious interfaith prayer services	Local experimentation and improvisation and what may look like anarchy
Agendas	Set by the Faith and Order Bureaus; focused on denominational strife	Set by women, Two-Thirds World people, political left and right; focused on justice issues
Concerns	Interfaith boundaries and practices	Partisan issues and often hostile differences
Purpose	Understanding and acceptance	Confrontation and breakthrough
Sacraments	Hope for intercommunion and that authority will be a secondary issue	Cannot hope for intercommunion because authority is a primary issue
Local attitudes	Experiment, but put your hope in global ecumenism	Concentrate on local experiments and put global agendas last
Problem solvers	Leaders will solve the problems	People at the grass roots have the solutions

GLOSSARY

ABRAHAM: Father of the Jewish people; first of the three patriarchs, Abraham, Isaac, and Jacob. See Genesis 17:5. Abraham = father of many.

A.D.: *Anno Domini,* "in the year of Our Lord," is a way of dating events according to the Christian calendar. This book uses C.E. (common era) instead.

ALEXANDER THE GREAT (356–323 B.C.E.): King of Macedon, one of the greatest leaders and conquerors of all time.

ALTAR CALL: Invitation by a preacher for members of the congregation to come up to the altar. People respond for a number of reasons: to repent and be saved, to help others accept Jesus, to pray for themselves, to confess their sins, or to ask for special prayers from the minister and others.

ANSELM (1033–1109): Archbishop of Canterbury, teacher, and theologian; first to develop theory of substitutionary atonement.

ANTIOCHUS IV (d. 163 B.C.E.): Attempted to Hellenize Judea and crush Judaism, a policy that instigated the Maccabean revolt.

APOCALYPTIC (Gk = uncovering): Type of Jewish and Christian literature dealing with the end of the world and the coming of the kingdom of God. Writing characterized by obscure symbols, visions, and vivid imagery.

APOCRYPHA (Gk = hidden things): Biblical books that are included in the Roman Catholic and Greek Orthodox Old Testaments but not in the Protestant one (see Appendix 2).

APOLOGIST/APOLOGETICS (Gk = speak in defense): Early Christian writers (c. 120–220) known as apologists defended Christianity against hostile or misleading characterizations; they explained its doctrines and practices. Modern apologetics is a defense of Christianity on intellectual grounds; it argues for the reasonableness of religious faith in general and for Christianity in particular.

APOSTASY (Gk = revolt): Denial of one's beliefs. In Christianity, a deliberate turning away from God and the Christian faith; the opposite of conversion.

APOSTLE: Envoy or "one sent." Refers to prime missionaries of Christianity (such as Paul and Junia) or to the twelve men chosen by Jesus as his primary followers.

ARMINIANISM: Theological system inspired by Jacob Arminius (1560–1609). The emphasis is on the freedom of a person to accept grace (versus the Calvinist notion of irresistible grace), though it also includes beliefs in universal atonement, conditional predestination, and human freedom. It has sometimes been used to describe liberal or rational tendencies in Christian religion. One needs to exercise caution, therefore, before applying the term to a person or group.

ASCETICISM (Gk = training): A system of practices designed to develop virtues and combat vice, used by Greek philosophers, Christians, and various Eastern religions.

ATONEMENT: Sometimes written as *at-one-ment* to indicate the reconciliation between God and people through the death and resurrection of Jesus. Christians agree that there is a need for reconciliation, but they argue about how atonement ought to be understood. There has been a long history of interpretation from the New Testament to the present. Substitutionary atonement, for example, was considered one of the Christian fundamentals.

ATTILA (d. 453): King of the Huns. He was going to invade Rome (452) but changed his mind either because of the diplomacy of Pope Leo I or because of lack of provisions.

AUGUSTINE (354–430 C.E.): Bishop of Hippo (North Africa) and one of the most important early Christian writers.

AUGUSTUS (63 B.C.E.–14 C.E.): First Roman emperor, reigning when Jesus was born.

BASIL THE GREAT (330-379): Greek theologian who wrote a monastic rule still used in Orthodox monasticism.

B.C.E.: Before the common era. A designation of time equivalent to B.C. but not centered on a theological claim as is B.C. (before Christ).

BENEDICT OF NURSIA (C. 480–550): Founder of the Benedictines, he wrote the first monastic rule used in the West.

BERNARD OF CLAIRVAUX (1090–1153): A monk and abbot of the monastery at Clairvaux in France who is renowned for his theological and mystical writings.

BIBLICAL CRITICISM: An approach to the study of the Bible that applies a variety of interpretive tools—literary, historical, textual—to the words, composition, and meaning of the Bible. Christians have always searched for various levels of meaning in the Bible and have often used the scholarly tools available to them at the time. In the modern world, those tools are many. Biblical criticism is opposed by those who believe in the absolute inerrancy of the biblical text.

BOOK OF COMMON PRAYER: Authorized liturgical book of the Church of England. Its various editions and revisions reflect the doctrinal battles within the Tudor Reformation.

BYZANTIUM: Site of present-day Istanbul. Constantine had a new city built there in 330 and renamed it Constantinople when he moved the capital of the Roman Empire there in 333.

CAMP MEETINGS: A form of revivalist meeting used on the American frontier. It originated as a form in Kentucky in 1801 during the Second Great Awakening. Camp meetings were designed to attract many people and were held outdoors; various ministers preached, and conversions were often accompanied by emotional exercises and manifestations.

CANON: The Greek word means "straight rod"; it usually means a kind of measuring stick. In Christian language, it means the official list of biblical books that are recognized as inspired. Canonical books must be distinguished from apocryphal books (books about which there is some question as to authenticity). Also an ecclesiastical title used to refer to non-monastic clergy belonging to a cathedral (the chief church in a diocese). Canons participate in officially sanctioned religious life in a way that is technically different from monks, nuns, and friars. Canon law is a phrase for church law.

CATHERINE OF SIENA (C. 1347–1380): Saint, mystic, and doctor of the Roman Catholic church. As a religious reformer, she helped end the Avignon papacy.

C.E.: The common era. It corresponds to what Christians call A.D. (*anno Domini,* meaning "the year of our Lord").

CELIBACY: Being unmarried. This condition is accepted by priests in the Roman Catholic church as necessary for ordination. In the Orthodox church, men may marry before ordination but not after; bishops must not be married.

CHARISMATIC (Gk = gift of grace): Possessing gifts of the spirit. In the New Testament, various gifts are mentioned that help a Christian to advance spiritually. In 1 Cor. 12:8–11, these gifts *(charismata)* are listed as wisdom, knowledge, faith, healing, miracles, prophecy, discernment of spirits, tongues, and the interpretation of tongues. They are sometimes called the gifts of the spirit and thereby associated with Christians who have a special relationship to the Holy Spirit.

CHARLEMAGNE (C. 742–814): King of the Franks, crowned emperor of the West in 800 by Pope Leo III.

CHRISTOLOGY: The study of the person and nature of Christ. The questions about the human and divine nature of Christ were especially important in the early years of the Christian movement (see Appendix 4).

CLEMENT OF ALEXANDRIA (d. 215 C.E.): Greek theologian who first attempted a synthesis between Platonic and Christian thought.

COMMUNION OF SAINTS: Mentioned in the Apostles' Creed (see Appendix 5). To some Christians, it means sharing together in the Eucharist, and to others, it is a description of Christian fellowship here on earth. Traditionally, however, it refers to the spiritual union between Christ and each believer and, by extension, describes the spiritual union that exists among all believers on earth and in heaven.

COMMUNITARIAN: Nonmonastic communities motivated by ethical or religious ideals. In the nineteenth century, there were a wide variety of religious communitarian groups in America.

CONFESSION: In one sense, confession means to acknowledge or to admit one's sins for the purpose of being forgiven. The sacrament of penance provides one possibility: the sinner confesses his or her sins to a priest, who is empowered (through his ordination) to forgive those sins in God's name. Confession also means to profess one's faith: a formal statement of beliefs is sometimes called a creed and sometimes a confession. A *confessional group*, therefore, is one with a common creed: it follows the established practices and adheres to the established credal statements of that group.

CONGREGATIONAL: A type of ecclesiastical government where authority flows throughout the congregation (see Appendix 6).

CONSTANTINE (d. 337 C.E.): First Christian Roman emperor. He conquered under the Christian sign of the cross and issued the Edict of Milan (313), which stated that Christianity would be tolerated in the empire and put an end to persecution.

CONSTANTINOPLE: Capital city of the Roman Empire under Constantine and his successors, formerly called Byzantium. Called also the "new Rome." Three ecumenical councils were held there.

CONSUBSTANTIATION: An explanation about the Eucharist associated with Martin Luther that differs from transubstantiation. Consubstantiation proposes that after the consecration of the elements, both the body and blood of Christ *and* the bread and wine exist together in union with one another.

CONVERSION (Gk = *metanoia* is one root, meaning "radical turning of the heart and will"): Several meanings: (1) turning from sin to God in faith and repentance (the controversy here is whether this turning is entirely an act of God, of the person, or cooperation between them); (2) drawing closer to God by living a more dedicated Christian life; (3) changing from nonbelief to belief, as in conversion from atheism; (4) sometimes used by Roman Catholics to describe the experience of someone who has turned from one church to the Catholic church; thus, *convert* is the word often used by Catholics to describe a Protestant now become Catholic.

COUNCIL OF TRENT: Roman Catholic council held periodically from 1545 to 1563 to respond to Protestantism. Until the Second Vatican Council (1962–1965), Trent was the most comprehensive statement of Catholic belief and practice.

COUNSELS OF PERFECTION: Traditionally, the vocations to poverty, chastity, and obedience, which form the basis of nearly all monastic and religious life for Roman Catholicism, Orthodox Christianity, and Protestant religious orders.

COVENANT: An agreement entered into voluntarily by two or more parties. God established a covenant with Abraham and with the Jewish people at Sinai; Christians believe a new covenant began with Jesus.

COVENANT THEOLOGY: Used, especially by the Puritans, to explain the election and perseverance of the saints. It was an important part of the religious, political, and social understanding of both Presbyterian and Congregational Puritans.

CRANMER, THOMAS (1489–1556): Archbishop of Canterbury at the beginning of the English Reformation, chiefly responsible for the Book of Common Prayer.

CRUSADES **(from the Latin word for cross; the Crusaders wore a cross on their official clothing):** A series of military expeditions launched from the eleventh to the thirteenth centuries by Christians for the recovery of the Holy Land (Jerusalem) from the Muslims. The first one was called by Pope Urban II in 1095. There were nine of them altogether. The fourth Crusade (1202–1204) ended with the capture and pillaging of Constantinople. The word *crusade* came to be used for other expeditions—against heretics, for example—sanctioned by the pope.

DARK AGES: Usually refers to the period between the collapse of the old Roman Empire (in the fifth century) and beginning of a stable society (about 1000 C.E.). The Dark Ages are often associated with the barbarian invasions, unstable government, and minimal levels of education and progress.

DEACON **(Gk = servant or minister):** Mentioned in the New Testament and recognized in many Christian churches as an office or ministry (often attached to reading the Gospel, visiting the sick, and so on). The role and nature of the deacon vary according to polity.

DEAD SEA SCROLLS: A collection of texts discovered in 1947 that tell scholars something about the Qumran community, a group of Essenes who lived around the time of Jesus.

DEIFICATION: In Eastern Orthodox mysticism and theology, it usually means divinization: becoming divine by way of a profound union with God.

DEISM **(Lat *dens* = God):** Belief in a supreme being who created the world and then left it to its own discoverable and reasonable natural laws. The Deist God is not personal and does not reveal religious truths or work miracles.

DENOMINATIONALISM: A denomination is a specific church group united in polity and belief. Denominationalism has several meanings: (1) the variety and independence of various churches; (2) the notion that there are and ought to be many differing church bodies; (3) the movement to unite local churches into one larger body. In this third sense, denominationalism has been opposed by those who clearly favor congregational polities or who value their own distinctness. Antidenominationalism is resistance to any centrally organized church body.

DEVOTIONS: Acts of prayer or religious fervor meant to focus one's energies on a relationship with God. In the Middle Ages, many Christians believed that their eternal salvation depended on how faithfully they had said certain prayers, kept certain feasts, and performed certain religious acts. Devotions sometimes required very small efforts: uttering a pious phrase like "Have mercy on me, O Lord" or saying special prayers on Sundays. Some devotions, however, required major commitments and could even endanger one's life, such as making a pilgrimage to Jerusalem. At the end of the fourteenth century, a movement arose called *devotio moderna* (modern devotion), which laid great stress on one's inner life and required the practice of meditation. The most popular book of this movement was Thomas à Kempis's *Imitation of Christ*. Many of the reformers, upset by some devotional excesses and/or convinced that such practices were of no use in obtaining salvation, condemned devotional practices and enjoined their followers to trust in God's mercy and to realize that they would be saved on the basis of faith alone, not because of their "good works" or devotions.

DIOCESE: A unit of territorial administration in churches with episcopal structures (see Appendix 6). A diocese is under the jurisdiction of a bishop and is usually a relatively large territory. The Romans divided the empire into provinces called dioceses to ensure smooth and effective government. Christians adapted the system to suit their ecclesiastical purposes.

DOCTRINE: A system of beliefs or dogmas; teaching of a particular group.

DONATION OF CONSTANTINE: Document forged in the eighth century defending papal interests. It claims to have been issued by the emperor Constantine (fourth century) giving the pope dominion over much of the western half of the Roman Empire. Proved to be a forgery in the fifteenth century by humanist scholar Lorenzo Valla.

DUALISM: Any philosophical system that tries to explain things in terms of two distinct and irreducible principles; in religion, good and evil or light and darkness, both of which are equally powerful.

ECUMENICAL COUNCIL (**Gk = universal**): Universal meeting of bishops, whose authority was accepted as official (see Appendix 4).

EDICT OF MILAN: Passed by Constantine (313) granting religious toleration to Christians.

ELDER (**Gk = presbyter**): An office in the presbyterian structure that is divided into teaching elders (ordained ministers) and ruling elders (elected from the congregation). Some Christians translate the word *presbyter* as priest rather than elder (see Appendix 6).

ENGLISH CIVIL WAR: Conflict between King Charles I of England and a significant group of his subjects. It lasted from 1642 to 1648 and was focused on Charles's monarchical views versus the demands of the Parliamentarians. Many of the king's opponents were Puritans.

ENLIGHTENMENT: A term applied to scientific and philosophical thought in the eighteenth century characterized by belief in natural law and order, confidence in human reason, and a rational approach to religious questions.

EPISCOPAL: A type of ecclesiastical government where authority rests with bishops and flows down from them through priests to members of the congregation (see Appendix 6).

ESCHATOLOGY (**Gk = last discourse or last things**): The doctrine of the last things or end of the world; eschatology is concerned with the end of the individual soul, all other people, the church, and the world. It is treated in the Old Testament and New Testament most thoroughly in apocalypses such as Daniel or Revelation.

ESSENES: Small Jewish ascetic sect at the time of Jesus. Essenes lived pious, communal lives in the desert, where they purified themselves in preparation for the Messiah. Community of goods, celibacy, and purification through baptism were some of their practices.

ESTABLISHED CHURCHES: Those churches whose practice and doctrines are supported by the state in some way. The Church of England is "established": the church is supported by and to some extent controlled by the state.

EUCHARIST (**Gk = thanksgiving**): Christian practice that repeats the action of Jesus at the Last Supper. Christians partake of the bread and wine in memory of Jesus. Some Christians believe the bread and wine are truly the body and blood of Christ; others believe they are symbols of the body and blood; still others believe they are a memorial fellowship meal.

EUSEBIUS (**C. 260–340**): Bishop of Caesarea and so-called father of church history. Wrote official biography of Constantine.

EXCOMMUNICATION: An ecclesiastical punishment whereby a person is excluded from communion with the church; that is, the excommunicated person may not partake of the sacraments or, in some cases, speak to anyone in the community.

EXEGESIS **(Gk = to narrate or explain):** The process of explaining a text, usually a biblical one, by way of translation, paraphrase, or commentary. An exegete applies interpretive skills to a text to understand it more deeply. Exegesis has been done from ancient times—commentaries on Scripture predate Christianity, and Christianity itself has a long and varied history of exegesis—but it changes as exegetical skills (linguistic, archaeological, historical, spiritual) develop over time.

EXILE **(the Babylonian captivity):** In the history of Israel, the period from the fall of Jerusalem (587 B.C.E.) to the reconstruction in Palestine of a new Jewish state (538 B.C.E.).

EXODUS**:** Second book of the Hebrew Bible (or Old Testament). In Jewish history, the Exodus was the flight from Egypt led by Moses (including the miraculous crossing of the Red Sea and God's victory over the Egyptians).

FAITH**:** For some Christians, an attitude of trust in God's mercy; people may be saved through Christ by faith. For other Christians, *faith* refers to a body of beliefs and is more like a creed or set of doctrines believed by people. For still others, it is intellectual assent to a body of beliefs.

FALL**:** The moment when Adam and Eve disobeyed God's command not to eat of the tree of knowledge, thus forfeiting the original blessedness that they had enjoyed. Theologically, a fall from a state of harmony to one of discord with the will of God (see Gen. 3).

FILIOQUE **(Lat = and the Son):** Words added to the Nicene Creed by Western Christians so that it reads "the Holy Ghost . . . proceeds from the Father and Son." Long a source of friction between Roman Catholics and Orthodox Christians.

FLAGELLANTS**:** Groups of people who, in medieval times, scourged themselves in public procession or in town squares to lead people to repentance and to do penance themselves for their own sins and the sins of the world.

FORTY-TWO ARTICLES**:** Collection of Anglican doctrines issued in 1553 but never enforced (due to the restoration of Roman Catholicism under Queen Mary I). They form the basis of the Thirty-nine Articles.

FRANCISCANS**:** The order of friars founded by Francis of Assisi (1182–1226), distinguished by complete poverty.

FRIARS**:** Religious beggars living an officially sanctioned, vowed religious life. Friars were called fraters (brothers); they were usually distinguished by the color of their cloaks (Gray Friars, Black Friars, and so on).

GENTILE **(Hb = the nations):** A term applied to non-Jews.

GENTILE MISSION**:** Refers to Saint Paul's spreading the Gospel message not just to Jews but to Gentiles.

GLOSSOLALIA **(Gk = tongue talking):** The ability or gift of speaking "in tongues," which may mean speaking in a real language unknown to the speaker (one might, for instance, speak Chinese under the influence of the Spirit) or in an unknown language (which then may or may not be interpreted to the congregation). In Pentecostal churches, speaking in tongues is considered a sign of baptism in the Spirit.

GNOSTICS **(Gk = knowledge):** An early Christian sect who believed that they were saved by the secret knowledge that they possessed a divine spark absent in others. Recent research on the manuscripts found at Nag Hammadi in Egypt has given us a more thorough understanding of the Gnostics, who were heretofore known mostly through the condemnations of their opponents. Many of the apocryphal Gospels were written by Gnostics.

GOSPELS **("good tidings"):** Any of the first four books of the New Testament preaching the "good news," namely, that there is salvation through the birth, life, passion, death, and resurrection of Jesus. The four Gospels in the New Testament are Matthew, Mark, Luke, and John.

GRACE**:** In Christian theology, God's favor or supernatural assistance. People receive grace so that they may be sanctified. Christians admit the need for some kind of divine help in their lives, but there has been much disagreement about what exactly this help is, how it comes to people, how people accept it, and whether it is there all the time or only for specific acts.

HEBREWS: See *Jews.*

HELENA (c. 255–330): Mother of Constantine. According to a later tradition, she found the true cross in Jerusalem.

HELLENISM: The culture, ideals, and pattern of life of ancient Greece. As a system, it competed with Christianity and challenged it to develop a philosophical language.

HERESY: Formal denial of a defined doctrine.

HERMIT (Gk = desert): Individual who, for religious motives, retires from the general society and goes out to a lonely place to focus on an intense relationship with God. In the early church, these people went into the deserts of Egypt and Syria.

HEROD: Dynasty reigning in Palestine at the time of Jesus. Herod the Great (d. 4 B.C.E.) gave the family its name and was king of Judea. His son Herod Antipas (d. 39 C.E.) executed John the Baptist and was reigning at the time of Jesus' death.

HOLY SPIRIT (HOLY GHOST): Theologically, the third person of the Trinity; biblically, a manifestation of God's power in this world. The Holy Spirit was promised by Jesus, and Christians believe it is present in the church in some way.

HUMANISM: A philosophical and literary movement that extolled human capabilities. In its Renaissance form, it signaled a return to classical antiquity. It inspired some of the scriptural research that led to the Reformation.

HUSSITES: Followers of John Hus, they were Czech nationalists who resisted armed attempts to squelch their religious protests. One of their main tenets was the reception of the Eucharist under both species; that is, they believed that people should receive both the bread and the wine. The Czech flag still used today has eucharistic symbols on it.

ICONOCLAST CONTROVERSY (Gk iconoclasm = image breaking): Opposition to religious use of images, from the fourth to the ninth centuries a raging battle in Orthodox Christianity. In the Reformation, some Protestants (especially Puritans) considered the use of religious images idolatrous.

ICONOSTASIS: Screen in Orthodox churches that separates the sanctuary from the rest of the church.

ICONS (Gk = image, picture): Flat pictures of God and saints venerated in Orthodox churches.

IGNATIUS OF ANTIOCH (c. 35–107): Bishop of Antioch and martyr. In an age of doctrinal questioning, he argued that the best way to safeguard true beliefs was through the teaching and ruling authority of the bishop.

IMMANENCE (Lat *in manere* = to dwell in): God's dwelling in and being active in the world. The doctrine of immanence sees the world as, in some sense, containing God within it (see *transcendence).*

INCARNATION: Christian doctrine that the eternal Son of God took flesh; Jesus Christ as both fully divine and fully human.

INDEX: Officially, *Index Librorum Prohibitorum* (Index of Forbidden Books). A list of books considered dangerous to the faith and morals of Catholics, drawn up by a censoring agency established by the church in the sixteenth century. The Index was abolished in 1966.

INDULGENCES: Remission by the church of temporal punishment due for sin. Based on the merits of Christ and the saints, the medieval Catholic church reasoned that it could grant indulgences drawn from a treasury of merits available to help sinners on earth.

INERRANCY: The belief that there are no errors in the Bible that are not corrected within the Bible itself. According to this view, the Bible is literally true and available to anyone who can read the text (see *biblical criticism*).

INFALLIBILITY: The ability to speak on religious matters without making a mistake. There have been arguments about biblical infallibility; that is, to what extent the Bible is infallible. Roman Catholics believe that the pope is infallible when speaking *ex cathedra* (from the chair): when the pope is speaking to the whole church on matters of faith and morals. The issue of papal infallibility is a matter of continued debate within Roman Catholic Christianity.

INQUISITION: The official mechanism for the persecution of heresy by designated ecclesiastical courts; established in the thirteenth century. Called the Holy Office from 1908 to 1965, when it became the Congregation for the Doctrine of the Faith with the function of promoting faith and morals, not just safeguarding them.

INSPIRATION (**Gk = breath, spirit**): Doctrine that Scripture was written under the influence of the Holy Spirit. How it works is a matter of some dispute.

IONA COMMUNITY: Founded in 1983 on the site of an ancient monastery off the coast of Scotland. Founder George MacLeod created an ecumenical Christian community of men and women committed to seeking new ways to live the Gospel.

ISRAELITES: See *Jews.*

JEWS: Three terms must be distinguished here. *Hebrew* refers to the Semitic people not yet formed into the nation Israel. *Israelites* refers to those Hebrews who were part of the nation Israel formed under the leadership of Moses and Joshua around 1200 B.C.E. *Jews,* as a term, derives from the last surviving Israelite tribe, Judah, and is a term applied to these people after the Exile (587 B.C.E.). In chronological order, then, one speaks of the Hebrews up to the Exodus, of the Israelites from the Exodus to the Exile, and of the Jews after the Exile. In a more embracing sense, however, Judaism traces itself back to the days of Abraham, Isaac, and Jacob, and Jews are descendants of Abraham and Sarah.

JOHN THE BAPTIST: Jewish prophet who, after retiring into the desert, emerged to preach repentance and to baptize in preparation for the Messiah. He baptized Jesus.

JOHN **XXIII**: Name taken by two popes: (1) Baldassare Cossa (d. 1419), who was elected pope by the Council of Pisa (1409) and was an antipope (that is, was pope in contest with two other men who also claimed to be the rightful pope); he called the Council of Constance; (2) Angelo Roncalli (1958–1963), who called the Second Vatican Council, which reformed and modernized the Roman Catholic church.

JUSTIFICATION (**Lat = make just; Gk = pronounce just**): A person's passage from sinfulness to righteousness (or justice). Also, that act whereby God makes a person just (conveys grace to a person's soul); or the act whereby God, because of the sacrifice of Christ, treats a person mercifully—as though that person were just or righteous. Christians share the belief that justification is bound up with rebirth or regeneration, but they disagree about what that rebirth means, how it is accomplished, and how, exactly, it affects the person.

JUSTIN MARTYR (**100–165 C.E.**): Christian apologist who tried to convert people to Christianity by way of philosophical argument.

LITURGY (**Gk = work of the people**): Used to describe worship in general and the Eucharist especially.

LOLLARDS: Followers of John Wycliffe in England.

MACCABEES: Jewish family of second and first centuries B.C.E. that brought about restoration of Jewish political and religious life.

MARTYR (**Gk = witness**): During persecution, used for those who suffered for their religious beliefs; finally restricted to those who died for them. Martyrs are honored as saints by the church.

MARY (**Hb = Miriam**): Mother of Jesus. She occupies a place of honor—principal saint—in Roman Catholic and Orthodox churches. Theological statements about her acknowledge her virginity and title Mother of God. During the Reformation, Protestants reacted against what they interpreted as excessive devotion to Mary. Her place in the devotional life of the church is a serious issue between Roman Catholics and Protestants.

MASS: A name—along with Lord's Supper and Holy Communion—for the celebration of the Eucharist. It is usually used by Roman Catholics but has also been used by Anglicans.

MENDICANT FRIARS: Members of religious orders that were forbidden to own property. Unlike monks, they worked or begged for a living and were not required to spend their lives in one monastery.

MESSIAH: (Hb = anointed one): In Judaism, a man sent by God to restore Israel and reign righteously for all people. Christians consider Jesus to be the Messiah and interpret the Messiah as a suffering savior (see Isaiah 52–55).

MILLENNIALISM (Gk = thousand): Based on Revelation 20:1–10, the belief that Christ promised faithful believers a thousand years of bliss and will return to establish it.

MOSES (thirteenth century B.C.E.): Leader and lawgiver of the Jewish people. Called by God to take the Jews to Mount Sinai, where God made a covenant with them.

MYSTERY (Lat = *sacramentum*) RELIGIONS: In Greek and Roman religion, secret cults that required elaborate initiations, purification rites, and accepted occult ideas.

MYSTICISM: A form of religious experience that emphasizes the possibility and desirability of a direct and intuitive apprehension of divinity. A mystic is one who strives for this direct personal union with God.

NATIVISM: Intense suspicion or dislike of foreigners, often directed against Catholics by American Protestants in the nineteenth century.

NEOPLATONISM: Ancient mystical philosophy based on doctrines of Plato. It had a lasting effect on the development of Christian mysticism.

NEW TESTAMENT: The Christian portion of the Bible: twenty-seven books.

NICENE CREED: Official statement of beliefs from the Council of Nicaea (see Appendix 4).

OLD TESTAMENT: The Christian name for the Hebrew Bible, as rearranged by Christians.

ORDINANCES: Nonliturgical churches—for example, Baptists and Mennonites—rejected the word *sacrament* and adopted the word *ordinance* because they thought *sacrament* had medieval connotations of magic.

ORIGEN (C. 185–254 C.E.): Christian philosopher and scholar, one of the first theological geniuses of the Christian church. Attempted to synthesize Neoplatonism and Stoicism with Christian creed so as to provide a Christian view of the universe.

ORIGINAL SIN: In Christian theology, the sin of Adam and Eve. The effect of it is the fundamentally graceless nature of human beings; that is, all people are regarded as having a sinful nature.

ORTHODOXY: Right belief (as contrasted with heresy). The word is used for the ancient Greek Christian church (Orthodox Christianity: Greek Orthodox, Russian Orthodox, and so on). It can also refer to adherence to traditional or established belief (as opposed to liberalism or innovation).

PAPAL PRIMACY: The claim that Jesus gave to Peter and to his successors (the popes) the power to rule over the entire Christian church.

PAPAL STATES: The territories over which the pope was the ruler in a civil as well as a spiritual sense before 1870; nearly one-third of the Italian peninsula. The power to govern this territory is called the *temporal power* of the pope.

PARLIAMENTARIANS: Group opposed to King Charles I in the English Civil War; many of them were Puritans, and the English Civil War is sometimes referred to as the Puritan Revolution.

PASSOVER: A Jewish feast of highest importance. In the Bible, it is an act of deliverance from the Egyptians, where an angel of death passed over the Hebrews in the last of the great plagues (Exodus 12).

PATRIARCH: One of the progenitors of the Jewish people, especially Abraham, Isaac, and Jacob. In the Christian church, a title of certain exalted bishops. In the early church, there were five great patriarchates: Rome, Constantinople, Alexandria, Antioch, and Jerusalem.

PAUL (d. 64 or 67 C.E.): Apostle to the Gentiles. Born and reared a Jew, he converted to Christianity after an "experience of the risen Lord." Author of major Epistles in the New Testament, great missionary, and early theologian.

PEACE OF AUGSBURG (1555): Settled the religious battles in Germany with the formula *cuius regio eius religio:* the people in a given region must follow the religion of the ruler of that region (those who opposed their ruler's religion should move to a more congenial place).

PEACE OF WESTPHALIA (1648): The general settlement ending the Thirty Years' War.

PEASANTS' REVOLT: An uprising of German peasants in 1524–1526. Although their grievances were economic, the peasants were urged on by some religious reformers and others who were impatient for change. Their list of demands included some religious reforms, but their methods were variations of mob violence. Luther called for their extermination.

PENANCE: In Orthodox and Roman Catholic churches, a sacrament of the forgiveness of sins. It can also mean a punishment of some sort (as in one "doing penance" for sins).

PENTECOST (Gk = fiftieth): In Judaism, a spring feast 50 days after Passover, commemorating the Sinai covenant. In Christianity, the feast celebrating the coming of the Holy Spirit to the apostles and into the church.

PENTECOSTAL: Member of a church that requires baptism in the Spirit manifested by *glossolalia,* speaking in tongues. Today, one can find Pentecostal Christians in non-Pentecostal churches as well; for example, there is a Pentecostal movement in Roman Catholicism.

PERSECUTIONS: Sporadic but systematic attempts on the part of Roman authorities to destroy Christianity. Began with Nero (64 C.E.) and ended with the Edict of Milan (313).

PETER (d. 64 C.E.): Most prominent of the twelve apostles of Jesus. Traditionally, the first bishop of Rome.

PHARISEES: One of two great political parties (with Sadducees) in Jerusalem at the time of Jesus. They were extreme in their attempt to keep all that was Jewish away from what was non-Jewish; they were liberal in accepting both written law (Torah) and oral law (tradition).

PILGRIMAGE: Journey to a holy place to obtain divine help or to honor God or the saints. Many religions encourage pilgrimage, and the desire to visit the place where a holy person actually lived appears to be common to many religious people.

PIUS V (1504–1572; pope from 1566): Recognized as a saint in the Roman Catholic church, he was an austere and zealous reformer, instrumental in promoting the reforms of the Council of Trent. In 1570, he excommunicated Elizabeth I, queen of England, and greatly aggravated the position of Catholics there.

PLAGUES OF EGYPT: In the Bible, the troubles visited on Egyptians by God so that the pharaoh would let the Jewish people go out of Egypt. There were ten plagues. See Exodus 7:19–12:36.

PLATO (427–347 B.C.E.): Greek philosopher. One of the most important and influential thinkers in the history of the world.

PLURALISM: The belief that no single theory can explain the universe, which, according to pluralists, is composed of many principles. In religion, it is the coexistence of a variety of religious forms and beliefs.

POLITY: Church structure or government (see Appendix 6).

POMPEY (106–48 B.C.E.): Conquered Jerusalem for Rome in 63 B.C.E.

PONTIUS PILATE: Roman procurator of Judea when Jesus was crucified. According to the New Testament, he evaded responsibility for Jesus' death because he feared the Jewish high priests' power.

POPE/PAPACY (Lat = father): *Pope* is the title restricted to the bishop of Rome since the fourth century; the papacy is the office of the pope.

PREDESTINATION: The idea that God decrees beforehand for all eternity the fate of individual souls. Some Christians believe that God predestines people to both heaven and hell; others say that God predestines to heaven but reprobates to hell. Predestination is deduced on the basis of divine foreknowledge.

PRESBYTERIAN: A type of ecclesiastical government in which authority rests with a group of elected elders (see Appendix 6).

PRIEST **(Gk = presbyter):** As a special ministry (apart from elder), priesthood does not appear in the New Testament, but by the second century, the office of the priest had developed to include a share in the powers of the bishop, specifically powers to celebrate the Eucharist and to forgive sins.

PROPHETS **(Hb = called by god):** Prophets were those called in the Old Testament to speak God's word to the people (usually to urge them back to the terms of the covenant). Sometimes, prophets predicted future events, but their main function was to speak for God, not to be seers.

PROVIDENCE: The doctrine that the world is divinely administered; that God, in some way, rules the world; and that the events that occur in the world are understood and controlled (or allowed) by God. The doctrine of providence need not destroy free will.

PURGATORY: A Roman Catholic doctrine that says there is a state of life after death that is neither heaven nor hell but a place where one can suffer or work out the temporal punishment due to sins committed on earth. Accordingly, Catholics tend to pray for the dead while Protestants, in general, do not. Purgatory is predicated on ancient beliefs about the divine attributes of justice and mercy. God's justice demands purification and so *could* refuse heaven to anyone who was not perfectly purified before death, but God's mercy will not permit such a refusal of heaven to those who truly long for heaven and simply need more time.

RAPTURE: Based on 1 Thess. 4:17, the belief among conservative Protestants that faithful Christians will be instantly transported to heaven before the end of the world. Popularized in the 1830s, this concept is at the base of the *Left Behind* novels and a staple of Dispensationalist Christianity.

RATIONALISM: Theory that reason alone (unaided by experience) can arrive at some basic truths about the world. In religion, it is often opposed to revelation: it holds that religion can be understood on the basis of reason alone and that revelation is unnecessary.

REFORMATION: A complex series of changes occurring in Christianity from the fourteenth to the seventeenth centuries.

RELICS: Material remains of a saint or sacred objects that touched the body.

RENAISSANCE: From the word for "rebirth," it was a development of Western civilization from the fourteenth to the sixteenth centuries that marked the passage from medieval to modern times. In it, there was a new importance given to individual expression, culture, and worldly experience.

RESURRECTION **(Lat = rising again):** Rising from death to life. In Christianity, the resurrection of Jesus is the central fact of Christian experience. Christians believe that all believers will rise from the dead at the end of the world.

REVIVALISM: A form of evangelical preaching that is highly emotional in style, characterized by its focus on sin and salvation and designed to bring listeners to a conversion experience.

SABBATARIANS: Those who observe Saturday as the Sabbath, or those who observe the Sunday Sabbath rigorously by abstaining from all work and recreation.

SABBATH **(Hb = repose):** Last day of the week in Judaism; first day of the week in Christianity. Observed on Saturday as a day of rest for Jews. Observed on Sunday as a celebration of the resurrection for Christians.

SACRAMENT **(Gk = mystery):** An outward sign instituted by Christ to draw people into relationship with God. Historically, there have been arguments about how many sacraments there are, whether or not they give grace, and what they mean. Some Christians prefer the term *ordinances,* and others may "have Communion" but never use the word *sacrament* or *ordinance*. Most Christians—except Quakers and the Salvation Army, who have no sacraments—accept baptism and the Lord's Supper (Eucharist or Communion) as sacraments, and some accept the forgiveness of sins. Roman Catholics and Orthodox Christians accept seven sacraments: baptism, confirmation, reconciliation, the Eucharist, ordination, matrimony, and the anointing of the sick.

SADDUCEES: Jewish sect or party made up of the priestly aristocracy (the Jewish establishment); political collaborationists with the Romans who accepted only written law (Torah).

SAMARITANS: Descendants of non-Jewish colonists who settled in Samaria in the eighth century B.C.E. They accepted only the first five books of the Bible and were considered heretics by the Jews.

SANCTIFICATION: Once a sinner has been turned to God through conversion and justification, there remains the possibility and task of drawing closer to God or to Christian perfection. Sanctification is a "second step" or second blessing.

SANCTUARY: That part of the church that contains the altar. In some churches, the altar is called a table and the sanctuary contains the table, the Bible, and a pulpit (for preaching). In Roman Catholic, Orthodox, and many Anglican churches, the sanctuary contains a tabernacle: a locked, enclosed space built into the high altar where the consecrated bread (called the Blessed Sacrament) is kept. In Orthodox churches, the tabernacle and sanctuary are behind the iconostasis. In all churches where the Blessed Sacrament is kept, one can find a sanctuary light or candle always lighted to indicate that the Blessed Sacrament is present there.

SANHEDRIN: Ancient Jewish legal and religious institution that operated as a court of law for Jews.

SATAN (Hb = adversary): A devil or demon, great adversary of people and enemy of God.

SCHISM (Gk = to tear): A rift in the unity of the church.

SCHOLASTICISM (SCHOLASTIC THEOLOGY): The educational system of the medieval schools, which consisted in methods of disputation and philosophical and theological speculation. It was stimulated by the discoveries of Aristotelian logic in the eleventh century and led to logical speculation and systematization of Christian faith on every conceivable level.

SIN: In religion, an unethical act, disobedience to a personal God. There is disagreement about what constitutes a sin but agreement that it is a rebellion against God.

SOCIAL DARWINISM: The application of the teachings of Charles Darwin (1809–1882) about organic evolution to society so that poverty, crime, and disease can be explained in relation to survival of the fittest.

STOREFRONT CHURCHES: Some evangelical churches have an outreach to inner-city areas by means of churches set up in abandoned stores; some religious individuals with a mission of their own to preach about Jesus also are sometimes drawn to downtrodden, urban settings. The churches set up in abandoned stores are called storefront churches; they do not form a denomination and often have little in common in terms of preaching, doctrine, and practice.

SYNOD: A formal meeting of religious leaders, usually of a particular region. To be distinguished from an ecumenical council, which involves the leaders of the church from all regions of the world.

SYNOPTICS (Gk = to see together): The books of Matthew, Mark, and Luke in the New Testament are considered synoptic Gospels: they bear greater similarities to each other than any of them do to the Gospel of John.

TAIZE COMMUNITY: International ecumenical community founded in France in 1940 by Brother Roger. Members are devoted to simplicity of living, communal sharing, and celibacy. Millions of young people have visited and stayed with the community for a while, exploring this dimension of Christian living.

TALMUD (**Aramaic from Hb = learning**): The vast body of Hebrew oral tradition containing the elucidations, elaborations, and commentaries of the rabbis. Accepted as authoritative by orthodox Jews.

TANAKH: The Jewish Bible. The word Tanakh is a combination of the three sections of the Jewish Bible: The Torah, the Prophets (Nevi'im), and the Writings (Kethuvim).

TEMPERANCE MOVEMENT: An effort to get people to abstain from drinking alcohol (totally or partially) that grew particularly strong in nineteenth-century America with help of the WCTU (Women's Christian Temperance Union) and the Anti-Saloon League. Their efforts (and others) led to the Eighteenth Amendment, prohibiting the sale and consumption of alcohol (Prohibition).

TESTIMONY: An account of the power of Jesus in one's life shared with fellow believers. It is distinguished by some Christians from witness, which is an account shared with nonbelievers. Testimony is meant to support the faith of one's fellow believers.

THEISM (**Gk *theos* = god**): Intended to oppose the concept of atheism, the conscious rejection of God's existence. *Theism* is the term for a philosophical system that accepts a transcendent and personal God. Unlike Deism, theism accepts the possibility of miracles and revelation.

THEOPHANY: An appearance of God in some visible form, temporary and not necessarily material.

THIRTY-NINE ARTICLES: The doctrinal positions of the Anglican church (see Appendix 5).

THOMAS À KEMPIS (**c. 1380–1471**): Spiritual writer, author of *The Imitation of Christ,* one of the most famous manuals of spiritual devotion in Christian literature.

TIBERIUS (**42 B.C.E.–37 C.E.**): Second Roman emperor (14–37 C.E.), in power when Jesus was killed.

TORAH (**Hb = teaching**): Hebrew name for the first five books of the Bible: Genesis, Exodus, Leviticus, Numbers, and Deuteronomy. Believed to have been handed down to Moses on Sinai, it contains laws of moral and physical conduct and love of Jewish people.

TRANSCENDENCE (**Lat *trans* = across; *scandare* = to climb**): The transcendence of God is his existence prior to and above the world. God is different from the world (see *immanence*).

TRANSCENDENTALISM: A literary, philosophical, and religious movement that flourished in New England from about 1836 to 1860. It originated with a small group of intellectuals who were against the teachings of Calvin and against the option offered by the Unitarians. They developed their own doctrine, which featured the divinity of human beings.

TRANSUBSTANTIATION: One explanation—along with transignification and consubstantiation—of how the bread and wine used in the celebration of the Eucharist are transformed into the body and blood of Christ. It was adopted as the official teaching of the Roman Catholic church in the thirteenth century, but arguments about it continue within Catholicism and Christianity in general.

TRINITY: One of the central doctrines of Christianity, the belief that there are three divine persons existing in one God. Various explanations have been given for the way God exists as one substance and three distinct persons, but the Trinity is generally said to be a mystery—that is, a belief that cannot be understood or explained simply in terms of human reason. The biblical basis for this belief is the working of God as creator, redeemer, and sanctifier and the words of Jesus about God as his father along with his promise to send the Spirit to abide with the church forever. Christians, with few exceptions, baptize members into the church in the name of the Father, the Son, and the Holy Spirit, an ancient formula that recognizes three distinct persons in one God.

TWO-THIRDS WORLD: Newer and more accurate way to refer to underdeveloped countries. The term "Third World," coined in the 1950s, is rejected by many developing countries today because of its derogatory connotations.

TYPOLOGY (**Gr = pattern**): A method of scriptural interpretation used by some early writers to show that events in the life of Jesus or the early church were prefigured in events in the Old Testament.

UNAM SANCTAM: The papal bull (or letter) issued by Pope Boniface VIII in 1302 during his quarrel with Philip IV of France. In it, the pope defined the four marks of the church as being one, holy, Catholic, and apostolic and argued that "outside the church there is no salvation."

UNIATE CHURCHES: Churches of Eastern Christendom that are in communion with Rome yet retain their own languages, church laws, and rites.

VATICAN: Modern papal residence in Rome. By the Italian Law of Guarantees (1871) and the Lateran Accords (1929), the Vatican, the Lateran cathedral, and the papal villa at Castel Gandolfo were granted extraterritoriality (not subject to the Italian government). Vatican City—including the library—is a separate city-state within Italy.

VATICAN II (1962–1965): Council called by the Roman Catholic church to respond to liturgical and pastoral needs of Catholics in the twentieth century. It made some significant changes in Catholic practice and attitude as well as in theological understanding.

VOLUNTARISM: The theory and practice whereby church membership is a matter of personal choice, not civil control or some other form of coercion.

VULGATE: Latin version of the Bible compiled and translated by Saint Jerome in the fourth century to provide one authorized version of the Bible to Christians (instead of the many versions in circulation at the time). It was adopted by the Roman Catholic church as the only official version, a position opposed by the reformers.

WALDENSIANS: Followers of Peter Waldo (d. 1217), who, like Francis of Assisi, gave his money to the poor to live in holy poverty according to the Gospels. When the Waldensians began to preach without permission from the local clergy, they were condemned. They continued to preach—often against abuses in the church—and were hunted down and burned as heretics.

WISDOM LITERATURE: Those biblical books that deal with what we might call profound common sense, instructions about life and conduct passed on from teacher to disciple, often dealing with moral conduct. The Wisdom books in the Old Testament include Job, Proverbs, and Ecclesiastes.

WITNESS: An account of the power of Jesus in one's life shared with nonbelievers. It is distinguished by some Christians from testimony, which is an account shared with fellow believers. The purpose of witness is to bring people to an awareness of Jesus by virtue of one individual's faith and example.

ZEALOTS: A revolutionary party extremely concerned with national liberation of the Jews from the Romans. They expected the Messiah to be a warrior-king.

Index

Historical Time Line

(Historical Time Line continues from inside front covers)

1073–1085	Gregory VII, pope, strengthens claims of papal absolutism
1095–1099	First Crusade
1100–1160	Peter Lombard, beginnings of Scholastic theology
1182–1226	Francis of Assisi, founder of Franciscan friars
1198–1216	Innocent III pope; height of papal power
1202–1204	Fourth Crusade; Western soldiers conquer and pillage Constantinople
1215	Magna Carta signed between King and English nobles
1225–1274	Thomas Aquinas, and the *Summa Theologica*
1265	Marco Polo visits China
1294–1303	Boniface VIII pope; humiliated and defeated by French king
1304	Clement V first Avignon pope
1330–1400	English mystics: Julian of Norwich, Richard Rolle, Walter Hilton
c. 1330–1384	John Wycliffe, English reformer, Lollard movement
c. 1372–1415	John Hus, Czech reformer, burned at Council of Constance
1377	Avignon papacy ends
1378	Great Western Schism begins, two men claim to be pope
1414–1418	Council of Constance ends schism, does not reform church
1450	Invention of printing press
1453	Constantinople captured by Turks; age of explorers, Magellan, Balboa, Columbus, et al. begins
1454	Gutenberg Bible printed
1484–1531	Ulrich Zwingli, Swiss reformer
1513–1572	John Knox, Scottish reformer
1517	Luther (1483–1546) posts his Ninety-five Theses on church door
1536	Tyndale's English Bible printed
1540	Jesuits founded to defend Roman Catholicism and pope
1545–1563	Council of Trent called to reform Roman Catholic church
1552–1610	Matteo Ricci, Jesuit missionary to China

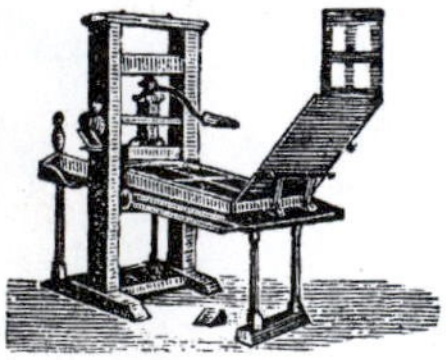